AuthorHouse™
1663 Liberty Drive
Bloomington, IN 47403
www.authorhouse.com
Phone: 1-800-839-8640

First published by AuthorHouse 8/6/2009

ISBN: 978-1-4490-0081-3 (sc)
ISBN: 978-1-4490-0080-6 (hc)

Printed in the United States of America
Bloomington, Indiana

This book is printed on acid-free paper.

Evolution of Faith and Religion
An Exploration
Global Religious and Cultural Insights

Ajit Randhawa, PhD

Dedicated to Raj
my wife

CONTENTS

Acknowledgements

Exploration of world religions made me search for a historical perspective on the beginning of rituals and faith in cultures that existed long before organized religion was established. I found my sources in many richly detailed books and the National Geographic magazine I grew up with.

I am indebted to several scholars for information about the history and religious practices in the world's religions explored in this study. I have learned much from the Great Courses offered by The Teaching Company taught by the distinguished professors namely, Dr. Isaiah M. Gafni of Hebrew University, Jerusalem (Judaism); Dr. Timothy L. Johnson of the Emory University's School of Theology (Christianity); Dr. John L. Esposito of Georgetown University's Department of Islamic Studies (Islam); Dr. Mark W. Muesse and Dr. Malcolm D. Eckel of Boston University (Buddhism).

I thank Professor Emeritus Dr. Seshagiri Rao of the University of Virginia, Chief-Editor of the Encyclopedia of Hinduism at the University of South Carolina for reviewing the chapter on Hinduism and Dr. Devinder Singh Chahal, author of Nanakian Philosophy and Editor of Understanding Sikhism – The Research Journal, Laval, Quebec, Canada for editing Sikhism and their valuable comments.

The course by Dr. John McWhorter of the Manhattan Institute provided information on the evolution of languages and religious texts. Dr. Glenn Holland of Alleghany College imparted the background on the ancient Mediterranean World. Lectures of Professor David Christian of San Diego State University were valuable for information on human evolution and Dr. Lawrence M. Principe of Johns Hopkins University offered his scholarly perspective on science and religion.

I am deeply indebted to Dr. Georg Retzlaff, former Professor of Homiletics at the University of the South, Sewanee, Tennessee, for editing the manuscript and his suggestions on the segments on Christianity. J. Zohara M. Hieronimus edited the chapter on Role of Women in Religion and graciously gave permission to use information from her book *Kabbalistic Teachings of the Female Prophets*.

My wife, Raj, has been an inspiration in launching this effort and I could not have completed this book without her support, encouragement and patience.

I hope that the information of this exploration encourages the Generation X, an intention which depends on the interest of parents, teachers, preachers, and peers so that the spirituality imbued in every faith becomes the foundation on which the next generation can broaden their outlook about humanity and the human connection yearning for unity and the wellbeing of all.

With humility,
Ajit S. Randhawa

PREFACE

When did early humans start rituals? What generated faith and early belief systems? How did the religions emerge and become the world religions? What is *The Word*? How did the word *God* originate which applies to every faith? This book attempts to explore possible explanations.

Some concepts started as a way of life that defined the cultures of early tribes. Rituals developed codes of conduct around them. Other concepts were conceived in dreams or through divine messages. Early civilizations, their beliefs, stories, and traditions have directed the evolution of present day world religions. Some belief systems emerged from philosophies of prophets. Their revelations and preaching were later compiled by scribes which became Holy Scriptures. Some of the original messages were parables and metaphors interpreted by the religious leaders of the time and supported by the monarchs who controlled the political landscape. A comparative study opens up vistas of cultures that developed organized belief systems. Religions consolidated themselves through hierarchal lineage, scholarly status, or charismatic delivery of sermons by priests. Variations introduced in worship practices with growing support of the followers developed new sects within religions.

Primitive humans were hunter-gatherers who later developed agriculture and formed communities. They were intrigued by the forces that were perceived to control their surroundings, established their belief in the power of deities or unseen spirits. For millennia, early tribes and their beliefs developed along rivers, lakes, sea shores and mountains. Archaeological evidence gives an insight into the rituals of the Neanderthal and Cro-Magnon. The celestial bodies like the Sun, Moon, and Stars were regarded as vital forces connected to life on earth. Lightning, storms, floods, and volcanic eruptions instilled fear in early humans. The elders sought protection from the invisible entities and developed practices to appease them. More elaborate rituals evolved into dances, and offerings for the spirits in a communal attempt to seek relief and protection from disease, natural disasters and death. These beliefs and rituals were passed on orally from generation to generation. The Sun god was worshipped in early civilizations. Emperors, pharaohs, kings and chiefs assumed power and proclaimed themselves to be direct descendants of the gods that controlled the earth and everything on it. The authority of the ruler was not open to any doubt or question. Messages in dreams or the voices heard by prophets were the precursors of the organized belief systems. After generations of oral transfer these stories were written by scribes. The compiled verses of the religious texts became the Holy books known as Torah in Judaism, Bible in Christianity, Koran in Islam, Gita in Hinduism, and Guru Granth in Sikhism. Other spiritual leaders laid down their philosophies for the followers i.e. Siddhartha Gautama (Buddhism), Lao Tzu (Taoism), and Confucius (Confucianism).

Religions branched into sects according to the criteria of lineage, spiritual ascendancy, geographical area, or political power with divine authority over their followers. Religious conversion was encouraged through missionaries or imposed by kings.
The drive for religious supremacy played a significant role in national and international events influencing billions of people. Kings and chiefs drew strength by combining state and religion for political conquests. Battles were waged to occupy more territories and the conqueror imposed his or her religion. Queen Hatshepsut was a Regent for her step son Thutmose III but she became the pharaoh of Egypt in 15th century BCE (National Geographic, April 2009, 88-111). Salome Alexandra became the queen when the King Jannaeus of Judaea bequeathed the kingdom to his wife in 103 CE (Biblical Archaeology Review July-Aug, 2008 (64 and 72).

The role of women in religious institutions was diminished during invasions. One third of world's population (3.335 billion) are Christians, Muslims, and Hindus. The remaining 3.2 billion people belong to other faiths and atheists are God's people too.

The supreme universal energy is equated with 'the Word' that permeates everything and everyone. It is this Life Principle that has been deified as Creator, Sustainer and Destroyer in different forms and shapes in various beliefs. The practice of the Word is universal in daily services in churches, mosques and temples. The blessed few experience the mystery and bliss of God's grace. The question of supremacy of religion shifted the focus away from the Word and led to the rivalry of religious practices, all professing theirs to be the only right path. Different ideologies triggered national and international conflicts leading to wars. The youth of today want clarification beyond faith. All spiritual leaders and sages have to convince them by demonstrating the attributes of God. The exploration within requires concentration of mind, staunch faith, strong will, patience, deep passion to seek God, and to feel oneness of life on this planet. Parents and teachers have a vital role to guide the youth and invest in generation X (born 1962-1976) to enable them to interact with the global citizens preserving the sanctity of their belief systems and cultural heritage. Imagine if there was no guidance to indulge in serious contemplation on the word of God, how the lure of vices such as Lust, Anger, Greed, Attachment (obsession), and Ego would transform this world! The global turmoil in the name of religion and the bloodshed throughout the world has cut through the core of humanity that is questioning the role of religion at this time. The purpose of this book is to provide basic information on the beliefs across the religious spectrum and generate a dialogue to explore the underpinnings of different faiths. It covers a range of ancient traditions, faiths and civilizations. Religion and state once were united as faith recognized the monarch as religious head as well. Different belief systems emerged throughout the world and were influenced by other beliefs encountered through traders, scholars and conquests of emperors. Sectarian fragmentation has occurred in all religions of the world. The youth of the 21st century are at the crossroads of religious and cultural dogma and need to be informed about the positive role of religion in their lives. The reluctance of youth to attend services is experienced by parents in all religions. This book is an attempt to offer insights into the past environments that shaped religions over the millennia. History is essential for reflection so that lessons can be learned. Unfortunately it also serves as a reminder of historical conflicts that fuel mistrust and lingering anger. Scriptures are exploited through selective interpretation and in the name of religion the innocent majority is plunged into untold misery and chaos as seen around the world at this time. We must strive to look for avenues that promote understanding, and to honor the sanctity of all faiths. We are connected biologically on this planet and chemically with the universe. According to the Lakota Indians of North America, the tradition and prayer is a quest for *Hanblecheya,* a cry for a vision of the Spirit. Their legacy is *Milayuke Oyasin,* which means we are all related.

Philosopher Socrates wrote 35 dialogues in the 3rd century CE and stated: Ethics is a vice of the refined, and virtue cannot be taught and his conviction: One should know thyself, suggested introspection. He concealed his superiority gracefully. Plato, a student of Socrates, believed that circumstances set the stage for the form a dialogue would take. His dialogues were not intended for use on stage in plays. Aristotle in his writings dealt with virtue and moral character. Philosophy and religion together gave rise to the theism movement. In the 19th century and the early 20th century Madame Blavatsky and Annie Besant founded the Theosophy movement that ventured to bring together the Eastern and Western worldviews about religion to harness the knowledge of spirituality. Interfaith religious dialogue continues to express views of scholars, scientists and theologians of all religions to find the ways that will recognize the unity in religions at the spiritual level. Olympic games offer optimism because they bypass all regional, national and international feuds and come together in the spirit of sportsmanship where athletes become a living bridge connecting nations across political boundries as global citizens. Spirituality movement at a global scale will influence the minds of humanity to comprehend God's plan for unity. Gandhi emphasized, Truth is truth, the West called it science which confines religion. Religions constitute different ways of looking at that reality. God is known by numerous names. A person can choose to call it Invisible Force, Ishwar, Allah, Khuda (Gandhi, 38). Simone Weil stated: Faith is the submission of that part of mind which has not seen

God to the part which has. Gregg Braden (2004) traced name of God to the Hebrew alphabet YHWH, revealed to Moses for the first time (Exodus 6:23). Later Jacob, Isaac, and Abraham knew God, and the enlightenment manifested through attributes as El Shaddai.

The exploration traced the beginning of the religions and their diversity from a historical perspective and the factors which influenced faiths and belief systems that later developed as world religions. Human civilizations have been shaped by two philosophies and both engage in knowledge claims. Religion through faith deals with discourse about God while science explores the natural world with reason. Both are wings that allow the human spirit to soar in search of truth. This is explained by phrases: *Credo ut intellegam* (I believe so that I may understand) and *Intellego ut credam* (I understand so that I may believe). According to St. Augustine of Hippo, with his formulations in the 5th century, religion has primacy but science assists true religion. His doctrine of Two Books includes the Book of Scripture and the Book of Nature. The teaching document of Pope John Paul II *Fides et A Ratio* (Faith and Reason) of 1998, pointed out that faith, knowledge, and reason together can lead to eternal and transcendent truth. History and chronology of events in the evolution of faith and religions are vital to comprehend the circumstances and human interaction to fully grasp the underpinnings that shaped the religions of today. Interpretation of different religions and their incompatibility tends to divide humanity. The book explores the basic philosophy of Judaism, Christianity, Islam, Hinduism, Buddhism and Sikhism to understand their faith and culture in order to interact in the global society intelligently. God's message is for the entire humanity.

> We shall not cease from exploration,
> and the end of all our exploring
> will be to arrive where we started,
> and know the place for the first time.
> …Eliot

SPIRITUALITY

Spirits were imagined to be the protective forces by the early Homo sapiens who developed faith in different entities of the universe. Belief in spirits later emerged as spirituality. Reliance on spirits was perpetuated orally for thousands of generations and faith in spirits sustained humanity. The Holy Spirit is a part of Trinity in Christianity. Beads of different religions make up the universal rosary of spirituality reminding us constantly to serve and safeguard all creation and serve humanity. The fragmentation of the universal approach created separate ways assuming an identity in the process. Spiritual persons are seekers of truth with a longing to purify the soul. The rosary snapped under the tension of vices and the scattered beads of diversity sought their distinct identity. The desire for supremacy in devotion became very powerful and developed ego. Every religion is promoting the message of their Prophet as interpreted by the religious leaders according to their moral compass in the shifting geo-political environment of the times. This has happened in the kingdoms past when religion and politics were integrated to solidify the support of the masses. Abraham is the patriarch of Judaism, Christianity and Islam. He preached at the Sumerian temple in Ur, the Zuggarat, a relic of the pyramid like temple of Abraham, where people assembled to worship. It was regarded as a place between Heaven and Earth where sacrifices and rituals were performed. Earth is considered sacred by Hindus, Chinese, Greeks, and the Shintos of Japan. In the West certain places were consecrated and made holy where shrines, churches and temples were built. Certain places are believed to enhance the spiritual experience. Such places include rivers, mountains, caves and springs.

The Jewish scriptures indicate that humans originated in the Garden of Eden, an area where four rivers were flowing namely Pishon, Gibon, Tigris and Euphrates. The latter two still flow in Iraq. In historic times the area of confluence of four rivers was Assyria. It is ironic that the same area where the Hanging

Gardens of Babylon flourished and housed King's exotic collection of plants and animals from across his kingdom, has become a hostile environment emotionally scorched with hatred and human strife. Empires were ruled by the elite of the dominant religion while others were secular states where all religions had freedom of worship according to their beliefs. Some nations decided to establish laws declaring the separation of religion and state while others adhere to their legalized religious belief systems.

The political developments in the world have created major shifts in recent times. The iron curtain lifted in the former Soviet Union, the Berlin wall was torn down, the barriers of caste system in India weakened, and the shackles of slavery in United States and South Africa were broken to establish human rights and dignity for mankind. However, the lust for power has swayed the religious elite to use any and every avenue to secure identity and supremacy of their belief system. Dalai Lama had to escape and abandon his territory of Tibet to avoid persecution at the hands of the Chinese who restricted the activities of monks. The Dalai Lama in exile established his administrative offices in Dharamsala, India and gained respect as a spiritual leader and as Nobel Laureate. The Middle East has secular states as well as Islamic states. In Saudi Arabia no other religion can be practiced except Islam. Turkey as a secular state is a bridge between East and West. With all the diversity in world religions, spirituality sums up the reality in the universally accepted divine force with the 'Word' which is common in all sects and faiths, each defining their separate identity.

THE WORD

Abraham Abulafia, a revolutionary mystic, believed that God is pure intellect. He developed a system to help unite the human intellect with the cosmic intellect to achieve prophetic consciousness. During this internalized psychological state of mind, he believed that the vision of God is manifest as letters that constitute names, the word. This system was called prophetic kabbalah. It aimed at experiencing a state of ecstasy

12

also known as ecstatic kabbalah. Moses was influenced by the philosophy of al-Farabi and ibn Sina who claimed that the overflow of the last intellect in a cosmological chain of ten intellects empowers a person to the prophetic levels of intellect. There were many prophets who had visions and messages from God to preach the word of God. There was focus on the light principle or the sound principle. Abraham followed the sound principle. His procedures included written, oral, and mental stages of letter-combination, reciting divine names, special breathing exercises, and body postures. Vision or imagination is an integral part of this process. In that state God and individual are one. It is an abstract that cannot be visualized.

The primitive tribes initially perceived spirits in earthly physical features, land, mountains, lakes, rivers, and oceans, and in animals and plants that formed a source of food, clothing, shelter, and transport. Celestial objects, Sun, Moon, Stars, Milky Way, Comets, and the sky were considered a heavenly realm. Events like Hail, Fire, Tornadoes, storms, tsunamis and earthquakes represented the wrath of angry spirits. In India, cows, mice, monkeys, snakes are worshipped by Hindus as they are linked to the deities. The dragon is part of the folklore and deity in China. The Indian tribes of Alaska identify the clan by carving and painting eagle, fish, and bear on Totem poles. The rituals became a way to appease the spirits with sacrifices and became woven in to the tribal belief system. The objects of worship, the ritual styles, and the authoritative figures varied in different cultures. With the growing number of followers, in time the belief systems were organized and acquired the status of religion. Mysticism emerged with the spiritual awakening of Prophets. Teachings of prophets were compiled by scribes and the Holy Scriptures became the word of God for their followers.

Self knowledge is a prerequisite to acquiring God knowledge. The Greeks referred to it as *Gnothe Seauton*, and Romans called it *Teipsum*. Self knowledge can be perceived after clearing the thick fog of our sensual lure and perceptions. Jesus expressed:

He that findeth his life shall lose it and
He that loseth his life shall find it.
According to spiritual master Kirpal Singh (Naam, 1999), the
manifestation of Absolute Truth is Sound and Light Principles.
Together this energy is known by different names:

Christians call it the WORD (Bible)

Muslims call it KALMA (Koran)

Hindus know it as NAD (Vedas), or UDGIT (Upanishads)

Sikhs refer to this as NAAM or SHABD (Guru Granth)

Siddhartha was born a prince. He became enlightened 2500
years ago and became the Buddha. His followers founded the
religion Buddhism. Jesus was crucified and his resurrection
made him Christ thus Christianity was born. Christ said: I am
the light of the world, and he that followeth me, shall not walk in
darkness, but shall have the light of life (John 8:12). Zoroaster
preached the divine force of sound current called Sraosha in
Persian. In Egypt, King Ikhnaton preached the principle of
sound current as Path of Aton 4000 years ago. The enlightened
ones acquire a spiritual glow. Focus on the Word offers stillness
and peace of mind that can heal the emotional stress caused by
the physical and mental trauma in daily life. Contact with the
Word restores and invigorates the mind. It is essential that the
seat of the soul, our mind, is primed to receive divine guidance
as advised by sages. Vedas call it Brahm which vibrates in
everything and everyone. Shamas Tabrez explains that world
originated from Saut, the sound principle. According to Abdul
Razaq Kashi the Ism-i-Azam (the Word) supports the creation.
The light principle, as narrated by Nanak can be seen without
eyes, and the sound principle can be heard without ears. Moses
heard this sound on Koh-i-Toor, Mount Sinai and Jesus heard
the same sound while in the wilderness. In the Himalayas,
during deep meditation, Shiva heard it and called it Anhad
Naad. The flute of Krishna created the same sound (Singh,
1999).

Mohammad spent fifteen years connecting to Awaz-i-Mustqim,
the Word, and experienced heavenly sparks for seven years in
the cave of Hira while in prayers practicing Sultan-ul-Azkar

(Surat Shabd). He received messages at the age of forty. His calling enabled him to become Prophet Mohammad. Maulana Rumi confirmed that Turks, Kurds, Parsis, Goans and Arabs have known this principle without the aid of lips or ears. Kun-feu-Kun is the Kalma of Muslims. According to Koran: God commanded and it was done. Hazrat Bahu pointed out that Kalma is repeated orally by many, only a rare soul repeats it with the tongue of thought but is unable to express it in words. Hazrat Inayat Khan, a Sufi mystic called it Saute Sarmadi and considered the creation as Music of God and manifestation of His power from the Garden of Allah. Maulana Rumi stated:

> We have five physical senses and
> an additional five subtle senses.
> The subtle senses are gold compared to
> the physical senses, made of copper.

Socrates was influenced by the peculiar sound that elevated him to higher spiritual levels. Plato called it Music of the Spheres. In 4th century BCE, Lao Tzu in Tao referrre to the Hidden Principle of Universe. Madam Blavatsky named it Voice of God. Mysticism is a soul searching realm. It may seem to collide with science but the latter is constantly searching for the truth as well. The scientific method requires validation of discoveries by their peers in the scientific community. The spiritual elevation is based on harnessing the power of mind. As we know more about cosmic energy and its unity in the cosmos, the Newtonian backdrop of science will be uplifted to a quantum mindset to reveal the truth. When our focus goes to the energy potential of the brain, we will be heading in the direction of spirituality. Concentration of mind, power of prayer, the knowledge of alternative practices, and the holistic approach are gaining acceptance acknowledging the concept of mind-body connection. According to Rabbi Rami Shapiro, a skilled carpenter goes with the grain of wood. One has to feel the energy and flow of the moment for that connection. *Go with the flow* is an expression of guidance.

The Word is powerful only if one can get in touch with its power source, God. Just repetition of the word is of no avail. Oral recitation of the word water in any language i.e. *ma* (Arabic), *eau* (French), *aqua* (Latin), *aab* (Persian), or *hudor* (Greek) will not quench the thirst. Abstract Sound can be heard only by the blessed souls because the man's consciousness is clouded by the material universe around him observing with the physical senses. Humans are the most advanced life form with superiority of intellect above all species. The power of imagination beckons to harness the mind and explore the realm of God. The practices of renunciation and seclusion thwart the ability to reach full potential to create a society that can live in harmony with one another and the environment. If everyone invokes the scrutiny of conscience in every action and believes in omnipresence of God, our outlook towards life will be transformed. Lao Tzu (28) advocated a balance in life:

> Know the Masculine, cleave to the Feminine
> Be the valley for everyone...
> Know the White, cleave to the Black...
> Know Glory, but cleave to Humiliation
> Be the valley for everyone...

During our evolutionary development the subconscious mind was down-loaded with emotions and instincts that make up our subconscious mind. Our environment adds a layer of impressions through family, nurturing, peer influence, society, and personal life experiences. Religion plays an important role in forming the core that develops character and it reflects in the attitude. Dr. Neilson, a physician in Ohio got an opportunity to join NSF Antarctic Research Station on South Pole. She arrived at the South Pole in November 1998. She felt a small lump in her breast in March, 1999. She trained fellow project members to do the biopsy and the information was sent to an oncologist in the United States. The tests confirmed malignancy. A special NSF air drop provided the equipment and medical supplies. She performed her duties and engaged in group activities with a smile. As her condition deteriorated a rescue mission in June, in 100 degree temperature below zero, brought her back for treatment and she lived to tell her story. Faith and spirituality anchored her values. Character and positive attitude enabled her to survive. The inherent spark of consciousness helps to subdue evil transgressions of the mind. The spirit attains

16

wholeness with its transcendence (Lao Tzu). Yoga creates a state of oneness when the waves of mind (vrittis) are absent in individual awareness (*chitta*) as they are channeled back to their subtle horizons (Davis, 1996). The doctrine of Karma implies the experiences of current lifetime that are the outcome of our deeds in the past lives. This serves as an incentive which promotes ethical conduct, a virtuous life and a chance at better after-life.

Interpretation of the Word is crucial. Each religious belief system claims that theirs is *the only way* to worship God to achieve salvation. This claim is made in religions with a shift to create a difference in the mode of prayer, rules of worship, icons and idols, and even unique architecture of buildings to establish identity. All righteous people of any faith are labeled as spiritual people because they believe in God known by different names due to national and regional differences in culture and language. This variation in beliefs has offered diversification and distinct identity to the religions. The traditions and practices originated from the revelations of Prophets. Their miracles solidified the faith. The holy places of pilgrimage likewise are the historical sites linked to initial events during the rise of a faith and built in honor of their Prophets. Teachings of all religious entities profess compassion, respect for nature, love for and service to humanity in the name of the Creator. These tenets of spirituality are basic to a caring compassionate society.

General providence and special providence has been debated since the Medieval Era. It spans the extreme view of Hasidim and Hayyim Halberstam that divine providence controls everything and every action at all times. The Italian Kabbalist Joseph Ergas (1685-1730) believed that nothing happens without divine providence. Chance is attributed to God. Gersonides view that God's focus is to preserve species, and does not control that a particular spider will eat a particular fly. Maimonides reserves special providence for humans and not for animals as they are subject to chance, not by divine decree. The divine providence, according to Jewish thought, comes into play in the realm of chance factor that is controlled. The question of free will has been a focus of philosophers and theologians wrestling with

God's fore knowledge and man's free will in making the decisions and choice for their actions. Our mind is influenced by the presuppositions that develop our nature, which are engrained during nurture. This limits exposure to a broader view about religions. Some adhere to the literal meaning of scriptures, others see them as metaphors, focusing on the essence of the message. Also there are skeptics and the atheists. A few respect all religions and rise above the artificially created religious and sectarian differences entering into the realm of spirituality, the embodiment of truth. Interest developed in practices like transcendental meditation, yoga, and prayer as alternative avenues to reduce stress, and improve concentration to achieve peace of mind. The concept of mind over matter has convinced the health practitioners that many ailments are triggered by emotional pressure. Periodically, we must evaluate our state of mind by looking inwards and focus on our balance sheet of virtues and vices. It is a great eye-opener. One has to be truthful and open to the personal analysis.

It is crucial that all religions contemplate and share the elixir of spirituality and respect the true ideals at the core of all religions. Immanuel Kant (1724-1804), a philosopher explained that God is Omnipotent and is everywhere. God and the property of being everywhere are one (Kant, 61). Abrahamic faith preached love of God, the teachings shared by Christians and Muslims (Bible: Lev. 19:33-34; Mt. 25:40 and Koran: 2: 177; 4: 36; 49: 13. Why have these teachings been ignored for millennia?
Philosophy and religion together gave rise to the 'theism' movement of the Medieval Period. Philosophies evolved over time. Modern medicine offers a quick fix for immediate relief, the eastern cure is focused on the holistic approach. Mind and body were considered separate in the West but eastern view of mind/body interaction is now deemed critical for cure as in the eastern philosophy which evokes divine energy for faith in God.

G: Grounded in Humility, Compassion, and Service to all.
O: Omnipresence and Awareness of God, and the Truth.
D: Disciplined use of senses to imbibe the Divine Spirit.

EVOLUTION OF RELIGIOUS THOUGHT

Myths were creation of the mind which became the legends and were passed on to the next generations through tales. Hills of Crosses offer support to the Lithuanians since the 14th century; Thousands of followers tread the footsteps of St. Patrick who fasted and prayed on the summit of Croagh Mountain.

According to a legend of Scarface of the Blackfeet Indians in North America, he fell in love with a girl that was taken by the Sun. Scarface traveled far and wide in search of the Great Power to claim his love. He met Early Riser, the planet Venus, son of Moon, the mother, and Sun the father. Scarface lived with them and was permitted to marry his love. Sun gave him two raven feathers with medicinal powers and directed him to establish a medicine lodge. He wore the raven feathers at the medicine lodge where he prayed and conducted spiritual healing. The feathers were passed on to his successors and the tale continued. Such stories in different faiths and religions created mythology. Romans recognized Jupitor, Mars, Apollo, and Venus as gods. Humans have always yearned for the Divine.

Early man managed to survive the Ice Age by living in caves wearing animal skins. The Ice Age lowered sea levels creating land bridges in Alaska, Australia- New Zealand-Tasmania, and in Europe. The nomadic behavior developed as the hunter-gatherers explored new areas in search of food and farming. In overwhelming situations of distress or life threatening moments, it was God's impulse that prompted the humans to seek help from a higher source. When adverse conditions passed, the assistance of the unseen force was acknowledged as the source for help and established faith in countless spirits.
A warm period of 15000 years refers to Adam in the Bible:
>...And the Lord God took the man, and put him in the Garden of Eden... (Genesis 2:15).

...Therefore the Lord God sent him forth from Garden of Eden to till the ground from whence he was taken...(Genesis 3:23).

This period was followed by the curse of the ground, the cool period that made farming extremely difficult for 3000 years. Studies indicate that the founder crops were cultivated in the Fertile Crescent, now in the region of Turkey, Armenia, Iran, and Syria, in farms in the northern regions between the Tigris and Euphrates Rivers 12000 years ago. The early migration brought their ideas, languages, farming technique, and domestication of animals to Europe, Asia, and to other areas. New evidence points out the attempts made by many different tribes to colonize the Americas as revealed by the divergent DNA pattern. America was inhabited by different groups that created inter-group clashes as indicated by the fractured fossil bones. The ancient fabrics discovered by archaeologists suggest that an advanced culture existed. The spearheads with intricate patterns as well as curved stone sickles to cut grasses suggested that Bering land bridge was not the only route of migration for the early humans to reach Americas. Another theory is suggested that kelps, the giant sea weed, along the Pacific Rim by the edge of ice during the Ice Age may have offered a safe route from Japan to the west coast in primitive reed boats instead of facing the huge waves in the open ocean. They used fire for keeping predators away and for cooking tubers, roots and meat. The warming global climate melted the glaciers raising sea levels that submerged land bridges separating human populations which developed in isolation. The modern humans ventured into other areas beyond their territories sparking conflicts and fights. The strategies of warfare replaced spears with bows and arrows.

Jericho was inhabited by farming tribes as early as 7000 BCE. Agriculture had developed in Europe and Asia by 5000 BCE. The first cities of Uruk and Ur developed in southern Mesopotamia, (modern Iraq) in 3500 BCE with the Sumerian civilization. The Phoenicians and Greeks developed languages between 1000 and 500 BCE. By 500 BCE the Romans established democracy. The citizens acquired rights and were no longer regarded as subjects of the rulers. Advancement in the arts, architecture, philosophy, wisdom, and the folklore was

encouraged in Mesopotamia, Egypt, India, China, and Europe. The description of the cultures of the East, Middle East, Europe and the Americas are included to show the origin and significance of faith in different tribes in chapter V. Religions developed a following through the message of their Prophets. The devotees of religions grew beyond the country of their origin and gained the status as world religions. Three events are significant during the Axial Period (800-200 BCE). In the East, the philosophies of Lao-tzu and Confucius emerged in China, Vedas developed Hinduism, from which the philosophy of Buddha established Buddhism. The philosophy of Mahavira developed Jainism in India. Elijah, Isaiah, and Jeremiah, the Jewish prophets spread their message of YHWH as non-exclusive monotheism. Deuteronomy refers to the pre-history of Israel and Judah. The constitution of the people of god as theocratic community is observed in three phases:
Noah, the basic rules of food; Abraham, the covenant of circum-cision; Sinai celebration established the ideology. Elohistic and the Priestly traditions came from the revelations of Moses who met God at the burning bush (Soggin 2001, 68-77).

Western philosophy took birth in Greece. Socrates introduced morality, Plato and Aristotle brought consciousness into focus. The evolutionary process during the post Axial Period has established the world religions of today. Turkey played a unique role in understanding the New Testament. More than half of the books were written in Turkey where Peter, Paul, and John had lived or had delivered sermons in the church. Differences in ideologies had an impact in shaping the religions in the 20th century. Religious identity sparked a race in modern times and developed sectarian denominations within religions.

DAWN OF RITUALS

The remains of Neanderthals and Paleolithic humans revealed that they buried objects with the dead. This indicates the belief in the after life. This is the first look at the emotional expression through the ritual.

Neanderthals engaged in hunting large game in which males and females of all ages participated as revealed by the frequency of healed fractures in bones of all ages (Archaeology: March 2007, 15). Females of early Homo sapiens were able to stay at the settlements and built families and clans. This gave them an advantage over the Neanderthals who were always searching for food to survive. The Neanderthal burial sites show other objects placed with the body in shallow graves as noticed in the remains buried 70,000 years ago. The Cro-Magnon burials included flints and ocher (iron oxide) covered wraps around the body in the graves as a ritual to honor the dead. All civilizations grew along the rivers, Mesopotamia along Tigris and Euphrates; Egypt along the Nile; Harappa civilization in India developed along Indus River by 1500 BCE and later migrated to the valley of Ganges River. They were called Aryans in Sanskrit. Chinese dynasties settled along Yellow River. The New World cultures also flourished around lakes and rivers. Catastrophic events and other calamities compelled the early man to seek help and protection from the celestial and physical objects perceived with supernatural powers as well as invisible imaginary entities, the spirits. Prayer was made with anticipated optimism (faith) for protection from suspected danger. The individual request for help evolved into a collective prayer by the clan or tribe. Ceremonial rituals were held to make a communal plea for protection with faith and hope.

Faith in the power of the unknown entities has captivated the imagination of early humans. Many kinds of rituals and traditions evolved in different tribes. Geographic isolation and distances among tribes created the diversity of ways to appease and honor these invisible spirits. The meteor blast five mile above Tunguska in Central Siberia in 1908 came as a fireball from the sky. The explosive force was of 15 megaton TNT, affecting 1000 square miles with violent tremors and bright night skies. The event still baffles the scientists today. Imagine the magnitude of fear felt by early humans in similar celestial events that turned them to place their faith for protection in a higher entity. Faith in rituals eventually became traditions in time to endure situations beyond their control. This may have given rise to superstitions that reinforced the fears creating legends and tales for future generations. The legendary stories may have been embellished to enforce the rules of conduct in many spheres of tribal life. Medicine men used their knowledge of herbs and added the dancing rituals to enhance the power of healing. The events included adornments with feathers, animal skulls or painting the face and/or body perhaps in the images of the imaginary spirits. A burial site in Goat's Hole Cave was discovered in southern Wales where The Red Lady of Raviland was buried with rings, other jewelry and body stained red with ocher to prepare for after-life (Hitchcock et al, ed., 23).

Early tribes recognized specific deities and spirits. The Hopi Indians sought help of the spirit *Katsinam*. The patron deity for Mexica was *Huitzilopochtli*, which appeared in a priest's dream to establish Tenochtitlan city. The Maya worshipped *Chacmool* whose statue stands at Chichen Itza. *Tlaloc* was the rain god for the Toltec people who offered sacrifices to secure god's favor. Peruvians worshipped a fanged deity, *Staff God*, which was a central figure in the Andes. The Indians in Normbega of the northern Atlantic coast of North America worshipped *manitou*. Hopi Indians give Kachina dolls as goodluck charms to seek blessings from the spirits. The Zoroastrians worshipped *Ahura Mazda* in ancient Iran. Mount Hermon is a nature preserve with water falls at the head waters of the Jordan River. This was the site of the Greek god *Pan*, half man, half goat, the god of fertility for flocks. He created panic and fear. People offered sacrificial gifts to Pan. Canterbury Cathedral was built on Celtic site of worship which contains 70 sculptures of 'Green Man' with leaves on his face and body. It is believed that Christians adopted holly to celebrate the birth of Jesus. Celtics consider ivy as the vine of resurrection which quickly revives after winter. Celtics tree worship involved a green tree with lights and ornaments just like the Christmas tree decorations and lights.

People of Nigeria, Benin and Togo in Africa seek help from 401 deities, *Orisha*, one of those is Thunder God *Shango*. The single god worshipped by the Zulu is *Nkulunkulu*. The Kung Bushmen in Botswana belived the falling stars were the gifts from the gods and brought bees and honey, ostrich eggs, blood, medicine songs as a result of the power of N*tum.* Candomble tradition which perpetuated in Brazil was brought by Africans who practiced Yoruba Voodoo. The spirit *orissa* calls a Youngman coming of age who enters a trance. Priests pour goats blood on the shaved head and scatter feathers of seven fowls on his head to initiate him into adulthood. The Unumbal people of northwestern Australia believed that the sky god *Wallanganda*, Milky Way, rained water on earth and *Ungud*, god of Earth, made the water deep as oceans. They slept and world creatures appeared out of their dreams.

Ancient Japanese believed there were 8 million *Kami*, the deities around in every form, Sun goddess *Amaterasu*, rice god *Inari*, and guardian god *Okuninushi*. The deity K*ami-hotoke* combined the Buddha and Kami. Ryobu Shinto linked Shinto and Buddhist deities.

The flooding of the Nile after the rains in the highlands made the land fertile for renewed vegetation and bumper crops. This may have led the Egyptian kings to believe that they will also rise after death. The Pharaohs started mummification 3000 years ago. Mummification was also done in South America. Mesopotamia had developed world's first large cities of Uruq and Ur with a population of 50,000 by 3200 BCE. Sumerian temples in Ur observed sacrifices of servants buried with the kings to serve in after life. Thirty city states had their own king and patron gods and goddesses. King Sargon was the usurper and created the first army of 5400 men. He captured Uruk city and conquered up to Syria and Turkey. This Babylonian King had sought immortality as recorded in the legend Epic of Gilgamesh. He unified the region and standardized weights and measures for the regional economy. After 30 years of conquest with hostage taking and ransoms, he passed 282 legal verdicts as living code including slavery regulation, social laws, and justice which involved eye for an eye, tooth for tooth.

Sacrificing animals as part of the rituals signified a higher level of devotion. Humans became sacrificial offerings to appease the spirits. Aztecs excised human hearts for the offerings. Virgins were offered as ultimate sacrifice for their purity. Alexander the Great held athletic contests and the defeated men were sacrificed as offering before starting an expedition or war. Nearchus, the admiral for Alexander's fleet sailing from India to Persia also took men for sacrifice to Zeus the Savior by holding contests. A desert island of Cataea was sacred to Hermes and Aphrodite. The desert island adjacent to Cataea was sacred to Poseidon, the Lord of Ocean. Nearchus did not go on those islands.

In China after major calamities like the earthquake of May, 2008 and other disasters the old Chinese rituals resurfaced. After a devastating fire in Dimen China, a ritual was revived after three decades where blind folded men go in a trance and ride horses to search for the cause in a traditional divination ritual (National Geographic, May 2008). Coffin trees were chosen at birth in the past to be cut down and carved as coffins for burial. As a show of ritualistic protest to the iron hand of the Chinese authorities at Tiananmen Square in 1989, artist Sheng Qi cut off his finger. In China the Confucian values offered balance. The era of old traditions and concubines of the 18th and 19th centuries have given way to modern cities like Beijing.

The elders and chiefs enjoyed respect and power in their tribes. They created the traditions for boys and girls when they came of age and devised initiation ceremonies to celebrate their adulthood status. The rules of marriage and family structure and their interaction within the family and the clan were established by tribal leaders. The tribes observed their own rules for social conduct and rituals and established their identity. The simple framework of society at the primitive level evolved into many ideologies that were social experiments. Rituals are tribal ceremonies which are practiced in special regalia with feathers, beads, head bands, jewelry, and involves singing, dancing, chanting with face/body painting participating in communal celebrations

Modern versions of societies, cultures and forms of governments are the projection of that process over thousands of years. North America began with a business venture of the London Company in 1607 and the colony of Jamestown was established after King James I. London Company changed its name to Virginia Company of London in 1609. Virginia was claimed as British colony and named after Queen Elizabeth I. They agreed upon three basic principles: religious liberty, private ownership and an organized self rule. This template later defined the United States of America for the next 400 years. The Indians had inhabited the western hemisphere for centuries before the European explorers arrived. Indians believed in the physical phenomena of nature on earth and in the sky inspiring them to live in harmony with all other creatures and the natural resources. They keenly observed the stars and constellations in the sky and used them for navigation and travel on land and sea. The calendars were based on celestial observations by early civilizations. Inka historians consider the settlement of Machu Pichu in Peru as solar observatory. The Mayan thousand year old pyramid at Chichenitza was positioned to reflect the Equinoxes. The Sun created an image of a serpent with shadow along the stairs of the pyramid. This was perceived as a warning about a catastrophic event. The three dimensional structure of the *khipu* was found in 2003, which depicts system of numbers. It is made of primary cord with up to a hundred strings in 24 colors with knots involving a variety of stones. It also revealed information about events that were more sophisticated than the Sumerian signs or the Egyptian hieroglyphic symbols. The Spaniards could not figure out the coding and burned Khipus in frustration in 1583 (Mann, 1491, Appendix B).

The spirits are still an intriguing phenomenon. When we talk of spirituality, we are really talking about the *spirit*. The Holy Spirit is a part of the prayer in every Christian congregation. This was added by King Constantine. When the spirit word is used in paranormal claims of communicating with the dead, it assumes a different connotation. The European Witch Trials were winding down in the 1600s. The rumors of witchcraft surfaced among farmers of the village Salem, near Boston, Massachusetts in 1692 when a young school girl appeared to be 'possessed' showing spasmodic movements. This was linked to witchcraft at that time and some people were hanged. In 1706, Ann Putnam confessed to her faked spasmodic reaction believed to be the influence of Satan at that time. Sacrifices are written in the Priestly codex Pentateuch. Animal sacrifices were done at Shiloh (1 Sam2.12ff, Bethel, 1 Kings 13.26ff). Death of Jesus is the ultimate sacrifice which is observed by sharing bread and wine in church. With the destruction of Temple in 70 CE the ritual of sacrifice stopped and was replaced by reparatory alternatives for sins.

The rise of organized religion introduced the word God to the vocabulary. It was probably, from the Lord God of Israel who won the contest over the pagan god Ba'al. The priest of Lord god was able to summon the fire to ignite the sacrifice and the priest of Ba'al god failed to do so. The word God is universal which is applicable to different names, in various languages in different religions. This has caused social, political or religious distinctions. Humanity needs to consolidate its enormous spiritual wealth to serve and preserve humanity.

The interfaith dialogue is an attempt to seek an understanding among all faiths honoring the sanctity of all religions. Dr. Alan Pace initiated the movement of Religious Pluralism 25 years ago that honors diverse faith communities throughout the world. Wayne Teasdale (1945-2004) was a pioneer in inter-religious initiative and a fine example of Christian openness to mystics and sages of other religious belief systems. He cared to listen attentively to the unfamiliar and seemingly strange religions but accommodated their beliefs as part of spirituality with tolerance, understanding and knowledge. The ownership of religions and the power base they command makes it extremely hard to relinquish their identity. Interfaith World Conference 2004 in Madrid, Spain held a common prayer reclaiming the sanctity of all faiths. One group, however, chose to hold their service at their own church at that specified time (Interreligious Insight). The 'Abraham Path Initiative' unveils the common ground of Abrahamic religions in the Hebrew Bible, the Koran and the New Testament. The spiritual ties to Abraham extend to Druze,

Baha'i, Mormons and Rastafarians. All religions developed with an affiliation to the prophets adopting a specific mode of worship, designation of sacred objects, texts, lineage, and their scriptures. The interpretation of Holy Scriptures has been an ongoing subject of scrutiny by the theologians, scholars, and historians during the historically changing social, religious and political environment. Recent archaeological discoveries have sparked debate among scholars about the biblical stories.

The Reformation movement in Christianity was initiated by Martin Luther, an Augustinian monk and teacher at the University of Wittenberg who challenged the church hierarchy in 1517 to break away from the Roman Catholic Church. He was excommunicated in 1520. Radical Swiss group, the Brethren, developed in 1527. They were called Anabaptists and perceived as threats to state religion. Executions and property confiscations by the state forced these groups to relocate in Holland, Russia and Germany. The movement persevered. History is a testimony to a quest for religious supremacy that killed millions in the fury of the crusades, jihads and holocaust over the centuries. The recent discovery of scrolls bearing the Gospel of Judas buried for centuries point out the changes in the New Testament which only incorporated gospels of Matthew, Mark, Luke and John. The gospels of Thomas and Philip were selectively left out by the bishops. The Jesus Papers, the Nag Hammadi scripts and Dead Sea Scrolls affect the stories written in the Bible and are being studied by the scholars. The "Last Supper", a significant moment before the arrest and crucifixion of Jesus was painted by Leonardo da Vinci from 1494 to 1498 in Milan's Church of Santa Maria delle Grazie. It shows the apostle sitting on the right of Jesus to be Mary Magdaline with whom Jesus had a child. However, this was questioned by serious scholars declaring it to be a hoax. Giovanni Maria Pala, a musician from Lecce, in southern Italy deciphered the hidden music of hymn to God in the painting Last Supper in 2007 (CNN) by following the Christian symbolism of bread, body of Christ, and hands to decipher the notes. It was revealed by reading from right to left because Leonardo da Vinci had used that method previously to hide musical clues earlier. The music was written for pipe organ used for church music in the 15th century. Pope Benedict XVI has responded to the newly emerging evidence about the gospels in his book Jesus of Nazareth (2007). He reaffirms the Resurrection and accepts two sides of Jesus, the divine and the human.

Religious practices in ancient times were based on blind faith in the law of the universe. In modern cultures, religion was dictated by the state. The civilized humanity understands that all religions adhere to the message in the scriptures of their holy books, honoring the prophets who served as guide for the good of all mankind. All prophets gave a universal message of spirituality. The religious boundaries were created by the Emperors and the religious elite. The turf war in religion continues in the 21st century. Christian faith, according to the Nicene-Constantinopolitan Creed, embraces Roman Catholicism, Eastern Orthodoxy, and Protestantism, three branches of Christianity. Al-Andalus under the Umayyad dynasty sustained multiculturism for 250 years where Muslims, Christians, and Jews coexisted and prospered during the 'golden age'. Social discriminatory practices in worship, taxation (jizya), and arrogance of superiority brought degradation beyond repair, and humanity is still looking for viable alternatives, both politically and through interreligious dialogue and understanding. After WWII the Universal Declaration of Human Rights was proclaimed by the United Nations General Assembly in December 1948. Article 18 states: Everyone has the right to freedom of thought, conscience and religion. However, enforcement of these words is still a challenge.

Initially man used the resources needed for survival. The basic needs grew into wants that created desires. Desires grow more and more as wants escalate starting the vicious cycle growing greed and ego. Desire develops as an individual's emotion and with the unchecked growth it engulfs the nations in a race for supremacy of ideology, financial power or the military might. Religious sentiments began to evolve in different cultures thousands of years ago. The mannerism and modes of prayer were different to seek blessings in the time of need. When the outcome was realized the faith grew stronger. Over time a variety of myths, customs, and beliefs took hold and were perpetuated through generations. *Chanoyu* in Japanese means the way of tea, a ceremony that is based on Taoism with the influence of Zen Buddhism. It is the attitude that has elevated it to a religious level and is observed to this day. It was fascinating to observe this ceremony which involved precise steps and was performed with grace and feminine elegance in the traditional kimono dress. The way of serving is of greater significance than the cup of green tea itself. Traditions are transformed into ceremonies, rituals, and communal practices that anchored the human race. Man had a great respect for nature which provided all the necessities to survive. This is still the mindset that prevails in the primitive isolated tribes in the few remote areas not exposed to civilization. The descendants of Indian tribes continue to respect nature as provider of life and adhere to the tribal legacy. Rituals and beliefs were depicted in carvings and pictures that offer a window into customs of previous cultures.

Human intellect ventured into philosophical exploration to experience the higher power. This gave rise to mysticism and 'kabbalah' which gives a description of the ten-dimensional structure related to Sefirot. A spiritual blueprint is depicted in the Tree of Life (Hieronimus 2008, 30). According to Abraham Abulafia's philosophy a higher intellectual experience is a religious phenomenon. It is caused by an overflow of cosmic intellects associated with the celestial bodies in the universe and angels. In an overview of the theosophic kabbalah in the 13th century, Dr. Elliott Wolfson confirms interest of mystics in the divine. Abraham developed a system he called Prophetic Kabbalah to focus on the barriers that separate God from man. He felt that there are separate intellects in the cosmos that overflow. If one contemplates and captures the overflow, one can acquire prophetic consciousness, the divine can be within our comprehension. Because it is a state of mind, it can be cultivated to achieve the power of prophecy. During the late 13th century, his ideas were combined with the Islamic mysticism of the Sufis. By the 16th century prophetic kabbalah of Abraham Abulafian had influenced philosophers like Solomon Alkabetz, Moses

Cordovero, and Elijah de Vidas as were Judah Albotini and Joseph ibn Zaiah in Jerusalem.

Lord Mahavira was born in 6th century BCE as a prince but he later transformed into an enlightened man. He put forth philosophy of *ahimsa*, the universal love to achieve nirvana, transcending beyond happiness and misery. He was the founder of Jainism in India. He preached non-violence, truth, right conduct and right knowledge. He gave up all worldly comforts when he was 30 years old and totally subdued desires and emotions. The same concept of non-violence was adopted by Mahatama Gandhi in India that resulted in freedom from the British in 1947. Martin Luther King also followed non-violence in the civil rights movement in the United States of America. Rev. Martin Luther King had a dream which was fulfilled when President Barak Obama, an African American, was elected as the 44th president of the United States.

Words of Jesus at thirty years of age (Matthews 25:35-36, 40):
 I was hungry and you gave me food, I was thirsty and you gave me drink, I was a stranger and you welcomed me, I was naked and you clothed me, I was sick and you visited me, I was in prison and you came to me.
This understanding demonstrates that God is enlightenment. Prophets have claimed that they are the only chosen ones to act on behalf of the Lord.

The message of the burning bush as was indicated by Isaiah established YHWH to be the Lord:
You are my witnesses, and my servant whom I have chosen, that you may know and believe me and understand that I am he. Before me no god was formed, nor shall there be any after me. I, I am YHWH, and beside me there is no savior (Isaiah 43:10).

Jesus threatened the belief system of the day when he said:
 You are from below, I am from above, you are of this world, I am not of this world " (John 8:23).
Jesus was firm when he said (John 8:24):
 You will die in your sins unless you believe that I am he.

Mohammad said (Koran xlix, 13):
> Say: O mankind, I am Allah's Messenger to all of you...
> There is no god but He...Believe in Allah and his Messenger.
> O people, your Lord is one and your ancestor is (also) one
> You are all descended from Adam and Adam was (born) of
> the earth. The noblest of you all in the sight of Allah is the
> most devout. Allah is knowing and all wise.

Lord Krishna in the Bhagavad Gita (Davis 1996, 162):
> The entire universe is pervaded by my unmanifest aspect.
> All beings abide in me. I do not abide in them; Influenced by
> my intention, primordial nature produces all animate and
> inanimate things. Because of this, the universe proceeds.

According to the Incas civilization (Hancock 1995, 58):
> ...the deluge was brought by Father Molina in *Relacion de
> las fabulas y ritos de los Yngas,* the Great Creator God
> appeared in human form as Viracocha from Tiahuanaco at
> Lake Titicaca replenishing the population on earth.

Guru Nanak preached spirituality encouraging both Muslims
and Hindus to look within and explore the universality of God.
He believed the five prayers for the Muslims be observed as:
Truth, Honest living, Charity in the name of God, Purity of
mind, and Adoration of God (AGGS, p. 141). Guru Nanak
referred to Hindu sacred thread (Janeoo) metaphorically:
> Make compassion the cotton,
> and thread of contentment;
> Tie the knot of continence,
> with a twist of truth.
> O Pandit, wear such a thread.
> It does not break or get soiled.
> It is neither burnt nor lost. (AGGS, p. 471)

Diversity in religions longs for identity by adhering to customs
and rituals of faith that differentiate them. Alan Race, Editor-in
Chief, Interreligious Insight in Leicester UK, contemplated on
the past three decades and observed that in 1970s we first

witnessed earth from the moon which made us think as inhabitants of this 'global village', the Earth. This generated the realization of inter-connectedness on our planet. The 1980s were more open to entertain the idea of plurality of religions and universal sacred heritage. Unity was a cherished feeling in faith. We felt encouraged to collectively welcome a harmonious future. 1990s revealed the deep seated emotions of religious and ideological superiority of one religion over the other. Every religion went in a defensive posture as they rallied towards exclusivity (Interreligious Insight, April 2007) . The phrase: Let's dialogue in earnest, but don't expect us to water-down our religion, clearly reveals the deeply embedded sentiments. Mehmet Okuyan of the University of Ondokuz in Samsun, Turkey, reiterates that cultural and political dominance elicits a negative image initiating defense mchanisms.

Theory of Secularization ignores the influence of religious sentiments on societies and culture. The conflict in former Yugoslavia was about religion and it became a political nightmare where people of the same descent and speaking the same language were divided only by their religion. Croats are Catholic, Serbs are Orthodox and Bosnians are Muslims. The Kyoto Declaration of the 8th World Assembly of Religions for Peace encouraged dialogue to promote reconciliation and healing, a message conveyed at the end of conferences. Rev. Dr. Marcus Braybrook, President of the World Congress of Faiths, a proponent of the Interfaith Movement has challenged every faith to revisit their teachings. Religion has often been misused as an excuse for violence. He quoted the words of Jesus as a Gospel reading at a service in Assisi:
Love your enemies, do good to those who hate you.
All religions must relinquish the preconceived superiority of their religion, violence for personal salvation, and perceived threat to their own religion. One religion may be skeptic of another religion, but atheists don't believe in any faith yet some claim to be spiritual. They seem to transcend all religious denominations. Recently religious leaders have been exposed about their business dealings, morals and ethics as they succumbed to the lure of vices eroding their standing and faith.

33

History shows that every conqueror has sought blessings for victory in war fully knowing that countless lives will be lost. Suicide bombers are glorified as martyrs and heroes convincing them that it is a holy cause with rewards in afterlife.

Abraham Garcia, a Mayan spiritual leader said:
    Peace isn't the simple silencing of bullets. It must be an inner change toward other people, respect for the way they think and live.

A Cambodian Buddhist leader Maha Gosananda stated:
    We have to remove the landmines in our hearts before we can remove them from the ground to modify our cultural outlook and usher in a culture of peace.

A 14th century Persian poet Hafiz was asked: What is the sign of someone who knows God? He said: who has 'put down the knife', so often used upon themselves and others. They no longer hurt anyone physically, emotionally, spiritually and they are safe themselves.

Cultures developed and flourished in India, Egypt, Greece, China and the western hemisphere for more than 5000 years. The archaeological evidence has revealed the rise of cultures with great spiritual philosophies, magnificient architecture as seen in the ruins of ancient exquisite monuments with intricate carvings, planned cities, beautiful plazas and palaces with vaulted ceilings. Guru Arjan Dev expressed unity of God which is portrayed in following verses (AGGS, p. 885):

    Some say Ram Ram, others say Khuda,
        Some worship Gosain, others pray to Allah.
    He is the Sustainer, the Protector of all.
    Some bathe at sacred sites, others go to Hajj,
        Some meditate in prayer, others bow their head.
    Some recite Vedas, others Koran,
        Some wear white clothes, others blue.
    Some are called Turks, others Hindus ..., says Nanak:
        One who accepts God's will knows God's secret.
    Humans are wired with instincts of aggression for territorial dominance. Faith and religion is an antidote to soften that

emotion. Harmful instincts have been subdued due to rules of accepted behaviour in societies. Religions lay down the doctrines to require morality, good deeds, mutual support and civility.

NUMBERS IN MYTHOLOGY

There are remarkable similarities in Greek, Egyptian and Indian mythologies. Is it a coincidence? In the ancient times myths developed in lands far apart but there were similarities in rituals, structures, knowledge of the planets as reported by Sellers, Santillana and von Dechend. Kings and chiefs had political jurisdictions, trade routes for commerce, armies, well developed agricultural practices, irrigation systems, knowledge of celestial movements, solar and lunar calendars, and planned routes for transportation promoting their faiths.

Old Babylonian legend talks about 10 kings before the flood. Egyptians describe 10 Shining Ones who ruled consecutively before the Deluge. The 10th Egyptian ruler led others on a vessel and survived the global flood. Hindus mention 10 Pitris who ruled before the global flood.

In ancient Babylon, Zisudra, a hero, managed survival with 7 humans on the Ark in the flood. In ancient Egypt, Toth, a hero, survived the Deluge with 7 sages. In India, Manu, a hero, survived Pralaya (global flood) with 7 Rishis (sages).

Hercules in Greek mythology is depicted fighting Lernaean Hydra. Hrsna (Krishna) is depicted fighting the Kalya serpent.

Dionysus in Greek mythology holds a Trident.
Shiva in Hindu mythology holds a Trident.

Dionysus with snake, leopard by his side, and the moon in the background at Mt. Olympus is portrayed in Greek mythology. The Indian mythology shows Shiva with a cobra around his neck, sitting on a leopard skin, and the moon behind his head at Mt. Kailash (abode of snow) in the Himalayas.

The phenomenon of precessional wobble appears in codes of numbers that appear in distant lands associated with different gods giving clues to the precessional shifts based on constellations in the zodiac degrees relating to the equinoxes accurately. The clues may have been passed on in stories of different lands but they take us back 5000 years for symbolism. The prevailing thought process was remarkably similar and the advanced knowledge exhibited by these ancient cultures is amazing. The celestial movements were calculated in ancient times which match the measurements with modern technology.

Jane B. Sellers, Archaeo-astronomer has confirmed the concepts advanced by Santillana and von Dechend. This honors the lost cultures for their intellect that inspires archaeologists in the 21st century. The following comparisons are drawn from the comprehensive work of Graham Hancock (1995). It is exciting and fascinating to learn that myths influenced both the Old World and the New World 5000 years ago.

Egyptian numbers are based on the Osiris mythology:

12 (months in a year); 30 (days in a month);
360 (days in a year)

Ra, sun god cursed his wife Nut not to bear a child on any day. Thoth god added 5 days so Osiris could be born to the beloved Nut. Evil deity Set planned to kill Osiris with 72 conspirators. The Pyramid Texts are reported to have Osiris mythology dating back to 2450 BCE. There was a tradition even in the past few centuries with clues in treasure maps that guided from one lead to the next to the site of the treasure in the era of pirates.

The knowledge of the transcendental number pi is indicated in the design of the Great Pyramid of Egypt built 4500 years ago with original height of 481.3949 and the perimeter of its base 3023.16 feet occupying more than 13 acres. The ratio was 2pi (2 x 3.14) and the specified angle for the sides of the pyramid was 52 degrees, the only angle that could work with that height to perimeter ratio. All four sides were finished with mirror like cladding with 115,000 polished casing stones weighing 10 tons each. The massive earthquake in 1301 CE loosened stones which were removed and taken to Cairo. The Pyramid of the Sun at

36

Teotihuacan in Mexico also used the transcendental number pi. The 233.5 feet height is in a 4pi relationship to the perimeter of its base 2932.76 feet. The knowledge of pi was used in two different continents long before the Greeks discovered this transcendental number (Hancock 1995, 290 and 319).

The numbers 12, 30, 72, and 360 give the following information:

Constellations in zodiac = 12

Degrees allocated to each constellation = 30

Years required by sun to complete 1 degree shift = 72

Number of degrees in ecliptic = 360

Years required to cover 12 zodiac constellations = 2160
   (2148 by current calculations)

Number of years to complete precessional cycle = 25,920
   (25,776 by current calculations)

Days added by god Thoth to a year = 5 (360+ 5=365)
   (365 days in a year, current number)

The Maya civilization used the following calculations in the Mayan Long Count calendar. These numbers also appeared in the Osiris calculations:

1 Tun=360 days	6 Tuns=2160 days
1 Katun=7200 days	6 Katuns=43200 days

Angkor city was built between the 9th and 13th centuries as the capital of the ancient Khmer Empire. French naturalist Henri Mouhot found the Angkor Temples in the jungles of Kampuchea in Cambodia. Some residents think that these were built by the King of the Angels. Its layout and dimensions suggest that the plan was based on precessional calculations as the ancient Hindu mythology suggests 540 gods churned the ocean with a serpent. Addition of numbers 36 and 72 is 108, and half of this is 54.

Roads leading to the Temple=5
   (Bridges over the crocodile infested moat around site)
Stone figures lining each avenue=108
   (54 on each side of the 5 avenues)
Total number of statues on 5 avenues=540
   (Hindu gods churning the Ocean)

In India, the Orion constellation is called Kal-Purush, the time deity. The figure 108 shows up in different combinations. Ravi Kumar, a Vedic Mathematician, regards 108 to be a sacred

37

figure that is significant in celestial measurements.
Diameter of Sun divided by diameter of Earth = 108
Distance between Earth and Sun divided by dia. of Sun=108
Distance between Earth and Moon divide by dia. of Moon=108
Stanzas in Rig Veda are 10,800 and wordcount is 432,000.

According to the Hebrew kabala, the names and numbers are essential to invoke divine powers.
Cycles of years per Rosicrucian tradition=108
(to show the influence of secret brotherhood)
Angels who invoke Sephiroth, divine powers =72

The Triad concept was important in the Hung League in China and in Singapore that involved figures 108, 72, 36, 360.
.
United Nations World Heritage includes sutras of Rig Veda.
Sixteen Sutras in Veda were used for mathematical problems.

Three steps to calculate square of a number ending in 5 e.g. 25:
1. 5 multiplied by 5 = 25
2. Number in 10th place is 2, multiply by the next, i.e. 3 X 2= 6
3. Place this number before the number in step 1= 625.
So, 25 multiplied by 25 = 625.
If one of the multiples ends in 9, 99, or 999: Example 73 & 99:
1. Deduct 1 from 73 = 72
2. Deduct 72 from 99 = 27
3. Place Step 2 number after Step 1 number = 7227.
So, 73 multiplied by 99 = 7227.

Avestic Aryans believed in Four Epochs.
First: There was purity, no sin, holy god Ahura Mazda.
People were tall and lived a long life.
Second: Evil attempted mind degradation but failed.
Third: Good and evil were influencing mind equally.
Fourth: In the current epoch evil is triumphant and vices have the upper hand (Hancock, 1995, 200). Hindu mythology also recognizes Four Epochs. 1. Satyuga: the era of truth and spirituality; 2. Treta: virtues were reduced 25% and vices corrupted the minds; 3. Duaper: virtues declined 50% and

38

desire for personal possessions increased; 4. Kaliyuga: Evil emotions, lust, anger, greed, ego, gained an upper hand.

According to Hindu mythology, Lord Vishnu's abode is located on mount Meru, 80,000 miles in circumference bedecked with gold and jewels. Brahmapuri, the domain of Brahma, is 800 miles long, 400 miles wide, and 40 miles high on the Mahameru Mountain where the city of Brahma, Manovati is located with 8 other cities. Amaravati is Indra's heavenly place (Singh 2006, p. 147-148).

Kabbalah's gematria (letters turned into numbers to caculate their value) in Judaism offers an insight into the lives of seven prophetesses of Israel by studying letters in the names and turning into numbers (Hieronimus, 2008). Seven Biblical Prophetesses of Israel are associated each with a specific day of the week, a specific species of the 7 foods, and correspondence with one of the 7 qualities, collectively paving the mystical path towards prophecy, the ability to know the 'Will of the Divine'. A detailed account of Seven Prophetesses is given in chapter III Role of Women in Religion.

LANGUAGES AND RELIGIOUS TEXTS

Hebrew Text

Koran (Arabic)

1. *仏の心とは大慈悲である。あらゆる手だてによって、すべての人びとを救う大慈の心、人とともに病み、人とともに悩む大悲の心である。 **Buddhist scriptures (Pali)**

Sikh Scriptures (Gurmukhi)

LANGUAGE AND RELIGIOUS TEXTS

Honey bees give the direction to the source, the distance and the abundance of honey depicted in dance, by waggling tail and the excitement to show the riches of honey at the source. This is communication, not language. Chimpanzees were known to develop a sign language in 1966. Washoe, a chimp could make 132 signs at the age of four. She could make a gesture but it was inconsistent, an imitation and not spontaneous communication. African Gray parrot can greet, recite sentences, sing but that is not consistent and depends on parrot's mood. It is a playful activity on bird's terms. There is no conversation in words in the wild, only sounds of expression.

Homo sapiens are the first as a species to use language. The Cro-Magnon could speak. The Neanderthals could only make grunts. The anatomical changes in modern humans evolved over a long period of time and brain had fully developed by 200,000 years ago. The behavioral changes happened suddenly through a remarkable mutation 50,000 years ago. A single gene initiated the development of speech and language (Nature, Oct. 4, 2001). A defective gene would exhibit difficulty in learning grammar, speech and sound variations. Speech developed as a result of anatomical changes. Apes, like the human infants can swallow and breathe at the same time without choking. The voice box, larynx, is high in the throat and reduces the risk of choking. The flat skull structure of the Neanderthals like the apes elevated the larynx. In humans, as the baby grows, the arched skull is flexed that moves the voice box lower increasing the ability to produce various sounds. This increases the risk of choking after 2 years of age. The hyoid bone in Neanderthals supported the tongue differently than in humans. Speech facilitated communication, a major advantage over the Neanderthals. The new tool and the behavioral change offered an advantage over the Neanderthals. The FOXP2 gene is linked to the ability to use language and it was present in Homo 100,000 years ago even though the dawn of human language is placed at 50,000 years ago. Chimps and apes have a different form of FOXP2 gene than the humans. Recent discoveries suggest that cognitive and language ability developed 80,000 to 100,000 years ago in Africa from where humans migrated to Europe and Asia. Scholars believe that spoken language and and its structural make up are universal.

Children learn effortlessly in any culture but it requires focus and dedication to learn another language at a later age. Our brain is able to transcend cultural intricacies or physical handicap unless there is 'specific language impairement'. According to Darwin, sounds were part of an excitement during courtship that also involved the territorial dominance, emotional expression of rage and passion as part of biophilia. It is believed that language and music evolved together but diverged later. Rhythm appears to be universal that is a twin to music used by ancient tribes for rituals with music and dance. Muscle helps us provide auditory perception which reflects emotional influences. Our brain is equipped to register tone, pitch and rhythm to appreciate the lyrics and sounds of melodies eliciting feelings. Neuroscientists started to explore music in the 1980s when music and its therapeutic effects were observed in patients. Dr. Cichoria became obsessed with piano after he got hit with lightning. Salima M developed a tumor in her temporal lobe that sparked a new fascination for classical music. Neuroscientists believe, it is a sensory-limbic hyperconnection that triggers musicophilia, unexpected feelings, talents, and religious feelings (Sacks, 2007). Dr. David Matlock of the Peoria Campus of the University of Illinois Medical School stated that American Heart Association recommends 100 chest compressions per minute. The music of the old disco song *staying alive* came close to the recommended rhythm at 103 beats per minute in CPR training.

According to Sapir-Whorf hypothesis, languages express the way people perceive the world. Language evolved gradually.

Clay tokens, like coins were called *calculi* used for counting till 3,500 BCE.

Cuneiform writing was pictographic, symbolic pictorial depictions of objects by pushing single characters into clay. This was used by Sumerians around 3500 BCE and other pictographic languages, Akkadian and Hittite developed in the fertile crescent region.

Ideographic symbols developed by 3100 BCE. This created an abstract rendition of the objects still in cuneiform was used from 2144 to 2124 BCE.

Egyptian hieroglyphs were discovered in the Temple of Remses II around 1250 BCE listing the Egyptian pharaohs. The writing form was for Coptic language. It developed from both the pictographic and ideographic symbolism. It also showed the syllables and consonants and developed around 3000 BCE.

Hieratic script was quicker in the shorthand symbolism. It was especially better for engraving on the obelisks. This change was reflected by 2500 BCE. The same technique was later used to write on papyrus with ink.

The Phoenician alphabet was developed from Hieratic script by 900 BCE which was adopted by the Greeks. This alphabet was the precursor for the development of Arabic, Hebrew, and the languages of India, Southeast Asia and Mongolia (McWhorter). Sir Arthur Evans (1851-1941), an archaeologist, discovered Linear B, a precursor to Greek alphabet.

European ethnic diversity started 5000 years ago when Indo-European family of languages were spread by people from central Asia i.e. the Italic (Italian, French, Spanish, Portuguese, Romanian); the Throcco-Illyrian (Albanian); and the Uralic (Finnish and Hungarian). All the diversity, linguists believe traces back to mega-ancestors. Moravian Prince Rotislav wanted to resist German influence by developing books in Slavonic. Cyrill and Methodius were brothers born in Greece. They were sent around 863 to translate books by developing an alphabet that became the Cyrillic alphabet, a version of Greek and Glagolitic that was able to express Slavonic sounds. Roots of linguistic families such as Indo-European, Tibeto-Burman, Dravidian, and Austro-Asiatic are found in India. Dravidian language literature shows its existence in 3rd century BCE and is the oldest on the subcontinent.

Languages are modified over time due to assimilation, vowel shift and consonant weakening. Tone makes a big difference.

The word *ma* in Mandarin Chinese can mean hemp, scold, horse or mother due to a variation in four tones. Cantonese Chinese has six tones thus the word *fan* expressed in different tones can mean share, powder, divide, grave or excited. This effect in tone variation has influence in other languages. Semantic drift changes the meanings of words. The word silly in Old English meant blessed but in the Middle Ages silly meant innocent. By 1600s it meant weak but now, it is understood as ignorant. *Sweetmeat* was used for candy when meat in Old English meant food. Now meat is animal flesh and sweet is sweet confection. Linguists call it Semantic narrowing.

Latin was spread by Romans from Italy all across Europe. It developed into French, Spanish, Italian, Portuguese and Romanian regarded as the Romance languages. Languages differentiate into dialects which are transformed into a new language over time (McWhorter, 2004).
The standardization of language and its predominance was the result of different influences.

    Standard English dialect is used in London.

    Francien French is used in national courts.

    Castllian Spanish, spoken by the Spanish armies endured. Denmark ruled Sweden and Norway before their independence and the common language was called Scandinavian. Sweden gained independence in 1526 and their language became Swedish. Norway became independent in 1814 and their language was called Norwegian. Danish therefore became the Language of Denmark. It is quite common to speak a different regional language and use another national language for official use, read the news in a different language, discuss politics in another language among friends or at home. This duality is observed in many countries.

    Standard Arabic and Egyptian Arabic (Egypt)

    Swiss German and High German (Switzerland)

    Katharevousa and Dhimitiki (Greece)

    Native American Guarani and French (Paraguay)

    Russian by masses and French by the Czars (Russia)

A political overbearance was noticed in Quebec where English was the official language and French was used at home. A law in

1970 made French the official language conducting government business in French and changed street signs in French. When the standard language is anchored firmly and is spoken, the language evolves naturally. Standard and the colloquial interact called *diglossia*. It is observed in 25% of the world. In India with 14 different languages, diglossia is regional.

In Javanese it is extended into three levels according to ones status in hierarchy, top, bottom, and the middle. The choice of words varies from eating to dining, kids to children, wife to better half, Ya (yup) to yes. This is termed *triglossia*. In India besides English and Hindi the third language can be any of the fourteen regional languages; in Spain it is Spanish, Catalan, and Basque, and in Luxembourg, French and German take on Letzebuergesch, the local German dialect (McWhorter, 2004).

According to Joseph H. Greenberg, a linguist at Stanford, Indian languages in the Americas are derived from three main linguistic families. Aleut spoken from Alaska to Greenland; Ne-Dene spoken in western Canada and Southwest United States; and Amerind spoken in the rest of Indian tribes in Central America down to South America. The evidence points out that there were three migrations. The ancestors of Aleuts crossed Bering Strait around 2000 BCE. The ancestors of Na-Dene around 7000 BCE and the Amerind speaking Indians of the Clovis culture in Blackwater Draw broke away from the northeast Asian groups around 14,000 years ago. This is based on the study of 28 key crown and root traits studied by Christy G. Turner II of Arizona State University. Clovis paleo-Indians were the first to inhabit America and Indians migrated from Alaska to Chile. Two geneticists, Sandro L. Bonatto and Francisco M. Bolzano of Federal University of Rio Grande do Sul in Brazil analyzed mitochondrial DNA that was first reported by Pena and the Brazilian team in 1990. Scientists believe a band of Indians left Asia between 33,000 to 43,000 years ago which disseminated the Haplogroup A in three migrations as the Ice Age permitted half to migrate to Canada and the United States before the Laurentide Ice Sheet towards the East and the Cordilleran Ice Sheet along the western coast merged. Others had to wait till the Ice-free Corridor Route opened between these two Ice Sheets. This opening created the second or third wave of migration. Tom Dillehay of the University of Kentucky with Mario Pino of the University of Chile concluded after twenty years of work on excavations at Monte Verde that paleo-Indians lived there at least 12,800 years ago. They had traveled ten thousand miles from the Bering Strait. The first Indians could have arrived 32,000 years ago. Archaeologists rely on radio-carbon dating, mitochondrial DNA, the soil samples of the site and the artifacts along with other geological data to confirm the results of their research. The debate continues while new data supports the current views and also raises new questions.

The Embera tribe of Panama has passed on the stories only orally and do not have a written language at this time. The population of this semi-nomadic indigenous clan is 15000. A missionary Douglas Schermerhorn has said, The Embera people often do not want anyone, including themselves, to write or print anything in their own language. They feel this would be akin to selling their language for profit. Christian missionaries tried since the 1950s to carry out the linguistic analysis of Embera language to translate the Bible but there is no agreement on the shapes of letters and the Embera people don't want the alphabet or the written language written. This culture survived for centuries in the jungles of Choco and Darien along Panama border with Colombia (www.nativeplanet.org). The modern influences are encroaching upon the accessible tribal sites. Tourism is opening up remote areas introducing the indigenous tribal cultures to the outside world. This interaction is tempting them to change their tribal ways for a life in the modern world. Their dancing and crafts exhibit the Embera culture to visitors. They share the old legends and tales of man-monsters and dance-rituals of medicine men. They believe in the spirits that assume animal shapes and engaged in wars of good and evil. The Mentawai tribe of Siberut, Indonesia rejected an exposure to the modern influence of tourism and chose to maintain Mentawai identity and live in harmony with nature. Next generation may be open to change.

The ancient written languages were a pictorial depiction as in the early Chinese and Japanese scripts. The Inka had developed a communication system by khipu where each knot of the string as part of the other subsidiary strings is attached to the main chord, adding the information about historical events, rituals and numerical data. The bundles of yarn with knots represented the library collection. The alphabet based languages like Arabic, Latin and Sanskrit developed prior to the derivative languages of today. The earliest revolution in mass communication can be traced to Bi Sheng in China who used movable wood blocks in printing around 1040 CE. However, Johannes Gutenberg in Mainz, Germany is accredited to the movable copper type that was the efficient main process that used oil-based ink in printing. By 1455 he had printed 180 copies of 42-line Bible in Latin. The same writing by a monk would have taken 20 years. This process allowed printing in other languages and available to all people. This assured the viable transmission of beliefs to the masses and to the future generations. Teachings of prophets and historical events were written in the scriptures. The emerging belief systems were established as religion in the areas of their influence. The variations were linked to languages and the geographical territories. The myths and memories in the indigenous cultures are linked to places. The sites linked to the prophets became the religious sites of pilgrimage.

It is estimated that during the course of human history 10,000 languages were used. There are 6,000 languages still in use suggesting the demise of 4000 languages burying the cultural history with them. Linguists believe that 600 of these are well established at this time (Kostyal: National Geographic). Only 200 languages are used in official documents and in literature at this time. Language is a vehicle that propels history, culture and religion. It defines ethnicity and generates affiliation to establish communities tracing linkage to the countries of migration. The religious affiliation also unifies ethnic groups creating a strong bond and an effort to preserve cultural heritage. There are 700 languages in Indonesia and 400 in India. China with one billion people is the largest ethnic group in the world speaking 200 languages. The Chinese were unified during the Han dynasty. In the Americas there were 1200 languages spoken by Indians that have been grouped under 180 linguistic families. Eighty six tongues were spoken in the area now California. Europe had four language families using mainly Indo-European. The other three were Finno-Ugric, Basque, and Turkic.

The Indian Myna bird and African Gray parrots are capable of mimicking a language with an authentic accent. Symphony of nature still plays in the tropical rain forests and the nature conservancy groups are doing everything to preserve these ornithological concerts performed daily at dawn.

I had the privilege to attend a function in 2006 which honored fallen veterans of wars. The guest speakers were Samuel N. Tso of the Navajo *Zuni Red Running into Water* Clan and Keith M. Little of Tonelia, Arizona, President of The Navajo Code Talkers Society. Navajo Indians were recruited by the United States Army to develop a code during WWII. The code could not be deciphered by the Japanese intelligence and was instrumental in the victory of Allied Forces. This was the pivotal mission that played a significant role in the Pacific advance to Iwo Jima and other islands towards Japan during the battle campaigns of World War II. The Navajo native language is Athapaskan used by the tribes in Arizona, New Mexico and Utah. There are 150 native languages spoken by tribes in the United States. Fifty five of these languages can be spoken by few native Indians.

Europeans passed through Cherokee Indians territory in 1540. De Soto saw the Cherokee Indians and was treated as a friend. Sequoyah, a Cherokee, is the only American Indian who devised a writing system by himself. His syllabary was introduced to the Cherokee Council in 1821. The Cherokee Indians became literate within months. The Cherokee Museum has installed a carved statue of Sequoyah who invented the script and language. Captain R. H. Pratt opened the first Native American boarding school in Carlisle, Pennsylvania during 1879. The Cherokee Boarding School was founded in 1880 but the English-only policy was enforced that suppressed the use of the native language (Cherokee Tourism).

Nez Perce helped Lewis and Clark's Discovery trip in 1805 to cross the Bitterroot in 11 days what Indians called Trail to the Buffalo which they used to hunt buffalo east of the Bitterroot mountains. Lewis stated : I think we can justly affirm to the honor of these people that they are the most hospitable, honest, and sincere people that we have met within our voyage. They gave food and guided them through 5235-foot Lolo Pass towards the Pacific Ocean. That trail is named the Lolo Trail. The American Indians were neighborly, open to new ideas and hospitable to new comers. Communication can happen with a few words as used in Pidgin English spoken by early traders in Canton from 1600s to 1900s with American Indians of Rhode Island and Creole in the South Seas pidgin.

The first artificial language was Volapuk, invented by a Bavarian priest in 1879. It included 40% English vocabulary and was based on Romance and Germanic languages. The subject-object-verb order is widely prevalent worldwide.

Lord's Prayer in Volapuk

O Fat obas, kel binol in suls, paisaludomoz nem ola…, means Oh our Father, who art in heaven, hallowed be thy name…

Esperanto, another artificial language, was developed by Ludovic Zamenhof in 1887 with mostly Romance and German vocabulary that is used by a million people. The Bible and the Koran was translated in Esperanto. Solresol, a musical language was invented in France in 1800s (McWhorter, 2004).

In kabbalah, letters are souls and words are bodies. Abraham explained that words can convey concealed message as in the Book of Formation referred to as stones and houses. Hebrew, like Urdu and Persian, is read from right to left. *Tet Pey Shin* means judgement. (read Shin Pey Tet). Arranged as *Pey Tet Shin* means flood. In English, racecar, kayak, level are the words that can be read and written left to right and also right to left.

SECTARIAN DIVIDE

From the early days there was a split in the Jerusalem church between Greek speaking Jews who opposed the Temple and Hebrews (Acts 6-7). The contention was about the extent to which Christians should observe the Jewish Law while Gentiles started to attend the church in Antioch (Acts 11:20). By the year 50 AD there were three basic concepts that were proposed by the Christian leaders at the time.

James, brother of Jesus, was the leader of Jerusalem church and wanted the Jewish Law to be followed.

Peter wanted to minimize Jewish rituals for the Gentiles allowing separate Eucharist meal celebrations for Jews and Gentiles.

Paul stressed that the resurrection of Christ marked the end of the Jewish Law with no distinction in church between Jews and Gentiles (Galatians 3:28). Paul's views were not accepted in the church of Antioch. He became apostle to the gentiles and started missions in Asia, Greece and Rome. Some Christians believed that Jesus appeared to be a man but was Christ who came from a divine realm in the flesh. This is called Docetism.

Gnostic religion gives importance to knowledge for salvation rather than faith and services. Gnostic theology believes in a transcendent God and a creator god for the material world. Gnostic cosmology sees the world as prison where human souls are held captive. Gnostic anthropology believes that human spirit is co-substantial with God. Gnostic soteriology deals with gnosis, the knowledge that helps to awaken the captive spirit which escapes from the body and from worldly attachments to go back to the divine. Christ is observed as a Gnostic revealer. The Gnostics were suppressed in the 4th and 5th centuries when the Ecumenical Councils of Bishops settled controversies. Irenaeus, bishop of Lyon wrote in the 2nd century against Christian heresies. He was an important figure in the ancient church supported by the ecclesiastical establishment. The 13 Nag Hammadi codices and Dead Sea Scrolls offer more information about ancient Gnostic religion. Gospel of Judas has

raised controversy among scholars about the identity of Judas
and his role in Christianity. Twelve disciples in the Gospel are
symbols of the proto-orthodox church founded by them where
the world creator god *Saklas* is worshipped, not the true God.
Judas Iscariot in the New Testament is a hero, closest to Jesus.
Judas in the Gospel is the thirteenth demon (daimon), and not a
hero in his prophecy about Judas:

You will do worse than all of them.

For the man that clothes me, you will sacrifice him.
Micgael Baigent a religious historian has worked two decades on
the historical perspective in light of Dead Sea Scrolls and the
time of Jesus in his book *The Jesus Papers* (2006).

The factions in Islam grew out of a struggle for leadership
between Ali, son-in-law of Prophet Mohammed and Mu'awiyah,
founder of Umayyad dynasty (Fakhry, 2004. 39-42). As the story
goes, Mu'awiyah tricked Ali by consenting to arbitration. This
raised suspicion and a perception of Ali's weakness causing
mutiny in his army. The mutineers became the secessionists or
Kharijites who believed in the allegiance to Holy Law as the
orthodox sect. They regarded tyranny as an alternative and
questioned the need for a caliph. Under their law if any Muslim
committed a political or other sin, he will be killed as an infidel.
A caliph could also be deposed and killed if he committed a sin.

The other sect, the Murji'ah was based on the knowledge, love of
God, and submission to God. According to their belief, good
deeds had no bearing on their legitimacy of faith as only God
can determine the genuineness of faith. If one believes in
submission and love of God, they have a claim to paradise.

After Muhammed's death, Shi'ah emerged as the third sect in
Islam who accepted only Ali and his successors from his progeny
to be the legitimate caliph they call Imam who is the only one
authorized to interpret the Holy Law. The two most revered
Imams are the 10th Ali al-Hadi and his son 11th Hassan al-
Askari. The Al-Askaria Mosque with Gold Dome was the holiest
shrine destroyed in sectarian violence in Iraq in 2007. Shi'ites
believe in theocratic rule in an Islamic state headed by Imam by

divine designation, not by election and with no provision to depose because the Imam represents God on earth.

Buddhism originated in India and gained prominence under the support of Maurya dynasty. With Gupta dynasty in power Buddhism declined in India and spread to Far East into China, Afghanistan, Tibet, Japan, and Southeast Asia. Hinduism became the main religion in India. With invasions by Muslim emperors, Hinduism in India was threatened by conversion to Islam. The 9th Guru of the Sikhs, Teg Bahadur was approached by Hindus Rajas for help to save their religion and kingdoms. The Guru agreed to support Hindu princes and did not accept convertion to Islam. He was beheaded in Delhi for refusing to convert to Islam. Guru Gobind Singh , the 10th Sikh Guru initiated Khalsa, the saint soldiers, to combat oppression and cruelty towards Hindus and Sikhs. The turban and unshorn hair established an identity which symbolized assurance of trust and defence of women and faith and a target of the regime.

Ottoman Empire and Islam were one, and the chief religious authority Abu al-Su'ud reconciled Islamic and Sultanic Codes of Law from 1545-1574. Under the Ottoman Empire, Albanians and Cretans were converted to Islam in Southern Europe. Bosnians and Croats converted to Islam in Central Europe so that they could become land owners or run a business during the Turkish rule.

As Islam spread in the Middle East, the Roman Empire declined, the Jews moved to different areas, Sephardim first moved into Iberian Peninsula and after expulsion in 1492 they moved to England, Holland, and the Americas. Ashkenazi moved into Germany and Eastern Europe later joining Sephardim to avoid persecution in Europe. The Jewish scriptures, the Torah and the commentaries on the scriptures, the Talmud, maintained their religious identity.

Judaism and Christianity have been differentiated for centuries. Christians were engaged in converting Jews to Christianity in the past. Modern Christology in its efforts to eliminate the anti-

Jewish bias imply that death and resuurection of Jesus do not replace God's words at Mt. Sinai and affirm Judaism as Jew's religion, a dual covenant, but assert that the way to heaven is only through Jesus Christ. Jews await another Messiah and do not accept Jesus Christ to be that Messiah. At its first assembly in Amsterdam in 1948 the World Congress of Churches addressed the extermination of six million Jews in Shoah acknowledging the suffering of the Jews. It was affirmed that Jesus was a Jew, a faithful son of the covenant at the Evanston Assembly in 1954. In 1965 the decree Nostra Aetate was issued by Second Vatican Council. The Church and the Jewish People (CCJP) in 1967 agreed that Jesus Christ fulfilled God's revelation stated in Hebrew Scriptures and emphasized the significance of Holy Land for the Jews. Pope John Paul II established Commission for relations with Jews in 1974. Its report encouraged Christians to condemn anti-semitism. At this time scholars have made assertion that both religions depict the complimentary aspects of the same divine. The statement of the World Congress of Churches Ecumenical Considerations on Jewish-Christian Dialogue in 1982 stated that the Christian traditions were the basis of the Nazi Holocaust and suffering of the Jews was acknowledged. Pope John Paul II apologized to the Jewish people. This is a major change from the sentiments of theocentric model of Christianity held for twenty centuries. The Orthodox Jewish theologian Eliezer Berkovitz gave Job's example who believed in God and said that God was hidden in Auschewitz but was actually present. He is a Saviour as Hidden God and Redeemer of Israel. Christian sensitivity to suffering of the Jews offers hope in Christian-Jewish relations. Spirituality is the unifying common denominator for all religions. The sacred texts defined different religions. It is imperative that societies around the globe contemplate on the central message in all religious texts which urges unity, harmony and peace.

RELIGIOUS TEXTS

Scribes wrote the texts for people to study. These books served as successful guides for a faithful life. When these books were declared to be authoritative in religions, they were established as religious scriptures. Major developments appeared during the Renaissance and Reformation movements of the 16th century, and during the Rationalization period in the 17th century which gave impetus to the era of scientific thought. Scriptures take us beyond the material (matter) to the realm of the Spirit (divine). St. Augustine, Bishop of Hippo clarified modes of interpretation:

The literal reading explains what happened.

The allegorical paradigm inspires to believe.

The moral view guides towards proper behavior.

The anagogical makes one contemplate on purpose in life and where we go from here. Modernity embraced science and cannot accept the mythipoeic mind. Search for the truth includes deeper scrutiny and probing the time of writing, its purpose, its religious and social context, author's identity and verification of narrative. Writer's narrative is influenced by the intended thought in language, scribe's ideology, theology, and knowledge of the historical events. The readers is not present at the time of writing. Imaginative reading of the texts, reading with faith, devotion, and correct interpretation leads to wonderous truth. (Shillington 2002, 219-222)

James Kugel, an Orthodox Jew, believes in the strength of the Documentary Hypothesis. Scriptures are divinely inspired, their correct interpretation is vital to comprehend the message given in the form of parable or metaphor. Scriptures are the compilation of prophetic proclamations that were passed on orally for generations. The scribes reflect the recollection of events and statements written long after the time the words were spoken. The sermons in parables and metaphors have lead to different perceptions, analyses, and interpretations. Literal meaning can sometimes obscure the real message. Subsequent writings have gone through revisions with additions and deletions based on the decisions of religious authorities. Revision of the Torah was forbidden. Sikh Scriptures, Guru Granth was recited, written and edited and approved by the Gurus and no changes have been made to the original text since its compilation and inception in 1604 by Guru Arjan Dev, except the addition of the scriptures of the 9th Guru Teg Bahadur.

Monotheism believes in one God and is practiced by the majority of religions and sects. The followers of Polytheism have many gods and goddesses for personal protection, prosperity and subsistence. During the Greco-Roman period there were many gods i.e. Zeus and Aphrodite for the Greeks and Jupiter, Venus and Mars for the Romans. Every person was free to follow their belief without any interference or force. Gods were offered sacrifices. Faith in personal gods helped in every part of daily life. There were no texts or directives but prayers were an important part of communal activity and personal devotion. There was no judgement about belief or heresy. Gods were worshipped for their help in raising crops and livestock, for granting a good life, the love of a woman or victory in wars. Kings were revered as intermediaries of the gods and heroes were honored. Rituals were performed with elaborate feasts and celebrations. Scriptures shaped peoples lives morally, socially, and spiritually offering divine guidance to strengthen the faith.

THE TORAH, (Pentateuch).
THE HEBREW BIBLE, (TANAK)
These two canons are important to the Orthodox Jews, the people of the book. The first four books of Pentateuch offer a context in pre-Deuteronomic traditions (Soggin 2001, 17).
        Gen 15.7, 18-21 (YHWH's covenant with Abraham)
        Ex. 13.5, 11 (before Exodus); 19.3-6,11 (arrival at Sinai)
        23.20ff (commandments); 24.3-8 (covenant at Sinai)
The Torah has greater influence as it relates back to Mt. Sinai. The oral Torah permeates the culture, the teachings, and the weekly Parsha. The oral Torah is also called the Torah of your Mothers. The written Torah is regarded as the Torah of your Fathers. The Torah Scroll written by a scribe (sopher) today would not differ from an ancient scroll. The Hebrew Bible (Tanak) is a compilation by many authors during the last centuries. The Jewish community was scattered during the 18th

55

century. Their faith helped them establish Israel as their country. A commandment of Torah reads: (Deuteronomy 4:2; 13:1 [Hebrew]) You shall not add onto the thing I command you, and shall not substract from it. Shalom is synonymous with the Torah and the Talmud which is the basis of Jewish Law.

COMMANDMENTS from Exodus 20:1-17.

20:1 And God spake all these words, saying

20:2 I am the LORD thy God, which have brought thee out of the land of Egypt, out of the house of bondage.

20:3 Thou shalt have none other Gods before me.

20:4 Thou shalt not make unto thee any graven image, or any likeness of anything that is in heaven above, or that is in the earth beneath, or that is in the water under the earth.

20:5 Thou shalt not bow down thyself to them, nor serve them: for I the LORD thy God am a jealous God, visiting the iniquity of the fathers upon the children unto the third and fourth generation of them that hate me.

20:6 And showing mercy unto thousands of them that love me, and keep my commandments.

20:7 Thou shalt not take the name of the LORD thy God in vain; for the LORD will not hold him guiltless that taketh His name in vain.

20:8 Remember the Sabbath day, to keep it holy.

20:9 Six days shalt thou labor, and do all thy work.

20:10 But the seventh day is the Sabbath of the LORD thy God: in it thou shalt not do any work, thou, nor thy son, nor thy daughter, thy manservant, nor thy maidservant, nor thy cattle, nor thy stranger that is within thy gates.

20:11 For in six days the LORD made heaven and earth, the sea, and all that in them is, and rested the seventh day: wherefore the LORD blessed the Sabbath day, and hallowed it.

20:12 Honor thy father and thy mother: that thy days may be long upon the land which the LORD thy God giveth thee.

20:13 Thou shalt not kill.

20:14 Thou shalt not commit adultery.

20:15 Thou shalt not steal.

20:16 Thou shalt not bear false witness against thy neighbor.

20:17   Thou shalt not covet thy neighbor's house, thou shalt
        not covet thy neighbor's wife, nor his manservant, nor
        his maidservant, nor his ox, nor his ass, nor anthing
        that is thy neighbor's.

The Old Testament tells the story of Adam and Eve in the
Ararat area. Genesis 2:11-14 refers to four rivers in the Bible.
Perath is Hebrew for Firat (Arabic) and Euphrates in Greek.
Hiddekel is Hebrew for Idiglat (Sumerian) and Tigris in Greek.
Gihon is the River Aras from Lake Urmia, was once named
Gaihun. Pishon is Hebrew name derived from Iranian Uizhun,
the U was converted to P. Uizhun changed to Pizhun, and then
to Pishon. Bible places Adam, the first man, as farmer in the
garden of Eden and his ability to cultivate crops, raise live stock
and other foods. It was the period of warming during 14,000 to
15,000 years ago. There was a period of 2,000 years of cooling
until 12,000 years ago which made agriculture difficult. This is
referred to as the curse of the ground. The warming trend
helped to resume agriculture as indicated in the following:

> ...let them have dominion over the fish of the sea, and
> Over the fowl of the air, and over the cattle, and over the
> earth, and over everything that creepeth upon the earth.
> (Genesis 1:26)
> And God said, Behold, I have given you every herb bearing
> seed, which is upon the face of the earth, and every tree, in
> which is the fruit of a tree yielding seed; to you it shall be for
> meat.   (Genesis 1:29)

Other historical references such as Davis and Bathsheba (II
Samuel) or apocalyptic events of Moses and David (Book of
Daniel) embody the historical overview of mythology, morality,
prophecy, society, theology, and the concept of One God. The
Tree of Life, *Etz Chayim,* is a guide for spiritual development. It
describes a ten dimensional environment in which the body and
soul interact. It's three pillars and ten sefirot (luminous spheres)
represent qualities of the Creator, designed into human in His
image. The light descends and ascends, much like the double
helix of DNA and describes intellectual, emotional, and spiritual

qualitiesof each body and soul and how they interact with God in life (personal communication with J. Zohara M. Hieronimus in reference to her book (45-50).

TREE OF LIFE

Left Pillar	Middle Pillar	Right Pillar
	1. Crown (skull)	
		2. Wisdom (eyes)
3.Understanding (ears)		
	Knowledge (nose)	
		4. Loving- kindness (Right Arm, hand)
5. Judgement, Strength (Left Arm and hand)		
	6. Beauty, Truth (Torso)	
		7. Victory, eternity (Right leg)
8. Glory, humility (Left leg)		
	9. Foundation, Covenant (Phallus, womb)	
	10. Sovereignty, kingdom (Feet, mouth, head of phallus)	

The Jewish Scriptures are inspired by God. The stories portray the scenes of the historical past. The Conservative, Reform and Reconstructionist Jews follow the Hebrew Bible, also called the Old Testament as the religious text. Kugel states that The Book of Deuteronomy needs to be updated to refresh comprehension: "to serve the Lord your God with all your heart and all your soul" (BAR Jan-Feb. 2008, 62-67). Old Testament is a narrative seeking response from the people of Israel.

THE CHRISTIAN BIBLE (New Testament):
Bible in Greek means 'the book'. The New Testament includes the teachings of Prophet Jesus narrated by the apostles Mark,.

CODECES

SACRED TEXTS

Codex Leningradenis

ΜΙΝΤΟΝΛΙΘΟΝΕΚΤΗ͞ς
ΘΥΡΑΣΤΟΥΜΝΗΜΕΙΟΥ
ΚΑΙΑΝΑΒΛΕΨΑCΑΙΘΕω
ΡΟΥCΙΝΟΤΙΑΝΑΚΕΚΥ
ΛΙCΤΑΙΟΛΙΘΟCΗΝΓΑ͞Ρ
ΜΕΓΑCCΦΟΔΡΑΚΑΙΕΛ
ΘΟΥCΑΙΕΙCΤΟΜΝΗΜΕΙ

Codex Vaticanus

CΛΠΙΓCΙΝΚΑΙΕCΑΛ
ΠΙCΑΝΟΙΠΤΑΡΑΙ·Τ
ΑΑΚΑΙΑΥΤΟΓΙΑΙ·ϵΜ
ΠΙCΙΝΚΑΙΕCΑΛ·Τ
ΘΙΝΙΓΗΛΙΤΟΤΗCϕϖ
ΝΙΙCΤϢΝΙΙϪΡΕΜΚ·
ΛϢΝΚΑΙΕΓΕΝΕΤΟ

Codex Sinaiticus

CHRISTIANITY

Matthews, Luke and John. The Bible is essential for important family occasions and graces every Christian home, every hotel room in the West and serves as guide to 1.375 billion Christians worldwide.

The Apostle Paul was one of the leading missionaries in the early church. He is believed to have made major contributions by writing 15 of the 27 books in the New Testament. He developed an understanding of the life of Jesus, his death and resurrection. Acts were written by Luke after Paul's death. He spread Christianity that included the Gentiles, differentiating it from the Jewish religion and converting pagans to believe in one God, the God of the Jews and Jesus. Paul prosecuted Christians prior to his conversion at the age of 33. There are many versions of the Bible. The old texts are written in order to fit the new text (intertexuality). New Testament (Letters of Paul) presented rhetorical analysis. The Gospels are a narrative telling the story of Jesus (Shillington, 2002). According to Juan Garces, British Library project curator, the Bible text has changed over time.

The Gutenberg Bible:
Following the oral traditions to pass on the teachings, the Bible became available in print. Johannes Gutenberg of Mainz, Germany invented the moveable type printing in Europe. The Bible in print gave the Scriptures authenticity and access to everyone for individual reading. The first Bibles were without spacing, page numbers or indentation. There are 60 original Gutenberg Bibles that exist today. The Vulgate, the Latin translation of the Bible, was published in 1455 CE. The first Bible is known as 42-line Bible, number of lines on each page.

The Geneva Bible:
William Whittingham translated the Geneva Bible into English with numbered chapters and verses. It appeared in 1560 CE with an anti-Catholic bias, the Bible of William Shakeaspeare. With an introduction by John Calvin it was used by Puritans, the radical John Calvin group pf Protestants. The priests of the Church of England did not agree with extreme reforms.

The Bishop's Bible:
Queen Elizabeth I took over the throne in 1558 and authorized the Bishop's Bible to counter the influence of the Geneva Bible. It was not as popular as the Geneva Bible and had 20 reprints.

Douay-Rheims Bible:
This English Bible was published by Catholic scholars in Douay and scholars exiled in Rheims, France around 1610. The translation appeared from the Vulgate was used for centuries.

The King James Bible:
King James I succeeded Queen Elizabeth I in 1603. He responded to the bishops' petition by the bishops at the Hampton Court Conference and authorized new translation. The mandate was that it would be conservative, with an aim to follow the Bishops' Bible closely retaining the prophets and apostles. Most of the text was retained. This task was completed in four years involving 54 scholars who resolved ideological and ecclesial issues. The translation was based on the Masoretic text of the Old Testament and the Erasmus text of 1516 *textus receptus*. The Hebrew scholars called Masoretes developed pointing, a series of superscripts and subscripts in Tiberias and the Old Testament is known as Masoretic text. The Erasmus text is also called the Authorized Version and was published by Robert Baker in 1611. The most commonly used Bible is the 1769 version by Benjamin Blayney. The red letters were added to the King James Bible in 1899 and in the 1901 edition. This is the Bible that has been used in all English speaking colonies and in the USA. The fundamental approach to Christianity has preserved the reading of the Bible as traditional religious text.

John C. Trever, an American, saw the Dead Sea Scrolls, the Manual of Discipline (IQS), the Habakkuk commentary, the Genesis Apocryphon and the Great Isaiah Scroll in 1948. The archaeological evidence will influence the interpretation of the scriptures. Jesus of Nazareth performed many miracles. He healed a blind beggar, a deaf mute (Mark), a paralyzed man (John), made the food appear to feed the crowd (Mark and Matthew). When wine finished at a wedding, Jesus turned water into wine (John). He asked the dead daughter of Jairus to rise in Galilee and she got up. Jesus laid his hand on the coffin of a widow's son in Nain and made him alive. Lazarus was raised from his tomb (John). Jesus walked on water to meet his disciples (John, Matthew, Mark). He performed exorcism and drove out the Demon of Capernaum (Mark, Luke). He expelled seven demons from Mary Magdalene, his disciple. Under a charge of inciting an insurrection Jesus was crucified at the site of the Church of Holy Sepulchre in Jerusalem.

The Green Bible:
The New Revised Standard Version (NRSV), which includes 1000 verses relating to nature printed in forest green color, was released by Harper Collins publishers in 2008. It includes essays by St. Francis of Assisi, Pope John Paul II, Desmond Tutu, and Anglican Bishop N.T. Wright (Time, Sept. 28, 2008, 57).

THE KORAN:
Prophet Muhammad received divine messages over a period of 22 years. After the Night of Power he was convinced that these revelations needed to be spread as written in the Koran:
O thou enveloped in the cloak, Arise and warn!
Thy Lord magnify, thy raiment purify, pollution shun!
He warned that neither riches nor power nor tribal history elevated one person or group over another. Commitment to Allah is of paramount importance. Angel Gabriel showed Mohammad the way of total submission by the practices followed in prayer by Muslims by standing, bowing, kneeling, and prostration. After prayer one night, according to a story, Muhammad fell asleep. He accompanied Gabriel to Jerusalem 800 miles to the north. It is mentioned in the 17th sura:
Glory be to Him Who caused His servant to travel by night from the Sacred Mosque to the Farthest Mosque, whose precincts We have blessed.
He went to the Temple Mount and was welcomed by Abraham, Moses, and Jesus that night in the beginning of 620 CE. He was offered wine, milk, and water. Muhammad accepted milk, symbolic of the middle way in Islam. Moses advised Muhammad that five daily prayers pleased God. All Muslims pause for

prayer at sunrise, noon, afternoon, dusk, and before retiring for the night. That night marked the highest spiritual experience in Muhammad's life when he was one of the three Prophets representing Islam with Prophet Abraham of Judaism and Jesus, Prophet of Christianity. This union at the Temple Mount established Jerusalem as the Holy Ground for the three faiths. The first revelation of Prophet Mohammad in 610 CE and the ones that followed were written into 'Suras' after his death which established the Holy Koran as the religious text of Islam. Prophet Mohammad praised God (Sura I:1-6):

In the name of Allah, the Compassionate, the Merciful.
Praise be to Allah, the Lord of the Worlds,
The Compassionate, the Merciful,
Master of the Day of Judgement,
Only You do we worship, and only You
do we implore for help. Lead us to the right path.

Prophet Mohammad was a political and military leader. All these aspects are reflected in the Koran. At first the prayers were done facing Jerusalem. But later the followers were directed for 'qibla' to face towards Kaaba, in the city of Mecca. From that time, all Muslims pray five times facing towards the Kaaba in reverence. Muhammad chose Mecca to establish a historical linkage with Abraham, the monotheistic patriarch honored by both Jews and Christians. The Kaaba is believed to be a part of the foundation of Abraham's original temple. Muhammad removed the idols and marked the end of paganism by following the original rituals to establish 'tawhid', the Oneness of God. Mecca is 800 miles to the south of Jerusalem. The basic principles laid down in the Koran are:

Belief in Allah; Total submission to the Divine; and Equality of all believers.

Men and women are addressed together (Koran 33:35) in the following verses:

For Muslim men and women,
For believing men and women,
For devout men and women,
For men and women who are patient and constant,
For men and women who humble themselves,

63

For men and women who give in charity,
Do we implore for help.
Lead us to the right path, the path of those You have favored.
Not those who have incurred Your wrath or have gone astray.
The following verses (Koran 2:261-265) address conduct:
Those who spend their wealth in the Way of Allah
are like a wheat grain, which grows 7 ears, 100 grains each.
Allah multiplies for the ones He wills. Allah is All Knowing.
The Sufi Order emphasizes a mystical approach. It practices
tolerance, values democracy, freedom, and preserves Islamic
identity (Koran 42: 52-53):
The straight path, the way to God, to whom belongs
all that is in the heavens and all that is in the Earth.

The orthodox conservative view subscribes strictly to the
Koranic teachings and infidels are subject to their wrath. Hijra,
the flight to Medina started revelations of imperial conquests.
Jihad is conducted with the conviction that any non-believer,
including Muslims, is infidel and deserves to die. The Taliban
and Al Queda fundamentalists have operated under this
interpretation of the Koran and their wrath has killed, what
they call in-fidels, including Muslims. Majority of the Muslims
around the world are do not interpret Koran in that light.

President Barak Obama reminded the people of Middle East in
2009 that peace was born there which constitutes the
cornerstone of all three monotheistic faiths, Christianity, Jewish,
and Muslim, and reiterated that it was incumbent on the people
of Abraham to unite to meet the challenge and realize the vision
of sustainable peace. He aso emphasized that it is easier to blame
others than to look inward to see what is different about others
than to find the things we share.
Prophet Mohammad's Revelation
(after the Night of Power)
O' thou enveloped in the cloak, arise and warn!
Thy Lord magnify
"He warned that neither riches nor power nor tribal
history elevated one person or group over another.
Commitment to Allah is of paramount impotance"

64

KORAN (ISLAM)

Koran 13th Century
Kenneth Garrett / National Geographic Image Collection

Koran's message does not promote extremism. It is the interpretation that is molded towards the intended objective of violence .Koran's message of spirituality as perceived by the Sufi Muslims offers hope for compassion, unity and peace.

THE BHAGAVAD GITA and THE VEDAS:
According to the Vedas, the creative aspect is God. The causal levels portray Vishnu, the Lord of Preservation; Brahma, the Lord of Manifestation; and Shiva, the Lord of Transformation and Renewal. Scholars believe the Vedic records to be the oldest religious philosophy that developed between 3000 to 4000 years ago. Additional information on Vedas appears in Hinduism.

THE BHAGAVAD GITA narrates the divine guidance which was given to Prince Arjun by Lord Krishna during the battle of Mahabharata in 3100 BCE:
> Your very nature will drive you to fight,
>> the only choice is what to fight against.
> On action alone be your interest,
>> not on fruit.
> Let not the fruits of your action be your motive.
>> Nor be the attachment to inaction.
> This is how actions were done
>> by the ancient seekers of freedom;
> follow their example, act,
>> surrendering the fruits of action.
> For certain is death for the born
>> and certain is birth for the dead;
> therefore, over the inevitable
>> you should not grieve.

Tha Bhagavad Gita is a part of the Epic Mahabharata, which presents a dramatization of human mind and its quest for liberartion. King Santanu represents Absolute Pure Consciousness. His 7 sons represent pervading consciousness. The 8th son projects the reflective aspect. This way an understanding of the primordial nature, time, space, cosmic elements, maya, egoism, and the power of analyzing circumstances is realized. The elements of doubt and uncertainty create delusional thoughts and selfishness. A sense

SANSKRIT

SANSKRIT on PALM-LEAF. Monastery in Nepal in Bbujimal Script. Two holes are for binding cord. (Wikipedia–PD).

VEDIC SANSKRIT dates back to 1500 BCE. It is liturgical language of Hinduism and Buddhism which was used in the grammar of Panini in 4th century BCE. Sanskrit language has been transliterated since the 18th century.

of discrimination gives pure intelligence. The dispassionate attraction includes the role of elements: ether, air, and fire. Sentiments and attachments include the elements water and earth. Pure consciousness dwells in individuals as soul. Soul's self knowledge leads to cosmic consciousness and salvation. The 8th son projects the reflective aspect. This way an understanding of the primordial nature, time, space, cosmic elements, maya, egoism, and the power of analyzing circumstances is realized. The elements of doubt and uncertainty create delusional thoughts and selfishness. A sense of discrimination gives pure intelligence. The dispassionate attraction includes the role of elements: ether, air, and fire. Sentiments and attachments include the elements water and earth. Pure consciousness dwells in individuals as soul. Soul's self knowledge leads to cosmic consciousness and salvation.

Krishna symbolizes purified senses as the Spirit of God. The path to super-consciousness is summarized in the message from Krishna to Arjuna as conveyed in the Bhagavad Gita: During meditation, while the attention turns inward, Om the primordial sound may be heard internally. This is perceived as Krishna's flute which awakens awareness of both the qualities of virtue as well as the tendencies of the delusional mind. Sounds of different frequencies are perceived prior to the sound of Om.

   Base chakra: buzzing sound of disturbed bees.
   Sacral chakra: Sound of a flute.
   Lumbar chakra: Resonance of a harp.
   Dorsal chakra: pitch of a gong.
   Cervical chakra: a mix of different sounds.
The sound of Om transcends all other sounds. The meditator, at an elevated level, withdraws attention and feelings from the physical awareness and mental consciousness and progresses to higher stages of superconsciousness through the third eye and the crown charka in the head.

   Superconsciousness related to the base chakra is *samadhi*, characterized by higher comprehension, confusion, and doubt.

   Superconsciousness connected to sacral chakra brings stability in concentration and clearer comprehension of events.

Superconsciousness associated with the lumbar chakra gives an increased concentration and a feeling of self-mastry.

Superconsciousness related to the dorsal chakra dissolves egocentric selfconsciousness and awareness of oneness of whole.

Superconsciousness of the cervical chakra removes all the veils to reveal the soul-nature and transcends to the stage of self realization, self knowledge.

Superconsciousness which involves the spiritual eye, behind the forehead between the eyes, and finally the crown chakra in the head sparks spontaneous knowledge of cosmic processes, realization of pure consciousness which ultimately leads to the enlightenment and the knowledge of God.

Upanishads refer to the episode of Chandogya. Svetaketu returned after 12 years study with spiritual master. His father asked : Tell me about the One. Svetaketu replied:

Just as by one clod of clay,
all that is made of clay is known,
the modifications only by name, arising from speech...
The truth is that all is clay.

The Teachings of Hinduism are based on Vedic philosophy which is embodied in the Vedas, Puranas and Upanishads.

Karma: the law of universal causality.
Maya: an illusion manifest in worldly domain.
Nirvana: the bliss that frees from the cycle of birth/death.
Yoga: the force that leads towards consciousness.

Deities are dressed up with jewels, ornaments and beautiful clothes in a special space devoted for worship in the home and at the temples. Hindus worship gods and goddesses as different aspects of the Divine. The sacred site at the confluence of Rivers Ganges and Yamuna is traditionally a place of pilgrimage and for sacred bathing. Varanassi is home to Lord Shiva, the holiest site. Vindraban is the birthplace of Lord Krishna. The Bhagavad Gita shows Three Great Paths to God realization (Gandhi, 13):

1. Janana: Intuitive discrimination of the real in unreal world.
2. Bhagti: Total self surrender with profound love for God.
3. Karma: Selfless service, right action without an attachment.

AAD GURU GRANTH SAHIB (AGGS) The Sikh Scriptures:
The revelations of Guru Nanak were composed in 19 melodies,
the ragas, handed down to the next Gurus. Guru Amar Das, the
third Guru compiled the first two Pothis, the Books of Hymns.
The fourth Guru, Ram Das contributed eleven more ragas. The
Granth was compiled by Guru Arjan Dev (1563-1606 AD) and
written by scribe Bhai Gurdas (1551-1637) in 1601 at Ramsar in
Amritsar.

The Pothi Sahib, as Guru Arjan Dev called it, was completed
and personally annotated by him and approved. It is known as
the Kartarpur Bir now located in the town of Kartarpur. The
final copy was completed and installed on August 1, 1604 at the
Golden Temple in Amritsar. Golden Temple is called Har
Mandir, Gods Temple. The first page of AGGS has a question:
>*How can a person know the truth*? the answer follows:
>*Accept the Will of the Divine and follow its directives.*
Mundavani verses, mark the closing seal. The Holy Granth
embodies Gurbani - the Word. The Sikh religious text has 1430
pages which include Arabic, Sanskrit, Persian, Punjabi, Hindi,
Sindhi, Bengali and Marathi languages. The compositions are
organized in classical music, the ragas, including the verses of
the gurus, sages, sufis and saints. The Scriptures are written in
Sadh Bhakha, the commonly spoken language and written in
Gurmukhi script. The final additions to the Granth were made
by Guru Gobind Singh adding the scriptures of his father Guru
Teg Bahadur and was compiled by Bhai Mani Singh. The final
version of the irrevocable Sikh Scriptures was completed at
Damdama Sahib. The Granth was confiscated by Ahmad Shah
Abdali in 1762 and taken to Kabul, Afghanistan. In 1850 a copy
of the Granth was presented to Queen Victoria which is
preserved at the India Office Library in London.

Guru Nanak recited the following verses during his visit with his
devotee Lalo (AGGS, p.722-723):
>Baber invaded India and demaded the contribution.
>Ethics and spirituality were masked by the untruth.
>The swindlers prevailed over the Qazi's and Brahmans.

> Muslims recited Khuda amidst torture and chaos,
> chanting slogans of massacre and bloodshed all around.
> They came in ..78 and will leave in ..97
> Another warrior will come and drive them out.
> Nanak prophesied the way message came from God.

The verses refer to Baber who came from Kabul and invaded Amnabad in 1578. His successor Humayun the King fled in 1597 when Sher Shah Suri came to power and established his secular kingdom with equal rights for Hindus and Muslims.

Guru Granth is revered as an embodiment of living Guru, which was declared by Guru Gobind Singh at Nander in Maharashtra before his ascension. Since then Guru Granth is sought for spiritual guidance by Sikh devotees. The Holy Book is brought to the Golden Temple everyday before dawn, carried by the devotees in a royal procession for view (*Parkash*) for the devotees to pay homage and listen to the hymns throughout the day. The Holy Book is retired at night (*Sukhasan*) with reverence. This religious devotion is practiced everyday in Sikh households where a holy room is designated for daily prayers. The interpretation of the First verses (Chahal 2008) reflect the revelation of Guru Nanak in Japu (Japji) in Aad Guru Granth Sahib (AGGS, p. 1).

> There is One God, the Infinite, Truth
> > The Creator, without fear and without Enmity.
> The Timeless, created be Itself.
> > Neither takes birth nor dies to be born again.
> By His Grace shalt thou worship and know Him.
> > Before time itself, there was Truth
> > As time runs its course, He is the Truth,
> > And that Truth shall prevail for evermore.

The Holy Book includes 5894 writings of 36 holy men of Hindu and Muslim faith from 12th to 17th centuries. The Holy Granth includes verses by Sufis Sheikh Farid (1175-1265), Bhikhan (1480-1573), Mardana, Satta and Balwand. Verses of Hindu sages include Brahmins Ramanand and Parmanand, Vaishya Trilochan (1267-1335) and Rajput Prince Pipa. The verses were selected on their spiritual merit.

71

PRAYER ROOM
(SIKHISM)

Prayer Room in a Sikh Residence

The scriptures honor the spirituality of Hinduism and Islam. The Holy Granth includes verses by Sufis Sheikh Farid (1175-1265), Bhikhan (1480-1573), Mardana, Satta and Balwand. Verses of Hindu sages include Brahmins Ramanand and Parmanand, Vaishya Trilochan (1267-1335) and Rajput Prince Pipa. The verses were selected on their spiritual merit despite the profession and social standing of the sages in the prevailing caste system at the time. Dhanna was a farmer, Ravidas (1476-1527) was a cobbler, Sadhna a butcher, Kabir a weaver, Namdev (1270-1350) a textile printer, and Sain a barber. This echoes openness of the Sikh religion with a focus on spirituality and oneness of mankind. Nankian philosophy was perpetuated by all Sikh Gurus as portrayed by Kabir (1398-1485) in AGGS p. 266:

The most revered religions believe in the
contemplation of God's Name and in righteous deeds.
Noblest of actions are derived from high ideals.
The company of sages purifies the mind.

Kabir expressed his view of God in verses (AGGS p. 1372):
Where there is enlightenment, there is righteousness.
Where there is falsehood, there is sin.
Where there is covetousness, there is death.
Where there is forgiveness, there is God Himself.

India was not exposed to Christianity until the British established the East India Company. Jesus and his message had not reached the Sikh Gurus otherwise a reference to the Gospel of Jesus would have been included in Guru Granth. Sikh Scriptures portray the condition of the times from Guru Nanak (1469-1539), to the 10th Guru Gobind Singh (1666-1708) , all of them perpetuating the Nanakian philosophy which continues to this day. Daily prayer of a Sikh culminates with the words:

Under your Divine Will, we pray for the welfare of all. During WWII the Sikh regiments expressed the need for daily view (darshan) of the Holy Granth. The High Command obliged and provided a 2 inch version of the Scriptures for Sikh units. The original handwritten manuscript is displayed daily at the Golden Temple in Amritsar, India. Thousands pay homage daily and it is open to every caste, creed, gender or religion. Every

Sikh yearns to visit Golden Temple, take a holy dip, and attend the services. The Holy Granth is available for Sikh diaspora around the world in a format that has the Punjabi script as well as the English translation. The following verses address the concept of death and after-life (AGGS, p. 885):

> The air mingles with the air,
>> life energy escapes into the universe.
> The elements return to the soil.
>> Who cares for the Dead!
> Who died? The life force returns to its source...

BUDDHIST NOBLE TRUTHS:
Prince Siddhartha Gautama was enlightened 2550 years ago at Bodhgaya in India. He renounced princely life and advocated to follow the path of spirituality, to ignore the lure of physical senses. Respect the feelings of others with compassion to avoid physical suffering. His first sermon was at Sarnath, where the famous temple was built. Buddhist principles are laid down in the Four Noble Truths which address suffering and emphasize the influence of ones karmas that impact the next life. The Noble Eightfold Path refers to wisdom, morality and mental discipline. Following affirmation strengthens their faith:

> I take refuge in the Buddha
> I take refuge in the Dharma
> I take refuge in the Sangha

The ashes of Buddha were distributed among eight centers and enshrined in stupas around the world. In India, Buddha ashes are in Sanchi. Buddhist hymns are chanted in the stupas all around the world. In old Tibet, Mandalas depicted Sun and the moon of equal size implying that they are equidistant from the earth. HH the Dalai Lama declared that to be wrong and anything disproved by science cannot be maintained (Iyer, 24).

TAO TE CHING: Philosophy of Lao Tzu.
Taoist poets selected the teachings of Lao Tzu and composed Tao Te Ching in 5000 words in the form of 81 capsules of thought (Tao Truth) that cover a wide range of topics. The set of two books includes Tao Classic and Te Classic. Tao is referred to as she, the feminine principle 'yin'. Tao observes the creation

in simplistic terms with a conviction that the exploration of morality leads astray due to unnecessary activities. The writings date back to late 4th and early 3rd centuries BCE. The following is based on the translation by Charles Muller (1997).

TAO CLASSIC Teaching:
Tao is formless and infinite.
The sage acts within the Tao as she is not the doer, the Divine is.
Two opposing forces in the universe are *yin* and *yang*.
Things have to be destroyed when they have served the purpose.
Opening and closing the gates of heaven refer to our five senses.
The soul does not perish with death, it merges with the Tao.
Consciousness arose from 'emptiness', it turns to it after death.
Spirituality and compassion grow by abandoning humaneness
    (*jen*) and rightness.
Six Harmonious Relationships are:
    Father-son; Brother-brother; Husband-wife.
    Ching is essence, the life force, vitality and spirit.
        hsin is belief that is proof, truth and faith.
    Good is in comparison to bad,
        So bad enables the perception of good and vice versa.
    Left position is auspicious, honors and celebrates joy,
        Right side is unauspuicious, honors death, destruction.

TE CLASSIC Teachings:
The abilities to foresee and use spiritual powers are distractions.
Anything that originates from nothing has to return to nothing.
The motion of Tao takes things back to its source.
Everything is subdued by yin, embraces yang, achieves harmony
Some lose yet gain, others gain yet lose.
Practice *wu-wei*, unattached action.
Excitement overcomes cold, stillness overcomes heat.
Opposing energies flow harmoniously.
Chi is believed as the vital force in Taoism and is inherent in all things and everywhere. Practice of breathing, acupressure and meditation influence chi positively. The creative energy of chi nurtures knowledge, compassion and healing.

The glimpses of the Philosophy of Confucius (551-478 BCE)

come from the Analects compiled into 20 chapters or books and written by many individuals (Muesse, 2007). David Carradine, the 'Kung Fu' actor of Hollywood portrayed the essence of Confucius doctrine. Confucius said:

I transmit but I do not create.

Being fond of truth, I am an admirer of antiquity.

Confucius stressed the need for devotion, submission, and the discipline to honor teacher or guru by the student, the disciple. He had two requirements for an aspiring student.

Eagerness to learn, and

Have the ability to think and contemplate.

Confucius believed that a humane person is an ideal person, then he concentrates on refinement to become a productive humane citizen. His own timeline in learning is in Analect 2.4 as quoted by K. R. Sundrajan in Interreligious Insight, 53-54:

At fifteen, I bent my mind on learning;

At thirty, I was established;

At forty, I was free from dilusion;

At fifty, I knew the decree of Heaven;

At sixty, my ears became subtly perceptive;

At seventy, I was able to follow my heart's desire,
    without overstepping the realm of propriety.

SEICHO-NO-LE: Masaharu Taniguchi (1893-1985):
Buddhism was introduced into Japan in the 5th and 6th century from China and Korea. It was assimilated into Shinto culture which believed in spirits. Masaharu Taniguchi, a Mahayana Buddhist, who merged the Shinto-Buddhist traditions and focused on the mind. Masaharu's spiritual spark came from a convict Oscar Wilde. Wilde was a self absorbed man who lived a llife of luxury and immersed in the pleasures of senses. He saw an old man, bent by age, struggling to carry a heavy load of water. Wilde saw a glimpse of his own end and was transformed to be a compassionate man. Masaharu received inspiration to establish a philosophy called *Seicho-No-le* (SAY-cho-NO-ee-yeh) which means the home of infinite life, truth and abundance. His doctrine emerged from a poem received repeatedly as a message in 1931. This poem became the Shinsokan meditation, requiring selfless actions and deeds of love for mind-purification ceremony

which replaces negative thoughts with positive feelings. He was known as the miracle man with power of healing (Davis, 2008).

Sacred texts are worshipped in magnificient architectural structures. Beautiful churches, temples and mosques hold sacred, historical objects, scripts, and other religious memorabilia where the followers offer their devotion and recite verses or meditate. All religions have historic sites that draw millions on pilgrimage, and the faithful desire to visit Holy sites at least once during their lifetime. Humans seek higher power for peace of mind and surrender to their God that will protect here and in the after-life.

These belief systems have been manipulated in early cultures as well as in recent times. A drastic divergence of any new approach is perceived as a cult. The vulnerable and helpless people fall victim to such sects in good faith to seek stability in their life. Some break-away cults attempt to isolate the initiates and impose restrictions creating an atmosphere of intimidation and fear. This happened at Waco, at Jonestown and with the splintered sect of Fundamentalist Church of Latter Day Saints (FLDS) from the mainstream Mormon Church of Latter Day Saints in the United States and the Doomsday Cult in Russia. The innocent followers faced tragic consequences.

The division between the Anglican and the Roman Catholic Church appeared in the 16th century initiated by Martin Luther during the Protestant Reformation. Pope Benedict XVI desires and envisions consolidation. Recent scandals involving the clergy proved deterimaental to the faith of baby boomers (born between 1945-1961) and have also adversely affected their ability to convince Generation X (born between 1962-1976) to attend church services in the wake of sexual transgressions that cost hundreds of millions to settle legal obligations. Evangelists use mass media to spread the spiritual message reaching much larger audience through televised services in huge auditoriums. Fame and ego, laced with greed and lust brought renowned evangelists to shame losing the respect of the audience they once commanded. No religion is immune to human inequities and moral breach of trust. The pious ones sail through while the morally weak fall from grace. Humans have spiritual inclination and the mind has to be awakened by a belief system that nurtures the faith. The light of God is in every soul. Its glow is dimmed under the soot of vices plunging the materialistic and lost souls deeper into hellish domain. Blessed ones escape the downward spiral and are rewarded by the grace of God.

Seclusion preserves contrast as in the Middle East, China, Russia, Africa, and Pakistan. Interfaith interactions strive for the common ground with a focus on similarities making different religious groups more tolerant and understanding. Spirituality is the base where different belief systems can open the dialogue and build harmonious religious culture mutually acceptable to all who are seeking Godhood. Ethnicity and religious diversity has sustained coexistence and harmony in multicultural nations like United States, Canada, Indonesia, and India. Language and traditions thrive in large clusters of communities and information technology has crossed the geographic barriers to create a global culture. Religions need more outreach and resume dialogue for mutual understanding as members of global society. A lack of humility and a big ego hinders tolerance. The sectarian strife among Shi'ites, Sunnis, Kurds and Arab Muslims has put Muslims at odds with one another, even bombing mosques and killing the Muslim faithful. All these sects practice Islam. Sufi Muslims follow a path of peace and harmony and others engage in jihad.

Goodness has prevailed through the ages. The precursor of the Red Cross was established in the mid 15th century. Chancellor Nicholas Rolin founded a charity hospice in Hotel Dieu in the town of Beaune, France in 1443 to treat the poor after the 100 year war. This hotel provided services until 1971. In 1704 a Sikh settlement was attacked by Muslim forces. Bhai Ghanaiya, a disciple of Guru Gobind Singh served water to all the wounded in the battlefield, Sikhs and Muslims alike. Red Cross was established 155 years later to offer services to everyone in need. Humanity has inherent capacity for care and compassion. A 13th century Sufi mystic Rumi believed in the unity of all things which is expressed in his poem:

> If there is any lover in the world, O Muslims - 'tis I.
> If there be any believer, infidel or Christian Hermit - 'tis I.
> The wine-dregs, the cup bearer, the minstrel, the harp and
> the music, the beloved, the candle, the drink and the joy
> of the drunken - 'tis I.
> The two-and-seventy creeds and sects in the world do not
> really exist: I swear by God that every creed and sect - 'tis I.
> Earth and air and water and fire-knowest thou what they
> are? Truth and falsehood, good and evil, ease and difficulty
> from first to last, knowledge, and learning and asceticism
> and piety and faith - 'tis I.
> The fire of Hell, be assured, with its flaming limbs,
> Yes, and Paradise and Eden and the Houris - 'tis I.

Old beliefs are now under the scrutiny of scholars and the new evidence points to a different direction. Sadducee's Opposition questioned the interpreters on some aspects. Pope John Paul II offered an apology about the role Catholics played during the Holocaust. Pope Benedict XVI visited the Park East Synagogue in New York, a first for a Pope. Ratzinger, as a 14 year old, was forced to join the Hitler Youth group. Rabbi Arthur Schneier presented the Pontiff a box of matzo and a Haggadah, the prayer book used during Passover. Rabbi Schneier, now in his late seventies is a Holocaust survivor. The congregation sang "Oseh Shalom" with the Pope, a song of prayer for peace.

RISE AND FALL OF PSYCHIANA

A remarkable phenomenon occurred in United States in 1928 when Frank B. Robinson created a new wave of religion called Psychiana. Mitch Horowitz quotes Robinson's ads in magazines saying: I Talked With God. Yes I Did – Actually and Literally… You too may experience that strange mystical power which comes from talking with God, and when you do, if there is poverty, unrest, unhappiness, ill health or material lack in your life, well – the same Power is able to do for you what it did for me (Science of Mind, March, 2007, 30) He offered twenty lessons for twenty dollars by mail. He sold more than half a million lessons to followers in 67 nations in a year from a little town Moscow in Idaho, USA and the New Psychological Religion was born. The time was right as the Americans were going through the Great Depression with WWII looming. This new hope and promise appealed to two million followers making it the eighth largest religion in the world. The power of suggestion: I believe in the power of the living God, and I am more and more successful, has spawned many movements to this day. The era of motivational speakers began. The power of practical and positive thought has always appealed to the troubled minds who are hungry for a fresh approach other than the traditional wisdom, or professional counseling. Frank B. Robinson chose to call it Psychiana because it brought spiritual power to the world in line with the movement called Religious Science which was prevalent at that time. He was ahead of his time and pioneered the use of effective advertising. The universality of religious belief systems brought Jews, Methodists, Baptists, and Catholics in its fold, all believing in one God and widening the scope of spirituality for the people of every race, creed, color, and philosophy. However, in short two decades Psychiana vanished with the death of its founder in 1948. The local news paper Daily Idahonian wrote about the history of the town of Moscow in 1961 with no mention of Robinson or Psychiana.

Humans have spiritual inclinations, which remain dormant until awakened by a belief system that nurtures faith. The light of God is within every mind. God's grace grants peace and contentment by eliminating the agony of desires and the fear of death. You cast away the ego of I to enter into the abundance of the Universe that God wants to be shared by all, Nirvana. Simone Weil (27-28) correlated the destruction of I (ego) to the feeling of emptiness, where the void is filled with the love of God and His presence that shows peace and the glow of contentment. Early humans perceived it as unseen spirits. Faith in Creator channeled messages to Prophets. Their teachings became the Holy Scriptures of religions.

True teachers are a spiritual royalty, above the kings and heads of nations. They already own the earth and the heavens. Such teachers included Abraham, Jesus Christ, Mohammad, Krishna, Buddha, Guru Nanak and others who made the difference in the society through their teachings. They linked with the divine. The entire Universe was their domain. Their style varied but content of their message was the same. Focus on the prophets and interpretation of their message by the devoted followers gave a unique identity to establish specific religion. This view of exclusivity created the drive for supremacy of one over the other and the message of spirituality, common to all, was shadowed by the individuality of devotion with distinct rituals of prayer and their own places of worship. These true teachers delivered their revelations, teachings, sermons in simple and natural surroundings to show the righteous path to humanity. Eckhart Tolle has revolutionized faith and blurred the boundaries between the religions. He confronted the conditioned mind which brought him to the brink of suicide during his depression and overwhelming anxiety. He was a graduate student at Cambridge University at the age of 29. Sudden surge of powerful energy swept him into the realm of bliss and heard a voice directing him not to resist anything. He was blessed with enlightenment. He relinquished everything and lived like a homeless for two years in the parks of London. He moved to Glastonbury, England and devoted 20 years to manifest his awakening. Then he moved to Vancouver, British Columbia, Canada where his book *The Power of Now* brought him into prominence as a spiritual teacher. He says, my ego was my foe due to his accumulated knowledge as an intellectual. He teaches not to identify with the mind but to honor the power of now. The present is of paramount significance, not the past or the future.

John Calvin, known as the 'Man of Geneva' was born in France and studied law and theology. He believed that state and church were jurisdictionally separate. The Geneva Bible was produced by the Church of Geneva in English with the support of Scotland's John Knox after the expulsion of Protestant scholars by Mary Tudor of England. Mary campaigned to reinstate Catholicism in the British Isles. This was a feud between Protestants and Catholics. England's King James felt threatened due to the Calvinistic leaning of the Geneva Bible. This resulted in the publication of The King James Bible. Pilgrims brought the Geneva Bible with them to Plymouth in 1620. The separation of church and state in the United States followed the Calvinistic view to enable the political system to function independent of the religious oversight as practiced in England. This gave rise to secularism in the free nations giving people the right to worship freely according to their faith. Spirited dialogues brought a shift from liberal to more conservative, from secular to faith-based, and from moderate to fundamentalist regimes. I wonder if God is amused (and disappointed) with the different religious booths set up on the World's stage at the Universal Convention on Spirituality whereas the Lord Almighty expected the entire humanity delved in the grace of One God for all the inhabitants of the planet forging a close bond and caring for all the creation.

The most powerful rulers declared themselves to be direct descendants of God, as in Egypt where New Kingdom pharaohs ruled between 1539 and 1078 BCE. Remeses II ruled for 66 years and built more temples than any other pharaoh in honor of God Amun-Re. Their belief in the after-life has kept the archaeologists busy in the Valley of the Kings and other sites where they collected valuable artifacts and treasures including the gold mask of Tutankhamun in the necropolis near Luxor providing valuable information about this civilization. The tombs were built and decorated with carvings and paintings by the workers housed in Deir el-Medina more than 3000 years ago. The Yamhad was an important Syrian kingdom in Mesopotamia under the King Halab during the Middle (2000-1550 BCE) and Late (1550-1200 BCE) Bronze Age. Mesopotamian Archaeology indicates that Citadel of Aleppo, the administrative capital of Yamhad, was built during Ayyubid period (1171-1250 CE and restored by the Mamelukes between 1250 to 1517 CE (Biblical Archaeological Review).

FAITH AND TRADITION

FAITH AND FIGURES IN TRIBES

HEIMATAU (Fish Hook): represents strength. Brings peace, prosperity, and good health. Provides a safe journey over water.

KORU (Spiral): depicts beginning, growth, harmony.

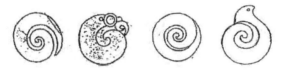

CROSSOVER: Triple twist represents friendship, two lives bonding one for all eternity in marriage.

MANAIA: Carrier of supernatural powers. Head of a bird, body of man, and tail of fish depicting sky, earth, and sea in balance. Protects from the evil spirits.

MAORI Tribe, Rotorua, New Zealand

FAITH AND TRADITIONS

Our understanding of prehistoric cultures is based on the remains of early humans found in burials. The pre-human species appeared during the Paleolithic Era, the Old Stone Age up to 17000 BCE. Agriculture developed during the Middle Stone Age (17000 to 8300 BCE). The artifacts from the cave dwellings of the Old Stone Age earlier than 8300 BCE suggest elements of rituals for burial. Neanderthals buried the dead with food and tools. They removed brains from the skulls and carried them into the caves. They consumed brains of the dead to acquire their skills. During the Middle Paleolithic era the early humans of the Mousterian culture buried their dead with feet pulled up in the contracted position, with food, stone tools and ornaments and covered under stone slabs, a practice throughout the Mediterranean. The rituals practiced by the Neanderthals were similar.

There was a change in the Mesolithic era (17000-8300 BCE) that started with a nomadic life of hunting while women gathered wild grains, nuts and berries. It changed to a settled life with the development of agriculture, fishing with nets and hunting with bows and arrows. The Natufian culture developed near marshes, rivers and lakes. They developed a concern about the fertility of the earth. Sun, moon and trees were revered and worshipped. Axes and spears were venerated for their spiritual power. Their interest in art is seen in use of beads and artfully decorated shells. The era focused on connectedness of all life, humans, animals, and vegetation with the divine. They perceived that there is life after death and developed the concept of unseen forces and named them spirits. Archaeologists discovered the city of Jerico, a walled settlement of 2000 people, founded in the Mesolithic Era around 9300 BCE.

During the Neolithic Era (8300-4000 BCE) a concern for humanity, environment and forces of nature had grown. Earth was conceived as mother for its fertility to grow crops and sustain animals and humans. Burials became more elaborate. The practice to include more articles of use, food and decorative items became a part of religious rituals. During this era the people of Jericho had built two buildings, one was temple and the other devoted to religious functions. The burial rituals involved painting of the deceased body. Death was accepted as a transfer from one realm to another. Animal sacrifice became a part of rituals. Different ceremonies marked rituals at the time of birth, puberty, marriage and death. Scholars believe that matriarchal societies were prevalent in that era based on female figurines and images that indicate worship of mother goddess as a symbol of fertility. This is observed from 7000 to1200 BCE.

Woman as the giver of life was regarded as the symbol of fertility and worshipped as the mother goddess. Religion focused on the feminine aspect of the divine for birth and life as a passage to another realm after death. It was recognized that life has a meaning. The early belief systems emerged around the Mediterranean in the ancient civilizations of Mesopotamia, Egypt, Syria-Palestine, and Israel. The earliest settlements developed around the Aegean Sea and the Indus Valley. The divine realm was conceived by each culture based on everyday life and conception of the sacred. A religion is a unified system of beliefs and practices relative to the divine which unite people into a moral community. An overview of different religious cultures offers an insight into the processes which generated religious beliefs in early civilizations. These evolved as a result of synchronicity of faith and the organized practices which developed stabilized beliefs and developed a following.

GREEK CIVILIZATION

MINOANS came to Crete in 7000 BCE and established a farming community. During the next 3500 years the number of settlements grew as the population increased. By 2000 BCE the Minoans had developed new crafts and improved techniques of construction. They built big palaces and large buildings. The cities were connected by roads leading to the trade routes, and trade developed in the Aegean Sea. The cities were not walled at that time indicating lack of any threat of invasion or war. Minoans developed a written language Linear A that has not yet been deciphered. The written language called Linear B was used for keeping records. Bull horns and the mythological figure *Minotaur* show that the Bull was considered sacred. Goddess figurines indicate that women represented fertility.

MYCENAEANS developed a single culture in Greece including Practices of Indo-Aryan cultures, an observation based on the excavations of Heinrich Schliemann in the 1870s. The Indo-Aryans invaded Achaea and created distinct communities of the native population with settlements in the plains and mountain valleys. They built fortified palaces on hilltops to observe activity in the valleys and the coastal areas. The city state, the polis, developed as a political entity which was established in the 8th century BCE. Smyrna (Izmir, Turkey) became the polis in 7th century BCE. Other Greeks were organized into *ethne,* the tribes i.e. the Aetolians, Thessalians, and Macedonians. Ethnic is derived from the word ethne. The word democracy came from the word *demos*, the people.

Ancient stories indicate worship of many different gods. The shaft tombs dating to 1700 BCE showed mass burials with up to 19 bodies that included artifacts. Beehive tombs around 1500 BCE were round domed underground burial chambers accessible through a tunnel guarded by a huge doorway. The fortifications indicate volatile conditions which led to the demise of these civilizations and Greece plunged into the Dark Age (1200- 800 BCE). Only the stories of gods and heroes were passed on orally in small groups in their isolated settlements. The religious beliefs became part of the Greek culture by syncretism. Zeus was Indo-Aryan god of sky and weather called *Dyaus Pitar.* His consort was Hera. Scholars believe Hera may have been an Achaean goddess. They believed in after-life and buried the dead with care. Humans and gods engaged in rituals of sacrifice indicating an established culture rich in mythological stories. The Epic poems of the Dark Age, Iliad and Odessey, are attributed to the blind poet Homer, a native of polis Smyrna.

GREEK EPICS

The ILIAD depicts the story about the anger of Achilles during the war of Achaeans against Troy. The Trojan prince Hector killed Patroclus so that Achilles will take revenge against Hector. Troy's king Prium asked Achilles to return his son's body and it was returned. Gods and heroes participated as equal members of society. Zeus was powerful and gods were under his authority and fate. Heroes yearned for eternal recognition based on their heroism. Humanity was supposed to enjoy life while it lasted. The Iliad projects that humanity is under the control of gods. However it shows that heroes control their own destiny. The poem points out the fallen heroes, acquiring glory and the human cost of war.

The ODYSSEY portrays the journey of Odysseus towards home after the Trojan War. He blinds Cyclops and faces the wrath of Poseidon but he manages to escape. He is seduced by a sorceress and then a nymph kept him at her island for seven years. Zeus ordered the nymph to let Odysseus go. He goes back to his wife, Penelope in Ithaca and finds many suiters for Penelope at the house. He has to do everything to win back his wife. In this poem the gods rule humanity. Odysseus goes to Hades, the underworld, which is a portrayal of hell, where sad and weakened spirits dwell in total darkness. A goat sacrifice revives the spirits to speak to him but heroism is of no avail in the underworld and he does not get any help. He is offered immortality by Calypso but chooses to return home rejecting the fate of a hero. He finds peace in human life with the pleasures of marriage and children. Homer's poems were valued by Greek civilization for their theology and the interplay of heroes in Greek culture. Greeks had no formal religion. The religious traditions were carried out by actions and by word. Homer's stories honored gods and admired heroes who worshipped gods. According to Hesiod's Theogony, Zeus was the king of the gods and guardian of the cosmic order. Hesiod carries out acts of incest, castration, patricide, and usurpation to portray Zeus.

The Archaic Age (800-480 BCE) saw the revival of worship of

the gods. Pan-Hellenic Games took place every four years regardless of the change in rulers and under the democratic system of rule. The city-state, the polis, was governed by a council of citizens. Greek colonies developed around the Mediterranean basin. Each polis worshipped its own god, observed its private activities and festivals. The Greeks joined under polytheistic religious culture with communal activities. They asked for god's will and honored god with rituals of music and dance in a sanctuary for religious activities like the Oracle of Delphi, sanctuary of goddess Demeter.

GREEK GODDESSES

ATHENA is a goddess of the Minoan and Mycaenean culture, the protector of fortresses and also associated with fertility, birds, and snakes. Her role in Athens came from the Acropolis. This was due to the contest between her and Poseidon to give the most useful gift. Athena created an olive tree and Poseidon created a salt water spring. Athena made civilized life possible. She is also a virgin and warrior goddess at par with men. She does not use her beauty towards gods or men for her actions.

DEMETER is the mother figure. She transformed herself into a mare to avoid Poseidon's advances. Poseidon became a stallion and raped her. Zeus also chased her but mated with her as a bull and their daughter Kore was born. She was abducted by Hades but Zeus ordered Hermes to bring her back. Demeter's cultic site as a mystery religion is in Eleusis because she served as a nurse for some time during the reign of King Celeus of Eleusis.

APHRODITE is associated with fertility, abundant plant and animal life. The cycle of the seasons relate to the death of her lovers Anchises and Adonis. She is seductive and her divine beauty is her essence, her physical expression is sexuality with desire for fragrances, sweet flavors and affiliation with birds. After the 5th century she was depicted nude in statues. Aphrodite is passionately involved in sexual acts carrying out sacred prostitution at her temples. Her lover's madness is a curse for avoiding her love.

The classical era in Greece sparked a surge in architecture, statuary and philosophy. Mathematical reasoning was regarded as part of divine science. The Acropolis was built to glorify the gods. The statuary symbolized the human form as the divine creation of proportion and form. The gods were represented the same way. Kouros depicted the male form and kore portrayed the feminine figure. The development of theatre was part of the worship of Dionysus for four days every year that included poetry, music and dance. The ideals of Greek philosophy were piety, justice, love and common welfare. True piety was seen in right actions and the ability to differentiate between right and wrong. Reason was perceived as the divine element in humans. Greeks believed that right behavior was the outcome of right knowledge, thus the philosopher was a virtuous man. Athenian democracy was a radical approach that gave them a sense of superiority.

Greek mythology clashed with rationality and soon was seen as superstition. However, the principles were put to reason. Zeus was regarded as the embodiment of good and that was worshipped in action by living a rational virtuous life. The combination of philosophical and religious principles appeared in the teachings of Pythagoras. He believed that human psyche was the essence of the divine, captured in the human body. He believed that the soul leaves the body at death and goes into metempsychosis. Ascetic practices included abstaining from the use of animal products. Socrates stands out as an influential philosopher and acknowledged to be the wisest man. But he always felt he knew nothing of value. This humility, perceived ignorance, constantly drove him to seek wisdom. Epicurus (341-270 BCE) found that peace of mind comes from freedom of anxiety about the power of fate. He considered philosophy to be a substitute for the superstitions of Greek traditions. Zeno held the position called pantheism that divine exists in and through everything. This is also referred to as Stoicism. It believes that:

Humans can control inner guidance that determines
behavior in a particular situation.
One must remain detached from external circumstances
by keeping the inner resolve connected to divine reason.

Fate is the perfect legislation of the divine reason, the *logos*. The rationalists were persecuted to maintain the religious values and their perpetuation among the next generation. They were regarded as atheists and their beliefs were a danger to the state.

In the war between Athens and Sparta during the years 431-404 BCE the Macedonians were victorious. The Greek culture was followed in Macedon since the 5th century. Philip II with Pan-Hellenic alliance in 338 BCE united Greece behind him. Alexander the Great invaded and conquered Persia moved on to the Indus Valley. He died in Babylon at the age of 33 after becoming the master of the world at that time. He wanted to create a uniform culture that was primarily Greek which absorbed the elements of native cultures throughout his territories creating new Hellenistic religion. The Roman Empire followed his plan of syncretism. In Egypt, Alexander was seen as a pharaoh. Apollo became the sun god identified with the god *Amun-Re* of Egypt. Hellenistic god *Serapis* developed from Egyptian god *Osiris* also known as Bull of Memphis. The Greek gods Demeter and *Dionysus* were also worshipped. The native cultures were taken up by the Macedonian kings of Egypt and Syria and simplified Greek was authorized as the lingua franca in government offices. Greek games, arts, and religious culture became important part of the hellenistic world.

Greek rationalism collided with faith in religious cultures. An interest was emerging in observation and philosophical ideas. Aristotle, a student of Plato (384-322 BCE) founded Lyceum as a research center for new ideas. He covered a wide range of disciplines including mathematics, physics, logic, natural science, ethics, and drama. Fate, regarded as the factor that directed events in life and the other forms of religion, declined. This was the reason for the condemnation of Socrates because philosophers were viewed as atheists.

The power of fate gave rise to alternative measures for remedies and for peace of mind. *Asclepius* was worshipped as god of healing combining religious and therapeutic techniques. Attention was diverted to magical practices, spells and rituals.

This was instrumental in the rise of superstitions, good and bad omens, meaning of dreams and their impact on future activity. The remedial measures called for expensive rituals, animal sacrifice and specific activities.

MYSTERY RELIGIONS:

Mystery religions showed a path to salvation that was rooted in blind faith. The mystery religions were based on deities, gods and goddesses in different cultures. They included recitations, objects of worship, singing and dancing performances. The goddess *Demeter* was the deity of a mystery religion. Her sanctuary was established at Eleusis where festival of sowing grain was held related to fertility and birth. Grain must be made into bread to serve as food. Another mystery religion was associated with *Dionysus*, the god of wine and ecstasy. Grapes must be made into the wine of Dionysus. The rituals included eating, drinking wine and sexual activity. Romans restricted the worship of Dionysus in 186 BCE. Mystery religions focused on life, death and rebirth.

One of the mystery religions from the East is based on Apuleius and the story of the Golden Ass. Lucius turns into an ass while working with magic. He was owned by *Atargatis*, a Syrian goddess as an act of evil fate. Lucius was released by *Isis*, the Egyptian goddess who appeared in a dream and promised Lucius to get his human form back during her sea jouney. She also assured that he wiould even shine in the darkness of Hades, the under world. Isis became the protector of Lucius. He prayed to the Queen of Heaven and regained his human form. The mystery rituals of Isis are associated with the death of Osiris and his resurrection. Isis searched for Osiris and his return was celebrated as Festival of Search and Discovery. *Osiris* assumed new identity as *Serapis*, the universal god, with sanctuaries at ports and in cities.

Another mystery religion was about the Great Mother goddess *Atargatis*. She had the virtues of Athena, Aphrodite, Selene, Rhea, Artemis, Nemesis and Fates. She is also known as Cybele, the Magna Mater. She was worshipped in Rome starting in the

3rd century BCE. It involves her beloved Attis who was marrying someone else. Cybele created frenzy at the wedding party and Attis castrated himself. He died and his body became the source for life. The Roman festival of Attis is celebrated for 12 days in March. The ninth day was celebrated as Day of Blood where devotees castrated themselves. These priests were called Galli who dressed as women and served in the temple. They also acted as fortune-tellers. A ritual for Cybele is called *taurobolium,* and a worshipper enters a pit and a bull is sacrificed on the slatted platform over the pit thus drenching the worshipper below in the pit with bull's blood imparting the divine life and vitality.

EARLY ROMAN RELIGIOUS CULTURE:
The Trojans who escaped from the capture of Troy came to Italy and are known as Romans. Others were outcasts who settled in Rome under Romulus. Roman epics, gods and goddesses are shaped after the Greeks. Rome was founded around 750 BCE. It was incorporated in 6th century BCE to establish the Roman Republic. Estruscans from the north had a great influence in the development of the urbanization and controlled the Italian peninsula by 250 BCE.

Romans believed in omnipresence of *Numen*, the spiritual power that prevailed among gods, human beings, places and in all things. The deities identified the location of spiritual powers that facilitated human actions. Even different parts of the house had specific deities i.e. god *Janus* for threshold, goddess *Vespa* for the hearth. The essence of the male members of the family was his genius and for the females it was her juno. The ancestral spirits were the Lares. The daily religious rituals were performed by the *pater familias*, the head of the household. Priests were categorized as the pontiffs, the augurs, the men for sacred actions, and the fetials. Priests were expected to maintain purity and officiated 104 days. The diviners were also religious officials who interpreted the omens. The Vestal Virgins were prominent women and they guarded the flame in the temple of Vesta. Romans were particular about their worship of the right god, at the right time and in the right way. Religious actions involved animal sacrifices. The gods were portrayed in human form. The Etruscans influenced the temple architecture. They introduced the goddess *Minerva* and developed the art of haruspicia, for omens. The Sibylline oracles were written in the 6th century BCE and suggested rituals for Greek gods to seek divine assistance to solve problems. Romans acquired Greek mythology but changed the names of gods and goddesses. They adopted the practice of votive offerings. It was a pious life in early Rome. The intellectuals were attracted to philosophy in stead of religion until Augustus revived religion.

RELIGION and ROMAN EMPERORS:
Augustus Caesar (63 BCE - 14 CE) started a new phase in religious culture. Other generals also sought power, and struggle ensued. Octavian, Caesar's adopted son made an alliance with Marc Antony and claimed the eastern part of the empire. Antony and Cleopatra were defeated by Octavian's general Agrippa and they committed suicide. Octavian with sovereign power became Emperor Augustus Caesar and revived the traditional religion in Rome. He became *pontifex maximus* and supervisor of all religious functions. Authority of Emperor and worship of his genius confirmed loyalty to Rome. After his death Augustus Caesar was declared a god by the Senate.

The divine men of mystery religions were concerned about salvation. They had the insight and ability to perform miracles or remedy a situation by mere presence. Appollonius of Tyana, a Pythagorean philosopher in the 1st century CE was born into a wealthy family but became a wandering philosopher. He wore linen clothing, sandals made from bark, abstained from meat, and lived a life of celibacy. He went to India and Egypt to seek esoteric knowledge. He performed miracles and had power to heal and predict events. He was opposed and tried by the Emperor Domitian and his body ascended to heaven. Pythagoras saved his followers from the cycle of death and rebirth. Epicurus protected followers from the fear of gods and after-life. Asclepius was a healer and cured the illness of devotees.

Plato pointed out the movements of stars and their rational design. Celestial observations paved the way for astrology.

93

Astral spheres were identified with divine powers. Their movements affected the impact of their influence. Because the pattern of movement of the stars was predictable, their influence could also be predicted by calculations. Astrology became a scientific form of the divine. Astrologers relied on astrology to anticipate adverse events and offer measures for prevention. Religious rituals were carried out to approach the divine for assistance. The inability to control fate through religion saw a decline in Hellenistic period. Magic offered an alternative to force the actions according to the desired outcome. Magical powers were acquired by syncretism, invoking powers of gods and goddesses in the process. Access to hidden name was essential. Isis had acquired the name of Amun-Re in order to exercise powers. The magic words like Alakazam and Abracadabra appeared in popular culture for casting spells, curses, love charms and healings. Hocus pocus of the medieval times came from the Roman Catholic mass.

MESOPOTAMIAN CIVILIZATION

This ancient civilization emerged between the rivers of Tigris and Euphrates in the the 4th millennium BCE and developed into city-states. This region is modern Iraq. Between 24th and 6th centuries these city-states established dominance over the people of Akkad, Sumer, Babylon and Asshur. Writing was first developed around 3200 BCE in Sumer. This region was in great turmoil and chaos which reflected in the Mesopotamian culture. The Neolithic settlements were the earliest developed by the Baidians. This change is believed to be due to the microcephalin variant ASPM that sparked the development of written language, agriculture, and the drive to develop city states. The Bible refers to Adam and his offspring(Genesis 3:23):

And the Lord God took the man, and put him into the garden of Eden to dress it and to keep it. (Genesis 2:15); Therefore the Lord God sent him forth from the garden of Eden to till the ground from whence he was taken. (*http://www.accuracyin genesis.com/adam.html*)

Sumerians came a century later and were joined by the

Amorites by 2900 BCE. Sargon the Great (2334-2279 BCE) consolidated the city-states under his rule. He raised army with outposts throughout his kingdom but Akkadian rule lasted only a century. Babylon was established as Royal city by Hammurabi during his rule that ended with his death. The Kassites from the west invaded Mesopotamia and ruled for four centuries. They were defeated by the Assyrian kings. Their power extended to the Mediterranean under Assur-nasirpal II in the 9th century BCE. The empire reached its pinnacle under Tiglath-Pileser III. The Assyrian empire was replaced by Nebuchadnezzar II of Babylon. He was victorius against Egypt and captured Judah. Persians invaded Babylon and Mesopotamia was ruled by other world empires until the 20th century.

The impact of earlier cultures was reflected in the religious culture of civilizations that followed. The region was at the mercy of natural calamities, unpredictable events, and at the cross roads of the civilizations of East and West. A monumental religious structure in the relatively plain area was the ziggurat, a brick building built like a pyramid representing a sacred mountain. It was dedicated to different gods and was a site for rituals. It represented the intersection of heaven and earth. It included elements of Egyptian religious culture and western mythology.

INANNA was the fertility goddess of Mesopotamia, Queen of Heaven and Earth, worshipped as goddess of sexuality in Sumer. She was revered as Ishtar later in Babylon. The rituals of the power of fertility included sex between Inanna's priestess and the city king in her temple. The erotic religious poetry reflects sexuality in Inanna and Dumuzi. Inanna is the patroness of prostitutes and the evening star. Without her sexuality there will not be any human or animal life. Her wrath is seen in lightning, storms, flood and wind. She loved wars due to the passions it aroused as anger, fear and revenge. Battle was regarded as the dance of Inanna. She acquired sovereign power by tricking the god of wisdom Enki/Ea just as Isis got magical powers from the Egyptian god Amun-Re. Inanna wanted to extend her reign in the underworld kingdom of her sister Ereshkigal who retaliated and unleashed 60 diseases and Inanna died. Ea god created Good-looks the play boy to tempt and distract Ereshkigal. Inanna was brought back to life but the replacement for Inanna had to be filled with Dumuzi. Dumuzi in the underworld marks the end of the agricultural year, his return restores fertility on earth. The story portrays suffering and death balancing the role of two sisters.

EPIC of KING GILGAMESH: Search for eternal life.
This is the story of the King of Uruk who takes sons from families for his army and he deflowers virgin brides. People complain to the gods who create Enkidu to confront Gilgamesh. Enkidu surrenders and becomes his comrade. They both set out to kill Humbaba, the monster of the wilderness, a guardian created by the great god Enlil. He poses threat to the humanity. At his mother's advice Gilgamesh makes offerings to Shamash, the sun god. Enkidu also summons the spirits. Humbaba is killed and the trees are cut down to make door for the temple as an offering to god Enlil. Gilgamesh had gone to wilderness in search of Ut-napishtim the only man who gained everlasting life from the gods. He had no wisdom but was told to get a plant from the abyss. He found it but it was taken away by a snake. Gilgamesh understands and resigns to his fate. He accepts human destiny and enjoys the time of life he has. The story shows Gilgamesh pushing the limits of destiny with a desire to become immortal.

The GREAT FLOOD: The Mesopotamian story.
The primeval flood is sent by the great god *Igigi* because humanity is very noisy. Ea discloses gods plan to Ut-napishtim and sent him to hear the planning of the gods. He comes back and takes his family to the boat he built to escape the flood. Eu tells him to bring all living things to the boat. The flood continues six days and nights and the boat ends up on Mount Nimush. Birds are sent out to see the waters and offers sacrifice. The gods smell the flavor and assemble around the sacrifice. Eu argues for the justice and proportion as it was indiscriminate devastation. Gods grant everlasting life to Ut-napishtim and his wife at the mouth of two rivers.

CREATION STORY OF EUMA ELISH: According to the story human beings are created from a sacrificed god. In the Atrahasis story, gods send wasting illness, two famines caused by drought, and plague. Enki intervenes to end the suffering. Then gods decide to send flood. The gods *Nintu/Mami* who created humanity are in mourning and gods miss sacrifices. At the end, Atrahasis and his wife retain immortality. Humans henceforth have a limited life.

CIVILIZATION OF EGYPT

The early settlements were developed as farming communities along the Nile River. They used plows and draft animals during the Neolithic era. They observed the ritual of burial. Other significant religious activities developed between 4000 and 1000 BCE. The Upper and Lower Egypt was united by Menes around 3050 BCE and the first Dynasty was established under the pharaoh. They regarded pharaoh as divine authority and the representative of god to supervise humanity as a part of the created order. They lived like humans but were perceived to have spiritual powers. Egyptian belief system took a long time to develop into a religion due to the changes made under every dynasty. Two concepts dominated the Egyptian culture, life under the control of the divine and threat of chaos.

Egyptian religion was based on cultic worship of celestial spheres, sacred animals and the dead. Pharaoh was the representative of god and higher than other humans. Priests conducted the cultic rituals for the pharaoh. Men and women participated as musicians, singers and dancers in the temple for the religious events. The rituals were conducted in the morning celebrating the rebirth of the sun. The statues were redecorated everyday with a change of clothes and anointed with oil. Sacred animals were worshipped and protected in the royal estate and mummified at death. Similar species were kept and fed by the general public. The royalty and high officials observed the religious activities. The general public struggled as labor class who depended on the mercy and protection of divine pharaoh, other gods and goddesses and kept the devotional items of worship at their home. The prayers of common people were heard by *Amun* and *Ptah* gods. People attended the ceremonies at the temple to obtain an oracle. The messages received in dreams were interpreted at the temple. The wise woman was regarded as a seer with a gift to foresee future.

The Egyptian culture was polytheistic religious culture. *Thoth* and *Khonsu* were the two moon gods. Gods changed their shape and action according to the changing environment and needs. The funerary god of the underworld was the jackal-headed Anubis. Osiris was the god of the dead and lived in the underworld with his consort and sister Nephthys. He was involved in the judgement of the soul alongwith nomes. The divine functions of various gods overlapped as well. There were specific Gods and officials for different professions i.e. god *Ptah*, the patron of the artisans and craftsmen; *Imhotep*, the patron of doctors; *Thoth*, the patron of scribes to the gods.

The solar gods invoked the power of the Sun and were recognized as the chief gods. *Kheprer* represented by scarab, the dung beetle, as the god of the rising sun. *Re* is the sun god at its zenith possessing the divine essence of the sun. *Atum* was the god of setting sun. Osiris was the sun god and Horus inherited it. The pattern of succession was established and every pharaoh was called the son of Re. At sun rise god Re traveled across the sky and went to the underworld at night. Later Amun-Re became the powerful native sun god of Egypt when Amun, the god of Thebes joined *Montu*, the god of war and became prominent and powerful. Amun-Re united the powers of different sun gods and became the single god. The powerful priests replaced Amun-Re with Aten, the sun disc thus changing the traditional god that gained the top symbolic place in Egyptian religion under Akhenaten from 1353-1336 BCE.

EGYPTIAN MYTHOLOGY:
The pharaohs of Old Kingdom (2670-2200 BCE) were called Son of Re where the sun god dwelled. With their divine powers they were charged to preserve truth, order, and cosmic balance as

ma'at. This was the motivating force that inspired pharaoh to govern with reason and dignity, to maintin the ideal state of being, and as the embodiment of both principle and a goddess.

MYTH of OSIRIS:

The mythological story starts with Osiris who ruled the earth with his consort and sister Isis during an era of prosperity and peace. There was abundance of crops in the soil enriched by the flooding of the Nile. Osiris was murderd by his younger brother Seth out of jealousy who cut his body in pieces and scattered. The cultic sacred sites were built for Osiris. *Seth* was a god of violence. While Isis was in mourning, Nephthys came to help her in the search for the pieces of Osiris's body. Osiris's body was assembled and restored at Abydos and Isis was able to conceive Horus with him. Osiris became the ruler of underworld. The story explains that pharaoh at death aquires the role of Osiris leaving behind an heir to maintain the continuity of the divine work of pharaoh. Also this establishes the domain of the dead apart from the land of the living. It also offers justification for the concept *the way things are* portraying a conflict between authority, jealousy, crime and chaos.

The Tale of Sinuhe depicts the love and patriotism of a courtier who leaves Egypt after a coup and death of Amenemhet in the Middle Kingdom. He goes to Syria-Palestine and a Bedouin Chief offers him his daughter. He lived there a few years but found their ways uncivilized. He comes back to Egypt with the grace of Egyptian god for his devotion to the king and love for the Egyptian religion.

The Underworld was conceived as a concern for the after-life. It was most pronounced in the Egyptian civilization based on the intricate tombs in monumental pyramids with elaborate burials only performed for the pharaohs reflecting their divine status. After 2000 BCE the mummification and burial was open to all. For mummification, the heart was retained as the seat for the *ba*, the essence, but the brain was discarded. The internal organs were removed and the body was washed and soaked in natron for two months. It was then sewn with or without internal organs and wrapped in linen strips. The body was made as natual looking as possible by padding and painting. The mummy was put in a coffin that was enclosed in one or more larger coffins, each bearing close resemblance to the deceased. As the *ba* was preserved in the mummy the shadow was provided furniture for the tomb with decorations. The models of male and female slaves called *ushbetis*, the answerers were enclosed for the shadow of the deceased. The 'Opening of the Mout' ceremony was performed on the mummy, the ushbetis, and other human figures. The ritual included recitation of spells, animal sacrifice and purification with water. The deceased is guided by Anubis to the courtroom of Osiris for judgement attended by Isis and Nephthys involving confessions before the divine judges. The heart of the deceased is put in a balance against the ostrich feather. If the heart is heavier due to evil deeds it is eliminated. If the heart is lighter than ostrich feather due to virtuous life then a life of eternity is granted. The favorable decrees of Osiris are recorded in The Books of Going Forth by Day. The eldest son offered nourishing food daily. The after-life was placed in the kingdom of Osiris where the deceased live in leisure and they are attended by ushbetis after an elaborate process of judgement. The fate of the deceased was based on the basis of the god he or she worshipped during life of the living and the virtues or evil deeds. God Amun-Re represented rejuvenation in after-life and Osiris granted the eternal life. The information was retrieved from various texts. The Pyramidal Texts are the inscriptions on the walls from the Old Kingdom. These were called the Coffin Texts in the Middle Kingdom.

EGYPTIAN GODDESSES

The divine order of creation represents duality in male and female. Goddesses are important in their role in creation. The first gods according to the Helopolis mythology are *Shu*, the male god and *Tefnut* was the female goddess. They created new gods. Tefnut represented moisture in the air of heavens and the underworld. Tefnut is portrayed as a woman with head of lioness, a crown of solar disc and with uraeus the sacred asp indicating supreme power.

100

NUT, the daughter of Shu and Tefnut, was the sky-goddess and the consort of Geb, god of the earth. Geb gave birth to the gods of political order. Shu separated Nut from god Geb and with his tears Geb created the oceans. The wings of Nut formed the sky. Nut is also depicted as mother of Re, giving birth each dawn and swallowing up at dusk.

HATHOR is the goddess of fertility, erotic love, and joy. The festival of drunkenness was celebrated in her honor. She is depicted as the historic cow goddess with horns, human face and cow ears. She is also the warrior goddess of divine vengeance.

ISIS gained eminence as Queen of Heaven. She is a celebrated model wife, mother, and goddess of Egypt's fertility. She is shown with a crown of horns. According to an Egyptian mythological story of 1200 BCE, Isis gained access to Re's secret name by a trick. This gave her powers to cast spells and knowledge of elixirs for health and immortality. Intervention of Isis is believed to have persuaded Seth to renounce his claim and Horus prevailed. She was seen to be faithful to her husband even in after-life.

WISDOM LITERATURE IN EGYPT:
It is the beginning of the thought process that contemplates about life and practical advice to best deal with the life to enjoy it to the fullest. Wisdom was imparted at a scribal school where the pupils learned to read, write and calculate. Father also taught son to reflect wisdom and distinction between a fool and a wise man. It was mainly justice based optimistic determination to emphasize the idea of free will. The teachings were focused to impress that good deeds bring out the good in life and evil as in the following examples.

The Instruction for Merikare , imparted by father Kheti III of 10th Dynasty to his son, is about his conduct in personal and official matters: good conduct determines destiny in life i.e. rule with justice; combine peity and practicality with ruthless approach in political matters.

The Wisdom of Amenemopet advises son to have an exemplary conduct stressing virtues i.e. honesty, humility, respect, mercy, generosity, careful speech and good judgement.

EARLY CULTURES OF SYRIA-PALESTINE

Syria-Palestine is located to the east of Mediterranean and to the west of Arabian Desert between a relatively secure Egypt that had an established religious culture. Mesopotamia had gone through political dominance of invaders over time. The area has four climatic zones and the diverse terrain includes fertile plains and rocky highlands. There were three traditional cultures that were very different in lifestyle thus developing conflicts.

The nomads were constantly moving in search of pastures. The farming community was settled and worked on land. The urban culture was concentrated in the cities. The political leader was also the religious head as in Egypt and Mesopotamia. The religion was polytheistic where the gods were organized in a royal hierarchy with *El* as the chief god and head of the Divine Council. His home in the mountains was the source of the waters of the cosmos. He was called Bull El for his power. He was the divine force who worked on creation. His son *Ba'al* became the god of Syria-Palestine as well as the Lord of Israel.

In the mythic stories of Syria-Palestine, Ba'al is the rain god who makes the earth fertile with rain. His father El forces him to work under Prince Sea. Ba'al kills Prince Sea. In one story Ba'al becomes a slave of Mot, ruler of the underworld but returns back to earth. In another story Ba'al and Anat fight Lotan, the monster of the primordial sea.

Different ethnic groups worshipped their own gods. The chief god of Jebusites was Salim. The Phillistines Dragon god was half man and half fish. By syncretism Ba'al was the god of Tyre, a Phoenician city, called Ba'al Melqart. The attributes of god were used to identify god i.e. *El Shaddai*, El of the Mountains, *Ba'al-zebub*, Ba'al of the Vermin. Children were named after the gods.

102

ISRAEL

The Lord god of Israel is linked to wilderness. Originally it was also the god of storm or mountain. Israel's religious outlook changed and was different from the Syria-Palestine religious belief system. Ba'al confronted Lord. At that time Israel leaders were city princes and war leaders. The people of Israel chose Saul to protect them against the sea people who came into Palestine. David was a younger military general but more successful than Saul. Conflict for authority and power put them against one another. People put David on the throne and Israel was united with Judah. David chose Jerusalem as the capital because he was a Jebusite and the books of Samuel and Kings viewed history from David's perspective giving significance to Jerusalem. Lord god chose Israel and Israel chose Lord. The synchronicity of the Israeli belief system developed into Judaism. Around 12th century BCE Abraham interacted with people who went to Syria-Palestine. Scholars believe that the tales of ancestry about Israel were added on during the early monarchy of Israel but the ancestral history during the Middle and Bronze Ages is correctly portrayed (2200-1200 BCE).

The history of Israel expresses traditions as viewed by different writers of different times. The story of Moses and what followed is described under Judaism. In Israel the family was patriarchal, the eldest son inherited the family fortune but he could designate a younger heir. To keep the purity of the blood line marriages were preferred within the family with cousins. This applied to adoptions as well. Polygamy ensured that the patriarchal line will continue. The hierarchy was based on the seniority of the wives. The nomadic families lived independently but the patriarchal household included the father, his wives, unmarried daughters, married daughters and sons and their spouses, all children of the joint family and the family servants.

PROPHECY in ISRAEL

Joseph has the ability to interpret dreams and read omens from the dregs of wine in a cup (Genesis 40-41:44:5.15). The consultation of dead spirits was prohibited. The sound and movement of trees was the source of oracles. Prophets had rejected the oracles and replaced with the Lord's word that was revealed to the prophet. Samuel believed in prophecies from three kinds of prophets:

Guild prophets prophesied under a leader and experienced the extreme forms as dancing, whirling, catatonic trance and taking off all clothing. These prophets fell out of favor.

Official prophets engaged in determining god's intentions and were part of the royal establishment. The Court prophets worked in the royal court to advise the king. The Cultic prophets worked in relation to the shrines.

Independent prophets were not affiliated with the court or shrine. The conflict with court officials was due to different ideas of Lord's direction for the people, not from authorities.

Elijah was a prophet for King Ahab of Israel and his son Ahaziah from 871 to 850 BCE. Ahab was the son of Omri, king of northern Israel, who worshipped the Lord god. He married Jezebel, daughter of the King of Tyre who worshipped the Phoenician form of Ba'al-Melqart. Ahab's queen, Jezebel of Siddon, initiated the worship of Ba'al in Samaria in 860. Prophets Elijah and Elisha were against the worship of Ba'al. The royal families in Damascus, Judah, and Israel were killed and worship of Ba'al was introduced. During clashes of the Babylonians, Assyrians and Egyptians, Nebuchadrezzar the king of Babylon, besieged Jerusalem and brought an end to the kingdom of Israel. *Marduk*, the Babylonian god adopted the attributes of all other gods to be worshipped by all. Priests slapped the Babylonian Kings to make them feel that they are under god Marduk had the power over the king.

Jezebel established her cult under 400 Ba'alite priests in opposition to the Lord god. At that time greater number of shrines of a god meant greater number of worshippers in prayer and Lord god was becoming more powerful. A contest was set at Carmel that was equidistant from Tyre, the cultic home of Ba'al-Melqart and Samaria, the cultic home of the Lord god (1 Kings 18:20-40). Two identical sacrifices were made and the invocation of each god was expected to burn the sacrifice by sending fire. The Ba'alite priests could not bring fire to the sacrifice. When Elijah called upon the Lord god to send fire, the sacrifice ignited and was consumed by fire. Faith in Lord god developed universal following and Lord god became God, the Almighty Lord. Elijah was an independent prophet without any official links and was the first prophet of Israel called Elijah the Tishbite. Elijah had to flee to wilderness to escape the wrath of Jezebel. Lord appeared to Elijah at Mt. Horeb. He prophesied during the rule of Ahab and his successor son Ahaziah in the northern kingdom of Israel.

Isaiah, Jeremiah and Ezkiel were classical prophets. Isaiah had prophesied (7:1-9) assuring Ahaz that enemy kingdoms will fall to Assyria. But Ahaz ignored the prophecy of Lord's covenant with David. Both prophecies were taken as confirmation of Lord's faithfulness to the people of Israel as promised. After the fall of Israel and Judah, faith in the Lord sustained. Fall of Jerusalem was viewed as punishment for sins of Judah. Ezkiel's prophecy and his own exile to Babylon in 597 BCE, the Wheel in a Wheel vision, as the chariot of the Lord made him their spiritual leader in exile. The prophecy of Second Isaiah that the nation will be restored, gave hope to the people and assurance of the covenant. He rejected idol worship and proclaimed monotheism with Lord's sovereign power over the universe and the God of the entire world. People returned after exile according to prophecy but everything was in ruins. Prophet Haggai told the people that building the Temple will ensure Lord's protection and bring prosperity. The temple was built.

THE JESUS MOVEMENT
There is mythic significance to the story of Jesus. He revealed God's intentions for humanity. The Jesus movement believed Jesus to be the Lord accessible in human form. The earliest proclamations focused on his suffering, death and resurrection. According to John (20:30-31) the Gospels recite the events that affirm faith in people. The historical perspective about Jesus comes only from the New Testament taken from Roman and Jewish sources and sayings of Jesus in Paul's letters, Acts of the Apostles, Christian writers of that time and Gospel manuscripts. He was a great thinker with miraculous powers.

John the Baptist was a reformer and baptized Jesus. Baptism was an initiation for a new life. Jesus was a reformer with an inspiring message. Jesus movement was identified with Judaism in early stages and included the Greek-speaking Jews. He welcomed all people and Gentiles. He cited commandment to love the Lord, one's neighbor and even enemies. Jesus was prayed as god by his followers. Messiah, in Aramaic language means The Anointed One which became *Christos* in Greek and later was known as Christ. Jesus designated himself as Son of Man. In both Hebrew and Aramaic, this term means human being. This was changed to Son of God, Savior, and Lord signifying divine authority and power. This identity in the Roman Empire clashed with the existing beliefs in traditional gods who protected the empire. The monotheistic movement of Jesus was a threat. At that time Judaism was the *religio licta*, a legitimate religion.

Most Jews did not follow the Jesus movement. Gentiles were receptive to it but opposed to the ritual of circumcision. He performed miracles and talked about the kingdom of God. Breaking bread and wine was an expression of community meal. Paul of Tarsus was a prosecutor and initially persecuted the Jesus movement. He was an official and followed the law. Paul experienced conversion. The Jesus congregation in Antioch commissioned Paul as a missionary apostle. Barnabus, a missionary became his mentor and partner in creating the Jesus community in the eastern Mediterranean. Conversion was a radical change that required severing all ties to the kins or to one's profession. The missionaries created a new kinship by using words brother or sister and Paul himself was an example to follow. The break with Judaism came when Paul accepted uncircumcised Gentiles and laid more emphasis on commitment to covenantal obedience. Separation from Judaism with an indepedent identity lost protection from the Romans and the persecution started. Romans charged Jesus for non-allegience to the King. He was executed by crucifixion, a common form of punishment to deter any attempt by others. The followers believe that he died for their sins. Resurrection made him Christ and became the main focus of worship in the Jesus communities.

APOCRYPHON OF JOHN – Jewish Mythology:
Apocryphon is the secret book of John. Christ after resurrection reveals secrets to John, son of Zebedee. The mythological story starts with Monad, the Primal Father, whose First Thought is a feminine figure called Barebelo and a son Autogenes is begotten (BAR: May-June 2008, 55). The primal family with luminaries established heavenly Seth, the seed of Seth and other souls. Twelve aeons, the heavenly entities personify the divine attributes. Sophia (Wisdom) is the 12th aeon. She produces Yaldabaoth (Child of Chaos) with other names Saklas (worshipped by 12 disciples in Gospel of Judas) and Samael (blind god) and declares: I am God and there is no other God beside me (cf. Isaiah 45:5; 46:9). After repentance, Sophia rises to ninth heaven. Yaldabaoth says, Let us create man in the image of God (cf. Genesis 1:26). An image in human form appeared in cosmic waters. Sophia put the breath of life into Adam (cf. Genesis 2:7) incorporating the divine spirit in humans. Yaldabaoth creates a woman, Eve, to undermine the power of Adam. Eve and Adam eat the forbidden fruit and acquire gnosis. Their son Seth becomes the father of Gnostics, the seed of Seth. Yaldabaoth creates fate and calamities for humans and Sophia intervenes for their salvation.

STONEHENGE, The London Monument
Stonehenge is an ancient site of the pre-Christian era located 80 miles southwest of London on Salisbury Plain which was built in three stages between 3000 and 1600 BCE. The Druids were a part of Celtic priesthood in ancient times. They performed their services as a priest and as scholar, arbitrator, healer and as magistrate. Rituals of maypole dances, bonfires, and courtship linger and represent pagan influence in Europe. The ancient religious practices are staged in Christian legendary tales of magicians and wizards. The fascinating tales of wizardry in the Harry Potter 7-book series by J. K. Rowling OBE (Joanne,"Jo") captured the imagination of a generation throughout the world The sunrise at the Stonehenge is celebrated on the longest day of the year, the summer solstice which draws thousands of people.

OTHER CULTURES

The early civilizations in China, India and the Americas expressed their faith in nature (Sun, fire, earth, water, rain, animals, or deities to help avert drought, destruction and death. The communal prayers included offerings to the priests to invoke God's mercy (Hinduism) and sacrifice of animals, humans, and excised hearts of men (Aztec and Incas) to please gods. The traditional regional music and dance was a part of all primitive cultures as a unique auditory enhancer in mystic rituals and communal activities to get a sense of euphoria and trance. The recitations of hymns, chanting, prayers, and religious scriptures written in specific melodies are a part of worship to keep distractions at bay and help in concentration of mind. Prayer calls from Mosques, blowing of horns and Church bells beckon everyone to assemble for prayer. The Tibetan prayer wheels remind about cycle of life, death and rebirth.

Sacrificial rituals have been performed for thousands of years. The sacrificed bodies, bones and ceremonial items have been discovered at the archaeological sites around the world. The platform mound at Cerro Sechin in Peru was the New World's first monumental structure in 1700 BCE (Archeology, Jan., 2007). 'The Street of the Dead' leads to the Teotihuacan's ceremonial center in Mexico ending at the 'Pyramid of the Moon'. The archeological site reveals dozens of men including a golden eagle in a ceremony probably attended by thousands around 300 AD (National Geographic, Oct., 2006). Other sites show remains of sacrificed animals and decapitated humans.

Some rituals were not necessarily linked to the religious protocol. In Africa, the mothers remember how their breasts were stone pressed to mask their puberty and save their daughters from rape and violent sexual aggression. The mutilation of sexual organs is still being practiced in some regions. During the partition of India the communal riots erupted among Hindus and Muslims. The rival factions confirmed their suspicion by examining the person for circumcision. Hindu men are not circumcised but Muslim male children are circumcised within eight days of birth. Male converts to Islam have to be circumcised. In North America, unlike Europe, male infants are circumcised.

The custom of *Sati,* an honor-suicide ritual in Hinduism was observed by widows in India for centuries. The widows jumped into the funeral pyre of their deceased husband. It is no longer practiced in India. Widows were not allowed to marry again for the rest of their life to preserve family honor. Cases of honor-killings of girls have been reported even during the past decade. In India the girls were disposed off at birth due to the looming burden of dowry that was required to marry a daughter when she came of age. The foeticide problem is on the rise since 1990. The United Nations Children's Fund declared in its State of the World's Children 2007 Report that out of 71,000 children born every day in India, the sex ratio is 882 girls to 1,000 boys. Boys are preferred in developing nations. Marriages were arranged by middle men in India who matched the couple at an early age. Parents gave a word in some instances that their daughter or son, when born, will marry into the other family. If husband died at a young age, the woman was not allowed to remarry even if she was a child bride and would be sent to special ashrams, the institutions for widows where they shaved their head and lived a life of renunciation till death. Widows were treated as if they were responsible for their husband's death. The dowry system is still prevalent and has been abused causing fraudulent marriages with the intention to get a big dowry. In some primitive tribes in jungles of Southeast Asia the bridegroom has to offer pigs, cattle, fishing nets to the bride's family and has to have a hut before asking for their daughter in marriage. Education and freedom has changed the social mindset, some for the better and some less desirable which has influenced traditional family values. Polygamy has been allowed in the Middle Eastern countries. Kings have had this privilege through millennia. A reference to a wide range of sexual beliefs and practices observed by primitive cultures appears in Chapter V under the topic Sex and Beliefs.

SAGE WISDOM

Body is a vehicle for the soul acquiring physical identity during the journey of life. It gives sanctuary to the mind where a flame is lit to continue the light of the Lord. That is why body is referred to as a temple to be maintained with care and reverence as its actions are a direct reflection of the mind. Mind reacts to external stimuli and stirs emotions such as tranquility or rage, bliss or discomfort, contentment or greed, humility or lust for power and fame, compassion or ego-driven pursuits, selfless service or self centered whims. Saint Francis of Assisi stated:

Start by doing what is necessary;
then do what is possible; and
suddenly you are doing the impossible.

Vincent Lombardi said: The good Lord gave you a body that can stand most anything. It's your mind you have to convince. Mind has the power of intuition but most importantly consciousness as a higher being. Your conscience reasons out the good and bad. When the good is triumphant, the actions and their coutcome are admirable, and lead to a path of good deeds. If bad overpowers the mind, a chain reaction corrupts the body that clouds ones conscience. On judgement day, we are responsible for our deeds. The consequences are based on the good and bad actions in life. In the words of Mother Teresa:

Life is a promise; fulfill it.
Kind words can be short and easy to speak,
but their echoes are truly endless.

Verses of Psalm of Peace (Sukhmani) in Sikh Scriptures show the path, through humility, to higher planes in spirituality:

He is a prince among men,
who has effaced his pride in the company of saints
He who deems himself as lowly,
shall be esteemed as the highest of the high.
He who lowers his mind to the dust of all people's feet,
observes the Name of God enshrined in every heart.

Aristotle said: The beauty of the soul shines out when a man bears, with composure, one heavy mischance after another, not because he does not feel them, but because he is a man of high and heroic temper. Soul remains above the human experience, untouched, but communicating with the mind through thoughts and visions. True souls are divinely inspired and charged with righteousness and compassion (Sikh scriptures AGGS p. 239):

> Soul drenched in the Word (of God) becomes eternal,
> (it) never wanders, it can't drown, it can't be stolen,
> (it) cannot be consumed by the flames of fire.

Oskar Schindler, an industrialist was compelled by his soul to save the Jews in Nazi Concentration Camps during WWII. Ihsanullah, a taxi driver in Washington D.C. won 55.2 million Dollars in lottery in 2001 and went back to Pakistan. He used his winnings to buy medical supplies and medicines, assembled a team of doctors to help the victims of the massive 7.6 earthquake that killed 73,000 people in Pakistan. Was he guided by the soul? Bhai Ghanaiya gave water to the wounded Sikhs and Muslims in the battlefield. When questioned, he responded, I see the Guru (Lord) in everyone out there and I serve thee. In these episodes it is this intrinsic energy called soul that is compassionate and magnificient creating elevated consciousness to rise above ones personal need and directs towards thoughts of service.

> The wind of grace is always blowing.
> You just need to spread the sail.
> ...Swami Vivekananda

We are the most evolved organism among myriads of species but we also are part of the universal plan. The only blessing as humans is that we have conscience and the ability to sharpen our consciousness and use it for the service of the universe. Mystics of both East and West have expressed the love of God. Sheikh Farid, a sage, persevered in his search for the divine and became weak and bony, animals picking on his feet for flesh. He pleaded to the scavengers not to touch his eyes as he still hoped to see the Lord. Sage Namdev, a tailor by profession, thinks of the Lord by saying: My mind is the measuring tape and tongue my scissors. I cut the cloth of vices into pieces to design my soul so that it can be accepteable to the divine spirit. Sages have a longing for a life of service and sacrifice without any expectations. Such spiritual transformation raised Moses beyond the lure of Pharaoh's wife. The legendary love affair of Majnu reached a level that Laila was no longer the object of physical attraction but represented his love of God. Saints and the wise talk about the desire of soul to reach the Oversoul and attain the attributes of godly love and become like God. In religious texts love for God is expressed like the love between true lovers.

There is an Indian saying: Food, Worship, Wealth, and Wife deserve privacy. The custom of covering the head and face from the elders in India was to respect the elder men of the family. The burqa, long gown that covers from head to the feet, worn by women of the Middle Eastern countries is to honor the privacy of women in public. The tradition of dating, dancing, and social drinking is a norm in the West. *Laissez les bon temps roulez* (let the good times roll). This has grown beyond the honorable purpose and brushing with socially questionable behavior which has given heartache to educators, parents, and society. In this era of global communication, all societies around the world have been exposed to all cultures in the East and the West that are transforming traditions. The assimilation of the culture is a natural outcome of access to education and global interaction among world cultures. Every culture has something positive to offer but requires personal discretion to acquire the positive aspects of other cultures to enrich their own. There are extremes ranging from the open relationships (heterosexual, homosexual or bisexual) on the one hand to the strict code of fundamental values that vary according to the belief systems and culture. The modern make overs of the societies have put the rigid religious convictions at odds with the progressive ways.

A belief system is based on the thought processes deemed to be the absolute truth. The entrenchment of those views intensifies ego and hardens their stand on their doctrines. Consciousness arises independent of the organized religions (Tolle 2005, 17-19). The spiritual message of sages, irrespective of their religion, caste, or creed is included in Sikh Scriptures based on spirituality and heightened consciousness. Tolle points out that any action or achievement, if unconscious, will create ego and is used for personal gain or fame. The actions empowered by consciousness show high creativity. Selfless good deeds are part of spirituality. Rick Warren, a charismatic Baptist pastor of the Saddleback Church in California launched a global Peace Plan.

UNDERSTANDING RELIGIOUS DIVERSITY

Religious thought has developed in all emerging cultures over the millennia. It was inspired by the call of the divine which channeled the wisdom imparted in a dream, or by a divine intervention. In a contest between two gods Ba'al and Lord god, the Lord god of the Israelites was victorious by burning the sacrifice as prayed by the priests. Possibly Lord god sustained as God, an expression for the divine, invisible but omnipresent. The Great Flood is a part of ancient stories in many cultures. The survival from that huge calamity initiated the necessity to worship and offer gratitude to a higher entity. According to Professor Glenn S. Holland the Egyptian goddess Isis came close to becoming a deity of world religion. The powerful messages of prophets resonated with the followers. A desire for separate identity gave rise to certain distinct rituals and practices. The groups developed a bonding based on religion which empowered their leaders to achieve social and political status.

There are 5000 ethnic groups in the world. Ethnicity created initial communal bonding on the basis of their unifying forces. Religions sought expansion and viewed strength in numbers recognized as a powerful influence. This ambition led to waves of conversion and/or allurement to increase numbers. The real purpose of religion became a competitive venture putting the universal message of spirituality second to the need for strength in numbers. The race for supremacy was set in motion to claim superiority over other religions. Cultural conflicts and sectarian violence developed into campaigns of dominance, conversion, massacres, ethnic cleansing and wars. The scars of these feuds, conflicts, Jihads and crusades, between Islam and Christianity are visible in the Blue Mosque in Istanbul, Turkey where the church frescos have been painted over to modify the church into a mosque by adding minarets. Hagia Sophia was a Christian church built in the 6th century in a sprawling Christian metropolis of Constantinople. Turkish Islamic warriors conquered the city and named it Istanbul.

Pope Benedict's message in the guest book at the mausoleum of Mustafa Kemal Ataturk read: Turkey is the meeting point of different religions and cultures and a bridge between Asia and Europe. Pope John Paul II visited Ankara in 1979 and sought spiritual bonds between Christianity and Islam. Pope Gregory VII in the 11th century remarked: Christians and Muslims owe each other the charity because we believe in one God, albeit in a different manner.

A beam of light passes through a prism and creates a spectrum of seven colors of the rainbow. One color represents only one range of wave length. Exploration of a wider range of the visible spectrum reveals other colors of different wavelengths. All these colors differenciated from the white light. Spirituality is that beam of divine illumination which has differenciated into different religions passing through the prism of humanity. Spirituality defines God and is the foundation of all religions.

Once Aurangzeb, Muslim Emperor of India, asked the 7th Nanak, Guru Har Rai, how nice it would be if all the population worshipped one Prophet and followed one religion. He replied: A garden looks so beautiful with all kinds of flowers in a variety of beautiful colors, patterns and pleasing fragrances. If there was just one type of vegetation everywhere it will not express nature's immense beauty the Almighty Lord created. Every faith praises and worships the One Supreme Force that created everything and everyone. Pir Mia Mir, religious advisor to Emperor Aurangzeb referred to Guru Har Rai as Allah's beloved and respected his spiritual wisdom.

The Universal Supreme Force has been identified as Ultimate Reality, God, Lord, Ram, Allah, Waheguru, Creator, Holy Ghost, Yahweh and countless other names for the spirits that were worshipped by the primitive tribes. All of these designated their unique doctrines, deities, prayers, greetings, languages, codes of conduct and religious practices in different cultures. At every stage in time, ambitious leaders and political figures have modified the religious landscape in different continents where existing practices and customs have prevailed and made their mark. It will be productive to focus on the teachings and follow the path paved for salvation under various religions so that, in God's name everyone seeks the welfare of the entire creation and transcends geopolitics. The universal demons Lust, Anger, Attachment, Ego, and Greed are five formidable forces that are considered to be the satanic vices. These elements were at the root of ancient conflicts and wars which historically engulfed tribes and nations and continue to permeate current geopolitics.

Scriptures were originally oral proclamations by the prophets but the allegorical and inventive exegesis added a different facet which modified the objects and practices for worship. The scriptures are treated with reverence and teachings have a divine luster that permeates the psyche of the faithful in a remarkably different way than any other text. The religious texts became Holy and the revelations were compiled into written words from the oral discourses by the disciples who accompanied the prophets. The impact of the written word has been interpreted primarily by the religious leaders.

Recent developments in disciplines of physics, biology, and astronomy have given us a new vision of truth, secrets of the mind, and its powers. As our knowledge and understanding of the unexplored and mystic realm grows we expect revisions to current perceptions in the future. Work of Nicolas Copernicus, a sixteenth century cosmologist raised a storm in religious circles. It was a radical departure from the established thinking at the time even though he labeled it as God's Divine Handiwork, the way our planets and the universe operates. He was a Catholic canon in a cathedral in Poland but was not permitted to discuss astronomy and mathematics with anyone. He went away and collaborated with Rheticus, a Lutheran, to write the book *De revolutionibus*. He dedicated this book to the Pope but did not mention Rheticus because it could not be published otherwise.

Owen Gingerich of Harvard, a distinguished astronomer and historian of science replied to Dava Sobel's question that many people viewed scientists as godless:

I find it ironical that fundamentalists at both ends of the spectrum of evolution tantamount to atheism. Philip Johnson, a fervent advocate of Design, hopes evolution will go away because he believes it carries a notion of atheism as it is often taught. Richard Dawkins, whose enthusiasm for evolution is over the top, hopes evolution will make religion go away.
Dr. Francis Collins of Human Genome Project liked a rational middle way, that evolution with its idea of common derivative of natural selection seems to be description of how the Creator brought about an incredible diversity of life forms.

There is a sense of optimism that science in its search for truth will keep on unfolding new information and help us admire the mysteries of the Creator. Religions can not be easily modified. The identity of a particular sect is derived from its scriptures which serve as their guide. Still we notice new variant groups emerge due to a preconceived purpose oriented interpretation. The Fundamentalist Church of Latter-Day Saints (FLDS) broke away from the mainstream Mormons in the 1890s and adhered to polygamy. Warren Jeffs became prophet of FLDS conducting marriages between older married men and young teenage girls. This social and legal dilemma ended in his conviction. Stand offs in Waco and Jonestown ended tragically killing hundreds of unsuspecting followers. There was also a self proclaimed Black Messiah of the 1980s (born as Hulon Mitchell Jr in the state of Oklahoma, USA) who murdered 23 people.

Six religions are explored with a brief overview of their origin, basic principles, and their practices for the reader. Based on their diverse criteria of an individual faith and belief system, a believer in one faith may be viewed as a non-believer in another. When a religion develops a following beyond regional and national boundaries and spreads to other parts of the world, it attains the status of a world religion. This started a race for religious supremacy which sparked the ambition of rulers and religious leaders to capture a wider area of influence to spread their religion and pursued it as a planned mission. Sectarian division with variations in practices appeared within eligions.

Early Homo sapiens believed in many spirits. Abraham's faith was open to all people. Morality was exhibited in sacrificial rituals offering his own son Ishmael. Prophets were reformers who voiced their thoughts which led to Monotheism. The followers claimed their prophet to be the only god and no other. Numbers were viewed as strength of the god and to gain supremacy resorted to conversion or other means of allurement. Monarchs conquered other territories to convert more people. The resentment that followed created unrest and turmoil. The emperors and kings understood the need for tolerance, open trade and cordial relations with neighboring kingdoms. Marriages of monarchs were a means of creating new alliances to establish truce and resume commerce to bring prosperity. This change brought the Golden Age as under Ashoka and Mohammad Akbar's rule in India, Constantine in Turkey, and tolerance of faiths in other lands. Fundamentalists were not happy unless their faith was reigning supreme.

The religious pendulum shifted again towards intolerance and tensions grew among monotheistic faiths. The dissensions within the faiths gave rise to sectarian divisions and more intolerance within the sects i.e. Sunnis, Shi'ites, and Kurds in the Middle East, Hindus, Buddhists, and Jains in India. This sentiment spilled in other parts of the world. Second Buddhist Convention created 18 different Budhist sects. Fortunately, world opinion is now shifting towards secularism, tolerance and understanding. This will help the flow of commerce, tourism, and mutual respect and tolerance for all faiths, and a road to global property and secularism.

It is ironic, there is no monument to humanity in Africa where human race evolved, the progenitors of human faith. It is important to explore the beginning, historical perspective and the under-pinnings of these faiths. The exploration of traditions, rituals, and practices in six religions is an attempt to present the journey in each faith and the vital role religions play around the globe. Let us explore God and the spirituality embodied in these six religions for a better understanding.

JUDAISM

יהוה

YHWY

Minorah

JUDAISM
(14 million)

Hebrew Bible, the Old Testament offers spiritual guidance to the Jews. The Jewish faith has redefined itself in the first thousand years and the belief system has evolved into Judaism. Worship was conducted only at the temple with sacrificial rituals. The Babylonians destroyed the First Temple in 586 BCE. The Second Temple was rebuilt and that was destroyed by the Romans in 70 CE. The synagogues became the places for worship and sacrificial ritual was replaced by prayer. Rabbi Akiva, a prominent Jewish sage in the 2nd century CE, discussed the Torah as law given to Moses at Mt. Sinai . Jerusalem is the site of the original Temple. The historical, religious, and political claims await an effort for independent Israel and Palestine.

Abram, later known as Abraham, was born in 2100 BCE. His childhood was spent in the city of Ur, located between the Tigris and Euphrates Rivers. It was the center of world's first empire called Sumer. Abram and his wife Sarai could not have a child. Sarai requested Abram to have a child with maidservant Hagar and Ishmael was born. Abram's father moved from Ur and settled down in Haran. God told Abram:
... you will be the father of many nations.(Genesis 17:5-6)
   Your bodies will bear the mark of my everlasting covenant.
   (Circumcision to be performed on the 8th day after birth)
                                    (Genesis 17:3)
God told 89 year old Sarai and called her Sarah telling her that she will have a son within a year. Sarah laughed, and God named her son Isaac which in Hebrew means laughter. God gave Abram the name Abraham at age 99. Abraham, means 'father of many' in Hebrew and God told him:
   get thee out of thy country...unto the land that I will show
   thee...I will make of thee a great nation (Genesis 12:1-2).
He was the first to break away from the prevailing culture of idolatry and recognized existence of God. Isaac was 37 years old when God ordered Abraham to sacrifice him. Abraham took

Isaac to Mount Moriah and was ready to sacrifice his son when an angel stopped him (Genesis 22:12). Abraham was buried in the cave of Machpelah near Hebron, the site of the Tomb of the Patriarchs (Miller, 2004). The site is under the jurisdiction of Palestine and the Jews are permitted to worship there. The descendants served Egyptian Pharaohs in bondage starting in 1600 BCE. According to the Book of Genesis Abraham was informed by God about the bondage. The earliest form of Abrahamic religion evolved into the mosaic religion which later developed into Judaism, the term used since the 6th century BCE. French expedition in 1933 excavated thousands of cuneiform tablets in Mari, Syria dating to 2nd millennium when Abraham was in that area. Abraham became a spiritual ancestor of almost one third of humanity, linked to Talmud and expressed in Genesis; to Koran where he is called *khalil*, friend of God, as the Prophet of Islam, referred in 25 of the 114 suras; and referred to as patriarch in the New Testament, the Christian Bible.

Moses was born in Egypt. His ancestor Jacob came from Canaan 350 years before him. Their population grew rapidly. Pharaoh ordered to throw all the new born Israelite boys into the Nile River (Exodus 1:22). The infant (Moses) was released ito the Nile on a reed boat towards the bathing site of a princess. She noticed and rescued the child and named him Moses. In Hebrew Moses means the boy drawn from the Nile. As planned, he was nursed by his own mother Jochebed who was nearby and was hired as wet mother to nurse Moses. she accepted the job. Moses was raised a prince in Egypt. Moses knew that he was a Hebrew. He once saw an Egyptian foreman beating a slave and he killed that Egyptian. He escaped to Midian in Sinai Peninsula where he worked as a shepherd for Jethro who gave his daughter Zipporah to be his wife. God spoke to him when he was 80 yers old:

> I am sending you to Pharaoh, you will lead my people,
> the Israelites, out of Egypt .(Exodus 3:10)

The Exodus is the most significant event in the Jewish faith and is now challenged. Moses took the Hebrews to what is named Mount Sinai or Mt. Horeb in the Bible. In Egypt this is called

Jebel Musa, Mountain of Moses. Jewish evidence points out that the site of the burning bush where Moses received the Ten Commandments from God was identified 200 years later and the monastery of St. Catherine was built in the 500s CE after Christianity was legalized by Rome. One of the oldest surviving copies of the Bible, Codex Sinaiticus written 300 years after Jesus, was discovered at that site (Miller, 2004). Codex is a Latin word for the books with shorthand notes written on the sides, the small masora (Masra Qetam) and the large masora contains lengthy notes on top and bottom (Masora Gedola). The codex is a book with pages written on both sides. The Dead Sea Scrolls are from the times earlier than the codeces. The Aleppo Codex is regarded as the most authoritative copy and cannot be used while chanting the Torah portion (BAR, Sept.-Oct., 2008). The Aleppo Codex was created by Masoretes in 930s CE in Tiberias on the Sea of Galilee. It was dedicated to the Karaite community of Jerusalem, a Jewish dissident group that did not accept Oral Law. The Codex was taken to Jerusalem in 1040 CE. It was seized by Crusader conquerors in 1099. It appeared in Fustat, near Cairo, a Rabbinic synagogue after that time. It was believed to be ransomed by Rabbinic Jews of Egypt. Moshe Ben Maimon, popoularly known as Maimonides (1138-1204 CE), the medieval authority referred to the Aleppo Codex there in Egypt. After that it appeared in the Aleppo (Syria) synagogue and remained there for six centuries and was brought to Jerusalem in 1957. The other copy similar to Aleppo Codex is the Leningrad Codex in St. Petersburg, Russia with vowel markings, cantillation signs and masora. The Biblia Hebraica is the standard scholarly text of the Hebrew Bible which uses the Leningrad Codex at this time (BAR Sept-Oct, 2008).

God's name was revealed to Moses as YHWH. This was confirmed by thousands of fragments recovered from the Dead Sea Scrolls. Moses received the Ten Commandments at Mount Sinai. The first commandment:

> I am the Lord your God who brought you out of
> the land of Egypt, the house of bondage.
> You shall have no other Gods but me...(Exodus 20:2)

122

WESTERN WALL
JERUSALEM

Richard Nowitz / National Geographic Image Collection

You shall be a special treasure to me above all people.
                                        (Exodus. 19:5)
who created the heavens....called thee in righteousness
    for a light of the nations to open blind eyes. (Isa. 42:5-7)

Among 613 commandments, 248 are positive, 365 negative
which one should not do. Habakkuk consolidated all these into
three fundamental principles:
    To do justice.
    Observe loving kindness, and
    Walk humbly with God.
Jews assumed a special status as a people and as a nation. This
was reflected later in Kabbalistic views. The Biblical period
begins with Abraham's having faith in God (Genesis 15:6) and
as the patriarch of the nation. His faith was tested with God's
commandment to sacrifice his son Isaac and his willingness to do
so. This created the enormous power of faith. The traditional
ram horn is reminder of that event in history where a ram was
sacrificed in place of Isaac.

The Holy Scriptures of the Jews begin with the Torah, the five
books of the Bible, the Mitzvoth. The kabbalist teachings of the
the holy women of Israel, Seven Prophetesses who lived between
1800 and 350 BCE, each is identified with the day of week, land
species, and their unique spiritual quality: (see Chapter III)
    Sarah: Sunday; Wheat; symbolic of Loving-kindness.
    Miriam: Monday; Barley; Judgement and Strength.
    Devorah: Tuesday; Grapes; Beauty and Truth.
    Chanah: Wednesday; Figs; Victory and Eternity.
    Avigail: Thursday; Pomegranates; Majesty, Glory, Humility.
    Chuldah: Friday; Olive Oil; Foundation, Covenant.
    Esther: Sabbath; Date honey; Sovereignty, Kingdom.

Twelve tribes of Israel developed from 12 sons of Jacob, the
grandson of Abraham. God called Jacob Israel and his
descendants are called Israelites. Their belief system was new.
Famine drove them to Egypt where Pharaoh enslaved them in
1600 BCE. The bondage in Egypt continued for hundreds of

years where Jews were slave labor for Pharaoh's massive projects. Moses freed them from bondage in 1250 BCE. After wandering in the desert they arrived at Mount Sinai where Moses spent forty days and nights and was handed down the commandments by God. The Torah became the source of divine law and a guide to God's directives.

The kingdom of Israel was established in 1025 under Saul as their first king. Jerusalem became the capital in 1000 BCE. King David was the descendant of the tribe of Judah and the kingdom was named Judah in political and geographical terms. The people living in Judah were known as Judaeans. He brought the Ark of the Covenant to Jerusalem which contained the Ten Commandments. His son king Solomon built the temple in Jerusalem employing Phoenician logs and craftsmen in 925 BCE. King Solomon died three years later and the kingdom was divided into northern part as Israel with Samaria as capital ruling the ten tribes of Israel. The southern part Judaea fell to the Babylonians who destroyed the first temple in 586 BCE. During the monarchy the prophets laid emphasis on morality and ethical values. This gave rise to the Reform movement. King Cyrus of Babylonia wanted to displace the well entrenched Israelites encouraging them to restore the temple as indicated in the stirrings of restoration in Hebrew Bible. The unity of the Jewish people was anchored in the central place of worship, the Temple and the ritual of sacrifice as religious event. Both of these essential cornerstones of faith were disappearing. The Second Temple was restored in 516 BCE . By the 1st century, three philosophies had emerged.

    Sadducees: Denied re-incarnation, resurrection and the belief of no involvement in world activities.

    Essenes: Believed that all is pre-ordained by God, man has no ability to intervene to fulfill his wish.

    Pharisees: God controls everything, but man can exercise his will to choose good or evil.

The Romans destroyed the Second Temple in 70 CE. In the Middle Ages the Jews dispersed in other parts of the world where the new dominating religions were Christianity and

Islam. Jews practiced their faith wherever they settled. The Christians of Western Europe allowed the Jews to join under the condition that they would give up some of the rituals and practices. Under the Reform movement, Halakha, the Jewish legal system, an essential part of Judaism, was not acceptable to all Jews for the first time in history. The word Judaism first appeared in the Second Book of Maccabees (2:21; 14:38) and Hellenism during the Hellenistic era in the 2nd century BCE. This term was associated with the people of Judaea and their culture, the nation called Israel (Gafni, 2003).

The Ten Commandments given to Moses at Mount Sinai defined Judaism. The first commandment states man's relationship with God: Belief in the One God, Worship only God and no other deities, Refrain from false oaths in God's name, and to Honor parents. Other commandments refer to relationships with other human beings prohibiting three sins, murder (shedding of blood), adultery (forbidden sexual relations), and stealing. The single principle, according to Hillel, summarizes Torah:

What is hateful to you, do not do to your fellow man.

The righteous shall live by his faith (Habakuk 2:4).

The need to differenciate Judaism from the younger religions Islam and Christianity was felt by the 12th century Jewish philosopher Maimonides. He developed thirteen principles. By the 16th century each principle was recited with the affirmation: I believe with absolute faith. The principles were included in the Jewish prayer books and Jews sing Yigdal hymn in synagogues. The Zohar makes the mystical statement that Israel, Torah and God are all linked.

The Hebrew Bible has three parts.

1. Torah: the Pentateuch, (5 books) Moses reflects on events from creation and ending with his death. Events include journey to Canaan up to the destruction of the First Temple, with emphasis on moral behavior.
2. Nevi'im: Prophets: (8 books) Joshua, Judges, Samuel, Kings, Isaiah, Jeremiah, Ezekiel and 12 other Prophets.
3. Ketuvim: Scriptures: (11 books) Psalms, historical scrolls, Books of Proverbs, Job, Daniel, Ezra and Chronicles.

RABBINIC JUDAISM

During the first six centuries CE the following were produced:
   Midrash: scriptures, fables, parables.
   Mishnah: Religious and social behavior, festivals, marriage.
   Talmud: Used for developing systematic legal texts.
   Palestinian (Jerusalem) Talmud was less used.
   Babylonian Talmud was widely used for legislation.
Maimonides made significant contributions. Rabbi Karo
compiled Shulhan Arukh, Hebrew for spread table, drawing a
line between the era of Middle Ages and modern time.
   Responsa: a book of responses to legal questions and issues.
   Jewish Prayer Book: developed in 8th and 9th centuries, it
      points out differences between Jews of Middle East
      (Sephardim), of Europe (Ashkenazim), Spain, and Jews of
      North Africa.
Jews did not discard old books but stored them according to the
custom *geniza*. The discovery of the Dead Sea Scrolls confirms
the observance of the custom.

After the destruction of the Second Temple in 70 CE, teaching
was oral for six centuries and continued to be based on the
written Bible with following changes:
   Prayers were held by Jews in synagogues which appeared
      by the Second Temple period.
   Yohanan ben Zakkai suggested acts of loving kindness,
      an alternative to sacrificial offerings during prayer.
   A quorum of ten is required for public prayer.
The Temple priests had the authority through lineage whereas
the rabbis gained their following by spiritual learning, devotion,
study and by earning the respect of the community. Prayers
were in the Hebrew language until the 19th century but rabbis
allowed prayer in other languages. During the 20th century
Hebrew was revived with the Jewish national movement.

PRAYERS:

Jews observe two daily prayers, morning and afternoon to
replace sacrifice of the two Temples. A third prayer, Amidah, is
also obligatory and is said standing referring to Jewish religious

and national goals. The recitation of three chapters, Deut. 6:4, 11:13-21 and 15: 37-41 attribute to the Jewish faith. Shma (prayer) proclaims:

Hear, O Israel, the Lord our God, the Lord is One.
This is the recited by a dying Jew and was said in Holocaust.
Prayer, Reading of Torah, and a sermon are part of the service.

JEWISH HOLIDAYS:
The High Holy Days (Days of Awe) fall in September.
The New Year (ROSH Ha-SHANAH): Yearly day of judgement.
    The service by blowing of the horn (Shofar) commemorates
    sacrifice of Isaac by Abraham on Mount Moriah,
    who was replaced with ram by Angel Gabriel (Gen. 22).
YOM KIPPUR, Day of Atonement: Starting with the New Year,
    10 days are devoted to repentance ending with the day of
    fasting observed on the tenth day with prayers.
SUKKOT (Tabernacles): This is observed five days after Yom
    Kippur in memory of the time spent roaming in the desert.
READING THE TORAH: Year's end and beginning of reading.
PASSOVER: On the first night, the Seder-dinner reflects the
    period of bondage in Egypt and redemption. Reading of
    Haggada is recitation of scriptures about the Exodus,
    symbolizing at the Seder on Passover with the Passover
    offering, the unleavened bread, and the bitter herbs. One
    week after Passover, the holocaust is remembered.
PENTECOST FESTIVAL: Celebrates the Torah.
HANNUKAH: Eight days observance of the conflict between
    Judaism and Hellenism.

JEWISH CUSTOMS:
    MARRIAGE: It fulfills the role of procreation in monogamy.
Betrothal (kiddushin) followed by marriage document
(ketubah). Both are now conducted at marriage by giving the
ring to the bride and reciting: Behold you are consecrated to me
with this ring in accordance with the law of Moses and Israel.
The Groom crushes a glass under foot, symbolic of the
destruction of Jerusalem.

    CIRCUMCISION: Abraham's covenant (Gen. 17:9-13).

Brit-Milah is a ritual of Brit, circumcision of the male on the 8th day after birth. It is symbolic of sacrifice of the body to the royal lineage by removing the foreskin.

Thus God said: if not for My Covenant (brit) day and night, I would not have set up the laws of heaven and earth.
(Jeremiah 33:25)

God made the covenant with these words. (Exodus 24:8)

Circumcize the foreskin of your heart. (Deuteronomy 10:16)
Moses equated evil thoughts as circumcized thoughts.

COMING OF AGE: Mitzvoth is Hebrew for commandments. Boys observe bar mitzvoth at age 13 and could wear tefilin (black leather box with text). Girls observe bat mitzvoth at 12.

DEATH: Shma is recited by the dying, confessing sins. The body is draped in white covered with prayer shawl. Burial is required in Judaism followed by mourning for 7 days with prayers at the house of the deceased, and ends after 30 days for all except the family. One year after death, Kaddish prayer (sanctification) is perfomed by the children.

DIVERSITY IN JUDAISM

1. THE REFORM MOVEMENT:
Some Jewish leaders in Germany decided to stop the erosion of this faith in early 19th century. The first Reform synagogue was established in Hamburg with a few changes in the service. Prayer was shortened and conducted in German eliminating major rituals received during the reform movement.

An organ was played at the service.

Sermon was delivered in German.

Synagogue was called Temple.

The emphasis on national identity and belief in personal Messiah was eliminated.

The Torah was regarded as written by humans rejecting the Halakha, the legal guidelines for Jewish tradition.

A child born to a Jewish mother or Jewish father is Jew. Jewish tradition accepts only Jewish mother's lineage.

A Jew can marry a non-Jew.

The traditionalist Jews broke away due to these drastic reforms.

2. THE ORTHODOX:

Rabbi Samson Raphael Hirsh headed this effort to preserve the Jewish historic traditions. Zacharias Frankel, head of the rabbinical seminary created a scholarly dialogue with his journal to preserve traditional views.

The Torah was given by God to Moses to be followed.

The Talmud, developed from oral Torah cannot be changed. Three groups emerged under the umbrella of Neo-Orthodoxy. Hasidim and Mitnagdim agreed to adapt to the Western culture. Israel as a nation in the aftermath of the holocaust has revived the orthodoxy as well as the reforms in Judaism, both as religion and as people.

Moses Cordovero was influenced by the revolutionary mystic views of Abraham Abulafia who established prophetic kabbalah and believed in the higher intellect which combines human intellect with the experience of the power of God. Historically, Hebrews are linked to Tel-el-Sultan, the ancient city of Jericho, where 7000 year old architectural artifacts indicate layers of settlements. This city was regarded as the latch of the land of Israel. Samson belonged to the Hebrew cult of the Nazarites leaving his hair uncut. The port city of Ashkelon was invaded by the Philistines in 1175 BCE. Its high gateway arch is the oldest, built in 1850 BCE. Delilah was a Philistine who aided to get Samson's hair cut. Goliath, who stood about ten feet tall, represented Ashkelon's might. David, an Israelite faced Goliath in battle and prevailed. Later he conquered Philistia and other kingdoms to consolidate Israel as a nation.

Solomon, son of David dedicated a temple to YHWY in 970 BCE where Abraham had offered Isaac in sacrifice. Solomon made an alliance with the Queen of Sheba, ruler of the territory of Yemen at that time. This alliance enabled Solomon to trade throughout the region. After Solomon's death, the split due to tribal differences created Israel and Judah. Assyrians conquered Israel in 722 BCE and later Nebuchadnezzar of Babylon ruined Jerusalem and demolished the Temple. He built a monument to the god Marduk. Educated upper class Israelites were taken to Babylon. They were called Yehudim of Yehud, Israel in Aramaic language. The temple of Jerusalem was rebuilt by the efforts of Ezra who reformed the priesthood to involve everyone in conducting religious activities cutting down the exclusivity enjoyed by priests. The Alexander the Great expanded his power in the Mediterranean, North Africa, Central Asia up to India in the 4th century. Jews who escaped from Babylonia settled on Elephantine Island near Aswan in the Nile.

African Jews of Ethiopia are called Falasha, in Ge'ez language which means 'gone into exile'. Their belief is based on the Torah, the five books of Hebrew Bible. They passed down the oral interpretations from generation to generation, observed Saturday Sabbath in seven-week cycles. Especially Langata Sanbat, the 7th Sabbath is celebrated with contemplation of the hard times in their past. Kosher diet is followed by the community. They are currently known as Beta Israel. This ethnic group practiced this religion for 2000 years. They were followers of Moses. They were not aware of the white Jews as they were isolated for so long. They considered themselves as one of the lost tribes left behind at the time of the parting of the Red Sea. The waters returned and they had to escape Egypt by going south into Africa. They were the Jews of Ethiopia but didn't have the Talmud, the Jewish scriptures. During the 13th century Beta Israel were in the hundreds of thousands and ruled the state now called Ethiopia. The Solomonic Dynasty of Ethiopia overpowered the Beta Israel around 1400. Their lands were seized during the 17th century. Majority of Beta Israel migrated to Israel as they were flown by Operation Moses and only a few thousand live in Addis Ababa at this time.
The papyrus documents written in Aramaic around 400 BCE and discovered in the late 19th century indicate a thriving literate Jewish community in Egypt at that time. King Ptolemy II Philadelphus included Jewish holy books in his library collection as by then the Hebrew Scriptures were translated in Greek. Antiochus IV Epiphanes, a Syrian ruler assumed power around 175 BCE and forbade the reading of the Torah, ordering worship of pagan god. Under the command of Judah, the Hasidim sect revolted and took over the Temple overpowering Antiochus's forces. The temple had a menorah with seven

branches. There was only enough sacred oil to burn for one day. But it lasted for eight days, a miraculous event. The schism brewed between the strict Sadducees, who followed the literal letter of the Torah and the Pharisees who followed the lineage of learning, giving credence to the oral as well as written word. This persisted for a millennium and some modifications developed separating the orthodox and others adapting to the modern times.

Herod was declared King of the Jews. After the death of Caesar, Octavian and Marc Antony established Herod as King of Judaea to put down the rebellion against Rome led by Antigonus, descendant of Judah. Herod won and the Emperor Augustus gave him more authority around 40 BC. He ruled for 34 years. He built the Temple of Jerusalem exactly at the same place where the first Temple stood. The Roman Emperor Titus attacked Jerusalem eliminating scores of Jews in the year 70 CE and ordered the demolition of the Second Temple except the Western Wall of the city. This wall is the holiest site for the Jews called the Wailing Wall. King Herod built the wall around the old city of Jerusalem at the time of Second Temple. Archaeologist Ehud Netzer of Hebrew University found King Herod's tomb in 2007 at Herodium in the Judaean Desert after decades of search. A first century historian, Josephus Flavius, had mentioned Herod's tomb in his writings. The Jews dispersed again to settle in different parts of the world.

Albert Einstein thought that no divine or human will could interfere in God's creation and cosmic plans. Albert Einstein was born to Jewish parents Hermann and Pauline in Germany who were irreligious and considered Jewish rituals as ancient superstitions. He believed in a God who reveals Himself in the harmony of all that exists. According to Jewish custom he invited a medical student, Max Talmud to share Sabbath meal. Max was 21 and brought science books for Albert Einstein to read, all 21 volumes of Peoples Books on Natural Science by Aaron Bernstein. He expressed his outlook on religion: The religious inclination lies in the dim consciousness that dwells in humans that all nature, including the humans in it, is in no way

IMMIGRATION OF
JEWS TO ISRAEL

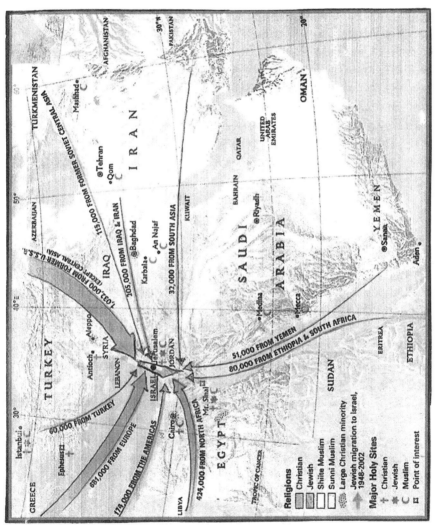

(courtesy National Geographic Society)

an accidental game, but a work of lawfulness that there is a fundamental cause of all existence (Time, April 2007, 46). He admired Spinoza on the subject of God who declared that soul and body are one. He published his views on what he believed: … that behind anything that can be experienced there is something that our mind cannot grasp, whose beauty and sublimity reaches us only indirectly: this is religiousness. In this sense, and in this sense only, I am a devoutly religious man. He distanced himself from atheists and explained: What separates me from most so called atheists is a feeling of utter humility toward the unattainable secrets of the harmony of the cosmos. He viewed the foundation of morality to rise above the personal, and to serve humanity. Jews record their Ethical Will to include important events in their lifetime for the benefit of their children. This tradition started more than 2000 years ago, but the written record has been kept for the last 1000 years.

Herman Rosenblat and Roma
A Tale of Love

Herman was a teenager in a death camp. Roma was a Schlieben, hiding from theNazis, posing as a Christian girl in the village. They gazed at one another. Roma threw an apple over the fence and Herman caught it and ran away from the fence. This went on daily for months without knowing each other's name. Herman was being moved to Czech Republic and told Roma not to come again. War was over and Russians liberated that Nazi death camp. Herman moved to New York. He was on a blind date. She told the apple story not knowing that she was on a date with the same boy who was at the Nazi camp. Herman said: that was me. He proposed the same night and were married in 1958 at a synagogue in Bronx ten years after their encounter as teenagers in Schlieben, Germany. Herman and Roma Rosenblat celebrated their 50th wedding anniversary in 2008.

CHRISTIANITY
(CROSSES IN HISTORY)

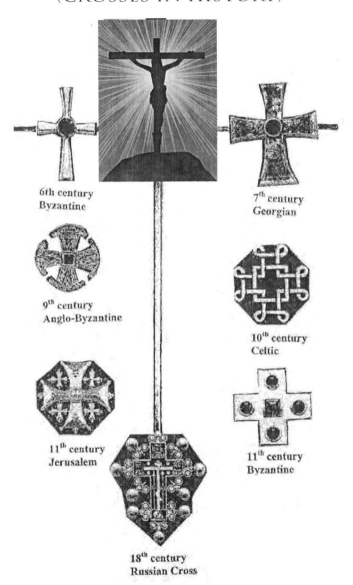

6th century
Byzantine

7th century
Georgian

9th century
Anglo-Byzantine

10th century
Celtic

11th century
Jerusalem

11th century
Byzantine

18th century
Russian Cross

CHRISTIANITY
(1.375 billion)

Early Christianity evolved from two religious experiences: Greco-Roman paganism and Judaism. Romans believed that human actions, personal or political, were under the protection of the gods, a polytheistic view. The mystery cults offered access to deeper realities. The power of prophecy and healing was perceived as divine acts. Judaism, based on the Torah, believes in one god and the followers consider themselves as a Chosen People. The practice of circumcision and the observance of Sabbath express convictions according to the Torah.

Jesus was brought up with the Hebrew Bible, embodying the Jewish teachings in the Torah. His teachings were recorded by his disciples and added to the existing Bible. The new Bible became the New Testament. After many interpretations the current version was shaped by St. Jerome's Vulgate Bible of the 4th century. Christianity as a religion began after the death of Jesus. During the 1st century, the message of Jesus was at odds with the religious leaders of Judaism under Roman law. He was crucified. Symbolically, it is the resurrection that created the Christian movement as a religion and is identified today with the story of Jesus as revealed in the Gospels based on the oral tradition which portrayed Jesus as the Son of God and as Christ. The crucifixion is viewed as a sacrifice on behalf of people's sins and Christ is accepted as a savior. The Chapel of the Beatitudes was built at the place where Jesus delivered the Sermon on the Mount and preached ways to an enduring happiness. Jesus fed thousands with a few fish and loaves of bread at Mount Eremos with slopes like an amphitheater. Jesus was arrested at the Mount of Olives where he prayed the night before his crucifixion on the eve of Passover. After resurrection he met with his disciples at the Mount of Olives from where he ascended again. The Church of Holy Ascension was built at that site with a footprint of Jesus. King Saladin converted it into a mosque in 1187 which exists today (Miller, 2004).

136

DEFINING CHRISTIANITY

The inclusion of Gentile believers without following Jewish rituals and activities differentiates Christianity from Judaism. The ritual of circumcision was no longer a part of baptism and fellowship meals were perceived as the presence of Lord Jesus after the resurrection. Prayers and healings were acknowleged as power of the divine. The churches looked Greco-Roman.

The NEW TESTAMENT includes Gospels of Mark, Matthew, Luke and John which independently express the events about Jesus' teachings as Lord. Canon of the New Testament has evolved from Eusebius (323 CE), Athanasius (367 CE), with the latest at the Council of Carthage (397 CE) with 4 Gospels, Acts, and Paul's Epistles. It is the revelation of God through Jesus as Messiah and is seen as the fulfillment of prophecy. The second coming of Jesus (Parousia) will be for relief from sins, suffering, and death. In the 2nd century Gnosticism was confronted with a clearly defined Christian tradition by the bishops and the church was organized as a hierarchical empire that flourished under Constantine during the 4th century. The Christian faith is monotheistic expressed as triune God with Father, the Son, and the Holy Spirit, all worshipped as God. They believe that God's manifestation comes through creation, salvation and sanctification. A complete understanding must involve two natures of Jesus, as true God and as true man. At this time Christianity awaits God's indulgence to prepare for the events in the future.

The BOOK OF ACTS refers to sharing of material possessions, the role of the Christian Church, and its missions.

The BOOK OF REVELATION is also known as Apocalypse of John. It describes the end of the world when God will intervene to destroy all the evil forces.

Four tenets of Apocalypticism:

Dualism: God has angels as forces of good and gives life.

Devil (Satan) has forces of evil, demons, gives death.

Pessimism: World is dominated by forces of evil and creating turmoil and suffering.

Vindication: God will overpower the evil forces and establish
the Kingdom of the righteous, resurrecting the dead.
Judgement Day: God will punish the evil people and reward
the good who will be accepted in God's kingdom.
The apocalyptic view was interpreted by some in a radical way,
in anticipation of the second coming of Jesus, with a dangerous
end, e.g. David Koresh, Jim Jones, and the Doomsday cult.

Other groups were based on specific ideals and practices:
Poverty (Mendicant). St. Francis of Assisi established the
Franciscan Order.
Virginity (Monastics) Benedict of Nursia declared celibacy
in monks life which was devoted to prayer.
Solitude (Hermits) *fuga mundi,* renouncing the world.
Christian missions (Missionaries) were guided by the verse:
…make disciple of all nations (Matthews 28:20).
Service in this work is viewed as a devotion to
spread Christianity that involves poverty, parting
from the family and facing hardships.

An access to salvation is believed to be only through Jesus
Christ, the son of God. The wave of mysticism, however, sought
a direct path to the divine. This and all other forms of separatist
views are the source of reforms. The new archeological discovery
of Nag Hammadi papers, Dead Sea Scrolls, and publications like
Da Vinci Code have called for revisiting the prevalent stories in
the Bible to interpret them in the new light as these are under
the scrutiny of scholars and theologians.

Christians were persecuted by the Romans as they did not
worship their gods Apollo, Jupiter, Mars, and Venus and did not
cremate their dead. They also resented the practice of memorials
to the dead. The Emperor Diocletian destroyed the Christian
churches and declared their assembly unlawful. The
decentralization of command established rulers in different
territories. The Emperor Galerius halted persecution and
introduced tolerance as he was dying. As the Emperor
Constantine was advancing towards Rome he had visions of *chi,*

rho as symbol of Christ. He met with the Emperor Licinius, and together they gave permission to the Christians and all others of different faiths to practice their religion. This was confirmed and religious freedom was promoted after Constantine defeated Lacinius in the battle of Chrysopolis in Turkey. The victory established Constantine as the Emperor in the Roman Empire. Byzantium city named Constantinopolis. He built Christian basilicas and his palace displayed the cross to assert his support. He was eager to discover more about Lord Jesus and his crucifixion. Guided by the people of Jerusalem, the site was dug up and three crosses were recovered. Anxious to find out which was the Jesus's cross, the corpse of a person who had just died was brought to the location to have a clue. The story is told, that when the dead body was touched by the crosses, one of those brought the dead body to life. That was the cross of Lord Jesus. Little pieces of that cross were distributed to the people of Christian faith everywhere. Constantine built the Church of the Holy Sepulchre.

> The Heavens declare the Glory of God; and
> the firmament showeth His handiwork (Holy Bible: 19).

He established Rome and Constantinople as two Primary religious centers as well as the seat of political power. Both cities engaged in a political and religious friction to become the world center for Christianity. He convened a meeting of church leaders of the Roman Empire. The deliberations at the meeting decided on he administrative framework to govern the activities of the church. It was decided in 325 CE that a patriarch will be the leader of the patriarchate, bishops govern dioceses, and archbishops govern archdioceses. The canons of faith and the statement of belief were set that hold to this day.

> One God, the Father Almighty, Maker of heaven and earth;
> One Lord Jesus Christ, the only begotten Son of God, who
>   shall come again.

Constatine added the Holy Spirit which proceeds from the Father and the Son. At that time one holy Catholic and Apostolic Church was recognized. Before Constatine's death, Sunday became Lord's Day; Eucharist commemorates Christ's sacrifice, death, and resurrection by partaking bread and wine; the altar for the items of worship; and the sign of the cross traced with the right hand that a priest or a worshipper could confer on the upper part of the body. These ceremonies have been observed since 200 AD. Holy Week commemorates the arrival of Jesus in Jerusalem starting on Palm Sunday, Thursday marks the Last Supper, Good Friday to remember the crucifixion, culminating in the celebration of the resurrection of Jesus on Easter Sunday.

The Emperor Theodosius I established Christianity as the only religion in Roman Empire in 380. In one century the Christians achieved a legal religious freedom from the period of persecution. Hagia Sophia church was built by Justinian as the architectural marvel of the Byzantine Empire in 537 and displayed icons as objects of worship in church. Monophysites believed that Christ had one nature. Their belief spread Christianity to Syria, Armenia, up to the border of China, and in Northern Africa. The Nestorians perceived the dual nature of Christ, one divine and the other human. Their influence of the Assyrian Church spread Christianity in Persia, India, Ceylon and United States. The Christianity of Constantinople (today's Istanbul, Turkey) is called Orthodox (correct teaching). It was spread by the missionaries to Greece, Serbia, and Bulgaria.

SACRED RITES IN THE MIDDLE AGES
1. Confession: A person's sins were forgiven.
2. Confirmation: Anointing a person with consecrated oil.
3. Baptism: Christian initiation, regeneration, rebirth.
4. Eucharist: Salvation through body of Christ (bread), and blood (wine), the sign of Christ's presence in it.
5. Ordination: Taking Holy Orders to become a priest.
6. Marriage: Symbolic union between Christ and church which unites man and woman for procreation.
7. Anointment: Final anointing of a dying person. It was changed to anointing the sick.

SACRED HOLIDAYS
CHRISTMAS
A sacred holiday for the Western Christians was celebrated in late December coinciding with the Romans. The Eastern

Christians observed it 12 days later whereas some groups wanted to celebrate in the spring. The day of December 25th was decided as the exact date of Jesus' birth was not known.

EPIPHANY

This commemorates the visit of three kings who came to worship the new born Jesus 12 days later.

LENT:

It is observed 40 days before Easter Sunday to make preparations for baptism. The mark of cross with ashes on the forehead signifies humility. It now recalls the time Jesus spent in wilderness by fasting and repentance.

PALM SUNDAY

The day celebrates the prophesied welcome with fronds of palm in the path of Jesus a week before Easter he came to Jerusalem. The decline of the Byzantine Empire started in the 8th century with the rise of Islam in the Middle East. Calif Umar with his Muslim forces seized Jerusalem in 638. Within the next two decades Muslim rule was established in Mesopotamia, Palestine, and Egypt. Still Jews and Christians were practicing their religions in the beautiful churches. Caliph Abd al-Malik built the Dome of the Rock on the site of the Jewish Temple near the Church of the Holy Sepulchre so that Muslims are pulled away from churches. Christianity was introduced to what is now Britain, France and Germany when confrontation with the Muslim rulers was beginning to escalate.

St. Gregory came from a monastic background. The monastic wave called for celibacy, poverty and simplicity in life. Monasteries were built on the Greek peninsula, mostly for women, in remote areas where women became devoted to God renouncing marriage and taking the vow of celibacy. Some monasteries were for monks with a vow of celibacy. He established rules for the monasteries and nunneries in Britain, France and Italy. The Duke of Aquitane in Cluny, France also founded a monastery. The monks spread the wave to Germany, Poland, Italy, Spain, England and Scotland. St. Francis of Assisi created Franciscans, an order for men, and Poor Clares, an order for women, with St. Clare as the first Mother Superior. These men and women vowed to live in obedience, without property, and in chastity. Christian monks produced cultural artifacts and liturgical music. Austrian monk Gregor Mendel conducted breeding experiments on sweet peas and is regarded as Father of Genetics. In the year 800 Pope Leo III strengthened the bond of religious and secular leadership in Western Europe by crowning Charlemagne as Holy Roman Emperor. The Pope had established a College of Cardinals as advisors who met the requirements to be pious and well versed in doctrines of Christianity. They had the power to elect the Pope at the death of the reigning Pope. This was the beginning of structured bureaucracy in Papacy. This was the era of architectural creativity. Cathedrals were built in Europe with stained-glass windows and decorated vaulted ceilings. Sacred relics were enshrined in bejeweled displays. The bones of three kings who came to see Jesus are displayed in the Cathedral in Cologne, Germany. The crown of thorns on Jesus' head was placed in the Sainte-Chapelle in Paris founded by King Louis of France in the 13th century. It was moved to the Cathedral of Notre Dame in 1806 to secure it during the French Revolution. Pilgrimages to renowned churches were popular to seek forgiveness for sins. The Christian after-world was depicted in paintings in some churches based on Dante's work *Divine Comedy* which is divided into 3 parts: Inferno shows satan and nine circles of hell, Purgatorio for those who had a chance at salvation, and Paradiso where saints, and the righteous people enter heaven, in the kingdom of God. Campus stellae is a place of pilgrimage as the sarcophagus of St. James floated from Palestine to Spain where the huge Cathedral of Santiago de Compostela in northwestern Spain attracts the pilgrims. The holiest of the churches are at the Mount of Olives and Bethlehem.

The dawn of 8th century sparked the conflict when 7000 Moors (Muslim) soldiers entered Spain resenting missionary efforts. A priest was murdered for attempting to convert Muslims to Christianity. For several centuries Christians were engaged in Crusades. This common threat from the Turks in the East and Moors in the South brought two branches of Christians together that were divided due to the differences in the doctrine.

THE CRUSADES

The FIRST CRUSADE: Pope Urban declared the First Crusade to the Europeans in 1095: …for your brethren who live in the east… I, or rather the Lord, beseech you as Christ's heralds to…persuade all people of whatever rank, foot-soldiers and knights, poor or rich, to carry aid promptly to those Christians and to destroy that vile race from the lands of our friends. Jerusalem was captured in 1099 where Jews and Muslims were killed bringing the Middle East under Europeans command.

The SECOND CRUSADE: It was prompted by Turks returning to Edessa, a new state, during 1146 and 1148.

The THIRD CRUSADE: This prompted Salah ad-din Yusuf ibn Ayyub of northern Syria to face the Byzantine Emperor Richard I in battles along the Palestine coast. A compromise was made in 1192 whereby Christians could make pilgrimages peacefully and the city of Jerusalem would be controlled by Muslims.

The FOURTH CRUSADE: During this crusade in 1198, the city of Constantinople was captured and destroyed. A new Empire was established with allegiance to the Church of Rome.

THE SPANISH INQUISITION:
In the 15th century, the Spanish Inquisition began officially under Ferdinand V and Isabella. Christianity was the sole authorized religion in Spain. Anyone suspected of practicing Judaism and Islam was expelled, tortured or put to death until the monarchy was shaken in 1820.

Due to the raids of Muslim pirates, St. Peter's was fortified with 40 foot walls and watch towers. This is where Constantine had been crowned Roman Emperor. The Papacy abandoned St. Peter's in 14th century and Pope Clement V built a palace of Popes in Avignon, France.

CHRISTIANITY

St. Peter's Square, Vatican, Rome
(courtesy Al Burye, San Diego, California)

VATICAN CITY-STATE:

Pope Gregory XI returned to Rome in 1377 and made Vatican his home. Borgias and Medicis, the powerful Italian families, the visionary Popes Julius II and Sixtus IV employed the talented architects Bramante and Bernini, and commissioned services of Michelangelo, the painter and sculptor who glorified the art of Christian iconography in the Sistine Chapel and built the dome. St. Peter's was the Italian marvel of excellence in architecture. This property was seized in 1870 when Italy consolidated. Popes refused to go outside the Vatican raising the issue of the relation of Holy See and Italy as a nation.

DENOMINATIONS IN CHRISTIANITY

The denominational diversity in Christianity was the result of an East/West schism. The pope and the king excommunicated each other dividing the Christians into two sects, the Greek Orthodox and the Catholic a thousand years ago due to the question of authority of the Pope. Christian denominations include:

ROMAN CATHOLIC CHURCH

Vatican City is a sovereign state under the Lateran Treaty of 1929 with 108.7 acres of land. The Roman Catholic Church remained faithful to the Bishop of Rome (The Pope). Catholic clergy is male by tradition. Catholic religion is followed in Southern Europe, Sub-Saharan Africa, and in Central and South America. The Basilica of Our Lady of Guadalupe in Mexico City is named after Mary, mother of Jesus. She appeared to a poor Aztec Indian in Central Mexico in 1521 telling him in native Aztec language to build a chapel in her honor. Millions visit the Basilica on December 12th annually as her feast day. The tradition identifies Mary, Mother of Jesus with Apostle Peter, carried on by Augustine. The Pope, as a religious head, created an independent religious authority as it exercised Christian political power in Crusades against Muslims. The American, French and Russian Revolutions challenged the influence of church on political affairs. This weighed in on the question of the separation of church and state while writing the constitution of United States of America. The

Bolshevik Revolution placed religion under state control.

GREEK ORTHODOX CHURCH:
Second arm of Christianity is the Orthodox Christians mainly in Greece, Eastern Europe and the Middle East. The rift began in 1054 when Constantinople was declared the New Rome and equivalent to Rome based on ideological shift between the two capitals with modifications in religious practices. Icons were used in liturgy, priests were married, and the bishops were appointed from the monks. The main emphasis in Orthodoxy is on worship. Leo and Justinian were heads of state and were the religious leaders. They held the Muslims at bay until 1516, the year Constantinople was conquered by the Islamic forces. The Hagia Sophia Church was modified and converted to Haja Sofia, the Blue Mosque by adding minarets.

PROTESTANT CHURCH:
When the Church cracked down on the dissidents, Martin Luther led the protesting Christians in the 16th century and created the third arm of Christianity, the Protestants. Reformed Christianity is followed in Northern Europe, North America, Australia and New Zealand.

THE LUTHERAN Reformation focuses on verbal revelation, and Scriptures. The German and Nordic populations follow these ideals proposed by Martin Luther and John Calvin.

THE ANGLICAN Reformation started with King Henry VIII and followed by Anglican Catholics and English speaking Episcopalians.

THE METHODIST Reformation sought piety like the monks. The Wesleyan tradition seeks transformation of the heart and doing good deeds. The Presbyterian tradition was promoted by John Knox with a belief in the doctrine of pre-destination.

THE ANABAPTIST Reformation enabled Baptists to organize independently in local congregations in Germany since the 16th century. They believe in adult baptism and exercised freedom from creed and hierarchy. They have developed the network of evangelical ministry in the Protestantism. There are numerous forms of Protestantism around the world with more known forms like the Holiness and Pentecostal sects.

Christianity became a state religion under Constantine. Use of icons and the stained glass adorned the religious architecture with art expressing the story of Christ. Scholastic development was valued in medieval Europe adding cultural aspect with music and poetic recitation and interpretation of Scriptures. Pope Julius II was a warrior pope leading his troops in battle. The Swiss Guards of today were once recruited by the Pope to push out northern Europeans from Italy to establish Papal States. He is also credited with commissioning artists like Michelangelo and Leonardo de Vinci who created statues, paintings, and musical compositions as artistic expressions of the story of Christianity blended with the culture of the times during the Renaissance. The Reformation movement aimed at simplicity to replace the extravagance of the Rennaissance period. Pope John XXIII ordered the Papal bejeweled crown sold and the proceeds to be given to the poor. The era of reformation allowed worship of the religion of ones affiliation freely at this time. Christianity will steer towards future transformation during the 21st century mainly to comprehend the essence of God's benevolence and the ways it can be acknowledged as truth.

The Second Vatican Ecumenical Council, convened by Pope John XXIII was concluded by Pope Paul VI with words of John:
I want to throw open the windows of church so that we can see out and the people can see in.
For the first time, women and non-Catholics attended a Vatican Council as observers. Clearly, the Roman Catholic Church showed respect for the religious freedom of individuals, and a commitment to human rights around the world. This council's urgency brought about the evangelical movement with the gospels proclaimed on the American air waves through the electronic media of TV, radio and the internet by celebrated church leaders like Billy Graham and Jerry Falwell. The core

principles of Christianity enable Christians to rise above the differences over theology and practices. Professor Johnson of the Candler School of Theology at Emory University (2003) points out that Christianity is extremely complex and often contradictory stating that it preaches peace but has engaged in crusades. It represents spirituality but has often given support to worldly vices of power, possessions and lust.

HOUSES OF WORSHIP

An imperial aspect of Christianity was expressed in architecture that symbolized Christianity.

BASILICAS are buildings with a nave, the long hallway ending with an apse at the end. The Eucharist (Mass) is a public ceremony which was originally a service identified with a meal (agape). The services sanctify time commemorating Jesus' death and resurrection at Easter and Christmas. Confirmation and marriage are also conducted as religious events. Jerusalem was declared the Holy City and the pilgrimages started in 4th century C.E. Other places were worshipped due to their historic value and/or linkage to saints and sanctification of space. Hagia Sophia (Holy Wisdom) was a patriarchal basilica during Byzantine time. The mosaic in the South Gallery depicts Constantine IX (1042-1055) presenting an apokombion (pouch with gold coins) and Empress Zoe holding a scroll with the list of gifts to the church. It is a museum at this time which has preserved Christian and Muslim art and the architecture. The famous St. Peter's basilica is in Rome.

CATHEDRALS also have a long nave but the building appears like the cross by adding a transept horizontally. The biggest event is Easter Vigil where baptism, the initiation, is carried out. The Notre-Dame Cathedral represents a masterpiece of the Gothic architecture in the heart of Paris. Its construction started in 1163 and was completed in 1345 AD.

Churches are designed beautifully and vary from simple places to highly elaborate structures. The Church of The Holy Sepulchre in Jerusalem and The church of St. Mary Magdalene

148

are beautiful places of worship. Cemetaries represent the memories of generations of Christians with the epitaphs that show the names and the lineage of families, dates of birth and death, and additional inscriptions to honor their title and accomplishments buried in the cemetery of their religious denomination and family linkage.

In all scriptures the concept of the Word is universal, the mystical voice of God within us, leading us to understand The Divine and acquire peace of mind as written in the Bible, Koran, Torah, Gita, Buddhist teachings and Sikh sacred texts. All faiths confirm that 'The Word was God'.

The new evidence sheds more light on the religious thinking and the political environment during 150 CE. The shroud of Turin is the most important piece of linen in Christian faith and the likeness image of Christ has raised questions. The Dead Sea scrolls, found in Qumran, have brought the established beliefs under the close scrutiny of scholars and theologians. Archaeologists have explored Nazareth, Sepphoris, Capernaum, Bethsaida, Kursi and Jerusalem for new evidence to know more about the life of Jesus in journals such as Biblical Achaeological Review (BAR).

The charges of sexual abuse against priests and bishops raised questions undermining their role in religion, divinity, spirituality and as priests in the faith spectrum. Social conformity and passion influence public sentiments over time. Joan of Arc was not condemned as a saint or a virgin, but she was perceived as a witch and heretic. Pope Benedict XVI feels that since 1950s the historical Jesus of the evangelists and the Christ of Faith started to drift away from one another losing sight of the object of faith and urges to reshape Christian social teaching. Only the determined and devoted seekers express that longing and emotional dark night in spiritual context like the 16th century Spanish mystic St. John of the Cross, and the 18th century mystic St. Paul of the Cross. The act of destroying I is confronted by the mind with great fuss and resistance (Simone Weil 1947, 27).

My God, why hast Thou forsaken me?
This is viewed as redemptive suffering of Jesus caused by the eviction of I from the soul. Agnes Bojaxhiu's first calling was to be a missionary at the age of 12 and wanted to work with the poor in other lands. She took vows in 1931 as Sister Mary Teresa and was thrilled to be little bride of Jesus as a nun. She taught 17 years with the Mission of Loreto Sisters. She requested the Mission to permit her to start her work under Missionaries of Charity in Calcutta, her second calling. Her confessor, Father Celeste Van Exem had heard her mystical conversation with Christ and accepted it as a genuine experience. She was given permission by the Vatican in 1948. Mother Teresa, a 1979 Nobel Laureate, was beatified by Pope John Paul II in 2003. She died in 1997. Sister Alphonso of Immaculate Conception was the first Indian saint beatified by John Paul II during his visit to India in 1986. Sister Alphonso was a South Indian nun who died in 1946 at the age of 35. Rick Warren explores the question, what on earth I am here For? in his book *The Purpose Driven Life* (2002) and suggests an introspection for 40 days to understand our purpose in life. He is on a global mission for service and peace.

Christian Church is a Christian congregation-at-large in which specific church denominations with particular ecumenical sensitivity in the local churches seek a common fellowship. This is reflected in one of the two main documents of ecumenical ecclesiology put forth by the Faith and Order Commission of the World Council of Churches with reference to Baptism, Eucharist, and Ministry (BEM). The other document is the Nature and Purpose of the Church (NPC) emphasizes the existence of diversity in unity stating specificity and Catholicity. There are different configurations in mainstream tradition:
> Concept of congregation reflecting individual practices .
> Parishes created boundaries defining each community.
> Diocesan bishop, the chief pastor of all churches in Parish.
> National Church with national identity.

Origen, an African, laid down the foundation of Christianity in Africa on the shores of Axum, off the Horn of Africa. before the white man arrived and before Islam. This shows the beginning of authentic African theology (Morris 2003, 139- 142).

150

ISLAM

Basmala or Bismillah

ISLAM
(1.060 billion)

During the year 610 CE, a merchant from Mecca at the age of 40 heard a voice in his sleep informing him that he, Muhammad ibn Abdallah, was the Messenger of God. It was the same place near Mount Hira where he always went to pray and meditate for fifteen years. He started experiencing flashes during prayers and meditation for seven years. He was frightened and went to his wife Khadija for protection. The message was clear:
O Muhammad, you are the Messenger of God. A figure appeared, revealing to be angel Gabriel, and ordered:

> Recite: And in the name of thy Lord who created, created man of a blood-clot.

> Recite: And thy Lord is the Most Generous who taught by pen, taught man that he knew not.

This was the first revelation which with all other revelations became the suras (chapters) of the Holy Koran. Muhammad received revelations for 22 years while he was in Mecca from 610-622 CE and in Medina from 622-632 CE. The Koran was compiled under the 3rd Caliph, Uthman ibn Affan. It has 114 suras (chapters) and 6000 verses. The long chapters are from Medina and at the end is the shortest sura from Mecca. Allah in Arabic means The God and Creator who is revealed in creation, revelation and action.

Mohammad belonged to a powerful tribe, Quraysh, in Mecca and was married to Khadija, a wealthy woman. Muhammad was her third husband and he was 15 years younger than her. She took him to see her cousin who knew the Jewish and Christian Bibles. He believed that the divine force is directing Mohammad to a mission. First followers were his wife and close family members and a friend Abu Bakr. The latter became his successor. Muhammad was raised by his uncle Abu Talib after his parents died and enjoyed his support. He received more revelations and was emboldened to preach three principles:
Belief in Allah; Total Submission; and Equality in all believers.

Prior to Islam, the Arabs followed the tribal religion that honored 360 patron deities and went to Mecca for an annual pilgrimage with no concept of morality or after-life. The prevelant belief was that Allah created and sustained life and the universe had no influence on daily life. Islam emerged while Judaism, Christianity, and Zoroastrianism were also a part of the socio-economic developments in Arabia. Muslims greet each other saying *As-salama-aleikum*. The following five Koranic observances identify Islam.

PILLARS OF ISLAM

1. Declaration of faith in Allah (Arabic for God) and in monotheism, belief in tawhid, unity of God.

2. Salat (Arabic for prayer). The Koran is written in Arabic and recitation is done during the prayer five times a day facing Mecca where Abraham built the Kaaba, the house of God. The postures include standing, bowing, knealing, placing the forehead on the ground in humility and submission and sitting on the prayer mat at a clean place anywhere. Muslims assemble at a mosque on Friday for a weekly communal prayer (ibadat).

3. Zakat (Arabic for purification). Muslims are obligated to give 2.5 percent of wealth to support the poor in the community.

4. The Fast of Ramadan is observed to commemorate the first revelation of Prophet Muhammad. Muslims observe fasting for a month from sunrise to sunset abstaining from any food, drink and sex. It is an exercise acknowledging God's support for life. It ends on the 27th day, the Night of Power, when Mohammad received his first revelation. It is a big event and is celebrated with a feast of Eid al-Fitr (Breaking the Fast) with joy and exchanging gifts.

5. Hajj (Arabic for Pilgrimage). It is the desire of every Muslim to make a pilgrimage to Mecca during his lifetime. The pilgrims wear simple clothes to symbolize equality of Muslim diaspora. Almost 2 million Muslims attend the Hajj every year. Eid al-Adha (Feast of Sacrifice) is observed at the culmination of this event.

The element of Jihad, called holy war, is not included in the Pillars of Islam. It is meant to fulfill the mission of spreading

Islam and is followed literally by the militant Muslims. It became a part of five pillars during early imperial campaigns and became an integral part of all the Islamic battles.

ISLAMIC LAW

The Islamic laws were developed by ulama, religious scholars. Majority of laws originated in Medina where Muhammad started the Islamic community.

SUNNI Muslims believe the traditions that were shaped after Sunnah, Prophet's example, and the succession is based on scholarship, piety and staunch belief in Allah, the only one who can judge people. In circumstances with no direct answers, *ijtihad*, independent judgement, is based on application of reasoning in similar events. Certain legal situations require *ijma*, the community's collective view, which depends on the opinion of muftis, the Islamic scholars.

SUFI Muslims wanted to adhere to the simplicity and purity that Muhammad advocated in the beginning seeking reforms in Islamic law. They have denounced materialism and imperialistic dreams. Their emphasis is on repentance for sin and prayer. The Sufi darvesh sect is known for using music and twirling dance for communication with God. Sufis have traditionally merged with non-Muslim communities in their neighborhoods practicing with strong emotions and deep devotion to God. During the Ghaznawid dynasty, the mystical treatises were written in Arabic and Persian between 11th and the 18th centuries. The interest in Sufism declined in the 18th and the 19th centuries (Fakhry 2004, 359).

Hazrat Inayat Khan (1882-1927), a Sufi is honorably addressed as Pir-o-Murshid. His ten Sufi thoughts are:

1. There is One God, the Eternal, the Only Being; none else exists.
2. There is one Master, the Guiding Spirit of all souls, who constantly leads all followers toward the light.
3. There is one Holy Book, the sacred manuscript of nature, which truly enlightens readers.
4. There is one Religion, the unswerving progress in the right

154

direction towards the ideal, which fulfills life's purpose of every soul.

5. There is one Law, the Law of Reciprocity, which can be observed by a selfless conscience together with a sense of awakened justice.

6. There is one human Brotherhood, the Brotherhood and Sisterhood which unites the children of earth discriminately in the Fatherhood of God.

7. There is one Moral Principle, the love which springs forth from self-denial, and blooms in deeds of beneficence.

8. There is one Object of Praise, the beauty which uplifts the heart of its worshipper through all aspects from the seen to the unseen.

9. There is one Truth, the true knowledge of our being within and without which is essence of all wisdom.

10. There is one Path, the annhilation of the false ego which raises the mortal to immortality and in which resides all perfection.

Following thoughts crystallize the objectives of Sufi Islam:

A. To realize and spread the knowledge of unity, the religion of love and wisdom, so that the bias of faiths and beliefs may of itself fall away, the human heart may overflow with love, and all hatred caused by distinctions and differences may be rooted out.

B. To discover the light and power latent in man, the secret of all religions, the power of mysticism, the essence of philosophy, without interfering with custom or belief.

C. To bring the world's two opposite poles, East and West, closer together by the interchange of thought and ideals, that the Universal Brotherhood may form of itself, and man may see with man beyond the narrow national and racial boundaries.

Eden, mentioned in the Bible is identified where four rivers originate in present day Turkey, and Western Iran. The Alexander the Great called it Armenia. The Sumerian epic *Enmerkar and the Lord of Aratta* narrates the journey of the envoy of the King of Uruk. He started in southern Mesopotamia, crossed the Zagros range through seven mountain passes, called gates by the Sumerians, and arrived in the kingdom of Aratta, the heavenly setting in the ancient times. The word plain is called edin in Sumerian language. Some scholars believe that Eden in the Bible came from the old name *edin* for the fertile plains with source of four rivers, Aras (Gihon), Euphrates (Perath), Tigris (Hiddekel), and Pishon (Uizhun) in the surrounding highlands.

A river flowed from Eden to water the garden, and
From there it divided to make four streams. (Genesis 2:10) Walker's treck through the mountain passes and observation of Eden describes it as one of the most productive regions in the Middle East with vineyards and fruit orchards. This area expanded agriculture which is mentioned as East of Eden. The Greek for the Garden of Eden is *paradeisos.* This was *pairidaeza* in ancient Persian meaning enclosed parland. Moghul Emperor Shah Jehan built Taj Mahal in India for his beloved queen Mumtaz. He planned it in the image of the Throne of God. Professor Wayne E. Begley of Iowa University examined the Koranic inscriptions around the arches which reveal that the monument was designed to create the garden of Eden. The huge white dome to represent Mount Shahand, the central pool as Lake Urmia, and four channels of water as four rivers. The arch representing the gate, the mountain pass to enter Eden. The Emperor tried to create Eden in India as a shrine to God.

The story of Charles Burak, a Jew, demonstrates the power of faith in God of humanity. He became seriously ill with pneumonia. A friend recommended him a spiritual healer who was a Jew but had converted to Islam. The Sufi healing came by praying to Allah. He chanted by taking YaH, a brief word for YHWH and Allah from the sufi prayer which became YaH Allah, and sounded like the sufi prayer. Charles felt the influence of the divine with surprising vitality. The spiritual energy did not stop to confirm if the person was a Jew or a Muslim but the divine healing power cured a human (Interreligious Insight, Jan. 2007, 22).

Shi'ite Muslims have their traditions directed by their Imams starting from Ali whom they regard as the authoritative successor by lineage. An offshoot of Islam from pre-Islamic times was a progressive Alevi sect which survived underground. It has emerged in Istanbul, Turkey among 15 to 30 percent of Turkish population. They do not believe in heaven and hell, do not face Mecca for prayers and believe that God resides in people and not in stones or mountains. Alevi's are liberal and girls do not wear the scarf. Mustafa Kemal Ataturk established separation of mosque and state founding secularism in Turkey (Time: June 7, 2008, 17). The flexibility in the authority for specific situations resulted in differences in legal opinions and their interpretation resulting in decrees called fatwas.

The following verses in Koran refer to the status of women:
Man and woman were created equal parts of a pair (51:71-72).
Men and women are equally responsible for adhering to the
    Five Pillars of Islam (9:71-72).
The Koranic reforms included the following directives:
    Female infanticide was prohibited.
    Child marriages were prohibited.
    Women were not to be considered as property.
    Women had the right to receive dowry and control property.
    Women could use their maiden name after marriage.
    Women were granted financial support from their husbands
        and controlled a husband's ability to divorce.
    Polygamy was prohibited.

SHARIAH: Muslims are governed by the divine law of God that includes the observance of Five Pillars. Family laws apply to marriage, divorce, and inheritance.

Barelvi Islam shares the mystic traditions of Sunni with Shiite and Sufi Muslims. Abu Hamid al-Ghazali started the revival of Islam in the 12th century. A shrine commemorates the work of Lal Shahbaz Qalandar, a 13th century Sufi saint, offering peace and tranquility. He preached peace between Muslims and Hindus. Sufi Islam is embraced by most Pakistanis where the rich and poor worship together. A famous poet Muhammad Iqbal (1878-1938) studied philosophy in England and Germany which made a profound impact on his religious thinking. He believed that religion is neither mere thought, nor mere feeling, nor mere action; it is an expression of the whole man. Focus was on knowledge and reflection in the Koran (Fakhry 2004, 364).

The revolutionary new preaching of Mohammad was initially ignored but his following threatened the Meccan high society and those in power. Muhammad first tried Ethiopia as his base but was not successful. He focused on Yathrib, a desert oasis on thriving merchant route to Syria where refugee Jewish tribes had established farming and other businesses. This attracted Arabs of the Aws and Khazraj tribes who dominated the Jews but didn't have cordial relations between them. These Arabs invited Muhammad to ease tensions. In 622 the first batch of followers moved from Mecca to Yathrib. This move is known as Hijra and Yathrib became Medina which established Islam as the religion and Prophet Muhammad as the messenger of God.

In 1453 Ottomans conquered Constantinople and changed the name to Istanbul. Suleyman the Magnificient adopted Shi'ite Islam and established Iran in 1530. After three years he added Baghdad and Basra to his kingdom.

The leadership of Muhammad as a religious, political and military leader became his legacy that inspired generations of the future. Muhammad sought the support of the Jewish community in Medina and asserted religion of Abraham focusing on similarities between Judaism and Islam. He adopted Jewish practices and rituals such as fasting on Yom Kippur, facing Jerusalem for prayers, not eating blood or pork, and prayers three times a day. However, Jews were not convinced that they will have the freedom to practice their religion and became his critics.

MECCA: The holiest Islamic Shrine
 Mecca is spelled Makkah Al-Mukarramah which was previously called Bakkah meaning 'narrow valley'. It is located in the Sirat Mountains of Central Saudi Arabia. The ancient Arab tradition is linked to the expulsion of Adam and Eve from paradise. Adam fell on a mountain on Serendip Island (Sri Lanka) and Eve fell in Arabia near the seaport of Jidda

(Jeddah) on the border of Red Sea. Adam prayed to God that a shrine be built. God put them together on Mount Arafat after they wandered for 200 years near the present city of Mecca. His wish was granted and the Kaaba shrine was built (*Wikipedia*). Mecca was an oasis on the Caravan trade route in ancient times that linked the Mediterranean with East Africa, Southern Arabia and Asia. It developed into the religious center called Macoraba. Mecca and Medina developed in the sacred land called Hijaz, barrier, in the Western region of Arabian Peninsula.

Muhammad was disappointed and his revelations labeled Jews as devious and treacherous. At this point the Islamic prayers and rituals were changed. Muslims started praying facing towards Mecca as the holiest site of Islam not towards Jerusalem. The holy day of rest was Friday not Saturday Sabbath. The muezzin and minaret replaced the trumpets to summon for prayer, and Ramadan became the month of fasting. Islam was linked to the pagan city of Mecca as an independent new religion.

The annual pilgrimage to Kaaba and kissing the Black Stone established Mecca as the holy site. It is claimed that Kaaba was built by Abraham and his son Ishmael. This brought Islam close to the Arab belief system projecting the monotheistic status and common ancestry. Muhammad recognized Abraham as the first monotheist and himself to be the next in succession to continue monotheism. He assassinated political rivals. His raids created a grand alliance against him and resulted in a siege of Medina. The siege failed and Meccans were no longer a threat. The treaty recognized Muhammad as Allah's Messenger. He subdued Jews of Khaibar. Jews could stay by paying the tribute with half of their produce. He attacked Mecca with a big force when a Meccan killed a Muslim. Mecca surrendered. The preacher Muhammad who fled Mecca fearing persecution, returned as undisputed powerful leader in Arabia within eight years.

MECCA

Mecca, Saudi Arabia. Site of Hajj in Islam.
(Credit: Martin Gray / National Geographic Image Collection)

The popularity and following of the prophet grew. He eliminated the pagan idols in the Kaaba. The infidels were not permitted to enter the Kaaba during the annual pilgrimage. The road to Islamic imperialism was paved. In 632 Muhammad with his first pilgrimage to Mecca, the hajj, established Islam.

HAJJ (Pilgrimage):
The annual Hajj is the largest religious gathering in the world that draws two million pilgrims from all around the world. It is one of the five Pillars of Islam. The Pilgrims come to the seaport of Jeddah in Saudi Arabia, 45 miles from Mecca. Upon arrival they take shower at the designated areas and change clothing. All of them recite the invocation and chanting echoes all over.

> You are without associate!
> Here I am, O' God, at your command!
> Here I am at your command!
> To you are all praise, grace, and dominion!
> You are without associate!

The first converts to Islam included Byzantines and Ethiopians. The Koran established Islam as the only true religion based on faith and piety.

> Say: O mankind, I am Allah's Messenger to all of you...
> There is no god but He... Believe in Allah and in his
> Messenger.

O people, your Lord is one and your ancestor is one. You are all descended from Adam and Adam was (born) of the earth. The noblest of you all in the sight of Allah is the most devout. Allah is knowing and all wise (Koran xlix: 13).

Akbar Ahmed, a cultural anthropologist (2007) is torn between asabiyya, group loyalty, and globalization but represents the majority of Muslims preserving Islamic principles and devotion.

IMPERIALISM

Muhammad had to escape from his home town of Mecca in 622 CE due to the resistance to his revolutionary teachings. He went to Medina where he developed a community of believers, the umma, that later emerged as a political arm with the concept of

Jihad to assert and spread Islam. This was a strategy to entice his followers in Medina to raid the Meccan caravans. The Prophet gave the farewell address in 632 and laid down his imperial ambitions:

> I shall cross this sea to their islands to pursue them until there remains no one on the face of the earth who does not acknowledge Allah.

It is this message that was echoed by Saladin in 1189, Ayatollah Khomeini in 1979, and drives Osama bin Laden. This is an outcome of frustration of Muslim extremists who recall the glorious past as a Great Civilization that excelled in every human endeavor and dominated for centuries establishing their regime and spreading Islam. The concept of an Empire originated in Egypt, Assyria, Babylon, Iran, Greece and other tribes. For centuries, this was the mission of rulers and conquerors. The two major rival empires during the rise of Islam under the Prophet Muhammad in the 7th century were the Roman Empire and the Byzantium Empire. The European (Christian) powers engaged in Crusades to counter Jihads and subdued Islamic regimes. History is a reminder that frustrated the Islamic powers.

Imperialism was an aspiration of monarchs that justified their invasions and subservience of the conquered people. The Arab conquest in the 7th century drew strength from Prophet Muhammad to fight nonbelievers wherever they might be found. Arabs occuupied Kufa, Basra and Uruk, (now Iraq) in the mid 7th century. Suleyman the Magnificient expanded the Ottoman Empire and established Iran with his adopted Shi'ite Islam. The decline of the Ottoman Empire brought colonialism and decline in social and moral values as well.

For *tajdid* (renewal) and *islah* (reform), the Muslim ommunity sought guidance from the Koran and the Prophet's examples. Reform movements sprang up in Arabia, Sudan, Africa, and India during the 17th and 18th centuries to reestablish the Islamic beliefs. Differences of opinion gave rise to revivalist movements.

The Wahhabi movement was started by Muhammad ibn Abd al-

Wahhab in Saudi Arabia in the 18th century. Wahhabis did not accept Sufism and destroyed their tombs. The destruction of Buddha statues by the Taliban in Afghanistan is believed to be Due to Wahhabi convictions.

The Mahdi movement was founded by Mohammad Ahmad in The 19th century that founded the Mahdiya Order in Sudan. In 1909 the Anglo-Persian Oil Company was formed as crude oil was discovered in the desert of Iran. Germany declared war on Russia in 1914 and the British occupied Basra and captured Baghdad from the Turks in 1916. Iraq was under British control in 1918. After WWI Ottoman provinces were divided between France and Britain. Prince Fizell II of the ruling family became the King.

During the 20th century the conservative Islamic leaders opposed western influence. Modernists proposed to review the culture to adjust to the changing international environment for progress as an Islamic community. Islamic activism started Jamaa-i-Islami among the elite in India and Islamic Brotherhood in Egypt in the lower class. The latter was disbanded by the Mubarak regime.

During the unrest against colonialism the 23 year old king of Iraq was hanged in 1958. The Baath Party was organized in the 1940s in Damascus, took power in 1963 and became very powerful across the Middle East. Prime Minister Abdul Karim Qassam of Iraq yielded power to Saddam Hussein who became Chief of the Baath Party and the Iraq state. His imperial dreams led to invasion of Kuwait in 1990 followed by the Gulf War of 1991. He remained defiant till he was captured, tried by the Iraqi Court and hanged. After the collapse of the dictatorial regime Iraq is struggling to develop as a democratic nation where the Iraqi cabinet is made up of the representatives of the Shi'ite, Sunni and Kurd sects who developed the first Iraqi constitution. Sectarian unity of Iraqis will determine the future of Iraq after the departure of the coalition forces.

Words of Prophet Muhammad were regarded as revelations to use force to achieve imperialistic dreams.

Stick to jihad and you will be in good health and get
Sufficient means of livelihood.

Abu Bakr, Muhammad's father-in-law and successor, supported
jihad for the booty to be won from the Byzantines. Ali ibn Abi
Talib, Muhammad's son-in-law (4th Caliph) said: Sacrifice
yourselves! You are under Allah's watchful eye and with
Prophet's cousin. Resume your charge and abhor flight, for it
will disgrace your descendants and buy you the fire (of hell) on
the Day of Reckoning.

It is common in Muslim tradition to represent rules established
after Muhammad's death as ordinances of Umar. This created
Islam as the religion of the Middle East. Umar recognized only
Arabs destined to rule, others are to serve, forbidding non-Arab
converts and Jews to marry Arab women. Umar ordered all
Arab slaves to be freed. Islam has been a patriarchal religion.

RELIGIOUS STRIFE

The internal struggle in Islamic factions grew due to leadership
squabbles. The 4th Caliph, Ali, son-in-law of the Prophet
Muhammad was in the line of succession to stake his religious
claim to power. Governor of Damascus was Mu'awiyah, the
founder of the Umayyad dynasty who faced Muhammad in the
battle of Siffin in 657. Mu'awiyah called off the fighting and
agreed to arbitration as a strategy. Ali's consent to the
agreement was perceived as his weakness by a wing of his army
which declared a mutiny. Ali's claim to the caliphate was in
doubt. The arbitrators ruled against Ali and his claim to the
caliphate. The deserters were the Muslim sect called Kharijites.
They believed if a Muslim committed a grave sin, he could not
be a Muslim. They believed that a decision is only with Allah
and by not agreeing to an arbitration. Ali forfeited his claim to
the caliphate or as a believer. The Governor of Damascus
became the caliph in 658. This was Islam's first imperial dynasty
as the Mu'awiyah's Umayyad family which ruled for the next
nine years. The strategy was established for Allah's caliphs to
dominate the Middle East to this day. The expansion was
legitimate as jihad in the path of Allah. The Umayyads resorted

to drinking, and indiscretions prohibited by Muhammad making the caliphate a kingdom. The question of free will was debated among theologians and Greek philosophers but this idea threatened the Umayyad caliph's authority and posed political implications. The Umayyad caliph had the proponents executed.

The mutineers were called Kharijites who questioned the political authority of the Caliph and equated belief with outward conformity to the Holy Law. They resorted to anarchy with the religious authority to assassinate if someone, including the Caliph, committed a grave sin, political or other, such person would no longer be a Muslim. Even the Caliph could be removed from the caliphate or legitimately murdered as an infidel. However, they resented the Umayyad for usurping the power of caliphate.

The sect Murji'ah believed in "the knowledge of, submission to, and love of God", a rather liberal view. Ultimately, only God can judge ones deeds. The Murji'ah, like the Kharijites, also agreed that any pious Muslim can become a caliph if the community deems him worthy, whether Arab or descendant of the Prophet's tribe, the Quraysh. Also, heterodox beliefs and the commission of the gravest sin did not lessen the faith if he believed in God's unity. Wasil b. Ata, a pupil of al-Hasan al-Basri, was an important figure during the theological discord. Wasil considered a grave sinner between infidelity (kufr) and faith (iman). He also supported the question of 'free will'. Bishr b. al-Mutamir put forth the doctorine:
     Whatever is generated from our deeds is of our doing.
Jahm b. Safwan, who founded the Jahmites argued that divine omnipotence of God determines all human actions and completely predestined events unfold during our lives.

The third sect that emerged after Muhammad's death was Shi'ah. The Imam, according to Shi'ah, is the only rightful successor to Prophet Muhammad whose succession can only run in his progeny. The Imam is the only authoritative interpreter of Holy Law. They stood for theocratic monarchy by divine designation and is a fountain of religious instruction (talim). An

165

Imam can never commit a sin as the supreme pontiff, cannot be deposed, and his position cannot be eliminated. Twelvers believe the twelfth Imam, Muhammad B. al-Hasan, who died in 878 as the Mahdi (Guided One), will return at the end of time. The Shi'ites maxim is "Whatever runs counter to (the practice of) the community is the token of rectitude". Their ritual of levitical cleanliness separates them from the main orthodox Islam.

In India, Isma'ilis, the extreme shi'ah introduced the Islamic philosophy in 977 during the Ghaznawid rule. It flourished from the 10th to the 18th century with the theological treatises written by great scholars in Arabic and Persian. A syncretic version of Islam developed after the Mutiny of 1857 in India. Ahmed Khan, after his return from England in 1870, launched the Urdu journal *Tahzib al-Akhlaq* (Culivation of Morals). He founded the Muhammadan Anglo-Oriental College in 1875 which has grown into the Aligarh University. He focused on morality and spirituality conforming to reason and nature. He believed that the spirit of Islam is compatible with liberalism at the core of Islamic philosophy. Muhammad Iqbal (1878-1938) , Indian celebrated poet and thinker interpreted Koran to harmonize with the modern worldview. Fakhry (2004, 364) quotes a statement from his book *Reconstruction of Religious Thought in Islam*: Religion is neither mere thought nor mere feeling, nor mere action; it is an expression of the whole man.

The Arab monarchs had the ambition of an empire. The Egyptian rulers from Abbas Hilmi (1892-1914), to Fuad (1917-36), to Farouq (1937-52) had the added strength as descendants of Muhammad Ali were monarchs with the ambition of an empire (Karsh, 2006, 212). They did not try to promote Islam with zeal. The activists were more focused on Islamic dominance as Allah's Empire.

Abul Ala Mawdudi (1903-79), founded fundamentalist Jamaat-i-Islami in Pakistan with the understanding: The power to rule over earth has been promised to the whole community of believers. This universal state or rather world empire, was to be established through a sustained jihad that would destroy the

166

regimes opposed to precepts of Islam and replace them with a government based on Islamic principles …not merely in one specific region … but (as part) of a comprehensive Islamic transformation throughout the entire world.

Hasan al-Banna who graduated in 1927 as a school teacher in Cairo, established the Society of Muslim Brothers. Its membership grew to one million by 1940 through its two thousand branches. The objectives were: individual moral purification and collective political and social regeneration through the establishment of truly Islamic government in Egypt, as a springboard for universal expansion until the entire world will chant the name of Prophet (Muhammad), Allah's prayers and blessings be upon him. Banna was influenced by Hitler and Mussolini and ran the Society of Muslim Brothers with a strong force and the credo was:

> Allah is our goal; the Koran is our constitution;
> the Prophet is our leader; struggle is our way; and
> death in the path of Allah is our highest aspiration.

Banna was murdered as a revenge for the assassination of Prime Minister Nuqrashi Pasha. Sayyid Qutb envisioned the universal supremacy of Islam as it gained power in the first umma as an association of believers and rejected racial, linguistic and regional partisanship. The Islamic expansion continued under the leadership of four successors of the Prophet Muhammad who created the first umma through military campaigns, and implemented Shari'a, the divine law.

Uthman ibn Affan, the third caliph faced opposition with his claim that Ali ibn Abi Talib, cousin of Muhammad should have been the caliph. Uthman was killed in the uprising that sparked the civil war from 656 to 661 and ended with Ali's victory. However, Kharijite assassins targeted Ali and Muawiyah. Ali was killed, and Muawiyah was the next caliph. The Muslim community was fragmented into Kharijites (succession on the basis of piety), Shiites (succession inherited through the line of Prophet Mohammad, and Sunni (selection by the community). The Sunni group was in majority in Medina. They followed the Sunnah what Muhammad practiced, hence the name Sunni.

167

These three sects differ mainly on the right of succession.

The Shi'ites influence spread to Arabia, Persia and coastal North Africa by the end of 1st millennium. The Shi'ites make up 10 to 15 percent of world's Muslim population. Sunnis dominated from 8th to 13th centuries with the Umayyad and Abbasid caliphates. Islamic influence moved from Medina to Damacus and to Baghdad. In 1258 Ghengis Khan, a Mongol, wanted to destroy Islam. He burnt libraries, killed the Caliph and 100,000 people.

The Umayyad Mosque in Damascus is considered the oldest one in active use. This was a temple built in second millennium BC honoring Dadad, an Aramaean deity, rededicated to Jupiter by Romans in the 1st century, and was converted to Church of St. John the Baptist in 379 AD. With Arab invasion in 636, it was coverted to Mosque and was restored to its grandeur by Umayyad caliph Al-Walid between 708 and 715. The caliph allowed four churches to be built in the city at other locations.

Efraim Karsh quotes the written sentiments of the Egyptian Islamist Ayman al-Zawahiri: Sayyid Qutb's call for loyalty to God's oneness and to acknowledge God's sole authority and sovereignty was the spark that ignited the Islamic revolution against the enemies of Islam at home and abroad (217). Egyptian President Anwar Sadat was assassinated by Zawahiri's men. The battle against Islamic terrorism in Egypt had begun. The Islamic groups developed a strong link in the West Bank and the Gaza Strip that Israel had occupied after the six-day-war in June 1967. Hamas is the Egyptian Islamic Resistance Movement as a branch of the Muslim Brotherhood which gained power under the Palestinian Authority led by Yasser Arafat. Ayatollah Ruhollah Khomeini created the Islamic Republic of Iran by toppling the monarchy of Reza Pahlavi, the Shah of Iran. Khomeini resented the modernization of Iran into a secular state as anti-Islamic. Khomeni was arrested and sent into exile in Turkey. He moved to Najaf, a Shiite town in Iraq and started a campaign against Pahlavi's regime. He was expelled from Iraq at Iran's request and he settled in Paris,

168

resuming his struggle in anti-Shah activities. Iraq was a powerful Arab state where Sunnis were in power controlling 60 % of the population that were Shia'h. Iran considered Saddam Hussein as a hindrance to the Islamic principles. The war lasted eight years till the United Nations Security Council negotiated a ceasefire. Hizbullah is a Shiite militant group created by Iran to operate in Lebanon as a visible step towards the Islamic revolutionary movement. The latest ambition under Ali Akbar Hashemi-Rafsanjani as the head of Iran's army included development of nuclear program. The quest for Allah's empire is now organized as al-Qaeda supported by Osama bin Laden and Ayman al-Zawahiri, both from Saudi Arabia. The recent terrorism that has killed many including Muslims has sparked a resentment towards Al Qaeda and its religious interpretations. Saudi Arabia, where millions go for pilgrimage to Mecca and Medina has denounced the fundamentalism that promotes violence. This chaos has severely hurt the devout moderate Muslims who want to glorify Allah with daily prayers, observing the religious practices and living a life of harmony and peace.

It was necessary to survey the sentiments of Muslims in modern times, especially after 9/11 to gain the current perspective. Akbar Ahmed, a celebrated anthropologist, who travelled to the Middle East, Far East and South Asia to feel the pulse of Muslims, to provide a worldview. Three schools of thought are:

 The FIRST model is the Sufi Order. It was founded by the mystical Moin-uddin Chishti that is spiritual, looking in ones own mind to seek God as the first model with its origin in Ajmer, India.

The SECOND model views Islam as observed at Aligarh University, developed after Cambridge in the UK, valued democracy and freedom fully preserving the slamic identity. The majority of Muslims belong to this category.

The THIRD model is conservative and orthodox with strict adherence to the verses interpreted as fundamental religious guidelines. This group led the militancy and declared jihad affecting believers and non-believers alike representing a small minority of Muslims. Ahmed himself believes in the second model expressing the need for ijtihad (independent interpretation) to allow cultural advancement and evolution. Clearly, religious issues are sensitive and a mutual respect and understanding among faiths is essential. The Dome of the Rock in Jerusalem, Qubbat as-Sakhra, was built between 685 and 691. It represents a masterpiece of Islamic art, glorifies the Prophet Muhammad, where two million Muslims go for Hajj.

Muslims came to Europe, European colonies and North America as un-skilled laborers in the sixties and seventies where cheap labor was needed. The second wave brought professionals and aspiring students to enter into scholarly and technical areas as productive citizens. This freedom and promises of a better lifestyle has polarized the community into pluralistic and the fundamentalist camps. Indiscriminate loss of life in the attacks by militants included Muslims, women and children, at the sites of carnage in America, Spain, and Africa. The Muslim community and other nations around the world have denounced violence in the name of Islam. Fundamentalist interpretations of Qur'an by Osama bin Laden and Al Zwahiri, the Al-Qaeda leaders, have divided the Muslim community where the majority prefers dialogue, understanding, harmony, respect and peaceful coexistence in a pluralistic society. The stereotype has posed a problem and will be resolved with the efforts of scholars and religious leaders reflecting on Islam in the global society. Muslim women have adjusted to Western society and wear hijab (head scarf) as a symbol of religion and as an expression of their identity and freedom. They participate in prayers, and have achieved recognition in the fields of medicine, education, politics, engineering, architecture and commerce. Muslims believe in one God, the Koran, and follow the life long actions of Prophet Muhammad as written in the Koran (42:52-53):
> The straight path, the way of God, to whom belongs
> all that is in the heavens and all that is in the earth.

French Cardinal Jean-Louis Tauran, President of the Pontifical Council for Interreligious Dialogue hosted a 2-day Interfaith

Forum at the Vatican in November, 2008 with the Muslim scholars and clerics to seek common ground between Christianity and Islam with the theme, Love of God, Love of neighbor. Arsalan Iftikhar promotes Islamic pacifism and calls upon the Muslim youth to reclaim culture of humanity and condemns terrorism to end Islamophobia and offer pportunities for rational discussions welcomed by the world for peace.

HINDUISM
OM (AUM)

HINDUISM
(900 million, 2008)

The fertile valley of the Indus River was inhabited by herders and farmers as early as 6000 BCE. The artifacts found at different sites by the archaeologists indicate a thriving Harappa civilization 5000 years ago. The Indus River originates in Himalayas and traverses through Punjab (the land of five rivers named Sutlej, Beas, Ravi, Chenab and Jehlum) that flow into the Indus River ending in the Arabian Sea. The original state of Punjab was divided in 1947 during the partition of India and Pakistan. The Harappa civilization built cities at 300 locations from modern day Karachi to Iran. The Bahu Fort is said to be 3000 years old which was built by the Dogras. The ruins at Mohenjo Daro and Harappa date back to the 2550 BCE. The Harappa Culture flourished between the Rivers Sutlej and Beas in present day Punjab (India) with planned paved streets around central mound lined with assembly halls, and buildings made of fired bricks. Houses for nobles were two stories high. The street sewers were planned for public hygiene and the population was up to 40,000 in some cities. The artifacts do not suggest an established religion at that point in time but the imagery on the seals, the motifs of animals and other carvings suggest the early pre-religious era when a complex script had been developed. Mohenjo Daro ruins reflect highly developed arts and culture. The Aryan invasion by 1500 BCE forced the inhabitants out of the river valley. They assimilated the Harappa culture and moved on to the Ganges River Valley in the vast Indo-Gangetic Plain. Appollonius Tyaneus, a Greek 1st century thinker said:

> In India I found a race of mortals living upon the Earth, but not adhering to it, inhabiting cities, but not being fixed to them, possessing everything but possessed by nothing.

Vedic religion observed ritual sacrifices. It was replaced by Hinduism which focused on meditation and devotion to deities. The Hindu temples vary in their architecture and rituals in different parts of India. The oldest temples were built with brick and wood 2000 years ago but stone was later used to build elaborate temples, some carved out of the solid rock. The Archeological Survey of India manages the upkeep of ancient temples. Hundreds of temples were destroyed in Northern India between 1200 and 1700 CE by the invading Islamic monarchs. Gulab Singh, the founder of the kingdom of Jammu and Kashmir started the construction of the Raghunath temple in 1835. The temples in South India were spared and continue to perform the elaborate rituals where deities are carried in processions during different festivals and the devotees chant hymns. Cows are considered sacred and seen on the roadways. The Golden Quadrilateral (GQ) is the major network of North-South and East-West Interstate Highways, a development since the nationwide railroad system in India. These corridors handle traffic with 1.5 million cars on the road.

Traditionally, deities occupy a special space in the sanctum. Big temples have their deities made up of five metals, gold, silver, copper, zinc, and tin called 'panchaloha'. Deities are bathed, dressed and decorated for view (darshan) by the devotees who visit the temple. Shoes are removed and placed in designated areas before entering the temple. Flowers, fruits and sweets are brought as offering to the temple often available in shops outside temples. It is customary to chime the bells that hang from the ceiling and devotees chant mantras like *Om Namoh Shivaya* or *Om Namo Narayana*, the verses from the Bhagavad Gita, Vedas, or Upanishads. Reverence is expressed by knealing and bowing the head in submission to touch the floor or by prostration with full body touching the floor with extended arms. The 'anjali' prayers are performed in the morning and arti is carried out in the evening by singing hymns (bhajans). Hindus identify two types of scriptures: Sruti (revealed) and Smriti (remembered). Hinduism is also referred to as Sanatana Dharma meaning 'the Eternal Law' in Sanskrit.

The Ganges River is sacred. People bathe, pray, and cast the ashes of their loved ones in it. The belief, the Ganges purifies, is still observed even though the clothes are washed, animals bathe and release wastes, and it carries the agents of serious diseases such as cholera, dysentery, hepatitis and typhus confirmed by the health authorities. The Indian government has plans to install treatment plants. The Kumbh festival draws millions of devotees to Allahabad, Hardwar, Ujjain and Nasik. Allahabad city is located at the site of the confluence of sacred Yamna and Saraswati Rivers where a tent city is erected over 18 square miles to provide temporary space for the pilgrims of every Hindu denomination. The time is calculated according to celestial combination to celebrate the festival. It was held in 2001 after 12 years and attended by 70 million people, the largest gathering anywhere in the world.

Hindus of Bali, an island in Indonesia, escaped from Java in the 16th century. They developed in seclusion for centuries that merged with the local religion and Buddhism. There are 20,000 temples in Bali. The largest temple is Pura Pnataran Agung, a shrine for Vishnu, Shiva, and Brahma. Every 100 years, a ritual called Eka Dasa Rudra is performed that involves an enactment of Gods, demons and humans. Animal sacrifices are a part of the celebration to appease gods. The next one is scheduled for 2079. Holi, a Spring festival, is celebrated by throwing colred powder or water on family and friends celebrating the victory of good over evil, a joyful event with music and dance.

The Vedas were written in Sanskrit and regarded as the world's first scriptures that reflect the philosophy of Hindu culture. Hinduism has developed as a religion on Vedic principles. The Vedic philosophy was passed on orally through recitation for hundreds of generations. These were written 2000 years later when the Sanskrit script was developed. Hinduism is the religion of 800 million people in India, a country with population exceeding 1 billion. All other religions are practiced in secular India which is the largest democracy in the world. Meditation and yoga are accepted and followed increasingly in the western culture due to the awareness of consciousness, health, and for the body/mind connection. The Hindu scholars and gurus like Bhaktivedanta Swami Prabhupada, Maharishi Mahesh yogi, and Shree Rajneesh have developed a worldwide following through the discourses on Hindu religion. Hinduism focuses on individual enlightenment, contemplation and the belief that:

You receive what you deserve during reincarnation,
Soul transmigrates at death and dwells in the new by birth.
Form of incarnation depends on one's karma in life.
Good karma improves the form and status in the next life.
Bad karma plunges one lower into the inferior forms of life.
This view allows one to restrain the mind from vices and work in
God's will and dharma by meditation to earn the Grace of God
and enjoy His benevolence. If one follows the wrong path and
indulges in vices , the path to God's realm changes into cycles of
birth and death. The word *Dharma* is derived from *dhr* , means
to sustain, to hold together. In the East it is Dharma and faith
that sustains society (Interreligious Insight Jan. 2009, 25).

The Bhagavad Gita narrates the dialogue between Lord Krishna
and Arjuna that took place in the battlefield of Kurukushetra
where the Pandavas and Kauravas confronted each other in the
epic war Mahabharata. The lessons include among others:
> The futility of birth and death.
> An action with no interest in the outcome.
> An aversion to create new karma.

Hindus believe that god 'Purusha' was sacrificed in four parts
according to the Holy Scripture that established the castes in
Hinduism (Hitchcock with Esposito, National Geographic, 87).
> Brahman: the highest class (from his mouth)
> Kashatriya: Warriors and nobles (from his arms)
> Vaishya: Farmers (from his thighs)
> Sudra: Performing menial work, slaves (from his feet)

BRAHMANS represent the highest learned class. They recite
and interpret the scriptures and perform ceremonies. They
became spiritual advisors to the kings and were respected by the
people. Palmists were knowledgeable about the influence of
celestial bodies. They prepared horoscopes based on the place,
time and day of birth of an individual and predicted the events
for the lifetime. They were consulted before deciding date and
time for auspicious occasions to ensure successful completion.
This tradition is still observed to avoid any negative celestial
influence before starting any important business or family event.

176

KSHATRIYAS were the strong warriors and represented the wealthy and nobles who helped to build temples and shrines under the guidance and supervision of priests to be in good grace of the gods seeking their protection. The Ganges River is lined with temples along its banks, attracting devotees for centuries to meditate, worship, and to bathe in the sacred waters. Many hope to die in Varanassi and scores of people release the ashes of their departed kins with the hope to end the cycle of birth and death.

VAISHYA include workers, craftsmen and farmers in this category. The businessmen traded material goods, farmers raised crops to provide food for all, cattle for milk and transport, and reared horses for the warriors.

The SUDRAS are the lowest class who used to perform menial jobs. They were called the untouchables and were shunned from social activities of other classes and were not allowed to worship with everyone and could not be near the nobles so that their shadow may not make them impure. Due to the efforts of a foreign educated person Ambedkar in free India, they are called 'dalits' and have reserved seats in the assembly and are a part of the workforce.

No one was supposed to marry outside their caste to preserve the integrity of the class system. Any transgressions were seriously denounced in the society, sometimes leading to honor killings. r In 1947 India became a sovereign nation, the caste system was officially abolished. Its influence, however, still lingers in Indian society. The Hindu Marriage Act was passed by the Parliament of India in 1955 which applies to Hindus, Buddhists, Jains, and Sikhs.

PATHS TO AN IDEAL LIFE
 CHILDHOOD: Early education, Study of yoga and Sanskrit.
  BOYHOOD: The Janeoo ceremony signifies coming of age and
          qualifies a boy to study Vedas.
  MARRIAGE: It is a sacrament, not a contract, a means of
spiritual growth. Man and woman are soulmates. The rituals

include wedding procession (Baraat), arrival of groom and bride, exchange of floral garlands (Jaymala), parents give daughter to the groom (Kanya Danam) with Fire deity as witness, bride and groom walk seven times around the nuptial fire. Priest advises to seek four goals as a couple:

> Dharma: to lead a sensible good life
> Artha: seek prosperity to make life happy
> Kama: to engage energy and passion with purity
> Moksha: the attainment of unity with God

SPIRITUAL PATH: Focus on God by renouncing worldly attachment to material possessions by becoming a sadhu.

VEDIC PHILOSOPHY

Vedas embody knowledge written in Sanskrit. They are the oldest written texts passed on by oral tradition for over 10,000 years. Sanskrit was the classical language of India, older than Hebrew and Latin. Manu compiled rules for proper moral behavior in the Vedic society:

> Wound not others, do no injury by thought or deed, utter no word to pain the fellow creatures.
> He who habitually salutes and constantly pays reverence to the aged obtains an increase in four things: length of life, knowledge, fame, and strength.

The world's first University was established at Takshila in 700 BCE where more than sixty subjects were taught. The Nalanda University was built in the 4th century. The following Vedas were written between 2500 to 5000 years ago.

> RIG VEDA: Knowledge of Hymns (10,800 verses).
> YAJUR VEDA: Knowledge of Liturgy (3,988 verses).
> SAMA VEDA: Knowledge of Classical Music (1,549 verses).
> AYUR VEDA: Knowledge of Medicine (100,000 verses).

THE UPANISHADS concentrated on individual disciplines:

Jyotisha:	Astrology and Astronomy
Kalpa:	Rituals and Legal Matters
Siksha:	Phonetics
Aitreya:	Creation of Universe, Man and Evolution

Chandogya: Reincarnation, Soul.
Kaushitaki: Karma
Kena: Austerity, Work and Restraint.
Dhanurveda: Science of Archery and War.
Mundaka: Discipline, Faith and Warning of Ignorance.
Surya Siddhanta is the ancient Indian text book of Astronomy which was compiled in 1000 BC. The information was handed down from 3000 BCE by mnemonic recital methods.

The Earth's diameter was calculated 7,840 miles. The current figures indicate 7,926.7 miles.

The distance between Earth and Moon =253,000 miles, current calculations show distance of 252,710 miles.

Other subjects were covered under the following Sutras:
Sulba Sutra: Knowledge of Mathematics.
Yoga Sutra: Knowledge of Meditation.
Kama Sutra: Knowledge of Love and Sex.

FOUR YUGAS

The ancient scriptures, Upanishads and Vedas, describe a succession of four yugas or eras. The duration of 12,000 Divine years is one Mahayuga. One thousand Mahayugas make one Kalpa and that is one day of Lord Brahma. One divine year (year of the gods) equals 360 earth years. There are four yugas:

Satyug: 1,728,000 earth years
Treta: 1,296,000 earth years
Duaper: 864,000 earth years
Kaliyug: 432,000 earth years

Each Yuga has distinct characteristics in terms of human outlook towards life and the environment, both external and internal. The latter refers to the consciousness of mind. Every era characterizes various activities and its attributes for people. In every era the goal is to advance towards achievement of salvation . The current era is Kaliyug that will culminate with cataclysmic ending starting the cycle again with Satyug. The characteristics of these four yugas are outlined:

SATYUGA: Humanity was focused on the spiritual virtues, the truth, contentment, conscience, love, compassion, patience, meditation, peace of mind and service to sages and humanity.

People engaged in meditation of the 'Word'. Everyone spoke the truth. This was the most peaceful period of time in four yugas and the longest. There was a saintly tradition in every household dedicated to truthful living for the common good of all. Presence of God was perceived everywhere and in everyone in conducting the daily business and chores. This era is noted for truth and spirituality.

TRETA: The lure of temptations increased, the overall impact of virtues was reduced 25% and the vices crept in to pollute the minds. The criminal activities and insecurity began. Jealousy became more prevalent. People got more engrossed in personal gains and were losing contentment and other virtues of humanity in their actions.

DUAPER: The spirit of compassion declined. Fewer and fewer people followed their spiritual guides to perform spiritual deeds for the community and follow God's directives. The influence of the virtues was reduced by 50%. People became self centered and selfish. Crime was on the rise and half the population on the planet felt fear and stress. The faith and devotion to God was disappearing from the society. Desire for personal possessions by unfair means was on the rise. There was less and less time devoted to God and falsehood prevailed.

KALIYUG: The evil forces got the upper hand corrupting the minds and thoughts. The era started around 3011 BCE based on Upanishads and Hindu scriptures (Rao 2007). Fascination with physical pleasures and attachment to possessions and wealth became an obsession. Kaliyug is an epoch where Lust, Anger, Greed, Attachment and Ego brought moral decline.

HINDU GODS AND GODESSES

Among the infinite creations of mind, the following have been worshipped as Hindu Gods in India. Hindus conceive the reality of God as one and in many animate and inanimate forms thus worship includes Sun, Moon, Water, Stones, Fire, Monkeys, Snakes, Cows, Elephant and a variety of Devs (male sages) and

Devis (female sages). Hindus recognize 330 million Devs (male sages) symbolically represented, at a sacred site in Jammu, in Jammu and Kashmir represented by rows of protuberances.

HINDU GODS:

BRAHMA: The Creator, is the supreme deity with four heads.

VISHNU: The Preserver, the god of kindness and mercy, and portrayed with four hands, holding chakra, conchshell, the club and lotus flower. His incarnations are Lords Rama and Lord Krishna.

SHIVA: The Destroyer shown with a trident, snake around the neck is also depicted as Nataraja, the Lord of Dance. Sati was his consort, became Parvati after sacrificial fire.

GANESHA, the god with elephant head, is worshipped by the Hindus as Remover of Obstacles.

HANUMAN, the monkey god, epitomizes the devotion to God. He is worshipped as the god of wind (vayu), and regarded to be reflection of Lord Shiva.

HINDU GODDESSES:

SARASVATI: consort of Brahma with many arms.

LAKSHMI: goddess of wealth with four arms.

DURGA: She is depicted riding a lion or tiger with three eyes and ten arms and was born out of the river. She is Shiva's consort, the supreme goddess, who is the mother of Ganesha. She is considered the warrior aspect of goddess Parvati.

KALI: with black skin, with protruding red tongue wearing a skull necklace represents a force that eliminates all evil forces.

THE INDIAN EPICS

RAMAYANA:

This was the first Indian Epic composed 6500 years ago with 24,000 verses compiled in seven books by Valmik.
This narrates the life story of Lord Rama. Ayodhya is the birthplace of Rama. It is in the foothills of Himalaya. The sacred temple at that site was demolished. Rama went into exile for 14 years with wife Sita and Rama's younger brother Laxman. Ravan, King of Sri Lanka kidnapped Sita in the guise of a saint and took her to his kingdom. The revered monkey deity, the

181

Gopuram-madurai Hindu Temple, India

Hanuman, helped to bring Sita back. After the exile, Rama returned to Ayodhya and the Ram Rajya began, the era of peace, prosperity and harmony. The Festival of Lights, Diwali, is celebrated to commemorate Rama's return from exile. This epic weaves together myths, demons, and deities. The story is re-enacted in stage productions. Ramayana epic symbolized the rise of Gupta Dynasty that ruled from 350 A.D. to 600 AD. This was the golden age for the arts, literature, architecture, and trade. The Gupta Empire expanded in the entire Indian subcontinent.

MAHABHARATA

This is the longest Epic in world literature with 100,000 two-line stanzas composed 5000 years ago. This was the Great War between two groups of cousins. Kauravas numbered 108 and Pandavas were 5 who were engaged in rivalry since their childhood. The words of wisdom Lord Krishna (Krsna) said to Prince Arjun in the Great Mahabharata War in Kurukushetra, India in 3100 BC are embodied in Bhagvad Gita:

> Your every nature will drive you to fight,
> the only choice is what to fight against.
> On action alone be your interest,
> Never on fruit.
> Let not the fruits of action be your motive,
> Nor be thy attachment to tnaction.
> This is how actions were done
> by the ancient seekers of freedom.
> Follow their example, act,
> surrendering the fruits of action.
> For certain is death for the born
> and certain is. birth for the dead;
> Therefore over the inevitable
> You should not grieve.

The royal family of the King Santanu is portrayed as the actors in the Epic Mahabharata, a drama in which each character depicts its role and its struggle towards a path of spiritual enlightenment leading to salvation of the soul. King Santanu represents Absolute Pure Consciousness. His first queen is Ganga, embodiment of intelligence, who appears in human form

183

of the sacred River Ganges. She marries the king with a condition that she will not be questioned on whatever she decides to do, otherwise she will leave for good. King Santanu agrees and she bears 7 sons. Ganga throws each one of them into the River Ganges after giving birth. When 8th son was born, the King told her not to put his son in the river. Ganga leaves as she had told the king and vanishes in the River Ganges. Six sons represent the inner regulating aspects.

The 7th son represents *'consciousness'*.

Bhishma, the 8th son, *'individualized reflective aspect'*. The second queen, Satyavati, portrays the primordial nature and bears 3 children:

Chitrangada, depicts the *'primordial nature'*.

Vichitravirya, *'independence of soul'*, and the *'ego'*.

Vyasa, expresses the *'knowledge of circumstances'*.

Vyasa has two children:

Ambika, depicts emotions of *'doubt'*. She bears
Dhritarashtra, who depicts *'delusion'* and his son,
Duryodhana, is prone to *'selfishness and desire'*.
...They represent the Kauros clan in Mahabharata.

Amblika, embodies distinction between good and bad.

Pandavas depict *'intelligence'* through two daughters:
Kunti, portrays *'indifference to attractions'*. Kunti bears 3 sons who represent 3 elements.
Yudhishthira (ether); Bhima (air); Arjun (fire).
Maduri, bears two sons who represent 2 elements:
Nakula (water); and Sahadeva (earth).
...They represent the Panndavas in Mahabharata.

Mother's word was always followed and never questioned in Hindu culture. The Pandav brothers brought Daraupadi princess home and announced, Mother, look, what we brought. Kunti, their mother, remarked: All of you brothers share it without even looking at what they meant. Thus princess Daraupadi became their common wife.

According to the legend, Pandavas and Kauravas were playing a game in which the Pandavas lose everything, even their common wife, Daraupadi, to the Kauravas clan. The Kauravas take

Draupadi to humiliate her in the royal court by disrobing her. Draupadi prays to Lord Krishna, her brother, to save her honor. As her 'wrap around' clothing is removed, more and more appears to protect her honor. This enraged the Kauravas suspecting Lord Krishna's support and led to this war. Lord Krishna offered a choice to Kauravas and Pandavas. One side will take my army the other side his guidance and support. The Kauravas get the army while Pandavas accept Lord Krishna on their side. During the war, Krishna was guiding Arjuna, the essence of the Bhagavad Gita. Mahabharata is dramatization of a journey that portrays the two aspects of human mind.

VEDIC PHILOSOPHY

KARMA: The law of universal causality, connecting man with the cosmos and condemns him to transmigrate.

MAYA: The world is not what it seems to human senses. The absolute reality is situated somewhere beyond the cosmic illusion woven by Maya and is beyond the human experience as conditioned by Karma.

NIRVANA: The state of absolute blessedness, characterized by release from the cycle of reincarnations, freedom from the pain, care of external world, and bliss. This state of mind leads to 'moksha', union with God.

YOGA: This implies integration, bringing all the faculties of mind under control for self consciousness. Yog Rishi Swami Ram Dev has popularized Pranayam and has helped millions around the world. Its techniques include Deep Breathing: *Kapalbhati Pranayam* (forced expulsion of air by quick squeeze of abdomen), and *Anulom Vilom Pranayam* (alternate inhaling through one nostril and exhaling from the other). These techniques written in the Vedas claim to offer physical, mental, and spiritual benefits. HH Sri Sri Ravi Shankar founded 'Art of Living Foundation' with centers in 150 countries teaching courses in *Sudarshan Kriya* (relieving stress through breathing), Yoga (uniting body, mind and spirit), Meditation (relaxing to quieten the mind), and Service. Roy Eugene Davis, a direct disciple of Yogi Paramahansa Yogananda has established Center for Spiritual Awareness also continues to explain Kriya Yoga in the United States and abroad.

Dr. Seshagiri Rao, Trustee, World Congress of Faiths and the Chief-Editor of the Encyclopedia of Hinduism quotes a verse from Rogveda: Reality is one; sages call it by different names. Hinduism expresses monotheistic and non-theistic traditions. The doctrine of spiritual competence (*adhikara*) and the chosen Deity (*ishtadevata*) are in harmony among different Hindu sects.

Rabindranath Tagore (1861–1941), a Nobel Laureate said:
Oneness among men, the advancement of unity in diversity - this has been the core religion of India.

Hinduism is a religion. that solidified the freedom movement under Mohandas Karam Chand Gandhi. His nurse Rambha shaped his religious outlook and helped him to transform into Mahatama Gandhi. On September 11, 1906 the Indian community in Johannesburg, Africa, developed the movement and decided not to obey the anti-Indian discrimatory legislation proposed by the Transvaal parliament. At the age of 37 he was forever changed and relinquished family, career, and wealth and after that he never owned anything. His crusade, with the fast in 1932, opened many temples to the 'untouchables' in a caste bound society. Another voice led him to fasting to end the deeply entrenched hierarchy of caste system. He could not bear the separation of economics and ethics. He renounced everything, and lived the life of a sadhu (sage). He startedted the movement of non-violence and self sufficiency in India. His determination and leadership with religious mass gatherings until the British surrendered India as a sovereign nation. The partition of India troubled Mahatama Gandhi deeply who wanted to see sovereign India as one nation intact. But India was divided into Pakistan on sectarian lines as an Islamic state and India remained a secular nation, the largest democracy, where Hindu, Muslim, Christians, Sikhs and other faiths maintained freedom of worship . During 2007, Abdul Kalam, a Muslim was President; Manmohan Singh, a Sikh as Prime Minister; and Sonia Gandhi, a Catholic, head of the ruling party. In India 82 percent of the population is Hindu.

186

Annie Wood Besant (1847–1933):
After a study of some forty years and more of great religions of the world, I find none so perfect, none so philosophical and none so spiritual than the great religion known by the name of Hinduism.

Albert Einstein (1879–1955):
When I read the Bhagavad-Gita and reflect about how God created this universe everything else
seems so superfluous.

J. Robert Oppenheimer (1904–1967):
Quoting from Bhagavad Gita: If the radiance of a thousand Suns were to burst into the sky, that would be like the splendor of the Mighty One... Now I am become death, the destroyer of Worlds.

The laws of life can teach us to live in harmony with nature and all aspects of life. When we know what the laws are, and conduct ourselves in accord with them, we experience lasting happiness, good health, and perfect harmony.

...Paramahansa Yogananda

BUDDHISM

Mihintale Buddha Statue near Anuradhapura, Sri Lanka.
Martin Gray / National Geographic Stock

BUDDHISM
(376 Million)

Queen Mahadevi, the wife of King Suddhodana in 6th century BCE dreamed of lying in a golden mansion where a white elephant came in with a lotus flower, circled around her, and entered her body. The Brahmans interpreted this dream and informed the King that a son will be born who will be Buddha, the enlightened one. King was advised to keep this son from watching any suffering and death. The prince belonged to a warrior community in Nepal called Sakayas. The prince was named Siddhartha, the one who achieves his goals. He got married and had a son. When he went out of the palace in his royal excursions, he saw old people with disease, suffering, and death. He met a sadhu who had renounced all worldly things. At the age of 29 he decided to seek a higher purpose in life. He changed his princely clothes and became a sadhu and departed from the palace taking up a new name 'Gautama'. He wandered for six years. He sat down under a tree near Uruvela at the banks of Nairanjana River. This place is called Bodh Gaya. He meditated there and was enlightened becaming the Buddha. The excavations along southern border of Nepal revealed the ancient city of Kapilvastu, the capital of the Sakya tribe, where Buddha grew up as a prince. The earth from the trenches and mounds dates back to the 1st millennium BCE.

Buddhism was founded by Prince Siddhartha Gautama 2550 years ago. He traveled 150 miles spreading his teachings for 45 years that everything is under the law of impermanence. He preached not to indulge in extremes of riches and pleasures of senses or to undergo physical suffering to achieve benefits of spirituality. He preached that the path to freedom needed to be free from violence, aggression and any harm to living creatures. The Buddhist path,dhammapada, develops compassionate mind.

Putting oneself in the place of another,
one should not slay or incite others to slay.

It calls for purification of mind as thoughts of cruelty and animosity come in the mind. Evil deeds and thoughts have to be driven out to make room for morality and wisdom. Buddha denied knowledge which he did not experience himself. He believed in perfect wisdom. He was considered nastik, a non-believer by Hindu priests. That is the reason that 1500 years ago Buddhism declined in India and spread in other countries.

TEN PARAMI (VIRTUES)
Nekkhamma (Renunciation); Sila (Morality); Viriya (Effort); Panna (Wisdom); Khanti (Patience, Tolerance); Sacca (Truth); Adhitthana (Strong determination); Metta (Loving-kindness); Upekha (Equanimity); Dana (Donation, Generosity).

FOUR NOBLE TRUTHS - Shunyata
1. There is suffering in the world.
2. There is a cause for suffering.
3. One can end suffering by eliminating the cause.
4. There is a way to end suffering.

He believed in birth-death-rebirth and reincarnation. He believed that a man's karmas in this life directly influence the next life. He called it the 'wheel of life'. HH the Dalai Lama says, Buddhists need the Shunyata, everything else is autumn leaves (Iyer, 25).

THE NOBLE EIGHTFOLD PATH
FOR WISDOM:
   1. Right Views: free from delusions and self-seeking.
   2. Right Aspirations: high and worthy intentions and opinions
FOR MORALITY:
   1. Right Speech: kind, considerate and truthful.
   2. Right Conduct: peaceful, honest, and self-less.
   3. Right Livelihood: without hurting any man or animal.
FOR MENTAL DISCIPLINE:
   1. Right Effort: exercise self control and constant self training.
   2. Right Mindfulness: right thoughts for the right actions.
   3. Right Concentration: Meditation on realities of life, God.

The following holy chants invokes the faith among the devotees:

      I take refuge in the Buddha,
      I take refuge in the dharma,
      I take refuge in the sangha.

The spinning of prayer wheels practiced by Tibetan Buddhists, represent a prayer. This path is accessible to everyone without distinction of caste as practiced in Hinduism.

Ananda, a disciple of Buddha, stopped to take a drink of water from a girl who was at the well drawing water. The girl belonged to a low caste and respectfully said: I am too humble and mean to give thee water to drink. Ananda insisted to take water and did not think of the caste. The girl went to Buddha ad told about her love for Ananda and sought his blessing. Buddha remarked, it was not Ananda, it was his kindness you loved. Buddha said:

> Verily there is great merit in the generosity of a king when he is kind to a slave, but there is even a greater merit in the slave when he ignores the wrongs which he suffers and cherishes kindness and good-will to all mankind...Thou art of low caste, but Brahmans may learn a lesson from thee. Swerve not from the path of justice and righteousness and thou wilt outshine the royal glory of queens on the throne.

The Buddhists doctrine is compiled from Tipitaka, the three baskets. These were originally written on palm leaves. Three parts of the Tipitaka include:

> Sutra Pitaka, revealing Buddha's life;
> Vinaya Pitaka, narrating monastic rules; and
> Abhidhamma Pitaka: analysis of Buddhist teachings.

The largest monastery called Somapura Mahavira at Paharpur was built by kings of the Pala dynasty that ruled India between the 8th and the 12th century. The central square building had 1000 foot long walls, 177 monastic cells, each with a pedestal. King Bhimbisara of Magadha supported the ministry. A merchant built a seven-story building for the monks to provide shelter during the monsoon season, the Jetavana Monastery with assembly halls, covered walkways, lotus ponds, wells, baths and porches. Buddha preached there at annual Monsoon gatherings for 25 years. As proposed by Buddha's aunt, Pajapati Gotami proposed, Buddha founded the order of Buddhist nuns. Pajapati shaved her hair. Buddha was cremated and his ashes were divided into eight parts.

Stupas were built in the cities where the ashes were sent. Originally these were earth mounds covered with stones but later these temples developed into magnificient architectural buildings such as the dagoba of Sri Lanka, pagodas of Japan, and chedi of the Southeast Asia. The sdevotees pay respect by circumambulation clockwise in reverence to Buddha's relics.

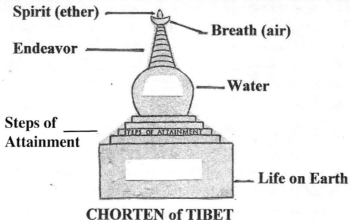

CHORTEN of TIBET

Chortens of Tibet show a square base indicating the foundation of Earth. There are several steps of Attainment above the foundation (mind and body concentration in meditation). There rests the Globe of Water with a Cone of Fire (endeavor). Above that is a Saucer of Air (breath). The highest tier is the wavering Spirit (Ether) which leaves the world of materialism behind. When the breath ceases, the spirit after a pause, is reborn to learn yet another lesson. This symbolizes the belief system of Tibetan Buddhists. Their calendar uses a sixty-year cycle. Twelve animals and five elements vary in combinations each year. The year of my birth was the Water Bird. His Descent from Heaven occurred on 22nd day of the ninth month. Tibetan Buddhists believe in the gods and goddesses on one side and the demons of hell on the other with humans occupying the middle.

The philosophical differences among the patrons at the Second Buddhist Council created 18 different sects in Buddhism. Those who followed the path of the master Buddha to become the Buddhas are called Bodhisattvas the enlightened disciples. Other sect believes in being a part of the world to help others.

Theravada Buddhism is followed predominantly in Sri Lanka, Burma, Thailand, Laos, and Cambodia. The Orthodox Theravadas believe Buddha imagery to be sacrilege. Mahayana Buddhism is practiced in Tibet, Bhutan, Nepal, mainland China, Taiwan, Korea, Japan and Vietnam. They believe that Buddha statues are essential for meditation and concentration.

Ajanta caves near Aurangabad in India were carved out to create hundreds of sculptures on the walls of these temples during the 1st century to the 6th century CE. Others created during the same period are the Hindu and Jain temples in Ellora located about hundred miles away from Ajanta caves. Some of the paintings are 2000 years old. The Gupta dynasty from the 4th century onwards established Buddhist Nalanda University to inspire research and debate and to develop various disciplines in the arts and sciences. Nalanda is world's first university that was established on 35 acres near the River Ganges where 10,000 people worked in the early part of the 7th century.

King Ashoka of the Maurya Empire, a grandson of the first Mauryan King Chandragupta was born in 304 BCE. Ashoka was a ruthless fighter and after watching the misery of wars he became a follower of Buddhism. He combined state and religion, thus the Buddhist civilization flourished. He retrieved Buddha relics from eight places and divided them into hundreds to spread throughout India where stupas were built. The Great Stupa of Ranchi in Bhopal dates back to 150 BCE. It has a 120 feet diameter dome, some with exquisite parasols on top. Ashoka held the Third Buddhist Council and sent missionaries all over his empire. Bamiyan in Afghanistan is located at 9000 feet above sea level where peaks rise upto 16000 feet. Buddha's statues in Bamiyan were the largest statues carved out of the mountains. which the Taliban blasted off during their control of the area.

Buddhism reached China in the 1st century. After the collapse of Han dynasty in 220 AD, there was a period of disunity. The Chinese had translated 1000 texts from Sanskrit to Chinese by 350 AD. The Sui dynasty brought reunification during 589-618 AD. In 1900 AD the Magao site revealed thousands of paintings

193

ans manuscripts. The Diamond Sutra is the oldest that bears its date the 13th of the 4th moon of the 9th year of Xiantong means May 11, 868. The Dunhuang Academy of China supervises the display, research and conservation of 570 caves where thousands of murals and statues were hidden for one thousand years.

The Buddha nature, Shakyamuni is the highest potential within all beings. The earliest literature of Pali Canon, the Ratana Sutta, refers to the Three Jewels (triratna in Sanskrit), in the Tibetan Buddhism:

> The Triple Gem: Buddha, Dharma, Sangha.
> The Three Roots: Guru, Yidam, Dakini.
> The Secret (Trikaya): Dharmakaya (piety), Sambhogakaya (earth body), and Nirmanakaya (humility).

The diamond mind can cut through all worldly delusions.
An angry and hateful person has mind like the open sore.
Correct understanding of Four Noble Truths is like a flash of lightning to the mind.

Madhyamika, the Middle Way concept of Mahayana Buddhism became the Three-Treatises school in the 4th century AD. After the reign of Ashoka, both Buddhism and Jainism survived along with Hinduism for centuries. Muslim invasions started from 11th century and destroyed Buddhist buildings and stupas to spread Islam. This was the reason for the decline of Buddhism in India. It survived and flourished in other countries.

In China it is Chan Buddhism. The first Japanese emperor to practice Bhuddism was Yomei. Horyu Temple is the world's oldest wooden building. Dogen Zengi, born in 1200, attained the bliss of Buddhist truth at the age of 28 and brought it back to Japan. In 1252 the Great Amida Buddha was built in Ushiku, near Tokyo. It is the world's tallest bronze statue rising 400 feet. Nichidatsu Fujii (1885-1985) founded the Nipponzan-Myohoji Buddhist Order in Japan in 1931 at the inspiration of Gandhi. He built Peace Pagoda, the Buddhist Stupa, to provide a venue for uniting humanity. The Peace Pagoda received the Courage of Conscience Award in 1998. Angkor Wat in northwestern Cambodia was the site of religious activity for centuries in the past. Buddhist glory peaked between the 11th and the 13th centuries in Burma, the present day Mynmar, under Anawrahta who built thousands of stupas along the Irrawady River (now called Ayeyarwady).

In 1871 the Buddhist scriptures written in Pali were brought to the Fifth Buddhist Council in Mandalay. Twenty four hundred monks started to transcribe Buddhist scriptures from palm leaves to marble slabs as a revised edition of Tipitaka. Thailand has 95 percent Buddhists who greet you with a *wai* with the same reverence as they would to Buddha. The Lumbini Development Trust is restoring and building monastic enclaves and cultural centers in India where Buddha was born thus reviving Buddhist mysticism.

Bhimrao Ramji Ambedkar belonged to the lowest caste. He was educated in the United Kingdom and the United States. He returned to India and renamed untouchables into Dalits, a Sanskrit word for the oppressed, and campaigned in 1930s for election of the Dalits as representatives. The caste system in Hinduism was entrenched and his campaign failed. Ambedkar renounced Hinduism and adopted Buddhism. Five million Dalits converted to Buddhism protesting inequality. India abolished the caste system after gaining independence and dalits were alloted reserved seats as representatives in the legislature and for administrative posts in government with equal consideration in all walks of life.

HH the Dalai Lama is the 14th spiritual leader of Tibetan Buddhists. He became the spiritual and political head of Tibet at the age of 4. He discussed strategic questions with F.D.R of the United States during WWII when he was 7 years old. He had to discuss as head of Tibet with Mao Zedong at the age of 15. His palanquin was carried on shoulders of the devotees from Lhasa 200 miles southwest to Chumbi Valley. According to Heinrich Harrer, his tutor, the devotees traveled from far off settlements to be in Dalai Lama's presence. The road was lined with parallel rows of pebbles to ensure his safety from evil spirits. He escaped the suspected violence and persecution from the Chinese army advancing towards the capital in 1950. Tibetan uprising did not change the minds of Chinese authorities and Buddhist monks and devotees were arrested. The Dalai Lama established his government in exile in Dharamsala, India in 1959 and has not returned to Tibet in 70 years. Although his efforts to bring the issue of Tibetan independence on world stage did not received attention until the Olympic Games resurfaced the questions of human rights in China but vanished from the political radar. There are 6 million Tibetans in China and Tibet. Lhasa once called 'the abode of the gods' is now dubbed to be Eastern Las Vegas with an influx of 300,000 Chinese changing the culture identified with Dalai Lama. He firmly believes that in order to comprehend the truth it is essential to investigate, analyze and explore if science can provide new truths so that the Buddhist concept can be changed. He states that one can become a good human being by studying within ones own religion or even without religion. He worries that despite making concessions with China he has not achieved freedom of worship and speech for his people. According to Tibetans the Dalai Lama is the incarnation of a god of compassion.

Lamaism is a sect of hope and a belief in the future. Lobsang Rampa's patron was the 13th Dalai Lama from Lhasa at Potala, located at 12,000 feet above sea level. Lobsang was selected to study medicine and surgery at Chakpori lamasery where 6000 herbs were in stock. His guide and tutor was the Lama Mingyar Dondup who trained him for the war between Japan and China. During training Lobsang Rampa had to follow 32 rules of the Priestly Conduct. After becoming a Lama, one of the elite, he had to follow 253 rules of conduct. (Rampa 1956, 100). He stated: ... before the Fall of Man, every one had the ability for astral travel, clairvoyance, telepathy and levitation.

Buddhists believe in proper breathing as breath is the source of life and emphasize breath discipline. This system of breathing was deciphered from the old records in caves and caverns under Potala. Proper breathing is only through the nostrils. Buddhists use herbs and breathing techniques to cure ailments. Satya

Narayan Goenka, (Meditation Now, 61) a student of late Sayagyi U Ba Khin is now a teacher of Vipassana meditation conducting courses of 10-day duration throughout the world in 90 countries. His teacher said: All these are games of the conscious level of the mind, the surface level, whereas your habit pattern lies at the root level. It follows three steps of the Buddhist teachings for truth about mind and matter.

1. Abstain from any actions that disturb others.
2. Mastery over mind by focusing on the breath.
3. Purifying the mind through self observation.

This technique is practiced to experience ones own reality to calm the mind and overpower the negatives that afflict the mind. A Buddhist finds self-confidence in faith and prayer that awaken the latent energies (Iyer, 159).

The Dalai Lama has personally guided Ogyen Trinley Dorje a.k.a. the Karmapa who belongs to Kagyu branch of Buddhism. Dorje's parents were nomads and Dorje persuaded his parents to be at a place where searchers will be looking for him. He was found by the searchers and was taken to Karmapa's Tsurphu Monastery. He was installed with the status:

Near divine bodhisattva, the Enlightened Being.

The Dalai Lama's eldest brother was trained as a high lama before the 14th Dalai Lama was born. The younger brother relinquished his monk robe and the current Dalai Lama was installed. This shows flexibility in the installation of the religious head of the people of Tibet and Buddhism (Iyer, 26-27).

When you understand the truth of suffering, its cause, its remedy, and means of its cessation…you will walk the right path. Right views will be the torch that lights your way. Right aspirations will be your guide. Right speech will be your dwelling place on life's road. Your nourishment will be the right means of earning your livelihood. Right endeavors will be your steps. Right contemplation will provide you abiding peace.

………Gautama Buddha

SIKHISM

Aad Guru Granth Sahib (AGGS)

The Sikh Scriptures

SIKHISM
(23 Million)

Sikhism is the fifth largest religion with 23 million followers in the world. It was founded by Nanak Dev (1469-1539) born at Talwandi (called Nankana Sahib) now in Pakistan. His father was in the good graces of a Muslim landlord Rai Bular. Priest Hardyal prophesied that he would be a prophet and a great reformer. His sister Nanaki loved him dearly and honored him as a spiritual soul. Guru Nanak exhibited divine outlook when he was five years old. He was attracted to the company of sages and listened to their discourses intently. His revelations identified the reality of God and questioned the validity of some practices that prevailed in Hinduism and Islam during his time. He delivered the message of rigteousness and unity to humanity. God's name was chanted as Ram by Hindus and as Allah by the Muslims. Both believed in God.

Nanak's revelation is revealed in the opening lines of AGGS portraying truth and purity of the divine (see page 71). Knowing this truth, Nanak urged humanity to experience regular life and observe compassion, ethical conduct, and strive for spiritual elevation so that mind can overcome the worldly impediments. This can be achieved through disciplined devotion to Naam, the word and meditation. This enables control over emotions and perform duties without ego. He did not accept duality of mind. Soul assumed its own individuality which developed ego, the root cause of afflictions in the human mind. Nanak explained the unfolding of the universe from primeval atomic source. There was nothing for eons except nebulous clouds but the Divine Pulse was for ever present. No time and space, no day and night, just God's vision of pre-conditions of primeval atmosphere and oceans with a promise of diverse life. Thus God created the Universe. The expanse of the universe and its limitlessness is known only to the Creator.

Nanak's life was prophesied by Pandits to be devoted to God.

This was apparent from the miraculous events that started from his childhood. One time his father's employee watched Nanak lying down asleep in a field and a cobra created a shadow on his face from the Sun. After watching this episode he tried to advise Nanak's father that his son was gifted with divine powers.

EVENTS IN EARLY YEARS (Sakhis)

A Hindu priest was summoned for the holy thread ceremony (janeoo). Nanak was twelve year old when he questioned the significance of this ritual. The priest said: My son, it is the sacred thread. It protects from the dangers of life and death. Nanak replied: It would become dirty, and will break after some time. How will it be able to protect? The good deeds and compassion help to protect the soul, not a cotton thread. This confirmed that he is destined for a higher purpose.

Nanak's father, Kalyan Das, was known as Mehta Kalu. His mother's name was Triptan. His father wanted him to be a business man. He gave him money and sent him to the market to make profitable deals. On his way to the market Nanak met some sages who had not eaten for days and had no clothes. He decided to help the sages by providing food and clothes and considered it to be a highly profitable investment.

The Enlightenment:
Nanak used to go alone to the woods for contemplation, and often went to a water tributary. He always returned refreshed and at peace. One day he did the same routine but did not return home. The town people searched for him and feared that he had drowned. Three days later, Nanak retuned with a heavenly glow and the gaze of a saint. Nanak preached:
There is no Hindu or Muslim, all are human.

The revelations in verses 8-11 of Jap emphasize the significance of *listening* followed by verses 12-15 (AGGS) of *acceptance*.

The language Prakrit of Panini was used between 300 BCE and 1200 CE. Persians named it Punjabi as it was spoken in the valley, The Land of Five Rivers called Punjab in Persian. The variation in the language of Scriptures reflects the different dialects of ancient Punjabi spoken in different regions. The Sikh Scriptures were compiled in 1604. God is addressed as patriarch due to the overwhelming patriarchal influence of societies in the 16th century. Guru Nanak stated his conception of God as Truth, perceiving it as a flow of immense energy that permeates the universe, a view now shared by the physicists from the quantum perspective. Dr. Devinder Singh Chahal, one of the progressive scholars in Sikh theology, publishes *Understanding Sikhism – The Research Journal* to engage Sikh diaspora based on Sikh Scriptures and Nanakian philosophy (http://iuscanada.com).

Guru Nanak drew attention to the dogmas prevailing in the belief systems of both Hindus and Muslims. His teachings focused on spirituality, faith and trust in the Omnipotent God. He lived as a family man in the world following the natural order with strong conviction of accepting the Will of God. He suggested that the symphony of celestial music, *Anhad vaje*, can be enjoyed by the blessed ones without engaging our auditory faculties.

His preaching style involved deliberate staging of events that exposed the futility of rituals to common man during his missionary travels. There was no intention of creating a new religion. It was a mission to promulgate a universal philosophy for Hindus and Muslims. This mission earned him the respect and devotion as a man of God by people of both faiths.

GURU NANAK'S MISSIONS (UDASIS)

FIRST ODYSSEY (1500-1505): This trip started from the town of Sultanpur towards Lahore, Kurukshetra and Haridwar. He addressed an issue in Haridwar at dawn. He joined the Hindus who were throwing water towards the Sun. Nanak started throwing water to the opposite side. People were intrigued by his ignorance and told him that they are sending water to their forefathers and it can only reach there if thrown towards the Sun. People asked why he was throwing water towards the wrong side? Nanak replied that my fields need water and I was irrigating my land. People were amused and questioned how this water can reach your fields from here? He replied, if water can reach your forefathers who are in another realm, why can't this reach my land which is here? People realized that he was making a point about this age old ritual. This was his way of raising awareness. He continued his journey to religious sites including Ayudhya, Bodh Gaya and stopped at Jagannath Puri, a sacred pilgrimage site for Hindus.

He watched the ritual of *Arti* that was performed by carrying lamps, incense, and pearls in a plate. Nanak pointed out that a wonderful Arti is going on all around us at all hours of the day and night. The blue sky is the platter, the Sun and the Moon are the lamps, stars are the pearls, the fragrant air from the hills is the incense, and entire creation sings praises in arti to the Lord. He continued his journey towards Bhopal and returned back to Sultanpur.

SECOND ODESSEY (1506-1509): He traveled South towards Ajmer, Ahmedabad, Amravati, Hydrabad, Madras (Chenai) and stopped at Kumbh. A tent city emerges during the festival to accommodate upto 70 million people. Pilgrims bathe in the holy water of the Ganges, Yamna and Saraswati Rivers. He went on to Sangla Deep (Sri Lanka), Goa, Bombay (Mumbai), Ahmedabad and Multan. There is a Muslim sect in Multan in Pakistan who worship Nanak with the belief that he was a Muslim Pir, a prophet.

THIRD ODESSEY (1514-1516): This journey was towards the Himalayas where Nanak visited Kangra, Kulu, Dehradun, Badrinath, Nainital, Sri Nagar, Kathmandu, Tashkand, Vaishnudevi, Jammu and back to Kartarpur in Punjab.

FOURTH ODYSSEY (1518-1521): He traveled towards Islamic countries through Karachi and visited Arabia (Mecca and

Medina), Syria (Damascus, formerly Damshaq), Iraq (Baghdad), Iran (Tehran) and in Afghanistan he stopped in Bukhara, Samark, and Kabul. Nanak visited Mecca, the holy site of Muslims where he was sleeping with his feet towards the Kaaba. Qazi at the the holy site was angered and questioned why he put his feet towards God's place and people gathered around. He replied respectfully to all and apologized: I was tired and didn't realize that my feet were pointing towards the Kaaba. You can turn my feet to the direction where God is not present. He was making the point that God permeates in all his creation. He is here, there and everywhere. The Mullahs and others in attendance bowed to the heavenly truth. Still intrigued, Qazi asked him to join him in namaz (prayer). Nanak agreed. Nanak was amused and did not participate fully in ibadat (meditation). Qazi confronted Nanak for not joining him in prayer. Nanak replied: You were worried about the newly born colt, how could I pray with you when you were not praying to God yourself? Qazi did not deny the truth and realized Nanak's spiritual greatness. Guru Nanak spoke in Persian (AGGS, p. 721):
My request to you O Supreme Lord, with no shortcomings.
> Every one living in the world is not without end, and
>> cannot do anything about the thought of dying.
> Why then they do not engage in good deeds?
> Why are they ignoring the inevitable demise?
Nanak said, knowing that I am the dust of thy servant's feet

After traveling through Syria, Iraq and Iran, Nanak and his companions stopped in Kandahar, Afghanistan. They stopped at Hassan Abdal where a highly acclaimed Pir named Wali Kandahari lived on the hill. Mardana, who accompanied Nanak, was thirsty and ventured up the hill to get water for himself and Guru Nanak. That site was Hassan Abdal and is now called Punja Sahib with the hand impression marked in the boulder. This was intended to soften the ego of Wali Kandhari who came down the hill in humility and bowed to the Guru. This was the final trip of his mission.

Nanak met a twelve year old boy named Bortha who was grazing his cattle. The boy wanted to know how to deal with the question of death. Nanak said that this is for the older people to contemplate and you are so young. Boortha respectfully replied, fire consumes straw and a big logs, death does not spare young. Nanak named him Budha, mature in thinking like an old man. He grew up to be a highly respected devotee of Nanak. He had the honor to bestow Guruship to Nanak's successors starting with Guru Angad Dev who succeeded Nanak and four successive Gurus including Guru Har Gobind, sixth in succession. Baba Budha was the first Head Priest (Granthi) at the Golden Temple the holy Sikh shrine in Amritsar.

Once he visited Lalo, a carpenter who was a devotee with meager means. He was a righteous man making a truthful living. Nanak turned down the invitation of a wealthy landlord named Malik Bhago but preferred the simple meal of Lalo. Bhago felt insulted and summoned him to his presence where all his people and servants had assembled. He asked why he refused to join the free sumptuous lunch? He replied: the food of an honest man, earned ethically with hard work, promotes heavenly virtues. The food of a tyrant has been prepared with the wealth made from hard labor and sweat of the poor which poisons the soul and disturbs peace of mind.
The metaphor was expressed with food of the rich Bhago held in Nanak's one hand and the food of humble Lalo in the other. When squeezed, the wealthy Bhago's food dripped blood while Lalo's food released a stream of milk. This miracle humbled the landlord who was devoted to charitable work and devoted his life to help the needy.

A proud ruler believed he gives food and shelter to his subjects and not God. His young daughter was a devotee of Guru Ramdas and told father that God is the protector and sustains life not a human being. This enraged her father. He threatened to make her life miserable. She still maintained her faith in the power and mercy of God. She was married to an invalid and she accepted him as her husband.

GOLDEN TEMPLE

Golden Temple, Amritsar
(courtesy Gurbani FM)

is after her not aware that her husband was cured. While the princess was away, he perceived black birds bathe in that pond got transformed into white swans. He crawled into the water and was no longer a tiny invalid in the basket. Guru Ramdas, the 4th Nanak in succession got the pool constructed at that site and named it Amritsar, the pool of nectar. The first temple was destroyed by Afghan armies. The present temple was restored in 1764 with contributions from Hindus, Muslims and Sikhs. In 1803 Maharaja Ranjit Singh built the temple with marble and copper overlaid with goldfoil.

Guru Arjan, the 5th in succession was approached by Diwan Chandu, an officer in Lahore to accept his daughter for his son Hargobind Rai. Guru declined which made him angry. He conspired with the Moghuls and made Guru Arjan insinuating that his Granth has derogatory verses for Muslims and Hindus. Guru Arjan was called to face the allegation and explain the verses. The verses were found to have Lord's praise. King Akbar was pleased and asked the Guru to recite hymns to offer him peace. Guru Arjan recited the following:

> One man invokes Ram, another Khuda,
>> some bathe in the Ganges, others visit Mecca.
> Some call themselves Hindus, others Muslim,
>> but one who recognizes God, says Nanak,
>> knows the secret of the Lord.

After Akbar's death, Jahangir became the King. Guru Arjun's enemies prevailed and submitted him to extreme brutality. He was seated on a hot griddle while scorching sand was poured on his body that blistered Guru's skin but he declined to accept any change in the divine words of Guru Nank in the Sikh Scriptures and accepted death. Foreseeing the political change, he advised the followers to acquire skills in horse riding and to be prepared for self defense.

Guru Hargobind, son of Guru Arjan was invited by the king for a meeting but was arrested upon arrival. He was detained in jail for more than a decade. When the Emperor visited him and talked with him, he was impressed by his divine discourse and decided to set him free. The Guru insisted that other Maharajas, detained before his arrest, should be released also. He got the robe made with 52 tassles as the Emperor had promised freedom only to those who could hold his royal robe. He secured freedom of 52 Maharajas, each holding a tassle of Guru's robe to freedom. At the time of Diwali, the Festival of Lights, commemorates freedom of 52 imprisoned Maharajas. This happens to coincide with Diwali, the Festival of Lights celebrated by Hindus commemorating the return of Lord Rama after an exile for 14 years.

Emperor Shah Jahan inherited the throne after Jahangir. Guru Hargobind had established Akal Takht, Throne of the Almighty in Amritsar. He had fortified the Lohgarh Fort. The word of this reached the Moghul Emperor. Mukhlas Khan was sent to attack the fort in 1629 CE. Guru Hargobind Rai faced Mukhlas Khan in battle giving him two chances to attack first which he missed and Mukhlas Khan was killed in combat. Khalsa College was built at that battle site, which is currently the Guru Nanak University in Amritsar, Punjab, India. Pande Khan set out to avenge his brother's death and boasted to capture Guru Hargobind. He attacked Guru's army at Kartarpur. A brave swordsman Tiag Mal joined in the battle, shoertly after he was married, and fought valiantly. Guru changed his name from Tiag Mal to Teg Bahadur (Brave Swordsman) who later became the 9th Nanak in succession.

The 7th Guru Har Rai continued the struggle for equality and freedom. He started the practice of free lunch and dinner, called Langar, at every Sikh temple where all sit down on the ground at one level without any discrimination for color, creed, race, wealth, religion or gender. The services and contributions were voluntary. Emperor honored this tradition and dined with the congregation seated on the ground like everyone else. He wanted to establish an endowment to support this tradition but Guru declined as it would undermine the spirit of service, charity and devotion.

Guru Nanak ascended at the age of 70, on September 22, 1539.

He ignored patriarchal succession and established Lehna as the successor Guru based on his divinic elevation and devotion and humility. At the time of performing the last rites for Guru Nanak, an argument surfaced between Hindus and Muslims as both loved and revered Guru Nanak and wanted to perform the final rites their way. Guru Angad advised both to put their fresh flowers along the sides of the body and cover with a piece of white linen. The flowers of the devotees that remained fresh by next morning will carry out the last rites. When the cover was lifted next morning, neither the body nor the flowers were there. The linen which covered the body was divided into two parts and given to Hindus and Muslims.

Bhai Gurdas, the esteemed Sikh scholar, was the scribe who compiled the first version of Guru Granth Sahib and it was installed at Amritsar in 1604. The foundation of the Golden Temple was laid down by a Sufi Muslim Mian Mir. Emperor Akbar on his visit honored Guru Granth by offering 51 gold pieces. The original version was taken away by Ahmed Shah Abdali to Kabul. The second version of Guru Granth was compiled by Guru Gobind Singh and written by Bhai Mani Singh in 1706. The Granth includes verses of Sikh Gurus and verses of Sufis and Saints expressing the unity and universality of the divine Spirit i.e. Sheikh Farid, Kabir, Namdev, Ravidas, Trilochan among others. Guru Gobind Singh established Aad Guru Granth Sahib (AGGS) as the Living Guru and abolished succession with an announcement:
  Khalsa Panth was installed by the Divine decree,
  All Sikhs will accept AGGS as Living Guru from this day.
Guru Gobind Singh's preparation for defense was triggered by the oppression and cruelty of the Moghul Empire. Emperor Aurangzeb was converting Hindus to Islam. A delegation of 500 Brahmins, led by Pandit Kirpa Ram, went to Guru Teg Bahadur in 1675 and told about the forced conversion by the Muslim regime. Gobind Rai, Guru's son who was nine years old, was listening to the terrifying ordeal of the Hindus said: Who else can have the courage and wisdom to save the Brahmins from

such a fate except you, father? Guru Teg Bahadur was pleased at the remark of his son and assured Brahmins that he will defend them. The Guru was summoned to appear in Delhi. The Emperor was away and the courtiers rushed to declare charges and Guru was beheaded. A violent storm appeared at that time. A devotee named Rangretta Bhai Jaita, secured the severed head of the Guru and took it to Anandpur in Punjab. He was later named Jiwan Singh. Another devotee carried Guru's body four miles away to his village and set his house on fire for proper cremation. The temple Rakab Ganj is established at that site.

SAINT SOLDIERS SELF PROTECTION

Guru Gobind Singh initiated five volunteers, called The Five Beloved, who were the first five to answer his call for sacrifice.

Bhai Daya Singh, a Khatri from Lahore.

Bhai Himmat Singh, a washerman from Dwarka, Gujrat.

Bhai Mohkam Singh, a textile printer from Puri, Orissa.

Bhai Dharm Singh, a farmer from Delhi.

Bhai Sahib Singh, a barber from Bidar, Karnataka.

Guru initiated them and was initiated by them himself, an example of collective leadership. It is believed that 40,000 people were initiated. Guru Gobind Singh was the tenth Guru who promoted Guru Nanak's philosophy with no modification to the verses. Sikhs got their identity with five Ks after their initiation at the congregation on March 30th, 1699 at Anandpur. The shrine at that site is called Takht Sri Kesh Garh Sahib. The creation of the saint-soldiers was to fight oppression, cruelty and forced conversion to Islam. The Sikh identity made them a target under the Muslim rule. They only came out of hiding to fight injustice or to rescue the abducted women from the Muslims and help the weak and defenseless victims. Sikhs faced ruthless brutality under the reign of Emperor Aurangzeb who sought conversion aggressively and used extreme torture.

Mani Singh's limbs were cut into small pieces.

Mati Das was sawed in two halves from head down.

Diala Singh was cooked in boiling water.

Sati Das was wrapped in cotton and burnt alive.

Taru Singh's skull was opened and detached.
The dark period in Sikh history is called 'great ghalughara',
Major Masacre, in 1746 when 10,000 Sikhs were massacred in
district Gurdaspur who were living near Beas River.

Guru Gobind Singh left the Anandpur Fort and proceeded to
the Chamkaur Fort. While crossing Sirsa River, his two younger
sons, his mother Gujri and a large contingent of Sikhs got
separated from the Guru. As the Guru entered Chamkaur Fort
with his two elder sons and other Sikhs, the Mughal army
surrounded the fort and the battle started. His two sons went to
the battle field and were killed fighting. The Guru left the fort
and traveled South with the aid of his Muslim devotees.
Guru Gobind Singh met Laxman Dev who was the disciple of
Aughar Nath and was spiritually gifted to perform miracles. In
1708 he became Guru's devotee and acquired the name Gurbax
Singh. He was a great general who started the currency of Guru
Nanak. He defeated Wazid Khan, the Mughal Viceroy of Sirhind
and established Sikh rule in 1790. He brought the demise of the
Mughal Rule.

Maharaja Ranjit Singh (1780-1839) ruled the secular state
where prosperity and harmony replaced torture and
subservience. He was forced into taking the command at the age
of 10. He married the daughter of Kanhaiyas, a powerful family.
His mother-in-law, Sada Kaur urged him to consolidate his
power as ruler of Punjab. The Maharaja defeated the Afghan
army and became the leader. The prominent people of Lahore
approached the Maharaja to take over Lahore, the capital of
Punjab, as the leaders were squandering their hard earned
money on wine and women. Ranjit Singh took over Lahore and
visited the Badshahi Mosque with Muslims. He became the
Maharaja of consolidated Punjab on April 12, 1801. The coins
were minted with Guru Nanak's image. He took part in
Dussehra, a Hindu festival, where huge effigy of Ravan was
burned to express disrespect for kidnapping Sita, Lord Rama's
wife. He visited Muslims to wish them Eid Mubarak. He joined
the Sikh community on Guru Nanak's birthday and bathed in
the sacred water at the Golden Temple in Amritsar. His court

reflected secular structure. Aziz ud-din, a Muslim , was his royal physician. He asked him about his view on religious differences. Aziz replied that I look at the land we all share and I see people, and no difference in Hindus, Muslims, and Sikhs. Maharaja addressed him as Fakir Aziz ud-din from that day and he was appointed the Foreign Minister. General Hari Singh Nalwa won battles in Afghanistan, Peshawar, and Kashmir. Nalwa name was used to instill fear and control their children.

The Koh-i-Noor Diamond, the largest diamond in the world was once worn by Pandava kings. It adorned the Peacock Throne during the Moghal Empire. With Maharaja's victory in Kashmir, Shah Shujah surrendered the diamond to Maharaja Ranjit Singh. In 1838 he was in a meeting with Lord Auckland at Ferozepur and suffered a heart attack and Maharaja died a year later on June 27, 1839.

His rule extended from Afghanistan to the West, upto Kashmir to the North, to the Chinese border on the East and reached the outskirts of Delhi. His youngest son was Maharaja Duleep Singh, the last Sikh ruler of Punjab (1838-1893). The state was annexed by the British in 1849 when he was seven years old. He was separated from the family and the community for the next eight years. He was converted to Christianity and sent to England to be close to the Royal family. He was groomed to move in the British high society. The British had already taken the Koh-i-Noor diamond when Maharaja was forced to surrender the Punjab State. This diamond is on display among the crowns of British Kings and Queens in London. When he grew up, he had a brief contact with his mother and came to know about his Sikh heritage and royal background. He converted back to Sikhism. His desire to go back to Punjab was never realized. The heart broken Maharaja died in Paris in 1893. He was buried in Elvendon Hall. The Ancient House Museum in Thetford houses the memorabilia which was bequeathed to Prince Frederick Duleep Singh (1868-1926), the second son of Maharaja Duleep Singh. A life size bronze statue of Duleep Singh riding a horse, in royal Sikh attire was unveiled by HRH the Prince o Wales in July, 1999 on Butten Island as a memorial to the Maharaja of

Lahore (Sikhpoint). The Golden Throne of Maharaja Ranjit Singh was made by Hafez Muhammed Multani in 1818 after the fall of Multan to the Sikhs. It was found in Lahore when Punjab was annexed in 1849. It was taken to the museum of the East India Company in 1853 and now is displayed in Victoria and Albert Museum in South Kensington, London.

The East India Company of England was established for trade. The British occupied India and ruled for nearly two centuries. After annexation of Punjab province in 1849, the British government also seized control over the Golden Temple. Sangat wanted the Golden Temple to be controlled by the devotees to maintain reverence and management. A committee of 175 people was elected to represent Punjab, other provinces in India, from Burma (Myanmar), Malaya (Malaysia), China, and North America including 36 government nominees constituted the Shromani Gurdwara Parbhandhik Committee (SGPC) with its political arm called The Akali Dal. The incugural meeting was held on December 12, 1920. The right to manage Golden Temple and all other temples was resisted by the British authorities. This sparked demonstrations called morchas during 1922-24 following passive resistance and observing non-violence. This became the Gurdwara Reform Movement known as the Akali Movement. The British declared these demonstrations unlawful. The top leaders and activists were imprisoned. In 1925 on November 1st the Sikh Gurdwara Act was passed reinstating the SGPC and the Akali Dal handing over control of Sikh shrines, Gurdwaras. The SGPC held its election for 180 members on June 18, 1926. It continues to administer issues of Gurdwaras and other religious matters (SikhiWiki).

INTRODUCTION OF SIKHISM IN THE WEST
Sikhs migrated to the western countries by the end of the 19th century. Teja Singh (1877-1965) was an educated Sikh pioneer who helped to establish Sikhs as organized communities by building Sikh temples (Gurdwaras) in U. K. and on the west coast in Canada and the United States. Teja Singh was born in Balowali, District Gujranwala in Punjab (now in Pakistan). His father Dr. Rala Singh practiced medicine. Teja Singh received

M.A. LL.B degrees in 1901 and started his job as a Civil Officer. In 1903 he was offered the position of Vice Principal of Khalsa College Amritsar. He knew that Guru's word was embodied in the Sikh Scriptures. He felt compelled to meet Sant Attar Singh. The saint wanted to see spiritual education as an integral part of the knowledge offered at the college. After the spiritual discourse Teja Singh was assigned three tasks which he accepted.

Maintain the Sikh attire and appearance.

Establish Sikh Gurdwaras (temples).

Preach to the West that miracles (*ridhi-sidhi*) are of no use. Teja Singh was admitted to Cambridge University in 1907. He was the first Sikh student on campus with turban. He completed the course work at Cambridge but he had to enroll for the final term at Columbia University in New York on a scholarship. He was in his twenties at that time. He was requested to deliver lectures on Guru Nanak and the Indian Society. He was an eloquent speaker. His lectures were attended inNew York by 10,000 students, professors and community at large. The news spread to Canada and he was invited for lectures in Vancouver, B.C. Canada. Mr. T.C. Crawford who had shares in the Mining and Trust Company in California was impressed and requested him to deliver lectures in California.

He was told that Sikhs in Canada were being pushed to go to Honduras. Governor of Honduras was invited by the government to visit Sikh families and give a report with an intention that they can be sent to Honduras. The report indicated that they are living well in British Columbia. He made a recommendation that if the Sikhs are pressured to leave, the 50,000 Sikh soldiers in the British Army will pose a big problem. Another government regulation was a major problem for the pioneer immigrants because the families were not allowed to join them. At a conference in London, Maharaja Bhupindar Singh of Patiala addressed raised this issue and the law was changed to allow families to join them. In the meantime Teja Singh convinced the community to establish their financial strength by investing in the Mining and Trust Company to shake off the label of poverty. Another devotee Dr. Knapp helped to arrange

250 acre parcel of land near Eagle Harbor in California. Teja Singh drafted By Laws and registered the Pacific Coast Khalsa Diwan Society to open up a way to build Sikh temple and establish the Sikh community.

In Canada he suggested to build a Sikh Temple and raise the Sikh flag (Nishan Sahib) for spiritual bonding of the Sikh community. In Victoria, British Columbia a procession was conducted with 5000 paricipants behind the decorated horse drawn carriage that was carrying the revered Holy Granth. There is a thriving Sikh community represented in all walks of life, professionals and businessmen in Vancouver with more than ten Sikh tamples to support the religious events. Mr. Dosanjh, a Sikh was elected Premier of the Province of British Columbia, Canada. Sikhs are active in government of Canada.

The religious and political activities were reported in the newspapers in London and in New York. Teja Singh was not permitted to go back to Cambridge University. He was denied scholarship in Columbia University in New York as well. An American offered to pay the fees to help complete his term and he graduated in 1911. Lord Bishop of the Unitareian Church of Chicago, Rev. Jenkin Lloyd Jones invited him to the Congress of Free Christianity and Religious Progress in Berlin, Germany to give a lecture on spirituality and Sikh philosophy of Nanak.

Professor Teja Singh returned to Mustuana near Sangrur town to meet Saint Attar Singh. He received spiritual training from him from 1913 to 1916. He relinquished all attachments, sold his house and devoted his *Tan* (service), *Man* (devotion), and *Dhan* (financial help) in the selfless service (*sewa*) of God. He earned the title of Saint (Sant) Teja Singh and carried out baptism (*Amrit Parchar*), built Sikh Gurdwaras, and established Sikh colleges. He traveled to Bangkok, Malaya, and Singapore in 1952-53. He visited Sikh devotees in African countries in 1954, and traveled to U.K., Canada, and United States in 1955-56. On his way back, he gave a lecture *The Way to Establish Permanent Peace* at the 8th Congress of World Religions for Peace organized by Ananai-Kyo at Shimizu in Japan. He passed away in 1965.

Mr. Dalip Singh Saundh joined the University of California in Berkeley in 1920. He earned doctorate in mathematics. He was a successful farmer for 30 years in Imperial Valley. He became an activist and fought against the discriminatory laws. He and other Indians finally earned the right to become United States citizens. He was elected and served as Justice of the Peace in Westmoreland, California. In 1956, he became the first Asian elected to the House of Representatives. He suffered a stroke while campaigning for the fourth term in Congress.

Late Yogi Bhajan, a Sikh missionary in United States worked with inmates and addicts of all denominations in a spiritual movement called 3HO which means Healthy, Happy, Holy with their headquarters in Santa Fe, New Mexico USA. His followers are called American Sikhs. They are devout Sikhs and observe services, meditate, and live an ethical life. This foundation has established centers throughout the world.

The Namdhari Sect has continued the line of succession with personal living gurus. Another movement was founded by Sawan Singh with a succession of living masters. Kirpal Singh, who succeeded Sawan Singh studied different religions. There were two successors, both of them continued to carryout his mission. Sant Thakar Singh focused on the message *Know Thyself as Soul* . He appointed his successor, Baljit Singh before he passed away. The other Sect is called *Ruhani Satsang,* congregation of souls. The current master of this Sect is Rajinder Singh in United States. Both sects have established centers around the world.

India secured freedom from the British in 1947 and Punjab state was divided between India and the newly created Pakistan with an unprecedented mass migration. The Hindu and Sikh population from the newly established territory of Pakistan became refugees. The Muslim population who chose to migrate to Pakistan also became refugees. This migration created sectarian riots, anger and bloodshed among the people whose ancestors had lived together for centuries.

Sikhism is guided by a value-based statement:
Truth is high but higher still is truthful living.

The value systems are influenced by the environment of the times and rationalities. The evolving values brought change in social, political, economic and psychological outlooks. The 16th and 17th centuries stand as testimony to that fact. The belief in One God and equality of all human beings was initiated by Guru Nanak. This was a major shift from the well anchored framework of caste system designating people to artificially created hierarchy of status which perpetuated for generations. The four castes were: Brahmans, the learned highest caste; Kashatriya, the warriors and nobles; Vaishya, the farmers and businessmen; and the Shudras, performing the menial tasks and personal services for all other castes. The barriers of distinction between these castes were rigid and no one could marry into a lower or higher caste. Verse in AGGS (p.800) show rearranged hierarchy to emphasize equality of all human beings expressing a dismay of the caste system that prevailed at that time.

BASIC TEACHINGS:
Meditation on God's Name: Omnipresence of God.
Honest Earning and truthful living.
Sharing with the under-privileged with humility.

SIKH PHILOSOPHY:
Family life: Gurus were family men as members of the society.
Purity of the family life.
Except wife, all females are sister, mother or daughter.
Except husband, all men are brother, uncle, or father.
Marriage (Anand Karaj): It is a union of two people and families and arranged with consent. The groom and the bride sit in front of the Holy Book. Priest recites 4 verses (AGGS, p. 800), one at a time, the groom leads bride around the Holy Book. The verses are the four stages guiding a person to reach the divine.
First verse: Commitment to truth and righteous life.
Second verse: Commitment to spiritual life together.
Third verse: Service to all humanity as God's work.
Fourth verse: Marriage as symbolism and a path to God.

216

PRINCIPLES OF SIKH FAITH

Freedom of conscience:

Respect for Humans: No discrimination based on religion, color, race and gender.

Service with compassion and humility, offering emotional or financial support for the needy.

Respect for Justice, the drive to eradicate unfair treatment of the weak, and the right to self defence.

Freedom of Speech: Forty soldiers wanted to abandon Guru Gobind Singh's campaign and requested to leave. Guru honored their right and bid farewell with blessing.

Prohibition for tobacco, drugs, advise others to abstain

A Sikh family's day starts with morning prayers and reading the verses in Guru Granth for daily guidance. It is followed by a prayer to seek Guru's help to conduct the daily business according to his teachings mindful of God's omnipresence. At the end of the day a Sikh thanks the Guru for blessings, asks forgiveness for any transgressions and seeks strength to improve the next day. This personal link with God nurtures faith which portrays humility, compassion, and acceptance of the Will of God. Every passing moment carries our signature in all actions. We do not step into the same river twice because it no longer has the same water. Every passing moment is gone for ever (Sorabji, p. 41).

SIKH IDENTITY:

Singh is the middle name of a Sikh man and Kaur identifies a Sikh woman. The 5 Ks are a symbol of the Sikh tradition.

1. Unshorn Hair (*Kesh*) covering by turban.

The color of the turban is a personal choice. Sikh priests wear a white turban and long beards. Turban has caused mistaken identity as terrorists due to a lack of distinction of the turban worn by Muslims and Hindus. Many innocent Sikhs became the target of hate crimes. Hindus and Muslims are clean shaven and mostly fundamentalists wear a turban, especially at celebrations.

The style of turban is different and Sikhs in the west with turban have maintained open or styled beard and mustache.

2. Comb (*Kangha*) to keep hair groomed (now symbolic).

3. Sword for self defense and the weak (now symbolic). The traditional sword was 3 feet long with a shield for self defence. Sikh identity symbolizes integrity, piety, and assurance for safety to those in distress.

4. Sikh breeches (*Kachha*), traditional cotton shorts.

5. Steel Bracelet (*Kara*).

People who do not maintain hair are called 'Sehjdhari' Sikhs. Sindhi men, though clean shaven, are devout Sikhs of Nanak. Punjab is the birth place of Sikhism. Sikhs are successful farmers which made Punjab the bread basket of India. They were respected for their bravery and honored by the British for their service in the armed forces. Bhangra is the spirited folk dance that traditionally is performed at the time of harvest in Punjab. Sikhs experienced a backlash after 9/11 due to the misplaced anger and hate. The Prime Minister of India, Dr. Manmohan Singh as a Sikh leader is respected throughout the world for his stewardship of financial intrgrity with dignity as a statesman.

RELIGION AND POLITICS

No peace among nations
    without peace among religions.
No peace among religions
    without dialogue between religions.
No dialogue between religions
    without investigation of their foundations.
         ... Bishop Hans Kung

        ******

We have to remove the landmines in our hearts
before we can remove them from the ground to
modify our cultural outlook and usher in a
       culture of peace.
        ... Maha Gosananda
          Buddhist leader, Cambodia

        ******

INTERFAITH ENCOUNTER

RELIGION AND POLITICS

Politics and power are inseparable. Religion is a very powerful force that has been used to solidify the masses to show political strength. The battles fought over millennia based on religion and/or political reasons have engaged Jews, Babylonians, Romans, Christians and Muslims. In the Indian sub-continent kingdoms supported Hinduism or Buddhism based on the faith of the Maharajas. The Moghul invaders forced conversions to Islam. Many converted to avoid taxes, persecution, or death. During he Sikh regime and the colonial rule under the British India was a secular country.

Prophet Muhammad fled from Mecca, his hometown, in 622 CE and settled in Medina. In addition to being an Islamic preacher, he also became a military and a political leader to establish Allah's empire. Jihad is a struggle in the path of Allah but instead of the jihad 'inside, it has turned to militancy and chaos. Mehmed I consolidated the rule of the Ottoman Empire. Mehmed II conquered Constantinople in 1453 CE and the walled and fortified city was renamed Istanbul. At the peak of Ottoman glory Suleyman II, the Magnificient, had conquered Hungary, Iran, Arabia, Greece, and part of North Africa. However, European armies with improved weapons and forces gradually diminished the empire forcing its leaders to flee by 1922. Such political tensions were seen in the Middle East during the Iraq/Iran war and in Iraq's invasion of Kuwait. After the fall of Saddam, an effort was made to establish democracy in Iraq. The unrest sparked communal factions and sectarian violence among Shiite, Sunni and Kurds based on their belief systems. Those differences laced with revengeful sentiments coaxed them to resort to the destruction of the Mosques of rival denominations. Shiites believe that Imam al Mehdi who disappeared at the time of his father's death is the 12th century and final awaited Imam who will reappear at the Al-Askariya Mosque to bring them salvation. This is their holiest shrine. The mosques were torched, and Muslims killed Muslims, some for revenge, others for no reason, because a suicide assailant already knows the consequences and clings to the promise of heaven (Surah 61: 10-12) and the allurements manipulate their mind to perform acts of violence in the name of Allah.

India's independence set off bloody sectarian violence in 1947 inspite of Gandhi's request to preserve the secular fabric of India as one nation. Mohammed Ali Jinah insisted to establish Pakistan as an independant Islamic state. The conflicts in former Yugoslavia caused immense human suffering due to religious differences exasperated by economic hardships. The political ambitions of leaders triggered bloodshed.

Simon Wiesenthal, survivor of the holocaust in WWII kept hunting for Nazis so that after his death upon facing those who were killed by Nazis he can say what he did about it. He persevered to find Adolf Eichmann, the architect of the holocaust who was hiding in Argentina. In contrast, Japanese named Sugihara, a Japanese, saved thousands of lives by helping Jewish refugees flee in 1930s and 1940s known as 'conspiracy of kindness'. What made Adolf Eichmann to choose the senseless path of killing? What guided Sugihara to save lives? Both were guided by their conviction which came from within. That message of conscience never registered due to Hitler's ego. ? This contrast is noticed by all at every level in humanity, expressed as individual, as a community, as a nation making headlines about the adversely affected millions of people in the developed or under-developed nations alike. We always have people like Sugihara and hope that no one ever dares like Hitler.

The Chinese believe that human events follow discernable cycles of Great Wisdom, Decadence and Decline. The Sage Kings are honored in history for wisdom and virtue namely Yao 2350 BC, Shun 2250 BC, and Yu around 2205 BC.

The Book of Genesis is cited to return to religious foundation in Christianity. The Taliban enforced fundamentalism in Afghanistan. Moghul invasion destroyed the Hindu shrines in India and enforced conversion to Islam. The historical episodes of the Crusades and Jihads show the courage, rage and spirit of sacrifice in the name of God bringing religion into politics and sparking conflict that tormented humanity in the name of God.

Abraham Maslow (1908-1970) pointed out a hierarchy of basic human needs. Food, shelter, and survival; Security; Acceptance in the society and a romantic personal life. These parameters build self esteem. With higher levels of self respect and recognition by the society, one develops an inherent desire for self actualization. This comes with maturity and contentment leading to inner happiness. Self actualization leads to intuition, consciousness, unconditional love of people and nature. So many have faced tragedies and made it their mission to devote their lives for the humanitarian cause to help others. The joy of freedom from wants and desires creates a drive for selfless work for humanity which paves the way to transcendence and for higher consciousness (Waters 2006, 39-42). Skepticism leads to a negative outcome. An open mind and positive attitude opens doors to pleasant new realities. Eckhart Tolle experienced it.

REFLECTION

Our senses are designed to enjoy the beauty and splendor of the Creator. These have been directed towards Lust, Anger, Greed, attachment to physical possessions, and Ego. This era brought out the worst in humanity in terms of selfishness, deceit, treachery, lies, revenge, fear, heightened desires for wealth, sex and power. The clergy, Mullahs, Pandits, Rabbis, Gyanis and Monks, who were expected to profess the word of God to people, became victim of these vices. Priests were accepted based on interviews, personal references, and spiritual credentials to determine psychological and social maturity. The aftermath of sexual-abuse scandals among the clergy necessitated a directive from the Vatican which instituted a ban on admitting homosexuals to the seminaries. In this era of personal choices and rights, women who are still restricted to participate or hold position in religious hierarchy may also stir dismay and dissatisfaction in service of God.

The quatrains of Nostradamus predicted horrors and destruction. Dolores Cannon explored the 400 years old riddles in quatrains of Nostradamus through twelve different people in her book *Conversations with Nostradamus* (1997), who were able to contact Nostradamus while he was writing the prophecies. Almost all of the 1000 quatrains had been successfully interpreted at that time. Peter Lemesurier (2003) has revisited the quatrains with illustrations on the 500th anniversary of Michel de Nostredame (Nostradamus), who was born in 1503 in St-Remy-de-Provence and started writing in 1550. The destructive forces are frequent as we witness tsunamis, volcanic eruptions, typhoons, hurricanes, droughts, floods and fires around the globe. The interpretation of his quatrains goes on. The concern about the environment was the subject of a debate 22 years ago released as the Bruntland Report, Our Common Future, in 1987. There is more and more suffering through disease, racial and religious strife. The desire for supremacy and power has led to the technological revolution and nuclear technology which has offered the most sophisticated tools of mass destruction. Nostradamus has indicated that earthquakes will cause nuclear accidents that will lead to modifications in plants and animals through radioactive exposure. Kaliyug has fast-forwarded in this era which is headed towards the apocalyptic doom unless there is a universal awareness to halt the trends leading towards devastation.

Francois Ponchand, a Catholic priest arrived in Cambodia in 1955. He warned about the looming crisis and mass murders but his call went unheeded until 800,000 people were murdered during the Pol Pot regime. Raphael Lemkin, a Polish Jew knew about the extermination at Auschewitz and other Nazi death camps but escaped in 1939 before Hitler invaded Poland and his entire family was killed. He heard from his mother that Turkish regime killed a million Armenian Christians in eight years period of atrocities. He was a successful lawyer in International Law in Warsaw, Poland. He decided to do whatever he can to stop this madness in the world. Lemkin coined the word genocide by taking *genos* from Greek, and *cide* from Latin.

He asked the question:

> Why is a man punished when he kills another man?
> Why is the killing of a million a lesser crime than the
> killing of a single individual?

On December 9, 1948 United Nations adopted the Convention on the Prevention and Punishment for the Crime of Genocide. Canadian General Romeo Dallaire warned United Nations in 1993 to prevent the massacres in Rawanda but left the United Nations with a heavy heart feeling utterly helpless. Radovan Karadzic, former President of Bosnia was named Butcher of Bosnia. Saddam Hussain, a ruthless Sunni dictator suppressed Shi'ite majority, killing Kurds in northern Iraq and countless others to stay in power. he was tried by Iraqi tribunal and hanged. After years of bloodshed in Darfur, Sudan it received world's attention. United Nations has done a wonderful job of providing humanitarian aid in the wake of disasters and have exerted economic pressure through embargos and by holding back assistance to the rogue regimes. It may require force of mind to change human perspective when all nations reject and exhaust militancy, terrorism, and extremism and offer the much yearned alternative of freedom, global interaction and peace. It is time for the new cycle as seen in history due to the global alliances that focus on human dignity and human rights. The era of old Empires, Dynasties, and Chiefdoms is gone. Unfortunately economic ambitions and sectarian strife ignite the fire of big egos to gain superiority, and threaten peace in the 21st century.

The Frankish kingdom fell in Charlemagne's hands after Pepin's death. Pope Hadrian II approached Charlemagne for help when the Lombards threatened Rome. As the Pope's control was restored, Charlemagne was crowned by Pope Leo III as *Imperator Romanorum*. This was planned to enhance the role of Catholic Church in the affairs of the monarchies in Europe. Charlemagne did not accept the title to avoid dependence on Catholic Church for directives and designated himself as Emperor ruling the Roman Empire. However, he is credited with the foresight of inviting Alcuin of York who introduced Latin script in the first printing press in the Carolingian Renaissance. Remarks of Pope Benedict XVI in

2006 at the University of Regensburg in 2006 cited a 15th century Byzantine emperor who referred to Islam, as religion spread by the sword, and some teachings of Prophet Mohammad as evil and inhuman. The criticism sparked violence. People were killed, churches were burnt and the Pope was threatened. The Pope offered an apology in Amman, Jordan to Muslim scholars who officially accepted the apology by signing a letter to the Vatican. The Pope's visit to Turkey opened the dialogue. An open letter, *A Common Word between Us and You,* from 138 Muslim leaders pointed out that without peace and justice between two religious communities, there can be no meaningful peace in the world. Dr. Thomas E. Reynolds of University of Toronto suggests engagement dialogue by listening to the grievances of Muslims, acknowledging that Jewish and Christian traditions also used violence and Crusades in the past that call for repentance and focus on mercy and compassion. The dialogue must sincerely reflect mutual respect, forgiveness and reconciliation.

Hugh Boulter's research at Bristol and Warwick was on the topic of religious identity. His research work produced his thesis: *The Spirit of Islam: A study in Christian-Muslim Dialogue and the Theology of Religions*. He discussed two models based on his interviews on the subject (Interreligious Insight, Jan. 2008).

Lockhead's Model suggests different attitudes towards interfaith dialogue. Isolation was due to the fear of persecution in the Middle Ages, and now it is due to social, economic, cultural and/or religious reasons. Hostility is due to historical Jihads and Crusades that lingers. Prophet Mohammad, both as a religious leader and statesman, is messenger of God for Muslims. Conversion between Islam and Christianity created competition for greater following. Muslims believe that Prophet Muhammad has shown the only valid path to 'Jannat' as written in the Koran. Christians believe that salvation is possible only through Christ. Both are religious concepts of faith. Partnership between people of different faiths is developed by facing common dilemmas of harassment and hate crimes or when children engage in dangerous activities. Dr. Shahid Raza of

Muslim College in Ealing, Secretary to the Sharia Council in U.K. feels that proper dialogue leads to understanding. This view in all faiths can develop a basic platform for negotiation. A premature irritability in dialogue comes from lack of patience in listening to the other side as is evident in the statements:

The revelation given by God in Jesus, while valid for its time is overtaken by the revelation given to Prophet Muhammad.

As Christians we are not interested in converting Muslims to Christianity but we want them through their religious life to discover that they are in fact part of Jesus' plan...
Another avenue is to look at differences and close the gaps.

Allport's Model of Racial Prejudice was published in 1954. This is a model of downward progression based on discrimination. When one group makes derogatory statements about other group or people, it is called antilocution. This has been experienced by the Jews, Blacks, Japanese, Germans, Latinos, and Sikhs at different times which leads to isolation of the minority groups who avoid any conflict. Integration can lead to a loss of identity by getting subsumed in the other culture. Hugh Boulter is Secretary to the Oxford Diocesan Committee for Inter-faith Concerns (ODCIC). He suggests that issues of concern which impact and divide the community include religion, conversion, salvation, marriage, customs, special diet, and attire according to ethnicity. These issues should be discussed with an open mind.

Madeleine Albright writes about Abraham Lincoln in her book *The Mighty & The Almighty* (2006, 51) when he saw a pig stuck in the bog struggling to get out. He had to decide whether to risk soiling his suit to free the pig or to keep going and leave the pig to his fate. He did go on but returned and freed the pig. Why? He wanted to take the pain out of his own mind. As it influences a person's conscience, the people in a position to make decision for a nation reflect the country's moral reputation, as theorized by Professor Joseph Nye of Harvard University. If this is a universal phenomenon, all the nations will be compassionate and

226

at peace. Citizens of all countries must strive to eliminate the suffering. This must prompt the conscience, individually and as a nation to usher in a cycle of compassion and a peaceful world.

This sentiment has kindled a wave of support for a humanity ravaged by tsunamis, earthquakes, disease, famine, politically displaced refugees with relief through medical supplies, and economic aid for reconstruction. The Alliance for a New Humanity is organized to bring about a personal and social make over to address the complex global conflicts and problems. Inter-religious Insight is a publication of World Congress of Faiths, Common Ground and Inter-religious Engagement Project. It publishes the views of scholars from different religions who are open to an intelligent dialogue highlighting core issues in an atmosphere of trust and mutual respect. This effort seems to have existed prior to WWII. The Global Congress on the World's Religions also strives to focus on the issues of religious harmony and needs of the humanity. The United Nations in all its political wisdom can draw valuable advice from these religious and spiritual think tanks. This dialogue has apparently continued in a limited circle of concerned theologians and academicians. Another effort in this direction emerged from Harvard as Abraham Path Initiative citing that historically the paths of Judaism, Islam, and Christianity emerged from the single spiritual Grand Highway. Another Grand Highway led to Hinduism, Buddhism, and Sikhism. The global turmoil has caught the attention of the United Nations to seriously examine the core issues.

Persons like Martti Ahtisaari, former President of Finland, the 2008 Nobel Prize winner, who was involved in restoring peace in Kosovo, Indonesia, and Namibia. He looked for opportunities through Crisis Management Initiative where others had given up. He pushed Slobodan Milosevic to end the war in Kosovo in 1999. He worked in Namibia for 14 years until the independence of Namibia. Former President Jimmy Carter of United States, has persevered in his quest for human rights around the globe. Former Vice President Al Gore of United States brought awareness about the urgency of saving the planet's environment and has succeeded in drawing attention to the problem. Ultimately it is the appropriate language of negotiation that can convince the humanity at large to come together for the good of mankind. All the Inter-religious organizations and the Spiritual leaders can leave a footprint of social change. Their approach works on the soul of disturbed nations while political envoys struggle to resolve political conflicts. Their knowledge and global diplomacy can offer fresh approach to help the bruised world. The Olympic Games over-ride political and religious barriers. It is an assurance that collective focus on conscience can be effective. Global peace is equally important and urgent for humanity to enjoy life peacefully. This message is preached in Churches, Synagogues, Mosques, Pagodas, Temples and shrines regularly but it is a faint glow in isolated communities rather than a powerful beam of awareness to illuminate the minds of humanity all over the world. Houses of worship have been used for political agendas resorting to sermons of hate and destruction. Gandhi felt the need for freedom of his people in India, it became the people's obsession; Martin Luther King had a dream and it became a dream of the entire African American populace in the United States. Nelson Mandella brought freedom to his people in South Africa. The path of negotiation was not easy but it was realized to preserve human dignity and respect.

The environment and code of ethics in a stable family have a major influence on the psychology of children and their life. My father's talks and actions have molded my outlook on life. He respected everyone, young and old, rich and poor, and he was respected in return. He served in the army during WWII. He prayed before every meal. He was never angry, but when provoked he only uttered Gods name to neutralize the effect of that disturbing moment. He shared the stories of saints with me to reaffirm faith in God and keep me grounded. There was a very noble person in the army during his tenure. One evening he was so deeply engrossed in meditation and prayer that he lost track of time and missed the roll call. After the prayers he realized this and was certain about the reprisal for his absence. He was expecting fellow soldiers to inquire about the reason for not attending the roll call. No one said anything.

When he mentioned about not attending the roll call, others told
him that you were in attendance and answered your call. This
was the moment when he felt, I can't let God fill in for me.
He requested to be discharged from the army. He spent the rest
of his saintly life in the service of humanity doing Gods work.
The power of prayer has worked miracles in many cases. Such
stories reinforce faith in God, life of truth and path of selfless
service. Not everyone is perfect. However, if we look for only
good attributes in a person, a positive picture will emerge. One
can learn from the successful and not so successful people by
making an observation, correct interpretation, positive thinking
and conscious contemplation.

GURU NANAK'S PRAYER

Thou art the Master, to Thee I pray, O Lord! For,
    this life and body are Thy gifts, Thy bounties.
Thou art the Father, the Mother, we are Thy children.
    No one knoweth Thy limits, O Lord!
Thou, the maker of our Destiny,
    art the Highest of the High.
All Thy creation is strung on Thy thread.
    All that Thou createst is in Thy command.
Thou alone knowest Thy end and state.
    So, Nanak, Thy servant, is forever a sacrifice unto Thee.
Nanakian philosophy did not approve the caste system. The
verses in AGGS (p. 800) show the rearranged hierarchy of status
Khatri – Brahman – Shood – Vaish, portraying equality of all.

A prayer at the end of the day helps to contemplate on the day,
on the good and the bad actions, compassionate or inconsiderate
deeds, honest or dishonest activities and seek the wisdom from
God not to repeat the actions that were not worthy, and ask for
strength to improve daily. Daily self scrutiny eventually helps to
improve social graces and character. Guiding thoughts prompt
us to seek our purpose in life is a transmission from the divine.
A worthy conduct reflects a response to that guidance. This
was manifest during Satyug, the era of truth and truthful living.

Larry Stewart started giving away money to strangers in 1979 at
Christmas handing out twenty or hundred dollars to strangers

at age 26. Over a period of 32 years he gave away more than a million and a quarter dollars to needy strangers. What was his inspiration? He was fired a couple of times one week before Christmas. He could not forget that devastating blow at the joyous time and could sense that pain on the streets every Christmas and he gave help to the needy. No one knew his name till the Christmas of 2006, his last round, Larry Stewart succumbed to esophageal cancer at the age of 58. He felt, that as human beings, we are here to help others whatever way we can. There is a tendency to think I will pray and do good deeds when I am old and have lived my life. There is a wonderful saying: If it is a good deed, do it now, if there is doubt or suspicion, then wait 24 hours, to contemplate and make a decision. A higher power always alerts us about the good or bad choices. The choice we make is our responsibility and we face the consequences. Criminals make apologies for rapes, murders or other heinous crimes when it is too late for the victims, their families, and for themselves. Some choose to forgive.

Our sub-conscious mind is loaded with the experiences of past incarnations. That is why we wonder sometimes: why I think like that? I am an 'Aquarius North Node' and I was astonished to see my image revealed so truthfully that some attributes hidden in my sub-conscious mind were not apparent to me and needed my attention (Spiller, 444-486). Sub-conscious mind is responsible for the thoughts that unconsciously influence ones behaviour. Such introspection alerts you to avoid the actions that hinder potential creativity and helps in self improvement.

In discourses about religion, and words like compassion, selfless service, unconditional love are ideals to aspire for. If God dwells in everyone and in everything, then everyone is a spark of the divine. How can one judge the divine, have resentment, anger and jealousy? If we need to forgive, does this not assume that a judgement is at hand for something that needs forgiveness? These are beautiful words but their impact is realized only if heeded to for what they stand for. We are all at different level of spiritual understanding like a marathon. It is easier said than done. Optimism, determination and patience is the key.

ATTITUDE AND LIFE

A positive attitude is crucial in leading a meaningful and ideal fulfilling life. It is essential to erase the disturbing memories of unpleasant, negative and painful events that rewind and refresh the experiences again and again resurfacing anger, negative emotions and mental anguish. In order to achieve peace of mind, contentment, and happiness one has to go beyond the past which is already gone. It is the present moment and the time that matters. A change in focus is vital to cope with tragedies , personal loss and day to day stress. Support groups, organizations, and professionals have helped countless people and given them hope to move forward. They have helped to change their attitude. Keith Harrell in his book *Attitude is Everything* (2003) suggests ten steps (127-153) and the following highlight personal commitment:

> Shedding the negative attitude and avoiding it.
> Finding goal and purpose in life.
> Seeking God's help and have faith.

We come across negative and positive people in our daily interactions. Positive people are blessed and they uplift people. Negative people are not happy themselves and make life uneasy for others around them. They deserve to climb out of the dark pit of negativity and see the light of inner spirit to experience happiness. But they have to have the desire, motivation, and determination to fight procrastination and make sure that as soon as the negative thoughts emerge in mind, they seek the love of God and bury those negative emotions.

> Love is patient and kind;
> It is not jealous or conceited or proud;
> Love is not ill-mannered or selfish or irritable;
> Love does not keep a record of wrongs;
> Love is not happy with evil,
>   but is happy with the truth.
> Love never gives up, ...
> Love is eternal.   (1 Corinthians 13:4-8)

RACE FOR RELIGIOUS SUPREMACY

Churches enhance fellowship and the spiritual connection. Common tradition developed different ecumenical practices thus developing different denominations. Support to local churches carried the obligation to accept the regulatory activities which imposed discipline, sanctions and with the authority to excommunicate. The common faith became obligated to follow denominational directives on belief and practices. Islam faced sectarian differences in succession of power and the head of the Shi'ites and Sunnis defined power of regimes within Islam based on their ideologies. Buddhism was not promoted by Hindu Kings and it flourished in other countries. Sikhism is a religion that emerged by reformation and was accepted by both Hindus and Muslims. Drive for a religious state led to the creation of Pakistan when India became a sovereign nation in 1947. India maintained her secular status as a nation.

Three world religions originated from the same area in the Middle East from one belief system of Abraham i.e. Judaism, Christianity, and Islam. This happens to be a triangle of conflict at this time. The change and transition has been gradual but deliberate. The recent discovery of texts translated from ancient scrolls, The Da Vinci Code and Jesus Papers have initiated a debate that is challenging the old beliefs, sermons and stories told for centuries. The title Son of God was once applied to a prophet in the 1st century known as Teacher of Righteousness. According to a text discovered in 1970 in the Egyptian desert this was once mentioned by the Bishop of Lyon (France) in 180 CE. Judas Iscariot is considered the informant who betrayed Jesus. Many generations preached that story but the records indicate that Jesus requested Judas to help free his soul with the words: Sacrifice the man who clothes me.

Elaine Pagels offers a Gnostic view (esoteric knowledge – *gnosis* in Greek) that Jesus emphasized the need for self knowledge, the sacred spark within, as a path to salvation, as in Gospel of

232

Truth, Gospel of Judas, and the Secret Book of John. His message urged people to seek freedom from the needs of body (flesh) and the worldly possessions. This view was diminishing the role and importance of priests. A literal expression alters the real message and obscures the symbolic worth of an occurrence in history. Events such as birth to virgin Mary, or Resurrection are expression in spirituality for a higher understanding according to the Gnostics. The episode of Nanak sleeping with his feet towards Mecca was symbolic to show the presence of God everywhere and in everything. Literal translations of religious texts and interpretations have modified the message of metaphors and parables. An emerging parallel between religion, spiritual freedom and apostolic authority challenges the prevailing pattern of Christian faith. The discovery of 13 papyrus books in the caves of an Egyptian town Nag Hammadi in 1945 questions the historical connotations. The Gnostic approach is a modern expression to spirituality that was suppressed by Orthodox Christianity.

Primitive Christianity was linked to the Jewish Essene sect based on all the ideals and doctrines that created the modern belief system around the teachings of Jesus Christ. Paul was the leader of a messianic community of Jesus who proclaimed freedom from the law creating an independent sector. The arrival of Jesus riding on a donkey to the temple fulfilled the prophecy that King of Israel will ride on an animal as lowly as a donkey and crowds chanting *Hosanna to the Son of David.* Samuel Clarke was educated in Cambridge where the philosophy of Descartes prevailed. Clarke published essays on Baptism, Confirmation and Repentance. In 'Amyntor' he related to the Writings of Primitive Fathers and Canon of the New Testament in 1699. In 1712 he published treatise on The Scripture Doctrine of the Trinity. Roger Williams was banished from Christ's Kingdom to hold the community of saints together. He advocated separation of church and state, questioning the right to dispose off Indian lands, and enticing Puritans to become Separatists because political authority was a part of the Church of England in the 17th century. He wanted to establish a dialogue with the Indians to teach them about Christ.

He is believed to have in part shaped the ideas of United States Presidents Jefferson and Jackson. In modern times, the concept of Non-violence and civil disobedience launched by Gandhi in India freed the nation from the British. The Civil Rights movement by African American Rev. Martin Luther King in United States and Nelson Mandela in South Africa achieved success in their quest for freedom and civil rights.

CONVERSION

Conversion is considered as a radical change of practice and perception. The Zoroastrian faith was founded by Prophet Zoroaster in Persia before Judaism, Christianity and Islam emerged as religions. This faith recognized Ahura Mazda, as the God of good and evil. It professes that there is a constant battle between good and evil. A Zoroastrian's duty is to ensure that truth wins. According to this faith the soul is bound by contract with God to be born into the religion and to follow its teachings. Any conversion is a breach of that contract. When Arabs invaded Persia, people were given three choices i.e. accept Islam as religion, pay 'Jizya', tax levied on non-believers of Islam, or death. Some people living in the Khorasan Province of Iran fled to escape persecution, going from island to island towards India. Ghengis Khan killed Caliph and 100,000 Muslims and burnt the libraries to destroy Islam. Hindu monarchs annihilated Jainism and Buddhism which moved to China and Southeast Asia. On St. Bartholomew's Day 2000 Huguenots were massacred in 1572.. Those, who fled to avoid persecution, settled in Africa during 1682 in order to practice their religion. Mary, Queen of Scots was the only child of James V and was raised a Roman Catholic in France. Charged with plots against Queen Elizabeth I, she was in prison for 18 years and beheaded in 1587 for treason. Edmund Campion started a Jesuit mission in England and was executed in 1580.

Conversion affected houses of worship that were demolished or converted. Temple of Dadat, an Aramaean deity, was converted to Church of St. John the Baptist in 379 CE and was converted into a mosque with Arab invasion in 636 CE. The Hagia Sophia Church in Constantinople is now Haja Sofia, The Blue Mosque,

CHURCH HAGIA SOPHIA
WAS CONVERTED TO MOSQUE

Haja Sofia, The Blue Mosque, Istanbul, Turkey
Courtesy Al & Diane Burye, San Diego, California

in Istanbul, Turkey by adding minarets and masking paintings.

The Spanish Inquisition investigated any deviations from the Catholic faith. Christian Spaniards and the converts from the Muslim and Jewish faith were targeted. There was a High Council of five members that had jurisdiction over local courts. Anonymous accusations were enough to presume the defendants guilty. Confessions were forced under torture and the defendants had a choice to accept conversion for freedom. Others were executed or burned on stake. During 350 years 5000 people were killed in Spain and in the Americas. Christianity was regarded as heretical under Nicene Creed. Orthodox Emperor Zeno evicted Christians in 451 BCE. The Christians, who faced persecution, achieved religious freedom in the 4th century CE.

Origen established the Christian mission in Axum, off the Horn of Africa and started Christianity. Missionaries have bravely traveled to unknown lands for centuries to spread the gospel of Christ. In that effort they have established schools, hospitals, housing and financial assistance. Building churches in the jungles of Africa, South America and other remote areas required dedication, and patience. Even though the mission contributed to the prosperity in the communities, it altered their original faith and modified their conventional way of life. Some well meaning clergy lost their lives as the resisting locals reacted in rage. This change is sudden and drastic, especially when the encroachment involves religious belief. It is easily accepted in some areas where life is threatened due to hunger and people are searching for a better life. The belief, that a person saved by conversion to Christianity assures their own salvation, drives this passion. More than 2/3rd of humanity in the world belong to other faiths and God is the greatest force in their personal lives under another name.

Benjamin Cohen is son of a rabbi in Georgia who observes and follows all Jewish traditions according to the Jewish Law (NPR). He attends a synagogue and admits not fully understanding the purpose and is missing the spiritual connection. His American wife is a convert to Judaism. Benjamin decided to explore Christianity for a year. He was immersed into weekly services and attended services at different churches. He went to the confession booth not knowing what to confess. Now he has a better understanding of Christianity. He returned with a renewed faith in Judaism. There are other examples where inter-faith unions in marriage between Christian-Jewish, Sikh-Muslim, Hindu-Christian, Sikh-Christian, Sikh-Buddhist have been celebrated. These instances involve a higher devotion to love and faith in their commitment. This is a challenge that they face in the society. Women, who fell in love with a Muslim agreed to accept Islam but adjustment to the rigors of that culture was daunting. An upbringing, when focused on the core principles of spirituality offers a lasting view of God that no longer seeks any change because all the elements exist in the word common to spirituality in all religions and faiths. Conversion is like uprooting from ones faith and transplanting into a new environment. The latter poses a faith-shock in adjustment where the foundation of faith is shaken and compromised. An elevated acceptance and recognition in the beginning gives a boost to ones ego. That initial feeling eventually leads to the reality of flashback of earlier upbringing, bewilderment and confusion which replaces community support, tranquility, and the inherent warmth of the faith one is born into. Under extreme religious pressure some have chosen to be atheists and resort to their personal view of spirituality for emotional stability. The X generation is at the crossroads and must be guided to appreciate the religion they are born into with their family and know the significance of God in their lives. That faith must be reinforced to offer balance and spiritual stability.

Anantanand Rambachan, Professor of Religion in Minnesota, USA stated in his Lambreth Interfaith lecture at Lambreth Palace in London (Interreligious Insight, July, 2008). A convert is perceived to show that the abandoned faith lacks something and the adopted faith offers more and is superior. In the past a large number of converts adopted Buddhism and Christianity in India to improve their life. Christianity, Islam, and Buddhism are mission oriented and have worked in good faith to improve healthcare in the communities by building hospitals, offering education and providing new schools. These material inducements often lead to a new Christian name. Conversion is a phenomenon that impinges on personal freedom of worship.

During the Muslim rule in India, Emperor Aurangzeb forced conversions to establish Islam in India. Under torture and hardships of prison or to escape heavy burden of taxes many Hindus converted to Islam. The Hindu Maharajas of Jammu and Kashmir and other small states were also threatened. Guru Teg Bahadur refused conversion and was beheaded. The tenth spiritual leader, Gobind Singh established the Khalsa in 1699 creating the identity of the Sikhs with a turban, unshorn hair and vows of spirituality. This identity was an assurance that whenever there was cruelty, injustice, and the honor of women in danger, they were recognized as a force for the defense of the weak and defenseless. They were hunted by the Muslims who collected big bounties for each Sikh killed. The history of torture includes horrible crimes such as throwing infants in the air to be caught and pierced by spears in front of their mothers, cutting infants to pieces and making garlands to put around their mother's neck, stretching on torture wheels. Two sons of Guru Gobind Singh were buried alive by framing in brick walls to force them to convert to Islam. Muslim rule was replaced by the Sikh Maharaja Ranjit Singh whose empire extended from Delhi to Afghanistan as a secular state where Hindus and Muslims had equal rights and enjoyed prosperity.

The 'invisibility' of the relationship with God is universal in all religions. The congregation makes it 'visible' as a community, or a nation through communal services in the houses of worship. Even though denominational diversity exists in every religion, the desire for unity comes from the universality of the Guidance in the Torah, the word in the Bible, Kalma in the Koran, the Nad in the Vedas, and the Shabd in the AGGS, Granth. Within each religion, there is a cohesive force of the spiritual message in the scriptures. Paul appealed to each community for essential unity of belief and witness (1 Cor. 1:2) and to be bound to the Church of God that is in Corinth (1 Cor 1:13). He pointed out to

238

the Galatians that it is the same Gospel, but some are confusing you (Gal 1:6). The Charta agreed to in its final form in 2001 by all the churches of Europe together as hoped in St. Paul's letter to the Romans (Morris 2003, 133):

> ...and there will be hope for ecumenism in Europe, and Hope for Europe: May their God of hope fill us with all joy and peace in believing, so that we may abound in hope by the power of the Holy Spirit (Romans 15:13).

We have come a long way from the belief of early tribes in spirits' which established faith. At this time there are different religious paths in the religions. The original message is simple, clear, and similar. It is delivered in different formats. The drive is to increase the number of followers with a promise of spiritual and emotional support and it requires financial obligation. God-loving people have shown signs of frustration. One must not fear a loving God, although we have heard an expression 'God fearing people' who are considered to be better than those who supposedly don't fear God but love God. This is reflected in an increase in the number of people without an affiliation to any religion who do good deeds for humanity. Therefore they really do not fall in the category of atheists. It is time to consolidate the spiritual capital of all faiths for the benefit of humanity. Prophets and sages have said: body is the shrine in which God dwells and through the illumination of mind one can access the Almighty, the Supreme Force. The effort is always individual and its effectiveness depends on ones selfless devotion, complete immersion and yearning from the heart. Every religious text guides us to achieve the following goals on the spiritual path.

RELINQUISH: Lust, Anger, Greed, Attachment, and Ego.
ACQUIRE: Truth, Contentment, Compassion, Faith in God and Purity in life.

Ultimately, it is the grace of God that enables us to rise above body consciousness and advance towards God consciousness. The prayer is like each breath which sustains the body. The moment it ceases, body becomes an empty shell temporarily used by the soul to complete its journey in Life. True followers of every faith focus on their purpose in life. There is no discrimination of the place of origin, color, race, religion, or attire in God's sight as humanity is his creation. Soul, is the energy of life, which leaves the body to join its source in the universe. The care of the body is essential to fulfill our purpose in life. It is often referred to as a temple to treat it with respect and use the mental faculties for ethical living and care for the emotions of others. Intake of food or any other ingredient which adversely affects body and mind is a transgression on the ability of mind to stay focused on God's assignment to carry out our purpose in this life.

Personal freedom of worship and modern lifestyle has to be blended in order to focus on the essence of spirituality in all religions instead of an assertion of superiority and supremacy of one religion over the other. Religious thought and the spiritual message needs to reach the youth so that they feel the urgency and real benefit of peaceful coexistence and understanding by knowing and respecting other faiths and cultural parameters.

Josepf Epes Brown, an anthropologist, lived with Black Elk and recorded Seven Rites of the Oglala Sioux. Edward S. Curtis portrayed photographed the American Indian life in United States from 1896 to 1930 and conveyed his message.

WORDS OF BLACK ELK, Oglala Sioux

...Indians know the One true God, and that we pray to Him continually. We should understand well that all things are the works of the Great Spirit. We should know that He is within all things: the trees, the grasses, the rivers, the mountains, and all the four-legged animals, and the winged peoples; and even more important, we should understand all this deeply in our hearts, then we will fear, and love, and know the Great Spirit, and then we will be and act and live as He intends. (Aperture).

ROLE OF WOMEN
IN RELIGION

Queen Hatshepsut, Pharaoh of Egypt
(Credit: Fernando G. Baptista / National Geographic Image Collection)

ROLE OF WOMEN IN RELIGION

Virgins and wives were viewed as both at the top and bottom of the sexual hierarchy. Virgins were seen to have transformative powers and were labeled as allegorical brides. They were consecrated and they established their orders. Mary became the first exemplar as consecrated virgin. Aristocratic wealthy women were big donors to church. Olympias was a wealthy widow and bishops of Constantinople sought her advice in ecclesiastical affairs. She was ordained as a deaconess. Women were prominent in church affairs, social service, in extra sacramental liturgies, and devotional activities. The practice of kissing the Eucharist before putting in the mouth was introduced by Lucilla in 311-312 CE in the dioces of Carthage. The True Cross was a miraculous discovery which marked the spiritual height of Helena's journey. Empress Helena was Constantine's mother. The Episcopal ceremonies included the chanting of virgins in processions (McNamara, 1996, 41-56).

Pulcheria, a virgin, destined to be an empress, served as personal representative of Pope Leo I at the Council of Ephesus in 449. In a statement of Chalcedonian orthodoxy she claimed to be the leader of all women dedicated to God, a sisterhood that was planning to terminate the covenant of procreation. In an effort to challenge the devil, men shared bed with women but avoiding physical intimacy to challenge the devil, an Irish ascetic lgend. Chastity was viewed as an antidote to subordination. Continent couples sought male bonding through scholarly retreats at Cassiacum.

The virginity movement weakened during the barbarian invasions in the early 5th century. By the mid 5th century, women were excluded from the leadership positions within four decades. The Council of Orange in 441 CE forbade the ordination of deaconesses. Pope Gelasius prohibited the consecration of bishop's widows. With the demise of the Roman Empire, women came under the control of Episcopacy. In an effort to minimize the role of women, church leaders portrayed virginity as an expression to forego an ambition . The desire to take part in administrative affairs was viewed as unbecoming of a virgin. Virgins were elevated as Brides of Christ. History shows their compassionate service to the suffering, sad, and sick children of the world. This legacy was carried on by the women who followed Jesus Christ and watched him suffer. Strict discipline and service marked the image of women as 'Soldiers of Christ' fighting religious battles. In the 11th century the church elders noticed the rise of celibacy among women as a threat to their supremacy. The sexual and child bearing role was minimized and women were equated with the powers of the devil. Women's drive to be equal with men weakened. An exception was the home called Marcigny which was associated with Mary Magdalene dedicated to the Virgin Mary. The label Soldiers of Christ and the rising popularity of celibacy were not acceptable to the male dominated hierarchy in church. This threat was countered by seduction, slander and rape to halt the growing popularity of chaste celibacy. Anti-Catholic sentiment encouraged some to attack women in convents. The women in monasteries were called widows and they were obsessed with their purity. They resorted to seclusion and self mortification to succeed in their spiritual conquest.

The bishops put religious women sworn to chastity behind walls of the monasteries. It assured that women will not be able to play any role in the clerical decisions. The threat of female autonomy forced them to *cura mulierum*, the care (and control) of women. The distinction between religious and lay people established that the religious could follow the Benedictive or Augustive rules and also require claustration. The reclusive life style of the monastery was not as rigorous as claustration to make acceptance for women in monasteries an easier alternative. The Pope also condemned marriage for the priests and barred lay people from participation in papal elections. The clerical hierarchy gained strength when women and lay people were not in competition in the process. The mass became prevalent in which only the male priests participated. The sacramental observances replaced the monastic liturgies. Odo of

Cluny secured authority from the Duke of Aquitane for the monastery that was owned exclusively by Saint Peter and was independent of any influence or oversight of Episcopal authority. When the exempt establishments came under the Abbot's supervision, the monasteries were consolidated in France, England and Spain following the custom as proposed. This created the belief that women could not handle Benedictive rules. The church was becoming independent of the proprietary lords. The notion of freedom from the flesh, nobility and the world was becoming popular. The wealthy and aristocratic women at that time preferred to donate wealth to male monasteries. These wealthy women were recognized in church for their support. The wealth began to flow to the monasteries.

There were religious alternatives in the ancient times like worship of Isis, Dionysus, Cybelle, and Mithras. Women were more prominent in conversions to Christianity, Judaism, and other Greco-Roman religions. Bacchic worship created a women frenzy and had spread to Italy in 2nd century BCE. The Baccanal rites with nightly homosexual orgies and their open relationships were investigated by church leaders. (Kraemer 2004, 270-298)

Syneisactism (men and women worshipping together without any physical transgression) was practiced among early Christians. However, it was deemed scandalous and was the subject of mockery among the Romans and the elders in order to diminish the celibacy movement in women and men devoted to syneisactism. This gave birth to the female identity and the rise of sisterhood, convents, and different orders where women devoted their life to follow the teachings of Christ and serve the needy. Women needed the services of male clergy to support religious activities and male servants to support their reclusive life style.

BIBLICAL PROPHETESSES

Seven women of the Bible are revered as Female Prophets of Israel who believed that communication with God is revealed through prophecy. Their stories from 1880 BCE to 350 BCE

244

portray Divine Immanence of God, the Creator. The seven emotions, Sefirot or vessels individually correspond with the seven prophetesses along with 48 male prophets. These are recorded in the Torah. Moses is the most revered. In Hebrew, kabbalah means received tradition which remained oral until the written script was developed. Tree of Life is the map of kabbalah, the blueprint for spiritual development. The stories of Seven Prophetesses are associated with seven days of the week, seven species of plants, and seven virtues that promote closeness to God (Hieronimus, 2008).

1. SARAH (Sarai): 1802-1675 BCE

Sarai was the daughter of Haran. She is the matriarch of the Jewish people. She was the most beautiful woman and was married to Abram, son of Terach. She is identified with wheat (Psalms 130:1) and first day of the week, Sunday. Her other name was Iscah meaning gaze, for her beauty and gift of prophecy. She is a symbol of Loving-kindness. Sarah was abducted twice, first by Pharaoh and then by king of Avimelech but her courage and trust in God brought her back to Abram safely. According to oral tradition, Sarai did not have a vomb. She asked Abram to take Hagar, the maidservant to produce a child. Hagar was pharaoh's daughter, a princess. She conceived and became arrogant and disrespectful. Sarai became angry and treated Hagar harshly. She fled in frustration. In her absence God spoke with Abram and Sarai and changed their names, Sarai to Sarah, and Abram to Abraham with a promise:

"you shall be a Father of a multitude of nations…"
An angel advises Hagar, who had fled to wilderness, to return and submit to Sarah and told her:

"you will bear a son named Yishmael….". Sarah is elevated and is blessed by God with the pronouncement:

" …kings of people will rise from her".
Both Abraham and Sarah laughed in disbelief but God said, the child will be named Isaac (meaning laughter). Isaac was conceived on Rosh Hashanah, the Jewish New Year, when Sarah was 89 years old and gave birth at the age of 90. The divine intervention for Sarah allowed other barren women to conceive, hearing restored among the deaf, sight came to the blind and

sanity replaced madness. Sarah's words of prophecy in Torah:
Drive out this slave woman with her son ... for the son of that
slave woman will not inherit with my son (Genesis 21:10).
She prophesied that Hagar and her son will be idol worshippers.
It came true.

Sarah invited people to observe the ritual of weaning Isaac. The
community doubted if Isaac was really her son due to her age
and brought an infant without wet mother to be nursed by
Sarah. She became vessel of God's milk and nursed the infant
with love, wisdom, and understanding. Loving-kindness defined
Sarah. Abraham took Isaac to Mt. Moriah without telling Sarah.
He was about to sacrifice 37 year old Isaac, the Akeidah, when
Angel Gabriel appeared and told Abraham to spare him and
sacrifice a ram instead. Sarah could not bear the news of Isaac's
death. She died at the age of 127. Some believe that she knew
about her end (Hieronimus 2008. 77-110).

2. MIRIAM (Zohar): 1398-1273 BCE.
Miriam was the older sister of two brothers, Moses and Aaron.
Miriam symbolizes judgement and balance between good and
bad, holy and unholy, worthy and unworthy. Her name Zohar
means splendorous light.

Miriam helped to deliver Hebrew babies when she was 5 years
old. This associated her with qualities of deliverance and water.
Men were leaving their spouses for fear of male offspring killed
by the Egyptians. Her father, Amran, left her mother. Miriam
challenged that in Jewish court and her father came back to her
mother. A son was born, Miriam's younger brother. He was
securely placed in a basket and released into the Nile River
toward water's edge where pharaoh's daughter always came to
bathe. Miriam was close by when princess noticed the floating
basket. Princess pulled the basket and found a Hebrew male
infant. She named him Moses, which means 'drawn from the
Nile'. Miriam then offered to search for a Hebrew wet woman
to nurse the baby and brought Yocheved, her mother, to feed the
baby. Miriam prophesied that this baby was the receiver and
enabler of God's word.

Miriam's leprosy was believed to be due to challenging Moses to wed a Cushite woman and making Moses the leader of the Jewish people. Water was required for purification. Water represents emotions to be released in a measured flow. Reading of the Torah is viewed to be water for the soul. Miriam repented for seven days while she was quarantined. She gained merit for her repentance and a round rock brought down from Mt. Carmel provided water for purification of the body and household items. Miriam's moveable Well, that gave water to the Israelites for 40 years during her lifetime was with them from the day of exodus. She merited the well due to her service to God. Miriam lived for 126 years. Pesach is Miriam's event which commemorates her exodus from Egypt. Miriam , according to prophecy, guided women across the Red Sea with her Song at the Sea (Hieronimus 2008, 111-154). Three stages as a path that show Miriam's correspondence include:

Using mouth to repent,
Wailing to feel the sin, and
Repentance and desire for devotion.

3. DEVORAH:

Devorah's correspondence was beauty, truth, leadership, and moral order. Her name, according to numeric value, conceals day and night, life and death, and absence or presence of the divine in life. The Ark of the Torah was established in the Temple in her time. Blessing of food, and blessing for nourishment were a part of the prayer linked to Devorah as spiritual nourishment. Harmonizing the opposites is a prerequisite for prophecy. Sukkot is observed for eight days as God's mercy and protection with a hovering cloud in the desert wilderness.

Palm tree is Devorah's species.
The righteous will flourish like the date palm (Psalm 92:13). Palm branch is erect yet supple representing strength and humility. The rustling of branches sounds like a bird in flight which symbolizes the Spirit of God. Devorah's corresponding species is grapes represented in the Tree of Life. She was the

only judge of Israel for 40 years. Justice was viewed as the foundation of Israel. She led an army in self defence as a Military General to defeat Jabin, the Canaanite king in the war on Mt. Tabor. She prophesied this event and informed General Barak with an understanding that it is not your glory or ego, but God's mercy through a woman. Barak agreed and war concluded as prophesied. She was the most revered scholar of the Torah and showed the strength of the moral order. (Hieronimus 2008, 155-195)

4. CHANAH: Born 1058 BCE.

She symbolizes the strength in the quality of prayer and not reliance on miracles. She was barren and wanted a child. She prayed to God for a child at the Temple of Shiloh and promised to offer that child for God's service. High priest created a proper vessel in which God's blessings were received. She conceived when she was 130 years old. She named her son Samuel (requested of God) who became a judge, a ruler, and a prophet. She had 3 sons and 2 daughters. She went to the Temple of Shiloh and offered her son, Samuel to Eli, the High Priest. The standing prayer, the Amidah, is attributed to the prophetess Chanah. The prophetic spirit can pray with a higher devotion, trust, and humility and destiny can be changed. She named God as Host of Hosts.

5. AVIGAIL: 906-836 BCE.

Avigail was married to Naval, a wealthy man. She was a symbol of humility, guided by a divine purpose, and saviour of bloodline of Jewish people. Her correspondence with Pomegranate indicated fertility, and the seeds represented one's deeds, the ones to avoid and the ones to accomplish in life. David's men approached Naval for a donation to the army. Naval was arrogant and refused. This angered David who ordered his men to destroy his propety and kill him. Avigail found out and without Naval's knowledge, who was drunk, sent food for 200 soldiers to David and followed to meet him. She bowed at his feet and offered her service and pleaded for sparing her husband. Avigail prophesied David's victory over King Saul to become king. David was not anointed at this time. David sent Avigail back in peace. Shalom, for Hebrews is God's reward for living according to the Torah. Avigail told Naval about her action after ten days. Naval had a heart attack ten days later and died. God removed him so that David could marry Abigail. David sent for Avigail to take her as his wife. She gave birth to son Chileab, who is better known as Daniel. She corresponds with the creation of royal blood line, qualities of majesty and humility. (Hieronimus 2008, 234-275)

6. CHULDAH: 457 BCE.

She lived during the period of Second Temple with grace of the Holy Spirit. Chuldah, a scholar of the Torah, was chosen for the interpretation of scrolls by King Josiah over Jeremiah. Chuldah prophesied: (oral tradition)

> Thus said God: behold, I am bringing evil upon
> this place and upon its inhabitants because they
> have forsaken Me.....and your eyes will not see all
> the evil that I am bringing upon this place.

Chuldah intervened, and due to king's repentance for worship of foreign gods, and his action to destroy the idols postponed the destruction of Temple till after his death in 70 CE. Observance of Pesach offering for the first time after the ritual of idol worshippers was perceived by God as loving-kindness to change judgement. Prophet Samuel had prophesied helplessness of the king and idol worship. She is revered for the practice of Reading the Torah, presence of the Redeemer at Mt. Olives, and the revelation of the Ark for the Third Temple which was hidden by King Josiah with flask of anointing oil and staff of Aaron above the hills of Jericho. Friday is Chuldah's day for the preparation of Sabbath for Saturday, symbolic of preparation for the after-life. Chuldah taught that we are immortal souls in a mortal body and urged to elevate ourselves above the material towards the spiritual for a transition to the after-life. Chuldah through gematria, showed redemption and sovereignty for a holy life. Olive oil, Chuldah's species corresponds to hiding or concealing.

> God is concealed within us, just like
> Olive oil is concealed in olive, and
> Light is concealed in olive oil.

249

God's light is manifest through actions.

Chuldah prophesied that the warrior redeemer, Ben Joseph, from the House of David will be the first redeemer, descendant from the covenant. The second redeemer, Mshiach Ben David, will be preceded by spiritual anarchy when the young do not respect the elders. Elijah and King David HaMelech will bring thousand years of peace. (Hieronimus 2008, 276-313)

7. ESTHER:

Esther was a descendant of King Saul. She brought together the correspondence of all other prophetesses that culminated in the final step, sovereignty, the Kingdom of God (Malchut). This is the tenth Sefirot, Malchut, in the Tree of Life. She represented complete surrender, body and soul, anchored by perfection of speech in word, in service of God and His creation with meaningful service for redemption of the world. Date honey, her species corresponds to sweetness of redemption and flourishing of Jewish people. Rituals of keeping Sabbath, prayer and fasting are symbolic of prophetess Esther. She was an orphan. Her father died after she was conceived and mother died after giving her birth. This was perceived as the destruction of I and the ego that gave Esther the wisdom. She was raised by her uncle Mordechai who named her Hadassah but changed it to Esther, to hide her Jewish identity. Esther's light was concealed, as she was destined to become a queen. King Achashverosh heard about Hadassah's beauty and summoned her to the king who took her as Queen of Persia, known by the name Ishtar, means as beautiful as the moon. She concealed her Jewish identity but observed Sabbath. Esther was a descendant of royal lineage of King Saul of Israel. She persuaded the king to have a Jewish seer and her uncle was appointed as advisor. Her spiritual link with Mordechai is regarded as life, and her role as queen of a non-Jewish King is regarded as death. Esther's modesty conceals her desire and was spiritually near the Creator. (Hieronimus 2008, 314-352)

WOMAN PHARAOH OF EGYPT

During the Third Intermediate Period, Tutenkhamun and Remses II were the pharaohs in Egypt. Cleopatra ruled as a queen, not as a pharaoh. Hatshepsut was the oldest daughter of Thutmose II and his queen Ahmose. Thutmose had a son with another minor wife, Isis. Thutmose II married his daughter Hatshepsut which was not unusual in that era but she could not have a child herself.

Hatshepsut became the Regent of her step son Thutmose III and established control over the young paharaoh. She switched from the regalia of a Regent to the royal attire of the King of Egypt and wore the striped *nemes* head cloth, uraeus cobra, and the false beard as pharaoh. She ruled from 1473 to 1458 BCE as the pharaoh of the New Kingdom. Her trading ships ssailed to Punt along Africa's Red Sea coast and brought riches for the woman pharaoh. She dedicated all these riches to her patron god *Amun*. Her mortuary temple at Deir el Bahri is a show of her triumphs during her reign. Djeseru temple is dedicated to Hatshepsut 's cult. History portrayed her as a usurping step mother and some of her sculptures were erased but the 100 foot obelisk made from a single block of granite towers above the ruins of Karnak. It is the tallest monument in Egypt preserving her unique place in the history of Egypt (National Geographic April, 2009, 88-111).

WOMEN IN GRECO-ROMAN TIMES

Women held prominent positions in clerical affairs in earlier era. Plutarch of Chaeronea (ca. 50-120 CE) has written on the bravery and religious role of women. Olympias, mother of Alexander the Great was engaged in divine inspirations with tame serpents. Vestal virgins of the 2nd century CE were consecrated by Numa, namely Deacon Maria (Archelais, Cappadocia, Turkey). The burial inscriptions shown on the epitaphs include Jewish women Sara Ura (Rome, 3rd or 4th century CE); Beronike (Venosa, Italy, 5th century CE). The widow of Byzantine Emperor Leo IV and mother of Constantine VI ordered her son blinded around ca 800 in order to occupy the throne. The epitaphs of Christian women elders include Kale (Centuripae, Sicily, 4th or 5th century CE); Thanasia Deaconness, (Delphi, Greece, 5th century CE); Ammion (Ucak, Phrygia, Turkey, 3rd century) in the historical record to include a few. (Kraemer 2004, 245-261).

According to the legend, Quintilla or Priscilla saw in a vision that Christ came in the form of a woman and revealed the place to be holy where Jerusalem is now located. Some devotees even to this day meditate to see Christ. The Quintillians developed several factions called Pepuzians, Artotyritai and Priscillians. Montanism (New Prophecy) was founded by three persons, one male prophet Montanus and two women prophets Maximilla and Priscilla founded Montanism, the New Prophecy. Criticism of Montanism grew and Christians expressed anger and frustration. (Kraemer 2004, 263-269). Montanus converted to Christianity and opposed the leadership role of women and their involvement in baptism. Hippolytus, a Roman presbyter, also pointed out that Christian heresies are the result of Greek philosophical influences. Montanists were eventually excommunicated barring women from any leadership role in church. This gave rise to house churches that involved collective worship. The musical harmony of choir emerged from the echoes of bass parts sung by men and treble by women for this pious activity. The Monastic community designated two types of attendants. One group attended the ailments of the body to get rid of disease, and other attended to their souls afflicted with desires, fears, passions, and evils. In the Roman world women's opportunities were very limited. Monastic discipline was accepted for freedom and survival. Olympias established the first convent for women in the city of Constantinople (Istanbul, Turkey) in her residence. Deaconesses Elisanthia and Martyria joined her in organizing the convent of 250 women which survived for centuries.

CATHOLIC NUNS

Aristotelian mindset viewed women as imperfect men. They could acquire the characteristics of men to become perfect. Men could become imperfect if they surrender their self control and vigor to women. Under the philosophy of syneisacticism, women renounced sex and marriage in early Christian communities. Clement of Alexandria supported the Christian mission and welcomed women who studied philosophy and worked against the pagans. Essene community offered a choice of syneisactic life but depended on women who sponsored men in the community. Virginity in those times was believed to be endowed with special powers. A group of women from Galilee carried the message of Jesus. Seventy women were sent to spread the message and they brought the converts with them. Mary, mother of Jesus gathered them at Penticost and prepared them for the Holy Spirit and contributed to the spread of Christianity. Mary was married to Joseph. The Acrocryphal Gospel, the Protoevangelion, attests to her virginity before and after the birth of Jesus. After her death, the community split, and in Medieval mythology Mary emerged as Mary the hermit due to her contemplative life as a mystic and Martha the dragon slayer for her active life as the minister. The testament of these two mythic figures was not mentioned by Paul (McNamara, 16). Lydia, a dealer in purple dye formed the church of Philipi in the Roman Empire. Paul recognized women like Tabitha, a seamstress in Joppa in his letters as yokemates who aided in conversion to Christianity. The first Abbess was Hersend, a noble widow. She was followed by Petronilla de Chemille who became the prioress. Hildegard of Bingen's hymns and short plays portrayed her visions to the nuns of her order. The authority of nuns sustained till the French Revolution. Due to the problem of *cura monialium*, religious women came under the papacy under the management of men controlled by bishops. House churches, *domestica ecclesia* bonded the Christian communities upto the 4th century. Christianity was viewed as mainly a religion of women and slaves. The Benedictine and Augustinian rules hastened the separation of autonomous women's houses and institutions. As the old women died out, the recruitment of women was restricted to allow only men as the followers of Jesus. The cloistered women stayed in walled compounds. They could see men only through the iron gates. The path for male priesthood was paved. Cardinal Hugolino became Gregory IX. The Hugolino Rule in 1219-20 established

253

claustration, silence and the vow of poverty. The monastic wave had weakened by the 15th century CE.

Women's role has been deliberately minimized over the millennia until the fourth quarter of the 20th century when Sister Mary Theresa Kane pleaded to the Pope in 1979 for the ordination of women. Historically women have played a significant role in church as mystics, teachers, and artists but struggled in the male dominated church. Thecla baptized herself before facing the lions in the arena. During the 12th century Hilderard envisioned music, medicine and moral insights.

The regulations for Christian widows were clearly spelled out in Constitutions of the Holy Apostles in the 4th century CE and widows had no permission to speak or to look up in any situation quoting the statements of the Lord (3.3-9, 13-15):

>Your orientation will be toward your husband,
>and he will rule over you.

and the apostolic saying:

>Adam was not deceived,
>but Eve was first deceived into transgression.

Such statements resurfaced in FLDS when they separated from the mainstream Mormons of LDS in 1890. In Afghanistan like other Muslim countries, laws take second place to tradition. Women were treated as possessions by their husbands and in the male dominated culture women had no rights. During Taliban rule, a suspicion and a report by a man with one witness would render a woman guilty. The executions by the Taliban were carried out in the school playgrounds in Kabul, watched on TV around the world where people gathered as spectators to see the accused woman shot. Domestic violence is a real phenomenon in all cultures. The camouflage of religion keeps it hidden due to false assumptions that this kind of behavior is not allowed in their religion. Parents and family members want no blemishes of allegations to link with their religion or community. There have been reports of honor killings when any woman found to have a relationship or an attempt to marry across religions. These are no longer anomalies as the educated women claim their rights in making their decisions. Access to world cultures through movies and internet is changing cultures which influence fundamentals of native traditions and change attitudes. The vast resources are available to enrich religious understanding of cultures and traditions which promote positive change and preserve stability in the families and acknowledge the role of faith in everyday life. Contributions of Interreligious Insight, Trustees World Congress of Faiths, Interreligious Engagement Project, Common Ground, and International Interreligious Council are important initiatives to promote dialogue and understanding which is so crucial at this time and deserves more visibility.

Hindu women used to wear janeoo, the sacred thread in Vedic times. It was required in order to have access to Vedas and Upanishads. Women were equal partners and had authotity to dissolve relationships. During the Moghul raids women were protected and in time became a weaker sex. They were not allowed to wear janeoo and lost the right to dissolve marriage. Women were expected to die with the deceased husband under the ritual of *sati*. Many women shaved their head and renounced the world. Guru Nanak questioned that tradition to preserve their respect:

> A woman gives birth to Kings and Saints,
> How can she be any less?

Women are blazing new trails due to intellect and confidence are now in pursuit of opportunities in all walks of life.

Mother's Day for Peace was proposed by Julia Ward Howe and was observed in 1870 in response to the carnage of the Civil War in United States and the Franco-Prussian War in Europe. Its observance was set for second Sunday in May. Her Majesty the Queen Noor of Jordan revived it as Rediscover Mother's Day with a sense of urgency to unite as mothers of all nations to stem the tide of hatred and violence and understand the value of human spirit. Other concerned women who gained notoriety as activists include Swanee Hunt, former U. S. Ambassador to Austria with her cause Women Waging Peace; Trish Malloch Brown of Refugees International; and Lisa Schirch of 3D Security Initiative by building schools and water wells in Africa.

Oprah Winfrey has built academy for girls to educat them and empowerthe youth in Africa. Princess Diana made a great impact during her short life of humanitarian service. At the conference held in New York City in October 2006 , women of major religions including Judaism, Christianity, Islam, Hinduism, Buddhism, Sikhism and representatives from Jainism, Zoroastrianism, Shinto and Baha'i faith assembled. The patriarchal encroachments that limit the participation of women in ecumenism and restrict their role in religious affairs were discussed. The deliberations pointed out that glass ceiling still exists for women in most religions. However, enthusiastic participation in forums and organizations is working to create greater representation of women in issues relating to religion.

There was no place for women in priesthood in the past. It was the domain of men only. Women then established convents and nunneries and gained notoriety in their own right in two spheres of service. One order is devoted to serve the sick and the suffering. Agnes Bojaxhiu knew at the age of 12 in Skopje to become a missionary to the poor in other lands. She answered her first calling in 1928 and became a teaching missionary and took her vows as a nun in 1931. She was happy to be a little Bride of Jesus. She taught 17 years as a missionary teacher affiliated with an uncloistered teaching community, the Loretto Sisters of Ireland. She sought permission to start her own ministry. She was granted permission and she established Missionaries of Charity as a one-nun crusade with no funding, but she was blessed with an enormous wealth of devotion and fortitude. In 1946 when Christ called her to work in the slums of Calcutta (now Kolkota) with the poorest of the poor saying:
>   Come, Come, carry Me into the holes of the poor,
>   Come, be My Light.
She was granted permission in 1948 to start that mission. She became Mother Teresa and began to care for the neglected, sick and dying in the streets of Calcutta in India. She devoted her entire life caring for the neglected and was honored with the Nobel Prize in 1979. She conversed with Christ, became His light, and admitted that Jesus gave Himself to me. She prayed to the deceased Pope Pius XII asking for the proof, that God is

pleased with the society, and rejoiced at the elimination of darkness she had struggled with, ending the silence and the emptiness. After her long and hard life of service, fulfilling the assignment of Christ, she was blessed and honored around the world. But her feelings of silence and emptiness simply demonstrate the height of humility. She never lost focus of her mission all her life and left a legacy of service to the poorest of the poor and the neglected ones. She died in 1997.

The mission of Ursuline, *Our Prompt Lady of Succor-Virgin Mary for help in a hurry,* was established to educate women to make a more civilized society. It is believed that 'Our Prompt Lady of Succor' helped Andrew Jackson to defeat the British army in early U.S. war. Ursuline nuns have lived in New Orleans, Louisiana for more than 200 years. They educated girls that included black, white and American Indians. In the aftermath of hurricane Katrina in 2005, Sister Aycock was asked: Why were you not protected from hurricane Katrina? She replied: Our Prompt Lady protected us from the hurricane, but it was the man-made levy system that failed and caused the flooding afterwards which necessitated our evacuation. The mission and the faith are maintained in New Orleans.

In 2006 Katherine Jefferts Schori became the first woman Bishop of the Episcopal Church in U.S.A. and the Global Anglican Communion. Rev. Sharon Watkins was the first woman to deliver the inaugural sermon for President Barak Obama on January 21, 2009 at the National Prayer. These roles for women in the 21st century show the change in church hierarchy and tradition. Catholic Nuns are exploring new avenues of services in Lord's name in United States. They shared their experiences outside the religious life established by the Catholic church during the 'Sojourn Congregation' held in 1997. This new freedom has raised questions caused concern in church hierarchy prompting 'visitations' of nuns, another word for investigation, who are perceived to venture beyond the traditional norm. Some have decided to move on to new life. Women under fundamentalist regimes are also making a headway toward freedom in their lives in other societies.

MYSTERY OF MIND

"Surrender" by Mykal Aubry

MYSTERY OF MIND

Rene Descartes believed the physical world is made up of mass and energy with atomic activity. The mental realm generates ideas, feelings, sensations and emotions. He believed:

Je pense, donc je suis: I think, therefore I am.

n the early 1800s Phrenology of Francis Gall proposed distinct activity centers in the brain in different parts. Brain was viewed as a homogenous tissue performing all functions. Francis Gall proposed 'Phrenology' in 1800s that there are distinct centers of activity in the brain.

Phineas Gage was injured in an accident in 1848 when an iron rod pierced through his head affecting the ventromedial region of his frontal lobe. Gage survived the accident retaining his memory and speech but his personality and behavior changed. He was no longer socially appropriate and his decision making abilities declined. The same area was damaged in Dr. Antonio Domasio's patient Elliot that caused changes in his personality. Elliot knew right from wrong but behaved as if he didn't (Grim 2008). Abnormalities in the frontal lobes have been studied in prison populations showing linkage to violent crime. In courts many cases have been argued with a not guilty verdict by reason of insanity. The brain scans have been used to understand age-related decline in memory, mild cognitive impairment and Alzheimer's disease. In order to remove a brain tumor, the neurosurgeon has to know what centers are in the vicinity of the tumor through specific paradigms, to locate areas that control movements in the body (Mayo Clinic Health Letter June, 2008). Einstein's brain revealed masking of the language area with enlarged region of mathematical function. He did not speak until the age of three.

The structure of the brain, its physiology and potentialities have engaged neuroscientists in this exciting frontier. Brain is made up of 100 billion cells called neurons. Each neuron is connected with other brain cells which range between 1,000 and 10,000 synapses to coordinate functions in the body at an optimum level. Brain is a powerful transformer which screens an enormous network of signals that originate by activation of genes. An understanding of the anatomy and knowledge of the electrical pathways do not explain the origin of thoughts, emotions, faith, will, conscience and consciousness. Our window into the activity of the brain tissue is through the scanners like Functional Magnetic Resonance Imagery (MRI) and Positron Emission Tomography (PET) which detect the flow of blood to different parts of the brain as an indicator of activity in the region. Use of oxygen and glucose indicates the thought process in action, called 'mapping' but it does not reveal the nature of thoughts. Dr. Andrew Newberg, an authority in neurobiology of religious experiences at the University of Pennsylvania has studied brain waves during meditation. A prayerful meditation reduces blood flow in the posterior superior parietal lobe which gives us the sense of orientation (Parnia, 2006).

The frontal and temporal areas are also activated. The levels of melotonin and serotonin are increased which induce relaxation. There is a decline in cortisol and epinephrine levels thus reducing stress. However, it does not prove or disprove the connection with the divine. Dr. Newberg uses scientifically diplomatic term 'neurologically real' phenomenon. This area in neurology is called Neural Correlates of Consciousness (NCC). Brain-based theories are limited by the unified manifestation in an extremely multifaceted network with no known pathways that lead towards the phenomenon of consciousness. The non-conventional theory proposed by Hameroff and Penrose is called Orchestral Objective Reduction (Orch OR) theory where sub-atomic processes are carried out in the microtubules in the neurons which switch states in nanoseconds in a quantum network. Sir John Eccles, a 1963 Nobel Laureate in Medicine believed that there is separation between mind, consciousness, and brain (Parnia 2006, 123). Dr. Bahram Elahi, professor of surgery and anatomy believes that consciousness is a separate subtle scientific entity that interacts directly with the brain like the electromagnetic waves that can transmit audio and video signals yet to be discovered in the future.

Dr. Jill Bolte Taylor, a Harvard trained neuroscientist narrates her ordeal when a blood vessel ruptured in her brain's left hemisphere. The stroke robbed her of the ability to talk, read, walk or recall anything from her past (Taylor 2008, 133-148). She snapped in and out of consciousness expressing two sides of her personality.

LEFT BRAIN: The language centers in her left hemisphere were silenced which reduced the chatter in her mind. Her sense of orientation decreased blurring an understanding of physical boundaries. Some call it the researcher mind that scrutinizes and argues. Left brain is the judging mind, the masculine, the *ying* aspect of mind. This side is obsessed with the I, mine, and me thoughts of self developing a big ego. To make that possible, the left hemisphere is equipped with multi-tasking ability, organizational skills, and is always calculating to make things happen. Left brain harbors and dwells on memories of past situations and keeps reminding unpleasant events and does not let them go away. This side pays higher attention to detail and is much faster than the right brain. It helps to discern language and notice the range of notes in music. Left brain is a dreamer. It makes up stories, scenes, and episodes by filling up the blanks. It is a drama queen which can create blissful or tragic scenes.

RIGHT BRAIN: The instinctive consciousness is identified in specific areas of the right hemisphere where the diplomatic mind, the feminine consciousness, the *yang* of emotions, the intuitive mind, and the small ego rests. Right side focuses on the present. It focuses on compassion and appreciates life and its surroundings without judgement or discrimination. It respects everyone and their potentialities and living in God's will. It observes the inter-relatedness of all humans, and other life forms with the universe. The perceptions are blended without boundaries.

In our left brain, Amygdala deals with critical emotions of panic, the medial prefrontal cortex is associated with the balancing act of social parameters and emotions. The ultimate decision we make about morality comes from the anterior cingulated cortex. The other utilitarian decisions are made in the dorsolateral prefrontal cortex in the right brain. Aside from the identification of the sites in the brain, behavioral psychologists strive to search for the triggers that break down morality and conscience.

Dr. Taylor was trying to remake her personality during her recovery and was fully aware of the influence of the left side and the right side of her brain. Extreme shifts in the left brain trigger criticism, insult, and hostility lashing out to others and to oneself. It will surface as negative personality if not balanced. Dr. Taylor tried to bury the painful emotions by not activating the circuits in her brain. She knew that anger response triggered by the release of chemical in the brain normally dissipates in 90 seconds and the emotion of anger pauses. It will only resume if you allow it to flare up again. There is guidance of great importance narrated in the tragedy and recovery of Dr. Taylor that we have the power to remake our personality. Obviously, the stroke of insight is a path to consciousness. She realized that functional ability of her right hemisphere manifests the deep inner peace and compassion. She recalled the studies of Drs. Andrew Newberg and late Eugene Aquili during the decade in which they used Single Photon Emission Computed Tomography (SPECT) technology to identify the anatomical connection of the brain during spiritual experiences which generate consciousness. Tibetan monks and Franciscan nuns who prayed inside the SPECT indicated neurological activity in specific areas of the brain. The left brain would love to engage in an argument and continue, by giving in to the limbic system. Right brain is compassionate and emboldens the cortical cells to overpower limbic esponse.

CONSCIOUSNESS

This phenomenon attracted attention of theVedic scholars in the 6th century BCE. Christian sages observed it after a 1000 years.

The Tucson International Interdisciplinary Conference on a renewed interest. The subject has attracted psychologists and scientists to probe the mystery of brain and acknowledged its role in consciouness. Transcendentalism movement developed from a combination of the European and Eastern influences that invove the divine, individual values, and faith. Thinkers like Ralph Aldo Emerson and his disciple Henry David Thoreau added strength to the transcendental movement. The trinity of human existence deals with the visible energy of our actions, the invisible energy of thoughts and dreams, and consciousness, the purest form, which is beyond the chaotic struggle of body and mind. Harmony in these three energies manifests the fourth form known as the spirit, spirituality, or the divine. All religions, in their own way, yearns for that fourth energy to reach God.

Consciousness is one of the great mysteries of science. It is subjective and hard to define. Anesthesia takes consciousness away. It is not localized in the brain. The pulse rate, heart rate, and pupil dilation indicate the degree of consciousness in clinical terms. Bernard Baars is actively involved in mind/body problem and examines its three aspect, mentalism, physicalism, and dualism viewing it both from the inner perspective as well as the from outside. Baars suggests that visual cortex can be viewed as a staircase. The visual information enters through eyes and its analysis starts in the recognition cells located in lower temporal cortex. The images are registered at the top of the staircase. Thalamo-cortical system under the staircase monitors the events going up and down the staircase in 100 milliseconds. Baars proposed Global Workspace Theory explained by the theatre metaphor. The event in the spotlight represents the conscious, engaging specific part of the brain. The audience is the unengaged part of the brain. But consciousness is projected as the Director wishes according to the script at hand. It is like Newton who used clockwork as a metaphor to explain the solar system (Blackmore 2006, p. 11-23). Gerald Edleman, Noble Laureate worked in the field of immunology. He became a neuroscientist later and believes that according to Dynamic Core Hypothesis, a conscious image is due to the coalition of neurons that outcompete the other neurons.

Francis Crick always wanted to solve two problems. First how the non-living became living, and second, how brain works so that consciousness can be explained. He solved the first problem by finding the structure of DNA and how it works in viruses (non-living until they invade a living cell) and how DNA determines heredity what Gregor Mendel, the father of genetics, called factors in his experiments on peas, he was thinking about genes. V. Rama Chandran, Professor of Psychology and Director of Brain and Cognition at the University of California is involved in brain research (Blackmore 2006).

Dr. Bruce Lipton, a cell biologist, became a believer by working on cloned cells and studying cell membranes. He believes that it is the signals from the environment (universe) that turn the protein switches on and off to make things happen or to stop the processes. Our identity is through our unique array of receptors, human leukocytic antigens (HLA) on the cell membranes that relate to the immune system. The success of transplant depends on the compatibility with the donor's physiological make up, the receptor-effector protein complex. The spirits of early cultures and tribes included animate and inanimate objects to respect the bounties of the universe because our bodies are formed using the byproducts of the universe. The beliefs control behavior and can override the messages of genes (Lipton 2005).

The next frontier of science is poised to explore the energy potential of human brain. Quantum theory explores the energy fields in the non-material dimension and it is just the beginning. Dr. Darold Treffert, the world's leading expert on savants, has worked more than four decades at the children's psychiatric ward in Wisconsin. He watched remarkable feats of the human brain. The mechanisms involved cannot be easily explained but he recognizes that sometime severe mental disabilities can reveal islands of genius. He observed extraordinary ability in math skills, calendar calculating skills, picture-perfect memory, spatial skills and musical ability. He feels, we come equipped with software. There is genius in all of us. How to unlock that

264

genius is a mystery. There are only 100 savants in the world. Dr. Treffert narrated following bservations to give an idea about the genius of savants.

Matt Savage: Diagnosed with autism, home-schooled, not exposed to any music till he was 6. Audio therapy and a toy piano triggered his ability to play the music 'London Bridge' perfectly. At the age of 14 he released his seventh album on his parent's record label.

George Widener: His autism is known as Asoerger's syndrome. He has an astonishing memory of days and dates: June 7th was the date Robert and Bruce died in 1329. He was the first King of Scotland. That was a Wednesday. I remember reading Daniel Boone, 1769 survey on June 7th in Kentucky…King Louis the 14th became King, It was a Wednesday. Sometimes an accidental injury to the left hemisphere of the brain sparks this ability what Dr. Treffert calls *acquired savant.*

Akrit Jaiswal: This child prodigy hails from a small village Noorpur, in Himachal Pradesh in India. At 2 years of age he learned the alphabet and was reading Shakespeare at age 5. He started collecting a library of medical text books and taught Math and English classes. At 6 years of age he was allowed to observe surgeries at the hospital. After his first surgery he was honored as medical genius. At the age of seven he performed surgery on a girl's fist successfully. At 13 years of age his IQ was 146. He was admitted to Punjab University at the age of 11. He was invited to Imperial College, London the same year to discuss medical research. His focus was to develop a cure for cancer. He had developed a concept called Oral Gene Therapy on the basis of his research. He hopes to join Harvard University and work in cancer research.

Education for the gifted is a difficult issue politically. Jan and Bob Davidson have set up the Davidson Institute for Talent Development in Reno, Nevada USA. They are convinced that talent rises to the top early. The rise of President Barak Obama has inspired the current youth. A reference to highest achievers confirms the belief.

265

Marie Curie:

Born Nov.7, 1867 in Warsaw. She could read by age 4, top of high school class at the age of 16. She was the only person to win Nobel Prize in two fields of science.

Albert Einstein:

Born March 14, 1879 in Ulm, Germany. Attended elementary school, dropped out at the age of 15, thought of an experiment at 16 which lead to the Theory of Relativity, published major papers at 26 on understanding the universe.

Pablo Picasso:

Born October 25, 1881 in Malaga, Spain.
Completed first oil painting at the age of 8.
Finished month-long exam at the Royal Academy in a day.
Pioneered Cubist school of art, and achieved global fame.

Yo-Yo Ma:

Born October 7, 1955 in Paris.
Graduated high school at 15, attended Julliard in NY.
Public performances on cello at 5. He made more than 50 Albums and won 15 Grammys.

Bill Gates:

Born October 28, 1955 in Seattle, USA.
Attended public elementary school and Lakeside Prep.
Hacked a computer security system at 13.
Founded Microsoft in 1975 at the age of 20.
Became world's greatest philanthropist, (worth 56 billion).

Tiger Woods:

Born December 30, 1975 in Cypress, California, USA.
Attended public schools, entered Stanford in 1994.
Putted with Bob Hope on national TV when 2 years old.
Shot a 48 for nine holes at 3, won 3 Junior Amateurs.
Turned pro at 20 and is a golfer of international fame.

Einstein's interest in quantum energy modified the Newtonian mindset among scientists and initiated research in the unification of mind and matter to explore the potentialities of the human mind. Researchers are exploring the Grand Unified Theory. Well known authors like Norman Cousins (holistic approach), Drs. Andrew Weil and Bernie Siegel (alternative medicine), Dr. Deepak Chopra (consciousness) have sparked interest in mind/body connection. Dr. Bruce Lipton (Biology of Belief), and Dr. Mani Bhaumik (Code Name God) have contemplated on the new scientific frontiers. Dr. Eric Pearl's book, The Reconnection (2007), has created a paradigm shift in energy healing. Barbara Ann Brennan has explored the human energy fields and the chakras (Hands of Light, 1988). Devendra Vohra's Accupressure Therapy is described in his book Health in Your Hands (1982). Yogi Ram Dev offers Vedic practices of Pranayama and Yoga to activate charkas and enhance healing. The science of mind is linked with the mysticism of spirituality to unlock the mystery of power within harnessed by holy men and prophets of different religions in the world.

The interaction of mind (energy) and body (matter) is by now well established, and the term Mind/Body Connection is used more frequently in medical practice. Dr. Lipton cites an example of hypnosis (Lipton 2005, 123) where Dr. Albert Mason cured the leathery skin of a boy which he believed was an extreme case of warts. The referring surgeon had failed to cure the boy with skin grafts. The surgeon informed Dr. Mason that the boy suffered from congenital ichthyosis. Once that full force of mind was thwarted due to the knowledge of misdiagnosis, Dr. Mason could not treat another case with similar prognosis. He admitted that his visible enthusiasm was an act, nothing the way he treated that boy first time. The physiological processes triggered by the brain cured warts.

There are reports about the remission of cancer which baffle oncologists and have no medical explanation. The belief system triggers the release of agents, yet to be discovered, that overpowers the disease and the staunch faith reinforces the healing process. The herbs or concoctions used by the medicine men (healers) worked with the power of faith. Derogatory comments are engraved on the subconscious mind of a child in early years, limiting a person's ability. It is very difficult for such persons to excel when constant reminder keeps knocking from the subconscious mind reminding them that they are a failure. Our subconscious memory is a repository of stimulus and response downloaded in our psyche that triggers automatic impulses. The conscious mind is controlled by the more powerful ghost of the subconscious mind. Our conscious mind has the ability to scrutinize every event and weigh the pros and cons of a situation to make a reasonably sound judgement as to how and when to respond and in what way. We exercise our free will when our acts are contrary to the automatic response of the subconscious mind. The professionals, scholars, sages, philanthropists, and judges override their personal bias, instincts, and perceptions of our programmed subconscious mind to evaluate circumstances and work towards a fair outcome. The decision between good and evil is always ours, and we are responsible for the outcome and its consequences. The concept of an Omnipresent God is to encourage and prompt a decision that will ensure a just and positive response for the good of all. It is our perception that becomes our belief and directs our response.

Studies on the disorders of the mind show that each person reacts differently in a traumatic situation. The diagnostic term has been changed over time. The horror of war in WWI was diagnosed as Shell Shock. In WWII it was given the name War Neurosis. Since the 1980s it has been called PTSD (Post Traumatic Stress Disorder). This diagnostic term also applies to victims of rape, violence and sexual abuse. Childhood traumas can be remembered into adulthood. Dr Herrington quotes Freud's psychoanalytical thinking that led to the development of psychosomatic medicine. She reported that frequent abortions are an indication of guilt they cannot express, to which body responds with miscarriage. Body remembers even if the mind forgets an experience. Franz Alexander was a pshchoanalyst who came to United States in the 1920s. He believed that the Freudian approach should be coupled with the physiology of emotions for clinical treatment. He recognized seven kinds of psycho-somatic disorders, each due to chronic excitation caused by a sad story: bronchial asthma, peptic ulcer, ulcerative colitis, thyrotoxicosis, essential hypertension, rheumatoid arthritis, and neurodermatitis. (Harrington 2008, 91-101). Dr. Herrington credits Flander Dunbar for her book *Emotions and Bodily Change* published in 1935 which was instrumental in promoting psychosomatic medicine as a new avenue of medical treatment. Depression is no longer a form of weakness. It is a brain disorder that manifests itself in a depressed mood and loss of interest in daily activities. It is linked to the chemical imbalance of neurotransmitters in the brain and shows decline in specific areas of the brain as compared to people not affected by depression. According to the Mayo Clinic (Health Letter March, 2005) depression is accompanied by heart disease, stroke, diabetes, cancer, Alzheimer's disease, Parkinson's disease, thyroid and endocrine problems. Psychotherapy addresses issues and helps to clarify self-image and identify emotions to deal with the situation which requires antidepressants and mood stabilizers.

Dr. Bernie Siegel promoted the concept of emotional stability for optimum health with his popular book Love, Medicine, and Miracles (1986). Psychotherapist Janet Collie responded favorably to her cancer after a Yale surgeon referred to cancer as God's reset button to reassess emotional life. In a lecture Dr. Siegel told the story of two physicians narrated by California oncologist William Buchholz as a parable. Doctors participated in a study to test four chemotherapy drugs with the initials EPHO. One doctor reported that 75% of his patients responded to the drugs well while another doctor saw only a 25% favorable reaction. The higher response was found to be due to the rearranging of drug initials to spell HOPE. Buchholz was trying to make a good moral point (Harrington, 2008).

Bernadette Soubirous lived in the village of Lourdes in southwestern France. A lady dressed in white appeared to her in 1858 when she was 14 years old and wanted her to convey spiriritual messages. She saw the Virgin Mary who led the child to an unknown fresh water spring. The healing properties of that spring water were reported later on. The site was officially recognized by Pope in 1876 as a holy place of healing. However, a commission of doctors was set up to determine the medically inexplicable occurrences of healing that took place at Lourdes.

Catholic doctors called attention to the inability of the new medical view of mind over body for the healing with spring water. Bernheim, a Jew, argued that the power of the mind is stimulated by belief with no religious implications. This is the power of faith. (Harrington 2008, 105-110)

In the 1980s a functional connection was observed that lymphocytes produce peptides that were previously known to be only in the brain. This connection was later reported to be between the nervous and the immune system. Due to this discovery, Dr. Robert Ader proposed Psychoneuroimmunology (PNI) as a new discipline. At this time AIDS appeared which caused chronic stress due to the concomitant stigma and rejection. This sparked a series of alternatives with mind/body connection such as contemplation, meditation and relaxation for healing. Transcendental meditation became popular in the 1970s and Maharishi Mahesh Yogi was put on the cover of Time magazine in the October 13th issue in 1975. Ulcers are no longer the cause of emotional failure in relationships, pressures of work or family stress but due to bacteria. This link was discovered by Barry Marshall who received the Nobel Prize for this work. Certain illnesses are not a metaphor but real physical ailments. Fibromyalgia was regarded as a psychosomatic condition but is clinically treated with drugs. The discomfort of our daughter was viewed as psychosomatic until it was diagnosed as endometriosis.

Meditation is now regarded as a potential alternative to maintain physical and mental health. It is a mind/body duo: if the mind calms down, the body will relax. It has been established that meditation has a clinical influence on the brain wave activity as monitored by EEG (electroencephalogram). The EEG frequency is lowered as the meditative state becomes deeper. Meditation, irrespective of faith or belief system, relieves stress. Prayer is therefore meditation which gives spiritual strength. St. Francis died in 1226. He preached that when connected to the spiritual source, your environment, yourself and people around you, the support manifests itelf. With true spirituality, body, mind and spirit are synchronized. Meditation and spirituality unites of mind and body, heaven and earth, human and divine. According to Mahatma Gandhi:

> Your beliefs become your thoughts
> Your thoughts become your words
> Your words become your actions
> Your actions become your habits
> Your habits become your values
> Your values become your destiny

Thich Nhat Hanh is a Buddhist monk from Vietnam. He preaches mindfullness for peace. He believes that the world needs compassionate listeners to feel what others are trying to express. The concept of interbeing requires communication. The following words describe his philosophy:

> Breathing in, I calm my body.
> Breathing out I smile.
> Dwelling in the present moment
> I know this is a wonderful moment
> (Science of Mind Aug. 2006)

He was captivated by the peace and tranquility in Buddha's picture in 1935 when he was 9 years old. He joined the Tu Hieu monastery seven years later. He seeks unity in all Buddhist groups and preaches mindfulness based on Buddhist teachings:

> Walk slowly and notice each step.
> Count the steps taken in each breath.
> Maintain a half-smile to generate calmness and

happiness. Nhat Hanh calls it walking meditation.

Unfortunately, the power of the mind is manipulated for evil motives. Suicide bombers are the outcome of a subconscious mind that is programmed to hate, kill, and self-destruct. The conscious mind will surely question such a killer instinct. The manipulators reinforce this through the heavy hand of religion with promises of a place in heaven and the company of virgins. Other criminals give in to the forces of greed, lust, power, ego and fame to commit heinous crimes without any remorse and in denial, that consequences are sure to follow. Joseph Stalin during his dictatorship for 25 years was responsible for the death of millions of people. Adolph Hitler demonstrated the height of human savagery by killing millions of Jews in concentration camps in WWII. Pol Pot of Khmer Rouge in Cambodia had no feelings and felt that his conscience is clear after eliminating a million human beings. Al Queda has killed Muslims in the name of religion in jihad. His drive is for Islamic supremacy throughout the world based on his interpretation of Koran and memories of the expansion of the Ottoman Empire.

There are scholars and theologians who are trying to improve interreligious relations while others are adamant on keeping the religious animosity alive. All believe in one God yet this vision differs so drastically that each religion and sect fights to preserve its identity, and longs for supremacy and find ways to criticize other faiths. According to Ernest Holmes, it is Spiral Dynamics in sequential levels of consciousness which alternate with the human focus on the external world. Mind probes the inner world and wants to be at peace. Those at one level of thinking try to impose their views on the ones at another level thus causing problems in their synchronistic coexistence, tolerance and harmony. There is a continuous emergence of Creative Principle that renews the spark of collective consciousness (Science of Mind April, 2008, 25-31).

Rhonda Byrnes was honored as the Spiritual Hero of 2007 for her amazing book and film The Secret. Her work focuses on consciousness that highlights purity of living and the Law of Attraction. She points out that the waves of consciousness vary from one generation to the next. People develop consciousness through their faith and experience bliss and the wonderful feeling of peace. She also points out the secret shifters which allow the negative forces to modify the events that threaten peace of mind. A psychiatrist has used the term emotional vampires for people who suck energy and peace of mind of others due to their irrational thinking and behavior. One has to focus on the positive to neutralize the impact of shifters and emotional vampires. The following attributes are common to all religions and fall in the fold of spirituality:

   Asking (with clarity, surety, and without ambiguity)
   Believing (that you are worthy and deserve)

Receiving (expressing pleasure by receiving)
Gratitude (gratitude for everything you receive)
Remember to remember (Feel wonderful and be grateful).
(Science of Mind: Jan. 2008, 13-20)

A hippo in safari reserve in Florida always waited for a bird to feed from his mouthful before swallowing the food. Humans have the basic instructions but the mind has to be attuned to the morality and social order by clergy, parents, teachers, peers and the society at large. The parental instructions and impressions gathered from their experiences make up the basic value system. It is influenced by peers and the environment in the early years of development. A positive impact results in wisdom and the negative exposure adversely affects the ability to distinguish between right and wrong. Wesley Autrey, the Subway Samaritan, saved a sick stranger by rescuing him from the tracks while a train was approaching whereas some follow path of crime. Mother Teresa dedicated her life with the selfless service for the common good.

NATURE AND THEOLOGY

The Aristotelian concept of nature was embraced in Christian thelogy during the 13th century. The English Civil War of the mid 17th century created opposition to the Church of England. Growing dissension developed the fear of a rise in atheism. The concept of the 'guiding principle' was viewed as the 'spirit of nature' to explain organization of matter and creation of complex organisms. Boyle (1627-1691) was a deeply religious man who established Boyle's Law that pressure and volume of gas are inversely proportional. He viewed scientists as natural philosophers who study the workings of the natural world as an act of God based on the doctrine of Two Books, the Book of Scripture and the Book of Nature. The Anglican doctrine of the cessation of miracles necessitated the search for other alternative to explain supernatural phenomena. In this quest Boyle got interested in witches as an evidence for the supernatural events. This was the time when alchemy was focused on transforming metals into gold. Descartes was a Catholic. He wrote about

273

God's hand in the conservation of motion and in gravity being constant as a common course of nature. Sir Isaac Newton in his physics text *Principa mathematica* 1687, described the laws of falling bodies and planetary motions as activities of God. He was interested in prophecy and eschatology, the study of the end of the world. Bentley used the solar system to show God's design and its stability as God's providence.

The mechanical philosophy of the 17th century was conceived as *machina mundi*, world machine where natural phenomena were based on matter. Pierre Gassendi, a priest, believed that atoms were created by God who gave them their motion. The mechanical view portrayed God as a craftsman, like a watch maker. Gassendi also asserted that the human soul is immaterial and not made up of atoms. When certain events could not be explained the argument ended by invoking a deity, the god of the gaps. The gaps are due to missing knowledge. Scientific discoveries close some of these gaps over time. Newtonian physics explained the unstable motion of Jupiter and Saturn in the 18th century. The greatest gap to be closed is the moment of creation as it was created from nothing. Scientists have explored tiny fraction of the vast expanse of nature and God's countless mysteries have yet to be understood.

INTELLIGENT DESIGN

The design argument was first proposed in the 18th century based on the historical, political, social and geographical circumstances in England. In the United States it was called Intelligent Design based on two views:
   a. Intelligent causes are responsible for the design of the universe, life and its diversity.
   b. The design phenomenon is detectable in nature.
Both of these premises came under criticism. The proponents of Intelligent Design resorted to legal and political strategies to create a highly conservative religious and socio-political agenda. The natural thelogy of the 17th century sought proofs about God in nature. It is difficult to offer proof of Primary Designer, primary cause or an explanation of primary causation. The

primary cause influences the secondary cause. If it cannot be explained, it is called a miracle. Ray published a book in 1691 *The Wisdom of God Manifested in the Works of Creation* citing examples based on studies in botany, anatomy, philosophy, physics and astronomy. The Bridgewater Treatises of the 1830s represent a most comprehensive work in Natural theology. The 8th Earl of Bridgewater left 8,000 pounds to finance the publication of *On the Power, Wisdom, and goodness of God as Manifested in the Creation.*

The theory of evolution was questioned by Creationists who followed the view that every organism appeared fully developed as we see. God created all living creatures and man in six days. Books like *Darwin On Trial, Of Pandas and People* and *The Wedge* were presented in court by the Discovery Institute during the trial in Dover, Pennsylvania against the Dover Science teachers and the school. The Dover School Board wanted to teach Creationism. According to the separation of religion and state under the United States Constitution, religious beliefs cannot be introduced in public institution of learning where the theory of evolution was taught as a tested scientific theory for generations supported by evidence from the fossils providing the missing links in the evolutionary tree. Darwin's Great Great Grandson Matthew Chapman was involved in this trial. Dover residents were not accepting the fact that humans are evolved from apes through evolutionary linkage. The National Center for Science Education had to bring in scientists to testify and explain scientific facts to the judge. The term 'Intelligent Design' replaced Creationism so that it did not appear to be religious and linked to the Hebrew Scriptures. Nearly 7000 pages were examined that revealed the deliberate change of words. That convinced the court of an attempt to disguise Creationism with Intelligent Design. Science teachers were under attack by the religious community. Creationism relies on doctrines based on faith. Evolution is based on evidence that could not be ignored.

Intelligent Design argues the irreducible complexity citing the flagellar mechanism fully equipped with motor for propulsion that could not be explained by evolution. There is evolutionary evidence from Darwin's record of adaptations and the causally related developments in the organ systems and organisms. The heart structure in fish with two chambers evolved to a three chambered heart in frog and a four chambered heart in mammals. Likewise external fertilization in fish and amphibians in water evolved into internal fertilization in the terrestrial environment. The causal interplay between organism and environment directed evolution over millions of years. All of the disciplines in the sciences have advanced our understanding of the universe, the physical world and the diversity of life during the past three centuries. However, the origin of life, self organization, and chemical processes involved in the creation of life still engage scientists to search for the clues. DNA and RNA have offered insights into the complexities of the early primordial environment and their role in perpetuating life. After a lengthy trial, the Judge gave his decision: Intelligent Design is not science, Intelligent Design is not a theory, and under the constitution it cannot be taught in a public school. More than 40 percent of American scientists believe in God. Most of the others believe in the transcendent. Scientific method leads to truth and understanding about nature, called methodological naturalism. This is good for science and religion. The American Scientific Affiliation is an organization of Christians who are fully dedicated to both the Bible and science. This organization debates questions from both spiritual and scientific perspective.

St. Augustine of Hippo was born to a Christian mother and a pagan father in 354 AD. He combined the Greek philosophy with the Christian beliefs and created a foundation for Christianity. He belonged to the Manichees, a popular sect in North Africa that refused blind faith, fideism, and accepted the power of reason to differenciate good and evil, light and darkness, ignorance and illumination. He was impressed by the interpretation of Scriptures by Ambrose and was baptized at the age of 33 and later became bishop. The current body of knowledge is essential for sound interpretation.

Credo ut intellegam means I believe so that I may understand.
Intellego ut Credam means I understand so that I may believe.
So what is the starting point? The answer:

Exercise of reason is necessary for *recta fides*, the right faith.

David Linden, a brain scientist, considers the human brain to be a true nightmare. Linden states that signals in the neurons propagate a million times slower than copper wires ranging from 0 to 1200 spikes per second. Neurons leak signals to their neighbors, and, on average, they successfully propagate their signals to their targets only about 30 percent of the time and are extremely inefficient. His scientific evidence also comes from the ASPM gene which codes for a protein in mitotic spindle crucial in determining the size of the cortex in the brain. Our knowledge at the human genome and of mouse, worm, and fruit fly clearly supports the theory of evolutionary development. Human brain evolved by adding more neurons on top of the existing ones so the frontal lobes can process additional information due to the added circuitry. The extraordinary perceptions and abilities have given us the ideas of mind, soul, consciousness, and our faith in spirits. Actually, the concept of spirits, even when elevated to the status of religion, retains its roots in the word spirituality. Archives of our brain have the experiences stored throughout our evolutionary history that become a part of our flash backs, memory and a jumbled matrix of events, places and settings in space and time. Feeling helpless in calamities and moments of extreme fear compelled humans to seek support and comfort from unseen entities in our mind. Successful outcomes reinforced the faith in whatever was perceived to be the source of help. Probably, mind created faith as a source of definitive help thus giving rise to rituals that were later made more powerful by adding sacrifice to assure the outcome. The elders, wise men, developed many variations unique to a clan, tribe, sect or religion differentiating various styles. (Linden 2007, 240-245)

The human brain is a complex analytical organ with auto pilot. The autonomous nervous system keeps us alive by running the vital bodily functions when we are asleep or unconscious. It also analyses the responses of our senses as they interact with the evnvironment and enables us to maintain our physical, physiological, and emotional integrity. Religion is based on faith and is beyond proof and scrutiny. Religious texts are an essential source of spiritual guidance to achieve balance in life. Science is based on evidence through research and is open to scrutiny by the scientific community to establish the validity of a theory. Every student deserves to be informed of the current status of scientific knowledge gained by the discoveries and the theories behind those breakthroughs in every field in the sciences, arts and humanities to become a well rounded citizen. It is the duty of parents, teachers, and society at large to educate children about the truth in science and religion. Religion and God offer the inspiration and faith for continued exploration. That is why the late Pope John Paul II said:

Religion and science are two wings on which human spirit rises to the contemplation of truth in search for truth.

MIND / BODY CONNECTION

Rene Descartes (1590-1650) believed that mind and body are two different entities. Dualism identified Physical Universe, with dimensions which occupies space. The mental realm is private, with privileged information i.e. thoughts, consciousness, hopes, fears and individual perception of motives, beliefs and faith. Mind has no dimensions or space. Descartes struggled with uncertainty about his knowledge. The Localization Theory was proposed by Francis Gall but his conclusions were based on the external bumps and depressions in skull with a limited sample of observation that labeled his Phrenology as pseudoscience. Advanced technology helped to discover specific centers in brain which control various actions in the body. Dualism as conceived by Descartes was wrong. The mind and the brain also have a linkage that perpetuates a seamless streaming of consciousness. Every discipline was a philosophy until systematization developed it to a status to establish disciplines in specific field of study. All the astronomers, mathematicians, physicists, anthropologists and biologists were philosophers for their love for knowledge and wisdom.

Meditation attracted attention for clinical research. In 1979 The Dalai Lama went to Harvard, and Herbert Benson discussed his research on meditation and its effect on stress and relaxation.

278

Benson knew about the Tibetan meditation called Tum-mo, the inner heat meditation that allowed monks to weather frigid temperatures. He asked for HH Dalai Lama's help to study Tibetan monks for his biofeedback research. Benson's research team videotaped monks on February 22, 1981 in Dharamsala, India in 39 degree Fahrenheit temperature and recorded the wet sheets over their shoulders releasing steam due to the heat released from the body of monks (Harrington 2008, 230-242). The Dalai Lama with his charisma, humor and happiness, facilitated the acceptance of the role of meditation and spirituality in medical community.

Purposeful relaxation processes have been used for 5000 years. Sleep temples were built in Greece in honor of Asclepios. The relaxation processes were regarded by the Greeks as divine intervention. Dr. James Braid, a Scottish physician demystified this phenomenon and called it hypnosis. There are almost 2500 books on mind/body connection and over a thousand on mind/body medicine (Harrington, 2008). The stories about mind/body medicine bring up issues that are medical, cultural and moral. The following discussion addresses an interaction of mind and body in different ways.

1. Power of suggestion: Mr. Wright was diagnosed with lymphosarcoma, cancer of the lymph nodes, and conventional therapies did not work. He gave up hope as he was running out of time, bedridden, gasping for breath. Then the news that the hospital he was in was selected to evaluate a new experimental drug Krebiozen. He begged to be included in the study and was given an injection on the weekend and he believed that it might be the miracle cure. Monday morning he was in high spirits walking around cheerfully. He was the only patient whose tumors had shrunk considerably. In the meantime the newspaper reported conflicting results about the effectiveness of the drug and Mr. Wright happened to read it. He relapsed but was promised to give the medicine when the next batch arrived. There was no new shipment of Krebiozen but Mr. Wright was given an injection of distilled water. He recovered and flew back home. He read the announcement of American Medical

Association that this drug was not effective. Mr Wright relapsed and was admitted to the hospital where he died in two days. The Placebo was viewed as quackery by some but it became a part of medical practice when doctors could not do anything by conventional means and tried the power of suggestion as an alternative.

2. <u>Mesmerism</u>: During the 18th century Anton Mesmer used purposeful relaxation process in Paris and Vienna creating profound change in body and behaviour. Mesmerization is the term used to indicate total submersion and submission to someones looks or actions named after Anton Mesmer. The medical community dropped it in early 19th century. It survived as a stage act for entertainment but remained on the back burner. Under the new name of 'hypnosis' it again became a part of treatment used by the medical community.

Hypnosis: French neurologist Jean-Martin Charcot was a highly respected physician of his time. He gave a lecture in 1882 describing hypnosis and its therapeutic application in patients suffering from hysteria (convulsions, paralyses, feelings of choking, tunnel vision). He described its three phases: Catalepsy, loss of will and rigidity of muscles; Lethargy, an unconscious state and increased muscle activity; Somnambulism, the hypnotic trance. Hypnosis was used in research manipulating the nervous system of patients in a controlled manner. Hippolyte Bernheim (1840-1919) was Charcot's critic but embraced the idea of suggestion and defined it as influence provoked by an idea suggested and accepted by the brain. Dr. James Fisdale prepared his patients for surgery with hypnotic relaxation. Dr. James Young Simpson discovered chloroform. It was adopted by the medical community as chemical anesthetic agent. During the search for a non-chemical anesthesia as an alternative for cancer patients by the National Institue of Health in 1995, hypnosis was found to be the most effective alternative. This was accepted as a treatment to alleviate pain in all patients.

According to Dr. Fredric Mau, a practioner in hypnosis, in Columbia, South Carolina, relaxation is essential to relieve stress. Stress elevates levels of the hormone cortisol which leads to higher blood pressure, lowered immunity, higher LDL (bad) cholesterol, lower HDL (good) cholesterol, decreases bone density and muscle tissue, and impaires cognitive performance. Clearly, mind influences body function. Electroencephalogram (EEG) registers brain wave cycles. A state of stress shows 20 cycles per second. When you are enjoying the activity you love and get totally engrossed in it, that is Alpha level relaxation registering 9 to 14 cycles per second. Sleep cycles vary between 4 and 1.5 per second. Deep sleep is Delta level relaxation when dreams happen. Feeling drowsy or half asleep and nodding off in the couch, one experiences Theta level relaxation which produces brain waves 9 to 4 cycles per second. In this state the cortisol drops and the feel-good hormones beta endorphins and serotonin increase. This is the state when hypnotists start their suggestions (commands). Hypnotic processes influence the mind and body through visualization and perception. Irritable bowel syndrome (IBS) is a stress related ailment. The research of Giacomo Rizzolatti and Vittorio Gallese with monkeys led to the discovery of mirror neurons, the brain cells that respond to an observed behavior as if the observer is acting. This capacity of the brain makes you cry while watching sad episode in a movie or break into laughter when watching a humorous, joyful act. Hypnosis creates a positive change in mind and body. It has been used to cure obesity, smoking and other ailments (11:11, July-August, 2008. 17-19).

3. <u>Confession</u>: Sin hangs heavily on the mind which reflects on the body. Clear conscience is deemed therapeutic as it brings relief from the weight of guilt. It was believed that sin corrupts body and mind. The Confession Booth at Church offers this treatment that is reinforced in Christian tradition.

> Confess your faults one to another, and pray one for another, that ye may be healed. (James 5:16)

4. <u>Psychoanalysis</u>: Anna O is quoted as one of the most famous cases in psychoanalysis. She suffered from bad memories (Harrington 2008, 72-75). The studies emphasized later that one cannot ignore emotional baggage. Hysteria is one of those illnesses. Sexual abuse by a family member in childhood and its

trauma is not expressed due to shame and the worst deterrent of such talk is that no one believes it, rather no one wants to face it. So, such trauma lies buried, undermining self esteem and confidence. This was not discussed in the 19th century. Freud shifted from trauma to fantasy in psychosexual development and remembering events for curing neurosis. Psychologist Pierre Janet introduced the idea of 'suggested forgetting'. Flanders Dunbar discussed instances in her book *Emotions and Bodily Change* that suppressed emotions produced specific ailments in the body, implying that body responds with disease symptoms.

5. <u>Power of Positive Thinking</u>: Dr. Robert Buckman attended a lecture by Dr. Bernie Siegel who talked about two oncologists testing a combination of four drugs in chemotherapy with initials EPHO. One doctor reported 75% of patients doing remarkably well while another doctor observed improvement in only 25 % of his patients in that trial. The first doctor had rearranged the letters of drugs to read 'HOPE' and the power of positive thinking was the therapeutic agent. According to Dr. Bernie Siegel there are no incurable diseases, only incurable patients. Norman Vincent Peale (1898-1993) was a Methodist preacher for 52 years. He wrote the book *The Power of Positive Thinking* in 1952. His message was: Believe in yourself, have faith in your abilities. This introduced medical applications, Placebo Effect, Holistic Medicine, and Psychoneuroimmunology.

6. <u>Cure by Faith</u>: In 1876 Pope declared Lourdes as a holy place for pilgrimage and healing. Since this was brushing with miracle, a commission of Catholic doctors was established to identify the healings that were acceptable on the basis of 'medical inexplicability'. Bernheim believed that religious belief and power of faith stimulated the power of mind. Jean-Martin Carcot was convinced by the psycho-physiological power of faith and published the book *The Faith Cure* in 1892.

Christian Science: Mary Baker Eddy (1821-1910) is the founder of the Church of Christ, Scientist. She was born in Bowin, New Hampshire. In church, a preacher stated: The saved and the damned are destined to be so by God. She resisted that theology and did not go to that church. She was a sickly person and heard of mesmerism based on Christian principles practiced by Phineas Parkhurst Quimby which cured the ills by right thinking and power of mind. She went to Quimby and was cured. She wrote the book *Science and Health* in 1875. This book is like the Bible in Mary Baker Eddy's church that was established in 1879.

7. <u>New Thought</u>: The movement sought health through prayers and visualization to open the mind to receive healing. William James, a Harvard psychologist, was a student of this movement and said: The greatest discovery of my generation is that man can alter his life simply by altering his attitude of mind.

8. <u>The Law of Attraction</u>: Rhonda Byrnes has sparked interest on a global scale with her book and film, The Secret. Simran Singh believes that we are powerful beings having the ability to co-create with the universe if body, mind, and spirit work with feelings, vision, and focus. Through this collaboration and thoughtful conversation... a human being's interior landscape becomes a personal movie that we write, produce, act in, and be an observer as well (11:11, July-Aug. 2008).
The wave of consciousness and meditation convinced professionals about the physiological benefits. Physicians and psychologists gave these practices authenticity to make them into a phenomenon of the modern times. There was an infusion of cultural practices like yoga, meditation and consciousness which targeted the stress caused by the brisk pace of the materialistic world and its daily grind. Hypertension was the medical term that referred to stress, a cause of so many ailments directly linked to mind and body. Homeopathy and herbal medicine also staked a niche in the popular culture worldwide. In a way, these professionals have given credibility to the old practices of the East and West, and humanity rises above the artificial diversity in faiths to bask in universal spirituality. Meditation is an escape where time is devoted to contemplation in order to connect to ones inner feelings, become aware of deeper thoughts, and listen to the sub-conscious mind.

9. Energy Healing: Dr. Eric Pearl has made a contribution in the realm of mind/body medicine through transpersonal healing using ones inherent energy. He explains the progression through 'Voluntary Attention' to manifest the 'Connection', by connecting to the source which in turn triggers 'Self Regulation' to establish 'Order'. The order brings about 'Ease' eliminating the 'dis-ease' through mind/body connection (Pearl 2007).

Techniques like transcendental meditation, prayer, yoga, positive thinking reinforce faith. Biofeedback has shown that body functions can be controlled by concentration of the mind and has popularized the need for Mind/Body connection. The reversal and total elimination of major ailments without conventional medicine are miraculous and defy explanation. Transcendental astrology and alchemy are the contemplation of eternal truths in the symbols offered by the stars and the combinations of substances confirming the essence of unification as stated by Simone Weil (Gravity and Grace, 1952). The philosophy of Epictetus, a Greek philosopher, a former slave, is embodied in the Serenity Prayer. Reinhold Niebuhr, a Protestant is credited with this prayer:

> God, grant me the serenity
> to accept the things I cannot change,
> courage to change the things I can,
> and wisdom to know the difference.

This prayer has been adopted by Alcoholics Anonymus with the understanding that if we accept God's Will, the major portion of the problem is solved by establishing parasympathetic dominance thus restoring optimal immunity and metabolic function. The heart rate slows down and the blood pressure falls signaling the comforting relaxation achieved by the magic of prayer. A study at Duke University noted the effect of prayer.

POWER OF PRAYER

Don Piper went to attend Baptist General Convention of Texas at Trinity Pines on the north shore of Lake Livingston in Texas. On his way back to Alvin, around noon, an eighteen wheeler

veered across the lane on a narrow bridge and was killed.
The collision occurred at 11:45 A.M. He had no pulse and was
considered dead in his smashed car covered under the tarp. Dick
Overecker had also attended the Baptist Convention and was
stuck in the traffic jam due to the accident. Dick arrived at the
scene and felt a compulsion to pray for the victim. He took it as a
message from God. He walked upto the car where the victim's
body lay covered under the tarp. He checked his pulse but here
was none. This did not deter him and he started praying with his
heart and soul. Looking at the badly mangled body he prayed
specifically for safety of his head and chest areas. Dick started
singing "What a Friend We Have in Jesus". Don, who had no
pulse, started to sing with him. He heard the sounds and felt a
squeeze on his hand after 90 minutes, the time he believes he
spent in heaven (Piper, 2004). Dick wishes for such prayer all the
time. Don Piper survived to share his near death experience
(NDE). He experienced a brilliant light and the feeling of being
in heaven. He saw Joe Kulbeth, his grand father, his great grand
mother Hattie Mann who stood upright with a smile and shiny
white teeth. He recalled her as a humped lady with wrinkled
face with no teeth in her mouth. The light became brighter and
the sounds were pleasant. Sound of Hallelujah and Glory to
God cast away all anxieties, worries and no needs. He witnessed
irredescent gate leading to the street paved with gold bricks. He
was part of the choir. Don himself became an angel for Walter
Foster, a 20 year old student who was obsessed with the NDE
experience of heaven. Walter died of heart attack and probably
was getting ready for heaven.

Jas had a heart attack and went into a coma for seven days. I
visited him in ICU where he was hooked to a resipartor. I felt
like comforting him and began to message his arms, legs, and
shoulders. I prayed to see him as the same jovial person he was.
I visited him a week later. He said: "I remember seeing you, you
sprinkled holy water on my arm, the drops had very beautiful
fragrance and shining like pearls which pulled me out of coma".
He believed in God and miracles for the first time. I was just an
instrument but God's grace gave Jas another chance at life.
Every life has a meaning and we are all here for a purpose.

MIRACULOUS EVENTS

Yogi Paramhansa Yogananda writes episodes in *Autobiography of a Yogi* (1946) that were miracles. He visited a perfumed sage who created the fragrance of jasmine in his palm as he requested. He met a levitating sage who defied the laws of gravity. He experienced the simultaneous appearance of the same person interacting at another place while talking to him at that time. The other person he saw came to see the yogi and confirmed it. He witnessed the arrival of his Guru in person to bless him years after his funeral.

A young engineer married a lady, a child psychologist. They started a new life in the United States. They tried everything and could not have a child . They resorted to IVF (in vitro fertization) treatment. They tried every reputable lab, the top physicians with long experience but were not successful. Finally they made appointment with the world's leading IVF expert in Brussels, Belgium and booked tickets to go there. Disheartened with the technology and the efforts of specialists with enormous expense, they turned to God with prayer from the heart after they had exhausted all other avenues. As they were scheduled to go to Brussels, her pregnancy was clinically confirmed. They now have a beautiful daughter and a son.

Our daughter suffered from endometriosis and leading fertility clinics precluded any chances of her pregnancy. She was heart broken and devastated at the prognosis. We consoled her that we have'nt sought blessing from the ultimate source yet and to have faith. We prayed for our daughter that weekend in all humility and fully accepting God's Will. Our prayers were answered and the Almighty God blessed her with a beautiful daughter defying the opinion of medical experts. She gave birth to a son two years later. The physicians at prestigious fertility clinics were in awe and had no explanation. The disappearance of the tumors, remission of cancer without any conventional medical treatment has surprised physicians about the healing power of prayer and faith.

My grandfather was directed towards the spiritual path by a holy master. As a young boy he was engaged in the activities usual for his age. The spiritual master sent a message to see him right away. The master told him to abandon other activities and to follow the spiritual path from that day forward. The suggestion was divine and overpowering. He started the spiritual training and earned his guru's acceptance. He gained spiritual awareness. He was preparing two potential followers who could be initiated to do the spiritual work after him. Both trainees engaged in meditation to acquire spiritual strength. One day one of them requested my grandfather to help cure his friend who had developed a terminal disease. He was advised not to interfere in God's plans. The disciple insisted and felt that he has acquired the power to cure his friend. He was advised not to engage in such a show of power to alter destiny. The disciple still went ahead, started meditation on his own, and focused on his friend's recovery. His friend began to improve. As his friend was recovering, he was getting sick himself with the symptoms of the same disease. He panicked and begged master for mercy and realized his mistake. But it was too late and he had to bear the consequences for interfering in God's Will. This disciple finally succumbed to this terminal disease but his friend, a tailor by profession, lived for decades. This tremendous energy that dwells in our mind can be harnessed for good deeds. This is the force that sages use for good actions without interfering with the Will of God. Spirituality is: acceptance, faith, forgiveness, peace and love (Siegel 1990, 178).

The power of positive thinking has become very popular and has helped lots of people in all walks of life. The prerequisite to the success still is faith. This has been worded differently to use phrases like *intuitive knowing* or *visioning*. The requirements still include the intensity and sincerity of your feelings, clarity of mind, and faith in the outcome. The procedure involves the same devotion that is essential for a truly sincere meaningful prayer that engages power of the mind with full concentration. My wife and I enjoyed a concert of Marina Lozamov, a pianist of international fame who was trained at the Kiev conservatory,

Julliard, and Eastman schools of music. Her words portray the vision that drives her: "There's always, for me, one sound or image that forms in my head as to how the music should go. It's a very strong impulse, even if I wanted to do less, I couldn't because it's either that way or no way at all. What does she think when she performs? She replied: You don't really think because there's no time for it. Thinking is what you do during practice. A good performance is a reaction honed to the point where everything becomes one: your emotion, your interpretation, your fingers, your mind – all fused into one. You don't think about what to do next or how to phrase it, it just comes and you can't stop the flow. You don't want to.

HEAVEN AND HELL

Heaven has been visualized as a most blissful place in all faiths and religions. The imagery varies according to the priest, Qazi, or pundit delivering the sermons. Hell has been portrayed where fires burn and the damned inhabitants scream in terror. The desire to go to heaven and the threat of burning in hell are etched on people's minds. It plays a major role in belief systems based on religious texts, and is viewed in different ways in world religions. It has been interpreted by the priests, pundits and mullahs to preach righteousness. Heaven is envisioned to be a place for the beatific vision in the presence of God where ultimate eternal bliss and peace is experienced.

JUDAISM: The Old Testament indicates heaven to be a transcendant abode of the living God. Believers can ascend to a place joined with God as in Old Testament accounts of Enoch (cf. Gn 5:24) and Elijah (cf. 2 Kgs 2:11). Heaven's grandeur is expressed as Heaven of Heavens in the Hebrew Bible as a magnificient place (Deut. 10:14; cf I Kgs 8:27). In the Pseudep there is an expression of seven heavens (Test. Levi 3; Slavonic Enoch). The Enoch in Old Testament mentions a transcendent dwelling of living God which is connected to a place where, through grace, believers can ascend (cf. Gn 5:24) and Elijah (cf. 2 Kgs 2:11) with a reward in heaven.

CHRISTIANITY: Christians believe that it is a reward for the righteous (Mt 5:12). However, God is not identified with heaven and cannot be contained in it (cf. 1 Kgs 8:27). First Book of Maccabees refers to Heaven as God's name (Mc 3:18, 19, 50, 60; 4:24, 55). Holy Father loves believers and they are raised with Christ to become citizens of heaven. Platonic philosophy embraced by Philo of Alexandria (20-45 BCE), influenced the thinking of Christian theologians. Jacob's ladder is a symbol; an expression of a staircase between earth and heaven. In heaven, the soul joins the divine realm of angels. Pope John Paul II stated in Vatican on July 2, 1999:

People who repent for sinful activity are sent to Purgatory according to Catholic view, to be completely purified for entry into heaven. The righteous are rewarded with an access to heaven and hell is a place where fires torture the sinners. Bible says: Do not store treasures on earth but in heaven where moth and rust do not destroy and thieves do not steal (Matthew 6:19-20). It is evident in biblical metaphor that God does not identify himself with heaven and cannot be bounded by it (cf. 1 Kgs 8:27). According to New Testament, Christ loves the believers, and they are raised with Christ to dwell in heaven.

Hell is a place for those who reject God (Thessalonians 1:8, 9):
   "In flaming fire taking vengeance on them that know not God,
   and that obey not the gospel of our Lord Jesus Christ:
   Who shall be punished with everlasting destruction from the
   Presence of the Lord, and from the glory of his power."

ISLAM: Heaven is called *Bahisht* in Islam. On the day of judgement the deeds of human beings during ones life are evaluated. Only Allah knows about the day of judgement. The righteous believers will go to paradise where they will live for ever and have pleasure from each of the senses (Koran 2: 81-82). In heaven the trees of gold bear perpetual fruits and provide comfort in shade. The highest of the seven heavens is called *Firdaus* where the pious people, the prophets, the martyrs and the most truthful faithfuls live. This offers ecstatic consciousness of God. There are seven levels of heaven in Islam. ...Who do good works and believe in Him, will be offered gardens, rivers, and pure companions (Koran, Surah IV-57 and 70-35). Paradise offers delights of flesh where the faithfuls meet young beautiful damsels called Hoors or Apsaras. This sentence has been misinterpreted by extremists to lure faithfuls to become martyrs in the name of religion. There are seven heavens and seven underworlds. These fourteen spheres are called *Tabuks* in Islam. Zoroastrians believe that the soul passes over the Bridge of Requiter that opens to allow easy passage for the good to enter into heaven. Hell in Islam is called *Dozakh* and has seven types where the damned are chained and tortured with varying level of intensity in the fire of hell:

1. Johunum: Purgatory hell
2. Laza: Blazing fire
3. Ai-Hutamah: Intense fire
4. Saerr: Flaming fire
5. Saqar: Scorching fire
6. Al-Jahim: Huge hot fire
7. Hawayah: Bottomless pit

HINDUISM: According to Hindu cosmology there are three realms called lokas namely, Heaven, Earth, and netherworlds. The latter includes sky and the underworlds. Seven lokas are above the earth as seven heavens, and in multiples of seven there are fourteen or twenty one below the earth. The Upanishads in the 3rd century BCE influenced the religious outlook. The God Indra reigns over many heavens, the shrine of waters. In another realm, according to Rig Veda, Yama, son of Vivasat is in power where prayers for immortality are recited constantly.

> Make me immortal in the realm, where movement is
> accordant to wish, in the third region, third heaven of
> heavens; where the worlds are resplendent.
> For Indra, flow thou on, Indu!
> Make me immortal in that realm where all wishes
> and longings go, where spreads the Radiant One's
> region, with holy bliss and happiness.
> For Indra, flow thou on, Indu!
> Make me immortal in that realm where beatitude,
> Joy, cheers, and transports of delight abound;

Where the highest desires have been fulfilled.
For Indra, flow thou on, Indu!
(Rig Veda 9.113.8-11)

BUDDHISM: The Wheel of Life: Being born, living a life, and dying. Dying is a process to be born in another plane of existence. Death is Birth. The 'spirit' is eternal. Body is a temporary garment which clothes the spirit. The wheel of life applies to all, an opportunity to acquire The Great Mirror Wisdom and Immaculate Consciousness on the Diamond Path. After that there is no retribution (Rampa 1966, 101-102).

Buddha body is formless and without substance. It is Enlightenment which will never disappear. It is reflected in 3 ways with one spirit and purpose. *The Teaching of Buddha,* Kyokai 1966, 50-54.
> Essence (Dharma-kaya)
> Potantiality (Sambhoga-kaya)
> Manifestation (Nirmana-kaya)

No one can stop the aging process and avoid death. The life of existence, which is impermanent, is a life of suffering.

SIKHISM: Heaven and hell have been used as metaphors in Sikh Scriptures. Heavenly feeling is acquired through the elixir of the word called Shabd Guru and through the company of the holy people. The theo-philosophical heaven is known through good deeds that gives spiritual ascendancy and peace of mind. A state of mind tortured by anguish due to animal instincts and misdeeds paints a picture of hell in this life with worries, fear and pain from family issues and physical suffering. In the words of sage Kabir (AGGS, p. 325):
> One does not know where heaven is, but
> > everyone claims to know and plans to go there.
> By mere talk, the mind is not appeased.
> > The mind is only appeased when ego is vanquished.
> As long as the mind is filled with desire for heaven,
> > one does not dwell near God's feet.
> Unto whom should I tell this?
> > The Holy Communion with the Holy is heaven".

291

The Sikh Scriptures mention God's existence in fourteen Lokas as well as in all his creation (AGGS p. 840). Heaven is depicted in God's creation and among people who sing praises of the Lord through his word and righteous deeds. True awareness is attained in the company of Sages which saves from worldly pain (Dhaliwal, 2006).

> Everyone in paradise, on earth and in the dark world are
> involved in maya, the desires, attachments and lures
> of the world and only by reciting the word,one can
> liberate the soul. Only a rare person, with the grace of
> God, can comprehend this logic (AGGS p. 576).

Wisdom is a reflection of the mind. The theo-philosophical heaven is the mental state of bliss. Mind wanders in both heavenly and hellish thoughts. Only God's Word can offer enlightenment. Indulgence in the animal instincts leads towards a life of hell, Godly instincts and good deeds provide peaceful glimpses of heaven (AGGS p. 1345). According to the Sikh philosophy there is no heaven or hell. These are mythological places that have empowered the organized religions to create a fear of burning in hell or rewards of virgins in flights of fancy because no one has seen heaven and no one can survive the fires of hell to tell about it.

Following verses of sage Trilochan (1267-1335) reflect on after-life (AGGS, p.526):

> In final momemts, if one think of money,
>   reincarnates as a snake.
> In final moments, if one yearns for a woman,
>   comes back to be a prostitute in next life.
> In final moments, if one longs for sons,
>   returns as a boar in the next life.
> In final moments, if one thinks of temple,
>   soul becomes a ghost, a spirit.
> If in the final moments, one remembers God,
>   God welcomes and grants salvation, God dwells in mind.

Guru Nanak declared that God is a spirit (energy) that permeates everywhere and in everything, animate or inanimate. Sikhs do not believe in heaven and hell to be physical places in the after-life. Guru Nanak questioned: If we are rewarded to be in heaven or condemned to burn in the fires of hell, then how the very first creation was judged as no deeds existed to be judged on? There was no heaven or hell at that time. If our lives are blessed and fulfilled, heaven is right here; if we are suffering from worries, illness, and family life in ruins, what else is hell? God is always forgiving, and will not punish his own children. If we know and observe God's presence at every moment, then there is no room for ego, deceit, crime, treachery, or adultery. If humanity can firmly eradicate expectations, there is no reason for any disappointment which breeds suffering of all kinds.

HEAVEN: A Global Perspective

Heaven as a metal strip Hebrew (Gen. 1:6-8; Pss. 19:1; 150:1)

Heaven as a curtain (Isa. 40:22; Rig Veda VIII.6.5; Egyptian Book of the Dead. Ch. 85).

Heaven as a garment (Iranian Zend Avesta. Yasht. 13:3; Yasna 30:5; burummu; cf. In Ezek. 27:24).

The windows of heaven (Gen.7:11; 8:2; II Kgs. 7:2, 19).

The bottles of heaven (Job 38:37) Turkish expression; In Rig Veda, It Rains (V. 83. 7-8).

The promptuaries of heaven (Ps. 135:7; Jer. 10:13; 51:16; Enoch 18:1; II Esd. 4:5, the hail, Job 38:22; darkness, Isa. 45:3).

The stages of heaven (Job 26:11; cf. I Kgs 8:27; Ps. 48:4; Test. Levi 3; Talmud, Hag. 12; Koran Sura 22:4; II Cor. 12:2).

The Pillars of heaven (Job 26:11; cf. Milton, Paradise Regained, book IV, line 455: the pillar's frame of heaven. Comus, line 597: the pillar'd firmament. (Dhaliwal, 2006: with permission from IUS Canada).

PROPHECIES AND ASTROLOGY

Israel is obligated to perform the ideals of covenants. The Jewish Temple was central to their faith. Moses predicted destruction of the Temple for ignoring commandments as he had warned that God would withdraw protection. The Assyrians attacked the Temple in 722 BCE. The Babylonians seized the Temple in 587 BC. and Jews were forced into exile. Isaiah had warned about the coming disaster urging obedience to covenants to assure unity (Isaiah 1:4, 1:7). Jeremiah made prediction that the Temple would be destroyed due to the degradation of deeds (Jeremiah 7:3-4, 14). Isaiah saw the Temple as God's residence that had to be always maintained with devotion. Ezekiel was exiled when he was 23 years old and he prophesied hope, forgiveness, and renewal :

> I will gather you and bring you back to your homeland from many lands to one place (Ez 36: 24; 37: 10-12).

The knowledge of the material world as we see, feel and experience it, is the comprehension of our physical sensory faculties. Spiritual thoughts, ancient stories, and manifestations of miraculous feats with abstract assertions and conclusions are based on the energy waves that we cannot see, feel, touch, or hear. Obviously these play a significant role in the abilities of healers, clairvoyants, astrologers and those famous seers endowed with prophetic abilities like Nostradamus and Edgar Casey to foresee future events. The abilities to predict events have withstood the scrutiny of scholars and historians. Astrology, numerology, and psychic phenomena all over the world have been practiced and experienced for thousands of years. Horoscopes still guide people to make important decisions. In India, astrologers predict and write the life history of the newly born child on decorated scrolls. This was done for kings, nobility and others who wanted it done. It is practiced today. Palmists require exact date, time of birth, and birth place, to prepare horoscope. Numerologists are particular about the numbers in the date of birth to predict the events in the future. This information is heavily relied on in eastern cultures to decide auspicious occasions like marriage, buying a house or travel. Pundits suggest wearing appropriate stones, precious or semi-precious, to perform rituals and give donations to ward off the adverse influence of the cosmic configuration of stars. Some cultures believe that we are passengers in life's journey and they0 believe that universe recycles our souls which transmigrate through incarnations. Our progress is based on the progression or regression we make during our lifetime traversing through the maze of sensory distractions that are part of the obstacle course of life.

PERSONAL PROPHECY
(The Bhrigu Story)

Sage Bhrigu, a revered seer in Hindu mythology, prophesied the events for countless configurations of stars and their location in the 12 sectors (houses) making a celestial grid called kundli. An old manuscript written in Sanskrit was recovered by a scholar familiar with Vedic treatises and historic figures in Hindu mythology. Bhrigu Shaster is believed to be a compilation of narrations by sage Bhrigu through cosmic knowledge that were written by scribe named Shukar.

The descendants of a family living in Hoshiarpur in Northern India had acquired a portion of this huge manuscript and indexed it to retrieve information based on combinations of stars in the particular celestial grid. The fragile pages of ancient writings are kept in plastic sleeves. The remaining part of this manuscript was torn page by page as wrapping paper by a grocer, oblivious of the prophetic information written on those pages. A large portion of this record was lost for ever. The documented story of my personal life as outlined in Bhrigu Shaster (manuscript) has been confirmed so far. The prophesied events are written as 'Reading' followed by comments under 'Response'.

I arrived in Hoshiarpur in Punjab, India on Tuesday, March 10, 1964 with my wife, two year old son, and my mother-in-law. I was curious to know about my plans of going abroad for higher education. Indices were brought by the attendant one stack at a time containing thousands of celestial diagrams (kundlis) and we started the search for my specific diagram as it appeared on my horoscope developed at the time of my birth by a Pundit in Kashmir. All of us searched for hours, and it was almost lunch time. We were tired and ready to take a lunch break. Finally the exact chart was found and all of us felt relieved. We informed the attendant to retrieve the record while we go for lunch. I was anxious to know what this document could reveal about my life. Bhrigu reader brought the pages secured in plastic sleeves.

Reading: The name of this celestial combination is Chakar Vartik. This person in his last life was born in Kashatri (warrior) caste. He lived in a city on the banks of river Sutlej in India with his family. He was a wise and wealthy businessman. There were all kinds of comforts in his home but he did not have a son. He had three daughters. I can see this due to the ability of cosmic vision. I am screening all his good and bad deeds of his past life. He will be rewarded accordingly during this life at various times. He passed away at the age of 77 years in the same city. This soul did not go into any other form of life. He is born as a man again. The same soul has taken birth under this combination of stars. Now I will narrate the events of his current lifetime. It will be the 5064th year of Kaliyug and this person will come to hear my words. His name will start with the word Ajit. He will be born in the month of Poh (December) on a Friday, the 6th day of Shukal Paksh in the house of his father by the name of Charan. This person will keep long hair. During his 31st year he will come wherever my manuscript will be at that time. He will be accompanied by his wife, mother like lady and his child. When this happens, he will hear my words. It will be a Tuesday, 2nd day of Krishi Paksh (10th day) in the month of Phagun (March). This is a pre-destined date and time and is not a sudden event.

Response: My name is Ajit and my father's name is Charan. I was born on December 22nd. The visit was on March 10, 1964, during my 31st Year, with the family members mentioned in the reading. According to this the Kaliyug started in the year 3,100 BCE which was confirmed by Dr. Seshagiri Rao (Editor of the Encyclopedia of Hinduism). I was utterly astonished, especially to see my name, my father's name which I could read, the day and date, and the specific family members who were with me. The reading mentioned a health problem and offered the special natural remedy to counteract any ailments. I followed the instructions with faith. I was advised to recite one spiritual verse in mind as many times as possible. That verse has been on auto recitation mode ever since except for moments of distraction. I have enjoyed good health all my life. I was directed for 3 things: Meditate on the verse, Medicine, and Charity from the heart.

Reading:This person will take birth under Raj (Royalty) configuration of stars. He will be thoughtful, intelligent and influential person pursuing higher education. He will work in the teaching profession. His rise will start at age of 23 and will achieve progress. However, the real recognition and achievements will come later.

Response: I joined as Lecturer after graduation with a Master's degree, and I was appointed Assistant Professor three years later at Punjab Agricultural University, Ludhiana, India.

Reading:At the time of this visit there will be thoughts of going abroad for higher education. His studies will be in the field of science. There will be some opposition to the idea, there will be road blocks but by following the suggested guidelines he will achieve his goal. He will devote four years for advanced studies abroad between the ages of 32 and 36 and will be successful. After that at the age of 37 he will lead a successful and comfortable life. His prestige will grow and he will achieve a high office in his profession.

Response: I got assistantship from the University of British Columbia, Vancouver, Canada and was admitted to Ph.D program in the Department of Biology. Upon graduation I came to South Carolina in the United States and joined as Associate Professor of Biology in 1969.

Reading: This person will have two sons and two daughters. Both sons will be blessed, handsome and well educated. The first son will be born under 'Kirk Arurh' influence of celestial configuration. This son was also his son during the lifetime previous to last. It is the same soul that will be his son in this life. This child will face some problems but after taking the suggested medicine as prescribed he will be fine and will avoid the ailments. This child will be healthy and will live a long life.

Response: We have two sons. Our first son Harmit (Mitti) was born on September 27, 1962 in India. My wife and son came to Vancouver, Canada to join me. My son graduated from Wofford College and was commissioned into the United States Army Chemical Corps. As Company Commander, he was in the

297

Middle East during the campaign Desert Storm. He joined the National Army Reserve and retired as Major. He is working with Johnson and Johnson Pharmaceutical Company as Institutional Business Director.

In patriarchal societies, sons were the heirs and the daughters future was linked with husband's life. Only the birth of two daughters was mentioned in the reading without any comments.

Simmi, our daughter graduated from Fashion Institute of Technology in New York, published a book on Fashion, and worked twenty years in family clothing business. She felt a calling and joined spiritual school to go on the spiritual path. She became a life coach and publishes a magazine 11:11 devoted to spirituality and anchors radio show 11:11.

Nikki, our second daughter, a graduate in accounting and finance is a social person with a vibrant personality. She served as Legislator in South Carolina House of Representatives for three terms successfully. She is running for Governor in the 2010 elections.

Reading: Second son will be born under 'Tula Arurh' celestial influence. This son will have the best luck of all siblings and will be a well known personality. He will be a blessed soul who has done great deeds in his last life. He will only be born after the charitable donations, meditations and taking the prescribed medicine. The blessed souls appear only after the parents have done good deeds.

Response: Our second son, Charan (Gogi) was born on December 23, 1976. My parents came to the United States to see their grandson. United States was celebrating Bicentennial in 1976. He is artistic, spiritual, and established his band. He graduated in Electrical Engineering and Computer Engineering. He started his web design company. He arranged fund raisers for the children hospital, organized events to feed the homeless and worked with businesses to provide clothing for them, and arranged recruiters of companies to facilitate employment for those living on the streets in Atlanta, Georgia.

Reading: This person will marry an educated, intelligent, good natured lady. She will be from a high class family. She had relations with him in previous life. It is a blessing that souls come together again after a separation for many incarnations. This person will enjoy long life with his wife.

Response: My wife, Raj studied Law at Delhi Unsiversity in India. She came from a respected wealthy family. She graduated with a Masters degree in Education in United States and taught in the Public School System for 7 years. She started her own business in 1976 and won the SBA's South Carolina Small Business Person of the Year Runner-Up award in 2002 and continues to run a successful business.

Reading: This person has the Sun line on his hand but its full influence will be realized by wearing Suraj Kant Mani (Moon Stone). This will offer peace of mind, bring success and protect from the bad intentions of the unfamiliar persons. This person will have an even more comfortable life after 40 years. At the age of 45 he will be at the highest position in his profession. He will be financially well off. He will have all the comforts, means of transportation, and people to help. At the age of 65, there is a big health problem and after that there will be no other health issues. At the age of .. he will complete his life. His wife will leave a short time earlier.

Response: I have lived a peaceful life. I was Professor and Chairman, Division of Natural Sciences at the age of 45 and was financially comfortable. I was diagnosed with Lymphoma at the age of 65. Dr. Robert Smith Jr., my Oncologist informed me about the malignant tumor, but he assured me in the same breath that he can take care of it which he did indeed. I accepted this as God's Will and had no despair or sorrow. Actually, I could not justify any complaint because I have had a perfectly healthy life without any hospitalization until then. The following verses came up (AGGS, p. 724) when opened (*parkash*) during the morning worship the day after I was told about lymphoma:

Blessings, Blessings, God's Blessings,
Do not worry, God will protect You...

This assurance, coupled with accepting the Will of God gave me strength and faith. I had forgotten about the Bhrigu reading and

299

suddenly one day I looked it up. That's where the 65th year was described to pose big health problem. The reading ended with the following general statement:

As the present life reflects the outcome of previous life's deeds and assessments, the same way, the nature and quality of deeds in this life will determine the outcome for the next life.

GREAT SEERS AND PROPHECIES

St. MALICHI was a bishop in Ireland during the 12th century. He predicted that there will be 111 popes. The 107th pope will be pastor and sailor. That Pope was Pope John, patriarch of Venice. Pope Paul VI was prophetically mentioned as 'flower among flowers. He was regarded a lily among lilies during his day. The final pope will be unnumbered and will be 'Peter the Rome'. Scholars of prophecy consider Pope Benedict and Peter the Rome as one and the same (History Channel).

MOTHER SHIFTON's prophecies mentioned the electric bulb, flight of man and women in trousers like men.

ROBERT ZOLLER is a Medieval astrologer and is regarded as a modern day Nostradamus. In 1997, he predicted younger Bush as President, conflict with Osama bin Laden and Saddam Hussain. He warned about the greatest period of danger in September 2001.

MAYA PROPHECIES

The Maya had advanced knowledge of astronomy and used it as a prophetic tool. They were obsessed with time. They believed what happened in the past will occur again as history progresses in cycles and rythms. Their mythical beginning was on August 13, 3114 BCE. Five cycles of 5125 years each bring an end of that period. Four cycles have passed and we are in the fifth cycle ending on December 21, 2012. The Maya believed that the Sun got its energy through sacrifices with stone-knife that excised the living heart.

The next cosmic event is predicted to be at the December solstice when the Sun aligns itself every 26,000 years in the center of Milky Way leading to the wobbling of the Earth on its axis, called precession. The Precessional Cycle, according to Bruce Schofield, is at the root of Maya culture. It is for transformation and renewal. Their prophecy refers to the following events:

      1690: Cultures in disarray.
      1776: American and French Revolution.
      1855: American Civil War.
      1960: Political assassination.
      1973: Time of bad government (Watergate, Iran
      2001: September 11, a day of change.
      1993 – 2012: Supreme deity will return to start new era.

The deity Kuku Khan, the blue-eyed Caucasian, left in 1050. Visit of Hernandez Cortes was wrongly perceived to be the deity's second coming which led to their downfall.

Their Solar calendar shows 18 months, each month of 20 days. Five days are regarded as unlucky days. It is 10,000th a day more accurate than the regular calendar we follow. It is based on 9 months of human gestation. Dr. Arlene Chase points out that the predictions of eclipses are based on the brightness of Venus. Their Tocan is like the Zodiac chart. Their calendar is based on 52 year cycle. Their game at the ball court was a hybrid of basket ball and soccer using knees and hips. The goal ring was positioned as the galactic center and ball was like the sun. The pyramid is a 3-dimensional calendar based on galactic activity. Ancient Maya texts were 22 feet long sheets covered with lime paint and folded like an accordion. The Spaniards burned all the writings except the four saved by the sympathetic priests. These were purchased in Vienna in 1739. A German scholar studied these writings in detail and decoded astronomical predictions.

SHAMANS OF PERU

According to the centuries old Maya tradition Shamans carry out readings with coca leaves to read the lives of people and predict the future. I observed Don Martin Pinedo Acuna, a Coca reader who wrapped coca leaves in a fabric pouch and the subject breathes into the pouch two or three times. This is supposed to leave an imprint of person's template. Then he opened the pouch and picked up a few coca leaves in his right hand and dropped them from shoulder level. He examines the spatial displacement of different leaves, their markings and shades carefully. The leaves give him an insight about the relationships within the family, ones future and physical problems, if any. The person confirmed that the reading was remarkably accurate and convincing. The seer claims to see the physical ailments and the rituals are performed to heal. There is no way to assess the technique delivers results as admitted by people who visit them for healing. He did healings over the luminous body (Kanchay) and vibrational healings with music in Andean tunes. He was trained as 'curandero' in Huasa. He is the keeper of the sacred mountain named Pachatusan (where the earth dances). Others in the group were Isabel Chinguel, a seer and Olinda Pintado who is a gifted healer. She got interested in 'mesadas', the San Pedro ceremonies at a young age. Marco Nunez was the interpreter with the visiting group. He is a counselor in Andean medicine and has visited many countries.

NOSTRADAMUS

Nostradamus was Europe's most important physician and astrologer to the Queen of France. He wrote 1000 verses between the years 1555 and 1558. His prophecies include the death of King of France four years earlier in a jousting tournament with Count Montgomery in 1559 wounding him in the throat and eye, rise and fall of Napolean, Hitler's (Hister) rise to power, visions of sub marines and environmental disasters. He foresaw WWI and WWII. His original 1555 text (Century I) described the omens surrounding Julius Caesar's death in 44 B.C. Quatraine 41 "...Clouds shall make two more suns shine in the sky..." indicates three suns, the phenomenon which scientists believe is caused by ice crystals called 'parhelion'. It was observed in Gaul and Picenum and other places during the time of Nostradamus. The great Pontiff he mentioned was Supreme Pontifex Lepidus. In his original September 1557 text he mentioned conquest of Punjab, India by Alexander the Great: "....From Indic land where five streams join in one...." (Lemesurier 2003). He referred to five rivers namely Sutlej, Beas, Ravi, Chenab, and Jehlam that unite into Indus. Many of the events in the Quatrains have not been fully understood. Dolores Cannon (1997) has worked in the field of hypnotic regression. She has written about Brenda, who provided most of the information and Elena, who had NDE (Near Death Experience), and ten other people who had met Nostradamus to clarify Quatraines. Almost all of the 1000 quatrains were successfully interpreted (personal communication with Julia Degan in February, 2009). NDE became more prevalent with the book 'Life after Life' by Dr. Elisabeth Kubler-Ross and Dr. Raymond Moody based on the NDE phenomenon.

EDGAR CASEY

Edgar Casey is regarded as the most gifted psychic of the 20th century with 8th grade education. He was compassionate and a humble person. He devoted his life to health and healing through 14,306 readings in his 45 years of life. He was born in Hopkinsville, Kentucky in 1877. He had visions as a child and memorized books by sleeping on them. He was also known as the sleeping prophet. Once he suffered with laryngitis and tried to get help from Dr. Lane, a homoeopathic practitioner. He went into self imposed hypnosis on March 30th, 1901. That was his first reading. He explained his ailment and its remedy. He became a kind of diagnostic physician. His stenographer Gladys Davis (1905-1986) recorded the readings where names were changed into numbers for privacy. He never charged for the readings. He had the ambition to open a hospital where he could diagnose and help people. He opened the New Psychic Hospital which closed in 1931. Edgar Casey stated that his information came from the subconscious mind of the person he was reading. The view of the world is seen in his statement:

There is no future, no past, and
time is an illusion that has purpose.

He was soon considered as a man with X-ray eyes. He described the procedures using technical vocabulary in medicine, surgery, and pharmacy. In trance when his eyes fluttered, he was ready for the reading. His information came from cosmic knowledge.

He warned people about the market crash and urged them to pull out their stocks. He predicted improvements in early 1933. That was the time of the New Deal and U.S. pulled out of depression. In 1935 his prophecy pointed to an alliance between Austria, Germany and Japan. He stated that the whole world will be set on fire. He also predicted that peace will be established in 1944 and 1945.

People benefited monetarily with his readings. Before 1923, oil prospectors sought him for insight about the geophysical condition of probable sites for drilling. People were using his abilities for profiteering. He did readings for Thomas Edison and Nelson Rockefeller. He started having migraine headaches and his health was deteriorating. His vision for readings became fuzzy. He became frustrated and disillusioned. He moved to Selma, Alabama and established the rule that there will be no reading for the sake of profits. His abilities returned and he started healing people with his selfless service. He used to do the readings two times a day. During 1944 he was reading seven to eight times a day. Every reading was emotionally draining. He had a stroke in 1945 and died (History Channel). Edgar Casey was a psychic urging humanity to value life, care about the environment and to contemplate on our role in it.

Edgar Casey mentioned about Atlantis as lying beneath the Bahamas, and the first Eden was in the middle of Atlantic Ocean. He revealed that records of that culture were hidden in the Yucatan Peninsula and under the left paw of Sphinx in Egypt. Dr. Robert Schoch, geologist and geo-physicist did find a major chamber under the paw of the Sphinx. People of that time had flying machines and crystals. They abused their power and Atlantis perished. Another startling prediction is about the change in the rotational axis of the earth that will create major shifts around the globe. These events will take Japan under water, the Great Lakes will flow through the Mississippi valley into the Gulf and the Atlantic Ocean will inundate New York city and coastal areas down to the southern portion of South

Carolina on the East coast of United States. His prophesied an escalation of volacanic eruptions, violent storms, earthquakes creating a period of global crisis from 1958 to 1998.

DREAMS

Dreams were taken seriously through millennia as signals for events that may happen in the future. Emperors and kings relied on the religious interpretation of dreams from the counselors gifted in psychic phenomena and clairvoyance. The dreams of Pharaoh were interpreted by Joseph. Pharaoh made him second-in-command of all Egypt and gave him Asenath, daughter of the priest of On, as wife. There are tales of dreams that were premonitions for the events that happened as visualized in the dreams. Buddhists believe, the roaming of spirit produces dreams. Time is a physical concept and long complex dreams aaccording to dream labs are fast streaming episodes.

Mary had a dream that she would conceive Jesus.

Mohammed had a dream, which repeated several times and Angel Gabriel advised him to initiate Islam by reciting what became the Koran.

Buddhas mother had a dream and her astrologers predicted that he will be a spiritual soul not interested in royalty.

The Wurundjeri Aborigines of Yarra River Plains, the site of current city of Melbourne, Australia, believe in the dreaming entity *Binjil* that protects and takes care of the territory.

By the end of the 19th century the dream theories of Freud and Jung were prevalent. Freudian theories involved the make up of dreams due to activation-synthesis that happens for a time until it boils over in a dream. Freud claimed that dreams have a problem-solving function. He believed that very charged thoughts are sub-divided and dealt with in the dreams later on as subdued thoughts which he called displacement. Many dream thoughts are compressed by condensation. If the dream makes sense, it was due to a secondary revision involving thoughts while awake. Freud is known most for his statement "wish-fulfillment is the meaning of each and every dream". The dreams that people can't remember, Freud called it repression.

The evidence from research with subliminal psychodynamic studies and relying on mental images when awake along with association with REM and NREM awakening was not conclusive. However, G. William Domhoff has challenged the Freudian theories on the basis of his neurocognitive model with access to neuroimaging and the clinical use of dream-enhancing or dream-depressing drugs (Domhoff 2003, 135-169). Domhoff points out that dreams are produced by the conceptual systems in the forebrain portion of the network.

SCIENCE AND GOD'S UNIVERSE

Scientific inquiry allows us to satisfy our yearning for the mysteries of nature. The greatest wonder is the human brain. Genetics, neuro-endocrinology, and experiences during ones upbringing create the forces which either make the humans compassionate, spiritual, caring, and kind or they become ruthless, brutal, Godless, insensitive, selfserving, and self centered criminals. Neuroscience has mapped the sites in the brain that control behavior. Frontal cortex controls how humans behave socially and spiritually by managing jealousy and anger, to be charitable or deceitful, speak the truth or tell a lie, seek peace and harmony or create turmoil, lead a life of bliss or suffer in agony. The immense potential of mind can open unexplored wonders of God.

Humans have the advantage of 'Collective and Cumulative Learning' due to the proportionately larger size. The ability to use symbolic language and development of grammar enhanced the potential of communication through infinite configurations to share information with others. Man has built on the knowledge gained through history and experiences. Cumulative Learning has enabled the scientists to explore the universe. The planet hunting spacecraft Kepler, named after the 17th century astrophysicist, was launched on March 6, 2009 to study 100,000 stars like Earth orbiting in other galactic systems in search of intelligent life in the universe. Bill Boruki, the Principal Scientist, hopes to learn if life on Earth is a rare phenomenon or life exists on other planets in the cosmos. The technology of today matches the clairvoyance achieved by the enlightened sages. Advances in medicine, especially stem cell research, hold the promise to help people with spinal cord injuries suffering with paralysis, Parkinson's disease and Diabetes and improve the quality of life.

Use of medicinal plants has existed since the days of tribal medicine men. Herbalists in China and India have used Licorice root for centuries. Scientists identified glycyrhizic acid in licorice

307

which is effective in treating patients with cancer known as Kaposi's sarcoma, killing cells infected with the virus. It has proven effective against Japanese encephalitis, chronic hepatitis, and HIV (Williams. National Geographic, March, 2006).

Dr. Deepak Chopra initiated the dialogue about the ancient practice of Ayurvedic medicine, yoga and meditation. He supports the use of modern technology for immediate diagnosis of orthopedic, respiratory or heart is an advocate of holistic approach with supplementary medicine to fix body and mind for the long term. He urges the mind to focus on:
Self awareness, to know your true self.
Willingness to keep an open mind.
Intention to establish link with the purpose.
Discrimination to understand the subtleties.
Acceptance of the reality.

Meditation helps to explore the mind, the inner universe, which plays an important role in stabilizing the state of body and mind. The ultimate benefits of meditation include: lowering blood pressure, improvement in attitude, and reduction in stress hormones in the blood stream. In the fast paced life, it is essential to calm our mind and take the time to relax and achieve calmness and tranquility. Religion empowers the mind to awaken the emotions that inspire faith in a belief system and it is above scrutiny. Einstein reflected: The sense experiences are the given subject matter. But the theory that shall interpret them is man made...never completely final, always subject to question and doubt (Einstein: Ideas & Opinions 1954, 323-324).

A SCIENTIST'S ODYSSEY
Dr. Mani Bhaumik grew up in India. He was the first Ph.D in Physics from the Indian Institute of Technology (IIT) and became a physicist of international acclaim. He invented Lasik surgery, indulged in materialism. Dr. Bhaumik reflects after emerging from the pleasures of abundance, success and riches in his words: "My life - not the things in it but the ceaseless pursuit of them ... stuff that the Vedas call maya, and I had attached myself to this illusion beyond all measure of spiritual health..."

His knowledge in science, world, and humanity, gives him the tools to attempt bridging the gaps between modern physics, spirituality, and cosmology. He explains that matter is made up of quarks and electrons which are packets of energy, an abstract force that manifests itself in different forms. This energy assembles as fields: Gravitational field, Electrical field, and Magnetic field. The later two combined to make up the Electro-magnetic field demonstrating the unification of forces and fields. The unification is due to the restoration of symmetries (giving up some distinctive features). Unification leads us to the reality of common source. Bhaumik was at the peak of his popularity and had a patent for excimer laser in corneal sculpting with LASIK surgery based on his work at Northrop Corporation. He made the laser operate at room temperature which was considered impossible at that time. Northrop Corporation rewarded him handsomely and he became a business man acquiring mansions in affluent neighborhoods in Los Angeles. This man of science, grew up in a spiritual environment, took a detour of worldly pleasures and re-entered into the marathon of spiritual journey again.

He met Norman Cousins who believed in the concept of holistic treatment for ailments. He had demonstrated that the potency of conscious effort, positive thinking, and focus on the area causing disconfort resulted in healing. He was diagnosed with terminal condition. He aggressively revolted at that decree and checked out comedy movies that entertained him for weeks. His so-called incurable condition went into remission. This power of reversing from a degenerative cell disease prompted him to publish a book *Anatomy of an Illness as Perceived by the Patient* (1979). His passion about the limitless potential of human mind generated interest in Psychoneuroimmunology (Bhaumik 2005).

Dr. Lipton was intrigued by the role of sub-conscious mind in determining the learned behavior (Lipton 2005, 59-171). When we are asleep, unconscious, deeply engrossed in a task, or reading a book, and lose track of time, the sub-conscious mind is on auto pilot that keeps the vital functions performing at an optimum level. Often, you may have driven to work with no memory of a conscious effort to take all the turns to reach your destination or the moments elapsed in day dreaming. The learned behavior took over and arrived at work unconsciously. The speech pattern, the demeanors, and the jestures of parents, while growing up in the family, become the behavior of children. Lipton believes that a trigger sets off the learned response like a juke box selection. The stress hormones are a trigger that initiates a protection response in a pregnant mother creating the same response in the fetus. It is widely accepted that mother's emotions during pregnancy reflect on the emotional make up of the fetus.

The will power, sometimes called freedom of will, is really a confrontation between the subconscious mind and the conscious mind. He gives an example of David Helfgott, a concert pianist, whose father, a Holocaust survivor, was engrained with a message that being outstanding or famous is life threatening. David went to perform in London inspite of the warning from his sub-conscious mind but had a deep seated fear of winning. His performance was perfect but collapsed at the last note. When he regained consciousness, he was insane.

According to Lipton, spirit is energy which psychologists label as superconscious mind, the biological foundation for conscious parenting and the healing processes. It requires consideration of the sub-conscious and the conscious mind to fully comprehend human intelligence. Subconscience has tremendous capacity to acquire belief and religion. The converts who consciously change their religion revert back to their original religion due to the pressing force of the sub-conscious mind which recognized the religion they grew up with. Several such cases have been reported in Islam and Christianity.

The exploration of the mind awaits more attention. Claude M. Bristol in *Magic of Believing* (1948) draws our attention to the metaphysical capacity of the mind to accomplish whatever goal is established. It was not in reference to religion but approached the subject from the concept of the metaphysical capacity of the mind. He was not a religiously inclined person but was interested in exploring the power of the subconscious mind. He focused on the tremendous power of belief and considered it a royal secret known to very few. Whatever you picture, within reason, can come true in your life if you have sufficient faith in the power within. The religious belief and faith go hand in hand as reported in the case studies by Thomas J. Stanley in *The Millionaire Mind*. He categorizes Religious faith Millionaires as RMs and Other Millionaires as OMs. Among the very important attributes he outlines are:

Believing in yourself and faith in God.
Discipline, Integrity, Passion, Eyeing Opportunity and Courage to take Calculated Risks.

Faith seems to fortify belief when a prayer seeks divine help. The medical profession is accepting the therapeutic role of prayer. Prayer is effective when it is offered with faith.

GODS, DEITIES, AND UNIVERSE

The nameless breathed windless by its own impulse (Rigveda). Universe developed from a primeval chaos when God decided it. God is perceived as a potter who used the same clay for creating humanity, changing styles and colors. Spirits sustained early humans. The Sun god protected primitive cultures in India, Egypt and the Americas. Mercury, Venus and Jupitor were the gods of the Greek and Romans. The mountains, rivers and lakes were sacred. Cows, tigers, monkeys, dragons and Anubis were worshipped. Dreams and revelations inspired religions. The central element for all of these was faith.

Human intellect searched for the reason to support faith. The more we explore, the more we discover and understand the creations of God. The unfathomed God has given humans the brain to continue exploration and acquire knowledge of the universe. Science has offered the how and why of natural phenomena for an understanding to strengthen our faith in the ultimate creator. Abraham Mslow (1908-1970) outlines a progression of human needs. The primary focus is on the needs to survive. These require food and shelter. Then security becomes important for survival. One seeks social and romantic acceptance and approval in the tribe or community. These are external needs. Once these are satisfied, one embarks on a search for self-actualization. Simple life style replaces the lavish with material abundance. Self actualization leads to unconditional love for people and nature, inner peace and joy, intuition and the wisdom within. This is consciousness, and transcendence (Waters 2006, 39-42).

THE COSMOS

Professor Lawrence Principe of Johns Hopkins University explains in his course on Science and Religion (2006) that universe was hot plasma of energy and particles as they are now in the center of the Sun. The particles were highly charged and the matter and energy were separated. 380,000 years later the universe cooled off a little bit. The positively charged particles captured the negatively charged electrons making the particles neutral. The atoms of Hudrogen and Helium are formed and the universe became neutral. The universe emitted a faint glow for hundreds of millions years. At that time 95% of the universe was dark matter and dark energy that exerted a gravitational pull. The stellar spectra show a shift towards lower frequencies thus called a red shift. Cosmic Background Radiation (CBR) was discovered by Arno Penzias and Robert Wilson who built a highly sensitive radio antenna to detect satellite signals. They wanted to eliminate the constant background noise. This was the hum of energy coming from everywhere throughout the universe. A Belgian priest, Georges Lemaitre proposed the Big Bang model in 1927 which was accepted by Pope Pius XII in 1951. Age of the universe is established at 13.7 billion years. The young universe has grown according to the Big Bang cosmology. Scientists look at it from 12 billion light years away. Telescopes enable us to probe the universe and we find that 75% of it is Hydrogen and 25% Helium. Russian scientist Dmitrii Mendeleev (1834-1907) gave us insight about the elements in 1869. There are 92 elementary forms of matter arranged as Periodic Table of Elements according to their atomic weight. The other version arranges it by atomic number, the number of protons in their nuclei. Simplest atoms were formed during the Big Bang.

ATOMS TO MOLECULES

Life forms are based on the recipe of complex molecules. Amino acids make up proteins, nucleic acids make DNA, organic molecules make carbohydrates make sugar and starch, and the lipids are responsible for hormones and fatty substances. This could only happen in the beginning before oxygen was added to the atmosphere. Oxygen disintegrates these molecules. The early atmosphere had methane, ammonia, hydrogen, and water, but no oxygen. Stanley Miller, a graduate student created that environment in the laboratory in 1952 by adding these gases and used heat and electric sparks as the energy source. Water hastens chemical reactions better than gases. In a few days he found the formation of amino acids, phospholipids and nucleotides in the apparatus. This demonstrated that the essentials molecules could be developed from atoms in early chemical evolution on our planet. The evidence of forming long chains spontaneously suggests a natual selection in molecules. DNA (Deoxyribonucleic acid) is a remarkable complex long chain molecule. This type of formation happened at the edge of the primordial warm waters. Now we know that such conditions existed in the mid-oceanic vents on the sea floor. DNA ensures integrity of reproduction. It can duplicate itself by unwinding and making two DNA molecules from one that are identical. But it cannot exist by itself. RNA (Ribonucleic acid) is a single stranded form of nucleic acid which can code information and it can serve as an enzyme to help produce the needed molecules. This speedy process led to the evolution of living organisms 3.8 billion years ago.

Masaru Emoto demonstrated that water in certain areas has a different crystalline structure when flash frozen and examined in a microscope (*The Hidden Messages in Water* 2004). The study included the healing water reported at the spring in Lourdes France. The modified structure of water was also reported in the samples from other famous spa sites i.e. Karlovy Vary in Czech

313

Republic, natural springs near Panama City, the spas around Buda and Pest in Hungary which are known to have beneficial effects on health and wellness.

Dr. Smirnov studied the effect of the disaster at Chernobyl Nuclear Plant in 1986 where the radiation caused cancer in the inhabitants around that site. The people of one community were not affected by the radiation hazard. They were using spring water from the Caucasus Mountains which apparently counteracted the effect of radiation on cells. It was realized that electromagnetism altered the structure of water which improved absorption of beneficial elements and helped to eliminate toxins. Molecular Resonance Effect Technology (MRET) was used in clinical trials and was found effective against Staphylococcus aureus, Escherichia coli, HIV, and brain tumors and reported in research journals (Fischer & Smirnov 2008).

EVOLUTION OF LIFE ON EARTH

The long chain molecules curled up and developed membranes through which they took in needed molecules and released the byproducts of reactions into the environment. This was the start of simple single celled organisms called Prokaryptes. They had the mechanism in place for metabolism needed to survive, grow and multiply. This activity introduced a new gas, carbon dioxide in the atmosphere.

The next major change came with photosynthesis. The evolution of chlorophyll , the green pigments in plants, carried out the chemical reaction by capturing the energy of sunlight and putting together carbon dioxide and water which produced sweet compounds as storehouses for energy. This capability enabled the evolution of organisms called Eukaryotes. They practiced symbiosis and the some independent entities with their own DNA became a part of new cells as organelles performing specific functions. Organelles like mitochondria draw energy as ATP (adenosine tri phosphate) compound from oxygen. Chloroplasts captured the energy of sunlight for photosynthesis. The eukeryotes were efficient, bigger, and grew

314

faster in the air which contained oxygen. DNA, the genetic material was protected within the cell which ensured accurate reproduction.

Multicellular organisms evolved organ systems thus making growth in size possible. Vertebrates appeared 500 million years ago and ventured on land and dinosaurs, huge animals roamed on earth before extinction. The mammals multiplied and exploded in numbers. Sexual reproduction offered greater variability and speeded up the rate of evolution. Mammals developed stereoscopic vision, hands evolved grasping capability and larger brains facilitated the processing of multisensory stimuli for survival, expansion and safety. Humans are at the top rung of evolution. Man is engaged in finding ways to escape from his own destructive creations. Gradually, humanity is beginning to feel that meditation is the most rewarding and harmless way to escape the pressures of its own making.

SUN: THE ENERGY SOURCE

A star dies when it runs out of Hydrogen. The Sun will meet the same fate. It will cool and collapse. The sudden compression will raise temperature to 100 million degrees Celsius. Helium atoms will fuse to form Carbon. The Sun will expand to reach beyond Mercury's orbit and will become a Red giant until all the Helium is used up as it happened to Aldebaran in the Taurus constellation. This will collapse again and another expansion will swallow Mars and Earth to become a Super giant vaporizing Mars and Earth. This happened to Betelgeuse in Orion constellation. This time it will turn into White dwarf, about the size of the Earth. After it cools for billions of years it will become a black dwarf after using up Hydrogen and burning all the Helium. Then Carbon, Oxygen and Silicon will burn to produce iron with a core temperature of 4 billion degrees Celsius. This will be the death of a big star which collapses catastrophically in a second exploding in a Supernova. Its mass scatteres in space and the core forms a Neutron star. The remaining elements will be transformed into gold, lead and uranium which are also scattered in space. A larger star forms a Black hole which is so dense that even light cannot escape from its gravitational pull.

Scientists have not detected 95 percent of cosmos and will know more about Dark Energy as the instruments become more sophisticated.

In the meantime we watch the galactic collisions in awe like the biggest since the Big Bang which is forming the galaxy Bullet Cluster #1E0657-56. The spectacular Hubble images reveal the beauty of Whirlpool Galaxy, M51 p. 62 and the Spiral Galaxy, M81 p. 107 (National Geographic, Devorkin & Smith, 2009). Eta Carina, a slowly erupting nova in southern Milky Way occupied astrophysicists in the 20th century which released clouds of gas and dust showes the violent events in the universe (p. 181). A mixture of stars in Large Magellan Cloud LH 95 located 160,000 light-years away showing young and old stars (p. 119). This gives us a perspective of our miniscule existence in the universe and the fate of our planet from a scientist's perspective.

The Sun God was worshipped by pharaohs as God's earthly representative. From the early tribal beliefs to the rituals of religions, calendars, the astrological signs and combinations of stars have guided seers and offered faith for mankind. Scientists continue to explore truth in God's wonders. Human societies had no written records in their early triumphs. The industrial development and Western cultures in the 20th century enabled the world communities to connect and interact globally.

It is God's gift of mystery and wonder that allows man to open new vistas in every field of science and the humanities to unlock the limitless unknown secrets of nature. Research in fields of neurobiology, neuroendocrinology, psychoneuroimmunology explore the mysteries of the mind to know more about the potential of the mysterious brain. The interaction of mind and body is controlled by sages and yogis . They can disengage the bodily senses from the mind. Jesus experienced brutal torture but accepted it all by saying:

God, forgive them, they do not understand.
Paramahansa Yogananda (1946) observed events attributed to the power of mind. Baird Spalding's writings during his trip to explore the Masters of the Far East in early 20th century

explore the Masters of the Far East in early 20th century witnessed the power of mind over matter (Spalding vol 1, 3, 5). God gave traits of humaneness long after the Evolution of anatomical characteristics differentiating humans from the Neanderthals. Major transformation was the creativity, conscience and the consciousness. Humans acquired the ability to make choices, right or wrong, but the conscience to know right from wrong.

ONE GOD – DIFFERENT NAMES

JUDAISM:
God exists by himself for himself, and is the un-created Creator who is independent of any force or entity thus the expression "I am that I am", "He is" (Exodus 3:14)
NAME: YHWH (The Tetragrammaton), Adonai in the 3rd century BCE, Hashem, Adoshem. YHWH is 45 lettered name of God with combination of letters (Kabbalistic view)
OTHER NAMES: Adonai, Ehyeh-Asher-Ehyeh, Elohim, Eloah, Shaddai, Zebaot (The Seven), Shalom, Shekhinah, Yah, HaMakom, El, Elyon. IAHOVAH became Jehovah.

CHRISTIANITY:
"I appeared to Abraham, to Isaac, and to Jacob, as God Almighty, but my name LORD was not known to them"
NAME: Jesus Christ our Lord, Lord Jesus.
Other names: Son of God, Savior, Messiah, Holy One, True God, Deliverer, Good Shepherd, Everlasting Father.

ISLAM:
"O Allah, I invoke You with all of Your Beautiful Names".
NAME: The highest name, al-ism al-'a'Zam, is Allah.
Other names: Ar-Rahim, Al-Quddus, Al-Aziz, Al-Khaliq, Al-Alim, Al-Azim, Al-Ghafur, Al-Karim, Al-Wadud, Al-Majid, Al-Qayyum, Al-Batin,Al-Ra'uf, An-Nur, As-Sabur, are from the 99 other names and the 100th name is Mahdi.

HINDUISM:

The creative aspect of the Supreme is portrayed in deities.
Gods and goddeses as different aspects of the Divine.
NAMES: Bhagwan, Ishwar, Parmeshwar, Hari Om.
GODS:
Brahma (Creator), Vishnu (Preserver), Shiva (Destroyer).
Ganesha (Remover of Obstacles). Krishna, Lord's Spirit
in (epic Mahabharata), Rama, (Lord in epic Ramayana).
GODDESSES: Sarasvati, Lakshmi, Durga, Kali.
The religious/philosophical connotations came from the
Samkhya Yoga System:
Samkhya from the Vedas, Puranas, and Upanishads.
Yoga to attain liberation from worldly attachments.

BUDDHISM:

"Our Master (TheBuddha) gave us liberty to investigate
  even his own word.........so I take this liberty fully".

The Dalai Lama

Buddhist philosophy believes in Law of Nature which causes
manifestation of events. Mind is creator of positive/negative.
  Positive Mind: Tathagata - Dharmakaya
                        Tathagatagarbha – Buddha Nature
  Negative Mind: Sunyata, Emptiness, Non-dual, No-Mind.
Dhammapada: Mind creates perception (Dhamma), woldview.

SIKHISM:

   "Truth is high, higher still is truthful living"
NAME: Ek Onkar (One God), Waheguru (Wonderous Master)
       Karta Purakh (Creator), Akal Purakh (Eternal)
        Parmatma, Parmeshar.
Other names: Satguru, Datar, Kartar, Dayal, Kirpal, Knowing,
       Father, Mother, Lover, Beloved, Karim, Saee(n),
       Thakar, Prabhu, Swami, Parshah, Sahib, Parvardgar,
       Gobind, Gopal, Nirankar, Ram, Narayan, Pritam.
See gods of Early Civilizations (p. 84), and tribal spirits (p. 335)

HUMAN ANCESTRY

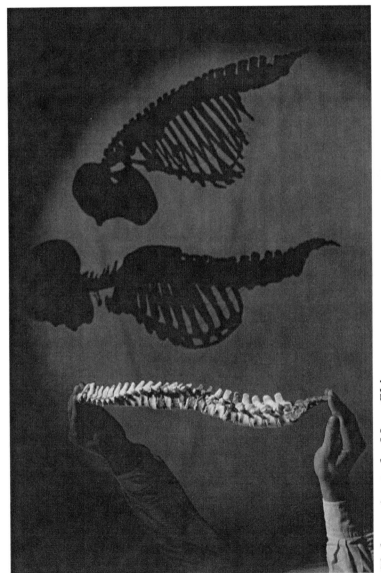

Skeleton, Australo, Man, Chimp
Kenneth Garrett / National Geographic Image Collection

HUMAN ANCESTRY

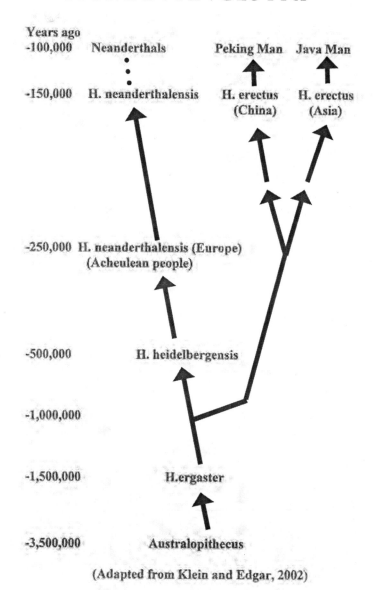

Years ago
-100,000   Neanderthals   Peking Man   Java Man

-150,000   H. neanderthalensis   H. erectus   H. erectus
                                        (China)   (Asia)

-250,000   H. neanderthalensis (Europe)
            (Acheulean people)

-500,000   H. heidelbergensis

-1,000,000

-1,500,000   H.ergaster

-3,500,000   Australopithecus

(Adapted from Klein and Edgar, 2002)

RISE OF CULTURES

3000 to 500 years ago .... Sacred Scriptures

⬆

5,000 to 3000 years ago...............Languages and Texts

⬆

16,500 to 11,000 years ago........... Magdalenian culture
Inhabited France, northern Spain, Switzerland,
Germany, Belgium and southern Britain

⬆

-21,000 to 16,500 years ago........... Solutrean Culture
France and Spain

⬆

-28,000 to 21,000 years ago........... Gravettian culture
Inhabited Portugal across Southern and Central
Europe to Russia

⬆⋮

-28,000 to 25,000years ago...Extinction of Neanderthals

⬆⋮

-37,000 to 28,000 years ago........... Aurignacian culture
Bulgaria to Spain

⬆⋮

-40,000 years ago ....Cro-Magnon
Early humans migrate from Africa
(Mousterian people)

HUMAN ANCESTRY

Let us trace our common heritage as we explore our beginning. Australopithecus walked in Tanzania 3.6 million years ago. Archaeologist Don Johanson and his associates discovered a fairly complete skelton (40%) in 1974 in Hadar, Ethiopia. Lucy was an australo female, A. afarensis, 3 feet 3 inches tall with very long arms as compared to her legs and ape like skull who died 3.3 million years ago.

Homo ergaster species evolved two million years later which evolved into H. heidelbergensis. H. ergaster became extinct 600,000 years ago. The latter developed into a new species H. neanderthalensis. The Neanderthals inhabited Europe 250 thousand years ago, known as the Acheulean people. Another offshoot H. erectus evolved from H. ergaster one million years ago. This species bifurcated into two bands after 500,000 years. These two groups evolved 300,000 years ago. One group went to China. The remains of Peking Man were discovered in the Zhoukoudian system of limestone caves in China in the 1920s. The other group spread towards Southeast Asia The skeleton of H. erectus discovered in Java was named Java Man by the archeologists.

The early modern humans, the Cro-Magnons , evolved in Africa 250,000 years ago according to the 'Out of Africa' hypothesis. The oldest remains are 160,000 years old found in the Blombos cave in South Africa which was occupied 70,000 years ago with remains of shell fish, stone tools and ocher paint. In a cave in Botswana a python god was found carved out of a boulder. Homo sapiens had developed larger brain and arched skull 40,000 years ago. Neanderthals coexisted with Cro-Magnon when they migrated from Africa to Europe. Neanderthals were outcompeted by the Cro-Magnon wiping them out 25,000 years ago. An offshoot of Homo heidelbergensis separated a million years ago which later evolved into H. erectus species in China and Asia 300,000 years ago. Burnt earth, bones, fire pits suggest that Peking Man used fire at Zhoukoudian in the cave in northern China. Montague cave in South Africa is called Cave of Hearths. Other sites include Vewrtasszollos in Hungary, Terra Amata and Menez-Dregan in France, Bilzingsleben and Schoningen in Germany which indicate that H. heidelbergensis used fire for survival in the harsh cold environment. Cro-Magnons and Neanderthals made hand axes by flaking stone that became more refined and efficient over time. Wooden spears 6.5 to 10 feet long, used by Neanderthals for hunting large animals, were recovered by Hartmut Thieme in the Schoningen deposits in Europe dating from 350,000 and 400,000 years ago (Klein with Edgar 169-180).

Tim White of the University of California at Berkeley is examining 4.4 million year old adult Ardipithecus ramidus recovered from the same site in Ethiopia where Lucy was found in 1974. Lucy was Australopithecus afarensis, 3 feet 3 inches tall with very long arms as compared to her legs and ape like skull who died 3.3 million years ago. The discovery of fossils in Africa in the region of Middle Awash River in Ethiopia from the sediment of a flood 3.3 million years ago helps to fill some gaps in human evolution with the discovery of 3 year old studying Australopithecus afarensis named Selam (Ethiopian word for peace). Human mind was beginning to take shape in Australopithecus and the vocal anatomy evolved later. Kamoya Kimeu assisted Richard and Meave Leakey in their paleoanthropological ground breaking work in Africa along with Alan Walker. After searching for human bones for four years in northern Kenya along the banks of Nariokotome River west of Lake Turkana, they found a whole skeleton in 1988 which was more complete than Lucy. It was a 11 year old boy who died 1.5 million years ago with a human looking skull features as compared to apes. He was 5' 4" tall. The body form was typical of Homo ergaster, still with brow bridge that remained basically the same from 1.8 million to 600,000 years ago, shortening of arms in comparison to legs, narrow hips and a barrel like chest promoting upright gate for bipedalism. The constriction of birth canal due to narrowing of pelvis delayed brain growth before birth thus requiring prolonged infant dependency. The brain was only 880 cubic centimeters while humans today have 1330 to 1380. Homo ergaster was the first to develop naked skin for sweating to efficiently cool down the body and brain in equatorial hot climate. Thinning trunk reduced body volume without decreasing the skin surface area thus facilitating heat dissipation. The Eskimos have a stocky body and short limbs suited to conserve heat necessary for arctic environment. The size difference in sexes also reduced.

As Homo ergaster emerged in East Africa, Homo erectus had reached China (Zhoukoudian) migrating from Africa one million years ago. That species was replaced by modern humans 60,000 years ago. Homo erectus was documented in 1892 at the Solo River (central Java, Sangiran) by Dutch physician Eugene Dubois. His work was confirmed by G. H. R. von Koenigswald who found another skull in Mojokerto in 1936.

Homo heidelbergensis was named after a find at Mauer near Heidelberg, Germany in 1907. Recent research by Paabo of the Max Planck Institute aimed at gene FOXP2 in mitochondrial DNA taken from fossil bones of the Neanderthals. Its absence may be the reason for their demise because Homo sapiens had an advantage of communication with language due to that gene. This capability around 40,000 years ago enabled them to compete and push the Neanderthals to extinction. Neanderthals lived at the site of Roc de Marsal (SW France) 25000 years ago. Paabo has already found differences in these two species precluding interbreeding. The Sima people based on the 300,000 years old fossils found at Sima de los Huesos at Atapuerca in Spain, place them between heidelbergensis and Neanderthals.

The genomes are closer to present day humans with more than 99.5% similarity. There is evidence that a form of the MCIR gene was responsible for red hair, pale skin, and freckles in the Neanderthals. The lineage separated 370,000 years ago. Larger frame of Neanderthals consumed 4034 calories a day where as the daily caloric intake for a 5 foot 4 inches female, according to USDA is 2200. Clive Finlayson of the Gibraltar Museum probed a cave on the Rock of Gibraltar which was inhabited by Neanderthals 125,000 years ago. The remnants in the cave include stone spear points, bones of rabbit, tortoise, dolphin, seals, and a fire place used 28,000 years ago. A three year intense cold wiped out Neanderthals (National Geographic, Oct., 2008, 39-59). Speedy evolution is based on the theory of 'punctuated equilibrium' explained by Stephen Gould and Niles Ethredge which speeds up the process in thousands of years instead of millions of years in speciation. This phenomenon, Allopatric speciation, was observed by Darwin in Galapagos Islands.

The concept of rituals dates back to early hominids. The archaeological discoveries have revealed that the Cro-Magnon buried the dead. Such activities allowed them to face the unknown together. The reality of death and its unpredictability was a mystery. The hope for life after death prompted the members of the clan to bury some objects to help the departed in the realm beyond. The evidence of objects such as utensils, ceremonial ornaments, or the items denoting the status of the deceased were included in burials which were pointed West to the East.

The Cro-Magnon of Africa were more effective cave dwellers and hunters who used innovations better than the Neanderthals. The latter developed in Europe and hunted large animals with stone tipped spears with more thrust from their stocky frame and muscular body. Dietary stress is suspected to have caused cannibalism observeded in the bone deposits in the Gran Dolina cave 800,000 years ago. There is evidence of cannibalism was reported in the Moula-Guercy 700,000 years ago. The Cro-Magnon hunted small animals with arrows and their population was greater than the Neanderthals.
Early Indians of the Americas, Aborigines of Australia, primitive tribes of the Amazon or the Aleuts of Alaska had faith in nature's bounties namely land, water, air, and Sun that gave food (animals and plants) to sustain life.

Man is a dressed up animal with animal instincts living in a society. The codes of conduct were established through religions. God, perceived in many ways has kept human emotions in check.

PRIMITIVE CULTURES

"Wonders are many, but none is more wonderful than man.
Cunning beyond fancy's dream is the fertile skill
which brings him, now to evil, now to good".
Sophocles, Greek playwright.

Human culture started with the Cro-Magnon, the Mousterian
people who migrated from Africa 40,000 years ago to Europe.
The Sungir' people in Russia produced Aurignacian beads by
the thousands. Archeologist Randall White of New York
University found beads in graves suggesting ritualistic burials
29,000 years ago, indicating respect for the deceased.
Archeologist Ofer Bar-Yosef of Harvard University calls it a
revolution when 11,000 years ago the hunter gatherers resorted
to cultivating wild plants for cereals and domesticated sheep,
goat, cattle and pigs for meat 9,500 years ago. When the
Younger Dryas period was over after 1300 years of cold climate
and drought, the population increased. This sudden surge in
human ingenuity is attributed to mutational change which
improved brain function for innovation. A single gene, as
reported by geneticists Cecilia Lai and associates of Oxford
University was responsible for the development of language and
speech which are impaired in its absence (Nature, October 4,
2001).

Easter Island is 64 square miles isolated in the Pacific ocean. It
was lush with vegetation for thousands of years. The Rapa Nui
were Polynesians who were part of a thousand year migration in
ten million square miles from Samoa to Hawaii and New
Zealand. They thrived there for centuries enjoying the Easter
Island palm which provided edible fruit, honey and wine. They
hunted porpoise for the protein diet. In the 13th century, the
tribe started building monuments, the megalithic statues
weighing up to 80 tons and 30 feet tall. Those were quarried in
the mountains 6 miles away and transported by rolling them on
palm trunks. The workers started cutting forests to use the palm
trunks to roll the stones to the current location of those 900

monuments. There were no palm trees left to make dug-out canoes for hunting at sea. By 1722 a few inhabitants were struggling to survive. Jacob Roggeveen, the Dutch explorer landed on the island on Easter Sunday and it is called Easter Island ever since.

SEX AND BELIEFS

MIDDLE EAST:
The clay tablets from Mesopotamia, dating back to 3200 B.C., indicate that sex was not a moral issue. Women were subservient and slaves for sexual service. Sex was regarded as alternative medicine. It was king's duty to have intercourse with Ishtar, the temple priestesses to ensure a successful year. Gilgamesh found that pleasures of the flesh were mightier than the sword and offered prostitutes for tender eroticism. Prophet Mohammad laid down rules for worship, sex and gender relations. Polygamy was approved allowing up to four wives. All wives were to be treated equally. Women were considered vessels and slaves. A concubine was less than a wife. Prophet Mohammad had nine wives. Women could ask for a divorce by repeating the request three times to terminate the marriage. Any accusation of adultery had to be supported with four witnesses. Adultery in women was punishable by stoning to death. Turks regulated prostitution in the 19th century and set up a class system. Prostitutes feared the prospect of catching venereal disease. Under the law of consent young virgins could be purchased. The age for consent was raised to 16 later.

Egyptians considered spirituality and sexuality as forces to reach higher levels of consciousness striking a balance between sex and longing of the soul. Virgins were rare due to the freedom of sexuality. Adultery was stated as *going to another house*. It was the duty of Egyptian Kings to breed heirs to maintain the dynasty name and for after life. Marriages between brother and sister, father and daughter were acceptable in royalty.

Nowhere else was sex a taboo than in the Arab Middle East. Women were segregated and kept in harems. A castrated male slave guarded women from outsiders or from escaping. The veil was for privacy and became a part of the culture. The burqa, the long robe, covered the entire body with netted areas for the eyes. Romance took flight of imagination to express admiration of the features under the burqa. Arab love was expressed in sensuous and flowery verses in romantic words, being helpless to reach the beloved. The longing for union with the beloved appeared as celebrated romantic stories of lovers.

Dr. Heba Kotb, a 39 year old mother, was a medical doctor. Later she got her Masters and Ph.D degrees in sexology in Florida. During her research she was thrilled and empowered by the verses in Koran that refer to sex between husband and wife: Our wives are as a tilth (to be cultivated) to you; so approach your tilth when or how ye will; but do some good act for your souls beforehand; and fear Allah. Her show, The Big Talk, is broadcast from Cairo on television in the Middle East and sex is discussed, a sensitive topic in the Muslim world. She has been dubbed Egypt's Dr. Ruth. Dubai's cosmopolitan atmosphere with all the western amenities has opened up islands of unbridled freedom and pleasures.

GREECE:
It was a man's world in classical Greece. Sex was openely discussed. Young women and pubescent boys were for companionship and courtship to express the sexual drive but it did not involve penetration. Wealthy women approached shoe makers to make pacifiers (sex toys) for their pleasure at the house. There was no stigma attached to homosexuality. Lesbians wrote poetry longing for young girls which was recited in public at religious events. In 264 BCE the Greeks spread their sexual culture in Europe with a premise that hard body dominates and penetrates, the soft body submits. Slaves were sexual property for pleasure of the flesh. Moral rectitude was enforced by Augustus in 27 BCE as the first Emperor of Rome. He enacted laws against lustful excesses and adultery. The wife and son of another citizen were off limits and any violation had severe consequences.

CHINA:

During the Zia dynasty cloud and rain were perceived as Heavens making love to Earth. Confucianism regards sex to be important for the continuation of the family. Taoism considers the role of sex to prolong life. Taoist sex manuals mention an intimate relations with six to eight women and ten to fourteen men without losing the semen. The Chinese pillow books like the Secrets of the Jade Bed Chamber show 30 sexual positions.

Polygamy was encouraged for producing more offspring due to the high infant mortality rate. First woman in marriage was the legal wife, all others were concubines. Kings could have 121 wives usually called sex secretaries. Chinese men go to brothels for networking and making business deals. The lamps in brothels were covered with red cloth giving a red glow. This gave rise to red light districts in Europe and Scandinavian countries. Men admired and loved small feet of women finding them erotic. Women began the painful practice of foot binding around 1000 AD. When China became more conservative, sexual tolerance and promiscuity spread to Japan.

JAPAN:

Izanagi and *Izanami* gods have influenced Japanese outlook towards sex. Female has a void and the male fills that void. Sex was not considered a sin. Prostitutes were practitioners of stress relief, as goddesses of mercy. In the 17th century during the time of Shogun, there were brothels where licensed prostitutes were employed. In the higher class, the services were rendered by the newly emerging Geisha culture. These well groomed and talented women were accomplished in music and the arts serving as sophisticated companions and escorts. Only in special situations they served as prostitutes. Sex assumed an expression of art and prints of sex figures were displayed in homes.

INDIA:

Sexual sensuality was seen as unity with the divine. Spirituality was metaphorically expressed in the intensity of sexual desire

329

symbolizing a longing for God. Lord Krishna in Hindu mythology is the embodiment of passionate foreplay and love teasing. Radha was obsessed with Kirshna's love. She uttered his name ceaselessly elevating her to spiritual realms. Shiva lingum symbolizes God's procreative force. Kama Sutra, the blueprint for love making was written by an ascetic who never experienced sex himself. He described 4 kinds of love; 8 kinds of oral intercourse; and 30 positions for love making. It also narrated ways to enlarge the penis and constrict the vagina. The sounds during intercourse revealed positions. If belt bells were jingling, she was on top, if ankles were ringing she was beneath the man during the sex act. The wealthy landlords, Nawabs, visited the entertainment houses called *deras,* where prostitutes sang, danced, and entertained. Indian women are depicted in stone carved figures in Ellora and Ajanta caves cut from solid rock. These were carved by Hindu and Buddhist monks, highlighting voluptuous breasts, large hips and narrow waist. The Tantric sex starting in the 6th century involved drugs and ritual sex for enlightenment. Sexual energy is believed to activate the chakras up to the crown chakra in the head, the exit point for energy.

THE WEST:
During Medieval times women were downtrodden and sexuality was not treated with respect. With the fall of the Roman Empire around 410 AD. The Europeans were influenced by the Christian church. Adam and Eve had fallen from grace in the Garden of Eden. The uncontrollable urge of Sex was believed to be the reason. The word sex and the formidable emotion went into hiding. Sex was only for procreation. The concept of virginity gained popularity and virgins assumed a higher status than the married women. Women disfigured their faces and bodies to protect their virginity. Deliberate efforts by the priest, to quell the tide of virginity in women, is narrated in the chapter on Role of Women in Religion. The vow of celibacy for clergy became a requirement. Church regulated sexual matters which were strictly enforced. The laws were written by celibate priests based on their information from the confessions and with added imagination of their own.

Sex with man and mule was a sin.

Use of a sex device or self stimulation was a sin.
Homosexuality was a sin.
Martin Luther called for marriage of the clergy and was
excommunicated by the church. During the Renaissance, the art
of Michaelangelo and Leonardo De Vinci blossomed. Galileo was
introducing concepts that threatened the church viewpoint.
Prostitution was regarded as an antidote to homosexuality.
Celibacy was breaking down and marriage was declared
divinely ordained and a gift of God.

With the invasion of Vikings, women were sent into walled
monasteries under the protection of Christian guards. The role
of women in church hierarchy was diminished and they could
not participate in the decision making process of the church.
Christian knights and wealthy lords marched towards
Jerusalem to conquer the Holy Land and confronted the Islamic
forces. The segregated women fantasized about knights in
shining armour. The courtly love was depicted in lavish
productions on grand stages. Sexuality and free love emerged
among the elite. Men were obsessed with the size of the phallus
and expressed it in long elongated shoes. This was labeled as
fashion of the devil. Chastity belts were developed for married
women to ensure legitimacy of their heirs. Sexuality exploded in
wealthy circles.

Protestants ushered in a new morality in 1630. Puritan pilgrims
sailed across Atlantic to escape the morally corrupt society. In
1640, courts were dealing with cases of incest and lesbian
relationships in the colonies. There was one woman for six men.
Sixty percent of the puritan women, who got pregnant, got
married. Women were questioned by women jurors for truth
during labor pains about the man who impregnated them.
Native Indian women controlled property. Some colonial women
got married with the natives. Sexploration, is a new word in the
web vocabulary like the Kama Sutra of the Vedic era in India.

AFRICA:
African women believe that procreation is their duty and
fertility is celebrated. Sexuality is not associated with pleasure.

331

Girls maintain virginity until their marriage. Cloridectomy is a required ceremony and a prerequisite before marriage. Communal bonding in certain tribes obligated men to have sex with a woman, and children are considered as children of the tribe. The courting rituals and customs for girls and boys coming of age and sexual behaviour is discussed under African Tribes.

In the Marind-Anim tribe of New Guinea's southern coast in Irian Jaya, a province in Indonesia, the semen was regarded as a source of male growth. Each boy was assigned a *binahor* a father figure from a different clan. It was his duty to inseminate the boy regularly in the anus until the boy attained maturity. This was supposed to enhance manliness in the boy. These people also believed that in order to conceive after having intercourse with the husband, the woman needed semen of all men in the patrilineal line to achieve conception. All the male kins injected semen vaginally on a regular basis. This belief caused infection of the genital tract which led to sterility. The tribe resorted to capturing children during head-hunting raids. This tradition was suppressed in the Dutch colonies and later stopped by the Indonesians in power.

Margaret Sanger introduced the first birth control device in 1916 during WWI before America jumped into the roaring twenties and sex became a recreation using contraceptives. WWII brought the sexual revolution with the explosion of explicit imagery. The information age has further enhanced easy access to pornographic materials. The designers modified their fashions with shorter hemlines and sexy flair. Cars served as sex chariots for teenagers. Twelve million men went overseas and the threat of STDs loomed large.

Kings and Emperors were obligated to produce an heir to their dynasties. Wealthy men married another woman if their wives could not give birth to a son even though man's Y chromosome in sperm determines the male sex. Mother can contribute only X chromosome in the ovum. The sperm has either X chromosome or Y chromosome. If the sperm with X chromosome joins with X chromosome in the egg at fertilization , it makes a XX pair producing a female offspring . If the sperm caries chromosome Y, the fertilization will make XY pair that will develop into a male offspring. Sex of the growing fetus is determined before sexual differentiation occurs. However, chromosomal aberrations in a female (X, XXY or XXX) will lead to incomplete reproductive system and may not be able to have children. Chromosome variation in males is XXY, X or XYY. Studies have shown that men with XYY chromosomes are more likely to be violent and aggressive but sexually functional. Such chromosomal aberrations in other pairs can lead to defects and conditions like Downs syndrome. Drugs and alcohol are responsible for birth defects due to their influence on the critical stges during differenciation and development. The babies of the mothers who use drugs during pregnancy become addicted.

Sexual orientation is a controversial issue. that is compelling and beyond the control of a man or woman. Their preferences may be influenced by the brother factor as reported in Time (July 10, 2006). Anthony Bogaert of Brock University in Ontario, Canada studied 944 men to explore if step borthers and biological brothers raised together influenced sexuality . He therorized that mother's immune system may develop antibodies to the male fetus proteins affecting future pregnancies. The antibodies that cross the placenta into the brain of the fetus may determine sexual orientation. There is a notion that gays and lesbians are born with the tendencies that make them feel comfortable as to their sexual orientation. Cryogenic preservation of eggs has been used by women who decide to put off motherhood for certain reasons. Dr. Llan Tur-Kaspa of the University of Chicago, Illinois has studied 550 cases and observed 5 major abnormalities in babies conceived from frozen eggs. The procedure involves stimulating the ovaries with drugs and then 10 to 12 eggs are extracted surgically and frozen until the woman wishes to conceive. Some of the eggs do not survive the freeze/thaw procedure. A success rate of 2% has been reported by UK fertility clinics. A case of octuplets reported in Los Angeles in 2009 raised social, ethical, and professional issues.

The Bible has many verses that denounce homosexuality. The conservative view labeled homosexuality as abomination carrying a death sentence (Leviticus 18:22, 20:13, 18:3-4). Romans 1:26-27 expresses this as dishonorable and shameless acts. Paul considered even grafting of cultivated and wild olives as contrary to nature (Romans11:24). Roger Juline quoted Rev. Irene Monroe of Harvard: What we know to be gay, lesbian, transgender and bisexual people in our time did not compute in ancient times. The Bible actually says nothing about gay and lesbian people. (Science of Mind, April 2007, 75-81). The debate goes on.

The interpretations discriminate according to the prevailing rules of a society which varies in different cultures. Sexuality is a natural urge and an instinct to produce progeny which can be done only by the union of a woman and a man. Transgressions of the bishops and clergy have brought shame to the religious institutions. Sexual relations in other animals are regulated by cycles of hormonal surge for procreation in all other life forms. It became a popular recreation when man succumbed to unbridled sensual pleasures. The oldest profession emerged to exploit this weakness and still flourishes in red light districts to this day. Homosexuality was not frowned upon in the Greco-Roman period in history. Discussion on sex is suppressed in almost all religions. Three major forces that impact the decisions are the culture of a society, common law, and religion. All three are interpreted by the people in authority in different cultures.

Research in the 1990s identified markers in the Xq28 region of the X chromosome of gay males but lack of confirmation of this study suggested that there are multiple factors involved which develop homosexuality. Studies at Northwestern University in 'sexual fluidity' in 2004 revealed that both straight and lesbian female subjects were aroused by heterosexual and lesbian erotic images . Gay men were turned on by viewing erotic films with men and heterosexual men were aroused by images of women.

334

SOUTH AMERICAN CULTURES

The early migrants came over the Bering Strait land bridge from Eurasia prior to the fusion of the Laurentide Ice Sheet in Eastern North America and the Cordilleran Ice Sheet along the Northwestern North America. The paleo-Indians eventually traveled south through the ice-free corridor in the Yukon River Valley along the eastern Canadian Rockies into Alberta in the Western Hemisphere. Prior to the Pleistocene age horses and camels roamed the North American Plains. During the Late Pleistocene the species like mastodons, rhinos, big armadillos, beavers, ostriches and turtles, now extinct, inhabited North America. These species vanished between 11,500 and 10,900 BCE. The extinction of big animals was related to the climate change. The big mammals like moose, caribou and bear migrated from Asia. The establishment of the Clovis culture in the South indicates a swift migration in four to five centuries towards the South and an explosion in population. There is a saying in the Northwest: *To get breakfast, take a walk in the forest; to get dinner, wait for the low tide*. This indicates the abundance of natural food resources at that time.

The centers of civilization in the western hemisphere were the Andes and Mesoamerica. They had developed thriving agriculture to feed the entire population. America's first urban complex was built at Norte Chico between 3200 and 2500 BCE. The Norte Chico gourd found in 2002 was harvested in 2280 BCE. It had the figure of the fanged deity with a staff carved on it, one of the main characters in Andean culture today. The Chavin de Huantar temple was built around 850 BCE by people of the Chavin culture. The Olmec people built sites at San Lorenzo and La Venta along the gulf coast of Meso America, now Mexico. The Maya civilization developed after the Olmecs (Charles Mann, 1491).

Maize was the only import from Mesoamerica (Mexico) to the Andes in 4000 years. Maize was genetically engineered by the

335

Indians through conscious breeding as reported in 2003 by Nina V. Federoff, geneticist at Pennsylvania State University. The Mexican Maize (Indian corn) comes in many colors and cob sizes. This reflects the diversity and creativity of different Indian cultures in diverse climatic regions. Maize was made into tlacoyos (tacos) consumed by the Andeans 10,000 years ago. At that time, the only other culture was that of the Sumerians. Cultures in the western hemisphere developed with no contact or communication with the Old World. Anthropologist Claude Levi-Strauss said: Cultures are like books, each a volume in the great library of humankind. The diseases introduced by European explorers and invaders wiped out the entire tribes with the epidemic of small pox, typhus, diphtheria, influenza, and measles. The natives had no antibodies for these pathogens which caused massive epidemic outbreaks killing 90 percent of native population by 1650. Christopher Columbus and Captain John Smith saw the thriving societies with bumper crops during their first visit. Earlier De Soto had introduced pigs in Florida in 1539. The pigs that escaped developed wild populations from Florida to Texas transmitting anthrax, trichinosis and tuberculosis. The labor crisis forced the colonists to bring slaves from Africa. Pope Julius II granted Spain the right to begin the missionary work in the New World.

Hernan Cortes arrived in Yucatan in 1518 with 11 ships, 600 men, horses and cannon. Enochtitlan, now Mexico City was a thriving empire of 11 million people ruled by Moctezuma. Cortes assembled a force of 200,000 and marched towards the capital. He was assisted by La Mahinche, an Indian woman to negotiate a meeting with Moctezuma. According to an Aztec legend a white conqueror was expected to come. Moctezuma believed Cortes to be him and agreed to meet. Cortes killed Moctezuma, plundered the riches, and destroyed cities. He believed he was doing god's work by destroying pagan culture. In 1531 Juan Diego, an Indian convert, had a vision of the Virgin Mary at Guadalupe advising him to build a shrine which was built and is maintained to this day.

The Andes were dominated by various Peruvian cultures over

time. The first was around 700 BCE consolidated by the Chavin along the central coast of Peru. They reigned for seven centuries. This was followed by the Wari Empire that ruled around Lake Titicaca on the border of Bolivia. The Chimu Society of Peru established Chanchan, the capital city with canals and roads connecting the agricultural communities in the northern coast and the artisan communities working with gold, silver and bronze objects such as funerary masks and other ceremonial objects. The Chimu state was conquered by the Inka around 1470. They created a powerful empire where the state provided the basic needs for everyone maintaining the Chimu tradition. Their method of coding information in the knots of khipus was unique. Their knowledge of the skies and celestial movements created the solar calendar of 365 days with compensation for the leap year.

The Spanish and the Portuguese started the slave trade around 1750 A.D. from the West coast of Africa bringing 4 to 5 million Africans to work as farm hands on sugar plantations and mines in Brazil and in the gold and silver mines of Peru. Some of these slaves were captured from Mozambique and Madagascar. Four to 5 million Africans were brought into the Caribbean to work on British plantations. The Indian slaves were sold to work at the plantations. Half a million were shipped into Southeastern United States and additional 200,000 transported into the Mid-West. By the middle of 19th century nearly 1/3rd of all the slaves were in United States. The Spanish South America also brought half a million African slaves for gold and silver mining in Mexico and Peru. They were called 'maroons'. However the climate, disease, harsh working conditions and brutal treatment of owners wiped out large numbers. Some who survived were able to preserve their culture and values.

THE INKA EMPIRE

The first paleo-Indians according to the archeological records arrived in Peru before 10,000 BCE. They had inhabited western South America by 8000 BCE. In 1983 scientists unearthed 96 well preserved mummies in Arica, Chile. The Cinchorro Indians

337

mummified the dead before 5000 BCE. They mummified only children first and later started to mummify adults. The Chinchorro had developed the technique and practice of mummification thousands of years earlier than the Egyptians (Science, 1998). Peruvian pyramids were built at Norte Chico. There was no hierarchy or inherited access to power to order people to submit for hard labor in construction projects at that that time. The Egyptian pyramids were built centuries after the Pyruvian pyramids.

The Inka (Inca in Spanish) empire in Peru was established by the Inka family from Lake Tititaca at the border of Bolivia and Peru. Inka's Cusi Yupanki built the empire in the 15th century after defeating the Chanka and renamed himself as Pachakuti (World Shaker), a dictator, while his father went into exile after fleeing from the battle with Chanka. The plaza of Awkaypata in Qosqo (Cuzco in Spanish) was the headquarters of Inka Empire carpeted with white sands brought up from the Pacific Ocean. Facades were decorated with polished gold plates. The planned complex was demarcated with four routes dividing the capital and the surrounding landscape into four quarters which according to the the Inka, mirrored the cosmic plan. A spiderweb of forty-one spiritually powerful lines linked the holy features of landscape such as the springs, tombs, caves and the shrines (Mann 2006). This was the land of the Tawantinsuyu in 1527 CE and Thupa Inka conquered the adjoining areas. His Empire in the 15th century, matched that of the Chinese Ming Dynasty, the Ottoman Empire, the Aztec Triple Alliance, or the Russia of Ivan the Great. However this civilization lasted only a hundred years when the Spanish brought devastation with the spread of small pox introduced by the Spaniards terminating half the Inka population. Unlike the Europeans, the natives had no immunity to the diseases. Civil war and factions grew after the disease that diminished the Inka as a power. The onslaught of other diseases like Typhus in 1546, Influenza in 1558, Diptheria in 1614 and Measles in 1618 killed 90 per cent of the population.The Aztecs Triple Alliance was the target of small pox outbreak before it spread to the Andes.

At the peak of Inka civilization, everybody had food, shelter and clothing. For Inkas, gold was *Sweat of the Sun* and silver was *Tears of the Moon*. The central administration provided everything for the populace by skillfully setting up supply and distribution among all the eco-climatic zones meeting the need for fish, beans, grains, Llama and Alpaca meat and hides from the coast to the peaks of Andean mountains was this multi-layered landscape. King Pachakuti established Picho in the 15th century as a resort for the elite Inkas of the time. It was skillfully planned as a corridor at 66 degrees angle that is now called Machu Pichu with an alignment to serve as a solar observatory. This was a self sufficient city where residence and food was available for all the artisans, weavers, craftsmen, priests and the Royals. The animal facilities could house and feed 1000 llamas. This was a center for solar worship where the sun passed exactly above with no shadows at the time of the December and June solstice. The site was discovered by Yale professor Hiran Bingham on July 24th, 1911. Inkas believed in geo-cosmic linkage and a relationship between the earth and the sky. There was a spiritual connection between rocks, people and the heavens. They were guided by astronomical phenomena and worshipped mountains. The excavation revealed the architectural expertise of the Inkas where the surrounding landscape blended with terraces and residential buildings. It was a hub for brisk commerce where llamas served as transport trucks of the Andes in this rugged terrain. The Spanish never reached Machu Pichu.

The only glimpse into the scholastic insight of the Inkas exists in the four hundred drawings presented to King Philip II of Spain in 1615 by the Inka writer Felipe Guaman Poma de Ayala depicting their pride in lineage. A powerful empire was subdued by the ambitious Spanish conquistador Francisco Pizarro with only 168 Spaniards who brought Atawallpa Inka into Cajamarca square and blasted his ceremonial army with a premeditated attack capturing the emperor Inka and manipulating a ransom of roomfuls of gold and silver objects as part of the agreement. Pizarro received the ransom and killed the emperor also. The mighty empire fell victim to deceit without a single casualty in the Spanish contingent.

The notable accomplishments of the Inkas as highlighted by Charles Mann (2006) include the following: textiles with a thread count of 500 per inch; armor of quilted cloth which was lighter and as effective as metal shields; corn was developed by the Inka from wild grass teosinte which hardly looks like corn.

Khipu (quipu) were the creation of the Tawantinsuyu that could be deciphered by khipukamayuq (knot keepers). Khipu were the devices that served to keep numerical records and the record of historical events, according to Harvard anthropologist Gary Urton. It is made up of a primary cord of textile, half an inch diameter, from which one hundred to fifteen hundred thinner strings hang, in turn having their subsidiary strings each bearing knots creating a binary code with colors and stones woven in knots. The knot reader could decode the message by running fingers on the strings up and down feeling the yarn used, the nature of the twist, the knots, and the colors of stones to comprehend the story indicated by that Khipu. The strings could be of 24 different colors. The spin and ply direction of the strings was a combination of 'S' or 'Z' twist, the yarn was cotton or wool. Each set of combinations created 1,536 units of information, more than the Sumerian signs or the twice the number of Egyptian hieroglyphs. Their libraries were bundles of mops that were more durable than leaves, bark or paper. Urton deciphered the 1996 treasure of 32 khipu that recoded the census for late pre-Hispanic era (Mann, Appendix B) .

Other devices used by the Inka include: the sling shot with stones which could bring a horse down by entangling the legs and could snap swords in half; the red hot stones wrapped in damp cloth would catch fire in midair like the missiles; dams and irrigation canals; the water crafts and ships were made of reeds tied together and the cloth sails to navigate ships hundreds of miles off the coast; the compression and tension idea was used to make rope bridges across Andean gorges shaped like bows. Their goal was to combine different tribes and create a typical regional art, economy and one religious belief system. Peruvian archaeologist Sonia Guillen discovered 83 dogs buried for a thousand years in the cemeteries of Chiribaya culture in her excavations near the southern port of Ilo (NG, May 2007, 31). These dogs showed features like a golden retriever with light-colored fur. They got mummified by the arid climate and salty soil of the area. The dogs were buried with textiles and food supply of fish, abalone and llama meat. Dogs, now extinct, may have been used for herding the prized llamas. Out of gratitude for their services as Chirabaya shepherds they were buried with honor. Ironically, the powerful and resourceful Inka Empire lasted only for a century.

INKA Reed Boat

MESO-AMERICAN CULTURES
THE TRIPLE ALLIANCE

Aztec Sun Stone
(courtesy Wikipedia)

MESO-AMERICAN CULTURES
THE TRIPLE ALLIANCE

By 2550 the lowlands along the Gulf of Mexico were inhabited by agricultural communities under the chiefdoms growing corn and other crops. They turned to the sea for fish. The first civilization was organized around 1200 BCE by the Olmec people, also known as the rubber people as the region was supported by rubber trees. The Olmec culture built temples and plazas. The basalt boulders were brought from the mountains to sculpt huge heads of deities. These were built at San Lorenzo and at La Venta in 800 BCE. Another was built in 400 BCE at Tres Zapotes. The Olmec civilization had developed a script and calendar that was used by the Toltec and other civilizations.

Aztecs settled in the Valley of Mexico after the fall of Toltec Empire in the 13th century establishing Tenochtitlan as their capital in 1325, the present day Mexico City. Tribute was levied on the conquered Chimu Society which funded the huge construction projects of pyramids, palaces and temples. The tribute system was vulnerable to future conflict with powerful enemies. The Aztecs decided to join with the Texcoco and Tlacopan to form the Triple Alliance. The empire expanded into Central America under Moctezuma I and II. The Mexica called the Spaniards teteo (meaning powerful, gods) and according to their belief they were expecting those gods to return from heaven. This confusion was responsible for their fall as they hesitated to attack the Spaniards. Indian are credited with having started the development of modern maize crop 6000 years ago by 'genetic engineering'. The Indians practiced *milpa* farming by planting many crops together. A corn field would also have beans, teosinte, squash, melon, chillies, sweet potato and other crops. Milpa crops nutritionally complement each other. H. Garrison Wilkes, who was engaged in maize research at the University of Massachusetts in Boston, considers that milpa is one of the most successful human inventions. The deficiency of lysine and trytophan in maize is supplemented by beans that have these aminoacids and maize provides cysteine and methionine that beans lack thus making it a balanced meal. Maize and milpa was common in all settlements in the Americas.

Hernan Cortes subdued the Aztecs in 1521. He set out to establish a political as well as spiritual victory. Hadrian VI, the Pope created a team of 12 Spanish Franciscan monks to meet their counterparts, the 12 Aztec priests drawn from the Triple Alliance to discuss God. The plan was to convince the Aztec priests so that large numbers of Indians could be converted through their priests. The Franciscans introduced the Pope as the only one who spoke the divine language saying that the only true God was very angry because of the idol worship the Aztecs were engaged in. He sent the Spaniards who brought so much misery to the Indians. By accepting Christianity there would be no more suffering. The Indian priests did not agree to adopt Christianity. The Franciscans argued that Aztec gods were not powerful enough to save the people from the domination of the Spaniards. The Mexica, having no choice, embraced Christianity with a small ceremony but the descendants of Indians still follow their traditional religious ceremonies. During the Mexican independence movement 1810-1820, the armies proclaimed The Virgin Mary of Guadalupe as the patron saint of Mexico.

Teotihuacan, a site around Lake Texcoco with 200,000 people emerged as military power and controlled central Mexico for four centuries. Their empire started around the time of Christ. The city was divided by the central Avenue of the Dead. There were Pyramids of the Sun and the Moon at the northern end, like the Egyptian pyramids, the third largest in the world (200 feet tall and 700 feet on the side) built during the 2nd and 3rd centuries CE. It stood on a lava tube indicative of the site from where humans appeared on earth. The reason for the downfall of the Aztecs is not known but the empire collapsed in 8th century. The Toltec ruled Teotihuacan but they also fell in 1200 CE. Then the Mexica settled at Tenochtitlan after being driven away into swamps during the time of the Toltec. They appointed a tlatoani (speaker), army chief, and cihuacoatl (serpent) and rose to prominence under Itzacoatl who eliminated the overlords in 1428. Tlacaelel was the cihuacoatl thus handling internal affairs for the alliance. He ordered all the codices (picture texts) of the enemies burned to start a new order for Mexica. In the 1400s at the birth of an Aztec male child, the umbilical cord was buried with arrow and shield for his future life to be a warrior (NG: Concise History of the World, p. 203).

Huitzilopochtli was the Mexica's patron deity, the Sun god. For him to protect humanity, he would need chalchihuatl, the life energy to replenish his strength. This life-energy could be obtained from the sacrificial rituals of humans. Slaves and criminals were offered as sacrifice to the Sun god. The imperial conquests became necessary for the sacred mission of ritual human sacrifice to fight evil. By comparison, death was an entertainment in Europe for people to watch burning, beheading, or quartering the accused, drawing large crowds. According to Cambridge historian V. A. C. Gatrell, England executed seventy-five thousand people in a population of three million between 1530 and 1630. France, Spain and Greece were engaged in similar public spectacles of death in public arenas.

Mexica's tlamatinime (the scholars who know things) taught and trained the future priests, teachers and administrators and wrote the codices. They were the first to establish compulsory education. All males until the age of sixteen had to be in some kind of school. The philosophers of the time thought about religion and spirituality. Nezahualcoyotl, (1402-72), a tlamatini, was asked: Truly do we live on Earth? His poetic response was:
Not forever on earth; only a little while here.
Be it jade, it shatters.
Be it gold, it breaks.
Be it a quetzal feather, it tears apart.
Not forever on earth; only a little while here.
Imagine the magnitude of rich heritage, art, philosophy, morality and ideas these cultures developed for five centuries. The collective wisdom of the western hemisphere was snuffed out very early by the ambitions of explorers sent out by Spain, England, Portugal and the Nordic sailors on the high seas.

THE MAYA

The lowlands of southern Mexico and the Peten region of
Guatemala are characterized by the rain forest with its typical
flora and fauna where mosquitoes abound during rains and heat
bakes the swampy bajos and the bottom lands. It is a land of
mud, serpents, and the jaguar. The Maya were forced to this
region due to the overcrowding in other areas. They settled near
bodies of water, lakes , rivers and swamps and developed more
areas by clearing forests to grow maize and squash. They
improved the lands by terracing, by adding silt and muck,
replenishing with compost and improving irrigation. Their
population grew and developed into city-states. The Maya
comprised about 60 city-states in the current northern Belize,
Guatemala, and the Yucatan Peninsula. They built grand
monuments like Mutal's Temple of the Great Jaguar in
northern Guatemala (now called Tikal), the Temple of the
Inscriptions in southern Mexico built by a 17th century king
Pakal, the House of the Magician at Uxmal where the Maya
tracked celestial movements and created the solar-year calendar.
They decided the timing of sacrifices and battles based on the
movements of Venus and Jupiter. The Kabah in Yucatan
displays images of rain god Chac to bring rain. The Temple of
the Warriors, in northern Yucatan at Chichen Itza, bear figures
of warriors with armor and feathered headdresses on its
columns. Yucatan was a bustling trading center around 1000. At
the pyramid called La Iglesia (Church) in the canopy of the rain
forest at Coba, a 30 square miles area in the Yucatan, priests
and kings climbed the stairs and held godlike powers over the
Maya subjects in those times.

Waka, at present El Peru in Guatemala, may have been the
largest city in the world with a population of 100,000 located on
the San Pedro River. The Maya arrived there 3000 years ago. It
had 300 feet high temple mounds, four main plazas and
courtyards with limestone carved altars and monuments. The

markets traded maize, beans, avocados, chicle to make glue, and latex to make balls for games. Other goods like Jade and quetzal feathers were brought from the mountains obsidian and shiny pyrite from the Mexican plateau. This was Classic Maya period.

Teotihuacan in the highlands of Mexico targeted Waka for its strategic location as a staging area for expanding their influence there and beyond. The warlord, Fire Is Born in his grand regalia accompanied by his armed warriors, walked into Waka in 378 A.D. as an envoy from the great power in Teotihuacan, the great jungle civilization of Mesoamerica. The Waka king, Sun-faced Jaguar welcomed Fire Is Born and a shrine was built to confirm their alliance with the sacred flame of Teotihuacan. By securing the troops and moral support at Waka, he headed to Tikal, 50 miles east of Waka. The Maya armor, with their cotton jackets filled with rock salt, was superior to the metal armor in the rain forest. With their javelin throwers and shields glittering with pyrite, the warriors arrived in Tikal a week after establishing an alliance with Waka. The Tikal king, Great Jaguar Paw, died that day. Fire Is Born toppled the stelae, the monuments put up by 14 earlier rulers. Stela 31 confirmed Fire Is Born to be Ochkin Kaloomte, Lord of the West. The inscription gives him the identity as son of Spear-thrower Owl, his patron in Teotihuacan. The new king was 20 years old. Copan, in the present day Honduras was conquered in 426 and the new king Kinick Yax Kuk Mo established a new dynasty. His title was also Lord of the West in reference to central Mexico's Teotihuacan. Maya flourished and developed the arts and religion bringing their glory to greater heights. In the 6th century the kan lords of Calakmul created a rivalry that split the Maya starting an era of profound achievements among both, the Tikal and the Calakmul. In that warfare between two brothers, both kings, one brother was killed and the retaliation rampage ensued. In 800 Cancuen city was overrun by killing king Kan Maax and all the royals, throwing their bodies in the cistern of the 200-room palace. This wiped out the Maya heartland in the Pasion River Valley, the present day Guatemala. In the declining wave of the Maya, the kuhul ajaw, the holy lords who commissioned murals and sculptures lost their drive and power, and the last inscription dates 869. The existing architecture fell into disrepair and nobles abandoned their palaces. Peten had supported ten million people in the 8th century, now there are 367,000 in the same lowlands. Land overuse and deforestation depleted the capacity of the land to meet the need of the growing population. Polygamy and intermarriages among the top tier of the royals and nobles created excessive demands for luxury items such as jade, quetzal feathers, and exotic ceramics. This rivalry among the nobles taxed the common Maya people who starved and moved to the forests. The bigger and elegant palaces and temples put a strain on the resources and the labor force. After 130 year rivalry Tikal defeated Calakmul. The hegemony in Dos Pilas and Petexbatun tried to rise but failed.

 The Cancuen was the last refuge for the fleeing nobles and this city in the upper Pasion River Valley flourished under the 15 year old King Taj Chan Ahk who ruled for 40 years without engaging in any war. He developed a 270,000 square feet royal palace with 11 courtyards. He entered the water as Maya referred to death . His son Kan Maax built more palaces and buildings and brought the Maya culture to its end. The culture simply vanished by 900 CE and the survivors had no knowledge of the glorious past of the Maya civilization.

Simon Bolivar, a Creole, was born in Venezuela. During the revolutions in France and America he was emboldened and led revolutionary forces to free Venezuela in 1819 from the colonial grip of Spain. Brazil gained independence from Portugal with the forces of Jose de San Martin. Although Bolivar could not unite all of South America as one nation but he is known as El Libertador.

NORTH AMERICAN
CULTURE

Totem Pole Figures, Northwestern Canada

NORTH AMERICAN CULTURES

The Indians were thriving as established communities in Eastern North America by the end of the 15th century. Women were involved in farming and household chores while men hunted and fished. They believed in harmony of nature and had faith in the supernatural forces. They had ceremonial enclaves and well built towns. Men engaged in wars and diplomacy between the chiefdoms. Lush healthy crops of corn, beans and squash covered the fertile lands for miles. Werowocomoco, the chief's village was in 45 acres with 100 natives. It was the capital of this chiefdom because and was regarded as a sacred place. Chief Wahunsenacawh was a leader of 14,000 Indians when the English landed to establish a settlement in the East in May, 1607.

The Micmac may have contacted local tribes to trade pelts for European beads, knives and alcohol during Trans- Atlantic fishing and whaling excursions in the early part of the sixteenth century. There are records of European voyages by Ponce de Leon (1513); Verrazano (1524); Ayllon (1526); Catier (1535-36); De Soto (1539-42); Pardo (1566-68); Hudson 1609); De Monts and Champlain (1604-07) on North America's Atlantic coast. The British, French, Spanish and the Portuguese explorers ventured out to sea to discover new lands. Two main cultures were isolated by the Panama-Colombia border and there was no communication between the tribes of Mesoamerica and the Andeans. For a thousand years both cultures developed independently. They adapted ingeniously to the terrain and the climate of two different ecological zones. There were no domesticated animals in the Americas until the Europeans brought the horses. The ones that escaped multiplied to roam in the wild. The natives captured the horses, tamed and used them for raiding the distant settlements thus expanding their reach. There were no beasts of burden in the Americas except for Llamas in South America until the landing of the conquistadors.

Explorers like Hernando de Soto came to Florida in 1539 with

600 men and with hundreds of horses and pigs. They saw healthy crops of corn, beans and squash. They established forts and Franciscans set up missions throughout the area (current Florida, Georgia). Charlesfort (Charleston, SC) was established in 1562-63. The Indian tribes in the area included Guale, Tumucua and the Apalachee. Indian tribes were concentrated east of the Appalachian Mountains. The French started trading in Northeastern North America, from Quebec to the Eastern coast with the Micmac, Maliseet-Passamaquoddy and Eastern Abenaki Indian tribes. The British arrived at Plymouth and established the New England territory in areas that now include the states of Massachusetts down to Virginia. This area was inhabited by Western Abenaki, Iroquoians, Algonquians and the Narragansett Indians. Virginia Algonquians were settled in Tidewater Virginia by the late 1400s. Tutelo, Saponi and Cherokee Indians escaped the ravages of epidemics due to lack of contact with the Europeans. In the southern Atlantic areas the Spanish plundered the richest and most beautiful temple in the Cofitachequi province of La Florida looting fresh water pearls. The Spanish used Timucua Indians as labor. The Spanish ceded La Florida to Britain in 1763. About 250 Timicua and Guale Indians went to Mexico and Cuba with the Spanish.

According to Smithsonian anthropologist Douglas Ubelaker's study, tribe by tribe, there were 2.4 million in North America between 1500 and 1800 CE. In 1500 CE the native Indian population in Eastern North America was over 1 million. There were no Europeans or Africans on the continent at that time.

The greatest concentration was in the southeastern North America because of the fertile lands, rivers and the mild climate that allowed a long growing season for crops. Within a century there were 58,000 Europeans and 1600 slaves living mostly in New England. The Indians succumbed to epidemics with only 379,000 survivors by 1650. In the southeast the disease wiped out Tumucua Indian population reducing their numbers dramatically from 200,000 to 27,000. By 1800 CE the European population increased to 4,763,000 and Africans, mostly slaves, grew to 1,002,000. The Indian population declined to 178,000.

The official first count for the Indians in 1860 census was 40,000. The Indian population was reduced by 90% between 1492 and 1650. Currently, the census figure shows 2.8 million Indians. Trade with the new world was brisk involving England, Netherlands, France, Spain, Portugal. Cacao, corn, potatoes, and tobacco were traded for cattle, horses, pigs, coffee. Rice, and sugarcane.

On May 14, 1607 Captain John Smith landed in Jamestown, Virginia with 104 colonists. This area was rich in fish and game. James Fort marked the establishment of the first colony in North America in the 8000 square mile Indian territory. The Indian tribe was Werowocomoco but the British named them Powhatan Indians. The pilgrims endured the hardships and confrontations with the native Indians during the early days in North America. Almost half of the new settlers died of hunger and disease. The Indians could easily eliminate the English but Indians hoped to develop an alliance.

Smith ventured into Chickahominy River hoping to discover a passage from the Atlantic to the Pacific Ocean. He was captured and brought to the Powhatan, the Head of the tribe. He was about to be executed under Powhatan's verdict when his 11 year old daughter , Pocahontas rushed and covered Smith's head in her arms to save him. Her real name was Matoaka, the Powhatan Princess. Pocahonta's marriage to John Rolfe was perceived as a treaty between the settlers and the Powhatan that contributed to the success of Jamestown as the first English settlement. (National Geographic, March 2007)

Indians recycled their land with crops and forest. The vacant land was used to hold ceremonies and events. Forest burning was done to clear the underbrush and add nourishment to the soil. This rotation replenished the forest and the land. The forest litter helped to conserve moisture and was natural mulch. The settlers used the same land year after year and the tobacco crops exhausted the soil quickly. Cattle, horses trampled the soil and grazed through fields. Pigs dug deep for Tuckahoe starchy tubers that Indians used during periods of food shortage. The introduction of European honey bees was for the honey but the bees proved to be universal pollinating agents that proved to be responsible for the success of citrus and peach orchards along the Eastern Atlantic Coast.

The immigrants coming from the marshes of England in the 17th century brought the malarial parasite in their blood. It got transferred by the mosquitoes to Indians and settlers alike. Malaria became endemic in the Carolinas. European black rats ravaged corn storages from New England to Florida. The new settlers destroyed the existing ecosystem that supported bumper crops. The new pathogens eliminated 90% of the indigenous population who had no antibodies for the introduced new diseases.

The 400th anniversary of the Jamestown settlement was attended in May, 2007 by Queen Elizabeth II and Prince Philip. A brief description of the original tribes is intended to show their faith, customs, rituals in the diverse terrain in North America.

CHEROKEE:
Much of our information comes from the written records of the Cherokee nation. Sequoyah had developed the writing system all by himself. His phonetic system involved 85 symbols. The Cherokee medicinal journals passed on the medicinal cures to the future generations. The Cherokee were literate by 1820 and women played an important role. The Cherokee believed:
> Pursuing *duyuktv,* the right way, one becomes *Ani-Yvwiya,* real person. Anyone hungary will be fed, anyone traveling housed.

The Indian Removal Act of 1830 was enforced by Andrew Jackson. It drove out 60,000 Indians to Oklahoma known as the *Trail of Tears.* The group named Eastern Band of North Carolina sustained this exodus and was officially accepted to stay in the Southeast. They stage this historical era in their production *Unto These Hills* to portray their past. The Oklahoma Cherokee Nation met the Eastern Band in 1984 after 150 years. Women play an important role in Cherokee Indians.

SEMINOLE:

The Seminoles are the descendants of the Creek tribe that joined the English to confront the tribes under the Spanish influence in the Southeast. They successfully destroyed the Timucua and Apalachee tribes of Florida. The victorious Creek were the Seminoles attracting more Creeks into Florida. They were sympathetic to Africans, giving shelter to run- away slaves and intermarrying with them. The Seminoles were also forced to move to Oklahoma but they resisted and organized guerrilla warfare under the Indian leader Osceola. After his capture and death, thousands of Seminoles were forced to go to Oklahoma. The Indian resistance continued by the ones who escaped into swamps and were hard to locate in the Florida Everglades. In 1957 they were officially recognized as the Seminole Indians. They are still governed by medicine men and by their council.

IROQUOIS:

The Iroquois tribe developed between 1400 and 1600 in the northeast embracing many tribes under the league's governing council. They focused on virtues like wisdom, integrity and the ability to settle disputes. American colonies sought Iroquois advice to develop their model of values, unity, and democracy. Their guidance is valued by the United Nations. The name Haudenosaunee refers to tribe's long houses where a dozen families live in a long house. The settlement could include upto 150 long houses. The lacrosse game was adopted from the Iroquois Indian sport. The tribe is devoted to preserving its identity, health, and a community spirit.

BLACKFEET:

This tribe was transformed after acquiring horses and guns in the 1700s. They could hunt more efficiently over a larger area and transport tepees, possessions and the tribe's elderly and infirm more easily. Their raids forced the Shoshoni tribe, who were without guns, into the Rocky Mountains. They respect their sacred sites. Tourism has educated visitors about their heritage, sites and customs. They observe sweat baths, maintain sacred medicine bundles, and leave tobacco offerings for trees and animals and engage in the annual Sun Dance. They purify themselves with sweet grass before entering the mountains. They decorate their bodies with paints.

LAKOTA SIOUX:

Due to the move of eastern tribes toward the west, the Lakota Sioux ended up in western high plains in the 1700s. They valued the bison for food, hide, tools and oil considering the animal as a gift from god. The Europeans hunted it for the hide. The numbers declined by 1875 CE due to over hunting. The soldiers also killed bison to remove the Sioux food and subsistence in order to overpower them. This group of Indians acquired horses by trading or raiding around 1750. They became accomplished horsemen and fierce warriors by developing their techniques in warfare. In an alliance with the Cheyenne Indians, they defeated Custer in the Little Bighorn Battle. The Sioux are a group of 14 tribes. Pipe smoking is an identity for all Sioux. They feel that smoking adds a spiritual dimension to human affairs and prayers rise up to the spirit world. They are convinced that the survival of human race is dependent on the earth's productivity and respectful management. Their traditional religion observes the Sweat Lodge ceremony.

NEZ PERCE:

In 1855 this tribe was forced to leave its territory which included the adjoining lands of Oregon, Washington and Idaho, the American Northwest region. In this region of rich valleys and mountains, women gathered berries, bulbs and roots. Men hunted for fish and wild life. Chief Joseph was a celebrated leader who tried to negotiate with the Army but failed. He took his people over the harsh Bitterroot Range, walking 1700 miles, and surrendered in 1877. He could not bear the sight of his people suffering with cold and hunger. Nez Perce bred horses keeping a record of blood lines of Appaloosas, prized for their endurance and speckled markings. They had to surrender their 1100 carefully bred horses also. A New Mexico horse breeder gave a gift of 10 mares of Appaloosas to Chief Joseph Foundation in 1991 for breeding. They are preserving their arts, history and language under their Cultural Resources Program.

NORTHERN PAIUTE:

They are the descendants of tribes and traditions going back 10,000 years in an arid environment with limited rain, no rivers and long distances. They have survived by adjusting to the delicate balance with the natural harsh environment in the Southwestern Great Basin. They inhabited 70,000 square miles area that now includes southern Oregon, Nevada, western Idaho and eastern California and shared the same language family. They gathered pinon seeds at communal gatherings. They hunted rabbits and antelope. They maintain their heritage with prayers, songs, stories, rituals and religious activities like sweat Lodge, Sun Dance and have Native American Church in their reservations maintaining their identity.

APACHE:

This tribe was the last to surrender in 1886. They were treated as prisoners of war till 1913. When freed they joined the other tribes at the reservation in New Mexico. They have a rich tradition which is maintained through ceremonies with painted wooden head dresses representing mountain spirits. They speak the Athapaskan language. Medicine men in an atmosphere of singing and beating of drums perform the healing by evoking supernatural forces. Singers recite the tribal history starting from the creation of the universe to the present time. The best known ancestor of the tribe is the celebrated warrior Geronimo.

HOPI:

This tribe believes in the spirit beings called *katsinam* who carry the prayers of Hopi Indians to their deities. These spirits dwell among them the first half of the year and then reside on San Francisco mountain for the remaining half year. These spirits are honored for bringing rain. The *katsinam* carvings are sacred and given to young girls imparting the gift of reproduction. Hopi Indians cultivate the corn with utmost care, almost like the family's children and rely on the spirits for rain. They dance in reverence to grow the crop in drought conditions. The Hopi believe that every individual has the capacity to contribute their spiritual thoughts and prayers.

NAVAJO:

The Navajo speak Athapascan and they arrived in the southwest around 1400. They settled in the Four Corners region separating from the other tribes. They were farmers and built their domed dwellings called hogans in the middle of their grazing land. Their wealth was based on the number of horses and sheep they owned. They strongly believe in the need to stay in harmony with super-natural powers. An illness requires healing that involves the physical, mental and spiritual realignment ceremonies with sand paintings, songs and Navajo rites. The painting designs are created by holy people. These are blessed and their powers permeate the sick person for healing. Their dwellings were burnt by the military forcing the Navajo for a long walk to Bosque Redondo, New Mexico. Many of them died of hunger and disease. With a treaty they established a reservation. The first Indian Community College, opened in 1969 which preserves their culture and language. The Navajo Code Talkers were recruited by United States Army during WWII to develop a code. The Japanese Army could not decipher the Navajo code and led to their defeat.

POMO:

There were 300,000 Indians in California in 1769 when the Spanish arrived. This was probably the only place in the world with the most diversity in languages in one population. All are considered belonging to the Pomoan family of languages. The rocky coastline provided plenty of marine life for food and people relied on acorns, wild plants and animals during summer.

TLINGIT:

These tribes inhabit Yukon, Alaska's panhandle and British Columbia Canada. Tlingit Indians are class conscious. The main segment are the commoners that are under the leadership of the clan leader who assumes that position by amassing wealth and throwing big Potlatches (feasts) that are designed to circulate wealth and make alliances with other clans. The number of people attending the feast and accepting gifts affirms the status of the host as their leader. The slave segment is comprised of women and children, captured from other tribes. They serve as the work force for menial jobs for their masters. They have revived woodcarving to make masks, and totem poles. Each clan shows their crests on totem poles, canoes, and hats. They weave their crests on blankets made from cedar bark and the wool of mountain goats. Winter was a time for potlatching when the stored catches of salmon, deer, bear, mountain goat, and sea mammals helped to get through the winter. The Tlingit territory is a diverse environment, starting at sea shore to mountain cliffs and dense forests. Tourism boosts their economy as travelers buy their gifts and unique clothing.

EUROPEAN CULTURES

Homo sapiens started to move in 40,000 years ago. Within 10,000 years the modern humans aggressively took over the Neanderthal territory and drove them to extinction in Europe. Migrations from central Asia, the Middle East and Egypt influenced the region with languages, art and culture. The Minoan culture, proficient in agriculture, had spread throughout the Mediterranean region. Greeks became influential since the fifteenth century B.C. Their descendants a thousand years later acquired excellence in art and architecture; science and mathematics; politics and philosophy. They introduced the democratic principles of government, an enduring legacy that continues to this day in the free world. The Roman Empire adopted Christianity as the state religion in the 4th century A.D. The 11th century brought the distinction of Roman Catholicism that prevails in western and southern Europe and the Eastern Orthodoxy in Eastern Europe. Since the 16th century the Protestants developed the reformed Christianity mostly in northern Europe. The widespread Islamic conversion and influence in Europe during the Ottoman Empire is seen in the Muslims of Albania and Turkey. The warring kingdoms have now sought economic and political strength by joining the European Union since 1993. Secularism is the unifying concept in the free world allowing everyone to practice their religion according to their traditions.

The Mycenaeans were Indo-Europeans who had developed cavalry with horse-drawn chariots. They invaded Egypt, Mesopotamia and the Indus Valley. They influenced the development of Sanskrit, Persian, Greek, Latin, and English. They settled in Greece. Later they overpowered the Minoan Kings and took over Crete. The Celts occupied Europe up to the British Isles and established their kingdom. Rome was founded by Romulus and Remus in 800 BCE. The Greek cities of Sparta and Athens were built around that time.

The Ecumenical Council of Chalcedon institutionalized the

doctrines of Christianity according to the Nicene Creed. Nestorian and Monophysite branches of Christianity were branded as heretical. Christians were forced into slavery and treated harshly.

The 16th century was a progressive era when artists like Botticelli, Cellini, Raphael and Michaelangelo made their mark in the arts. The latter painted the ceiling of the Sistene Chapel in the Vatican Palace. Leonardo da Vinci painted the famed Mona Lisa called La Gioconda in 1503. During the 17th century between 1605-1612 Miguel de Cerwontees Saavedra's Don Quixote was published and Shakespeare wrote masterpieces like King Lear, Macbeth, Winter's Tale, and The Tempest. The King James version of the Bible was published in English in 1611 and authorized.

Maximilian I became the Holy Roman Emperor in 1508. Pope Julius II declared that in the future Germanic Kings would be Holy Roman Emperors. Martin Luther, an Augustinian monk and teacher at the University of Wittenberg questioned the church's doctorine and on indulgences nailed 95 theses on a church door for the Bishop of Mainz. Martin Luther was excommunicated in 1520 by Pope Leo X. Martin Luther commenced a translation of the Bible into German that was completed in 1534. John Calvin was a Protestant leader who wrote *The Institutes of Christian Religion*. He protested the separation of church and state. King James I feared the Calvinistic views and introduced the King James version of the Bible. Europe represents 7% of the earth surface where more than 750 million people are living at this time making it the most densely populated region after Asia at this time.

NORTHERN EUROPE

CORNISH:
In southwestern Great Britain, half a million Cornish people are concentrated in Cornwall as an ethnic group engaged in mining. They appeased the *knockers*, the mine spirits, by giving corners of pastry. The story of *knockers* persist in the mining towns from

Colorado to Montana in the Cornish immigrant communities.

FAROESE:
There are 18 small islands, part of the kingdom of Denmark, inhabited by 45,000 people. They speak Icelandic and are descendants of the Vikings who settled there in the 9th century. They are of Celtic heritage with religious affiliation to the Lutheran Church. They live in small communities relying on fishing and sheep herding. Chain dancing is a social activity in their culture.

FINNS:
Finland was annexed in 1809 by Russia but it had been a part of the Swedish kingdom for 500 years till then. It became an independent nation in 1917. Kalevala, the epic poem, depicts a national story about a mythic hero who brings music and prosperity and rescues the sun and moon, a legendary tale passed on for 3000 years. Most people follow Lutheranism while some still practice the Eastern Orthodox religion, a remnant the tsarist Russian occupation. The people have more affinity to Hungarian heritage and speak a Finno-Ugric language. They constitute a cultural bridge between eastern and western Europe. They are creative and receptive to change. Their artistic intellect shows through their architects and designers of world fame. In the tradition of St. Lucia, girls wear white gowns and a crown of candles on the head on December 13 every year entertaining their families with songs, gifts and food.

ICELANDERS:
A small independent nation of 250,000 people since 1944 was established by the Vikings in 874 CE. The early settlers included Celtic slaves brought from Scotland and Ireland on this volcanic island of Iceland where glaciers meet natural hot springs. They have harnessed that energy to produce electricity, heat and light for industry. A thousand years of intermarriages have established a kinship that does not recognize any distinction of family names. Their version of the Norwegian language is an ethnic distinction that is evident from their love for literature and story telling. Their religion is Lutheran. Reykjavik is a

modern city with fashion, music, tourism and technology and has replaced the earlier main activity of farming and fishing.

IRISH:
After being a colony of England for a long time, the Easter Rebellion of 1916 initiated the events that led to the formation of the Republic of Ireland in 1949 now a part of the European Union. The Book of Kells, a medieval Gospel book, is exhibited at the world renowned Trinity College in Dublin. Most of the Irish are Roman Catholic and speak Irish or Irish Gaelic but the principal language is English. People love literature, theatre and music...and the pubs. A medieval festival celebrates pre-Christian traditions in Athenry near the site of a Norman castle. The potato famine of 1846 lasted for five years, during which large numbers of people emigrated to England and America.

PICTS and NORS (Northern Islanders):
The northern islands of Orkney and Shetland were originally inhabited by Celtics called Picts. Vikings took over the islands and replaced the Picts making it a Nordic settlement until 1469. It became a part of Scotland when Princess Margaret of Norway married King James III of Scotland. Norn, the Scandinavian dialect, was spoken during a bilingual phase but was later lost to English. Shetlanders continued to use the old language. In Summer, St. Magnus Fair is celebrated. A January festival *Up Helly Aa* reenacts Viking battle during the long nights by setting a Viking boat on fire as a celebration. The daily life revolves around fishing and sheep herding. Fine lace and Shetland wool woven in Orcadian patterns are famous.

SAMI
These people were nomadic pastoralists relying on reindeer herds. The Sami were well adapted to live in the Arctic Circle, the tundra way of life. They inhabit the northern parts of Norway, Sweden and Finland as well as the northwestern Russian Kola region. Scandinavians call them Lapps. They see power in mountains and rocks in their shamanistic religion. They invented the skis to accompany the sleds and used every reindeer part for food, protective skins and to carry dwelling

362

poles and skin covers. Researchers trace back their origin in the Alps of Siberia a thousand years ago. Most people are now employed by logging and mining companies. A small number of people still rely on reindeers.

SCANDINAVIANS:
The inhabitants of Norway, Denmark, and Sweden are all one people despite their boundaries on the map. They speak almost the same language and follow the same religion, Lutheranism for eight centuries and social democracy. Denmark dropped Lutheranism as the state religion in 2000. Their crafts represent their culture. They have enjoyed a high standard of living attracting immigrants from other countries who work in timber, mineral and oil industries. The country cottages reflect the agrarian background from the herding days of the past.

SCOTS:
The famous Scottish plaids identified their clans wearing tartans. The kilts represented their ethnicity and identity before 1707. The bagpipe is typical Scottish music popular since the 18th century. Sheep ranches and the dish *haggis* dominated their economy in their agrarian past. They produced Dolly, the first cloned sheep. Scotch is the malt whiskey enjoyed by the Scots. Poet Robert Burns was honored for his poetry in Scots English. He died at the end of 18th century. Most Scots are Presbyterians. Scots have been considered to be like the western cowboys of America, free spirited and rugged.

WELSH:
These are the people of Wales, a word that came from *woel,* an Anglo-Saxon word meaning slave or foreigner. Wales is *Cymru* in Welsh language. Welsh is spoken in Wales while the official language is English. The religious affiliation is Protestant. The annual festivals of *eisteddfodau,* the chairing festivals, honor the poetry champions lifting them up on the chairs hoping to compete in Europe's largest festival where poetry is recited in Welsh only, a hallmark of Welsh ethnicity. The Welsh maintain the most productive sheep raising region in Europe embracing modern technology in their economy.

WESTERN EUROPE

BASQUES:
They are considered to be the descendants of Cro-Magnons who inhabited this region 30,000 years ago. They may be the oldest ethnic group in Europe. The Basques language *Euskera* is not related to any European language. The Basques were the story tellers and spontaneously recited verses in Euskera. They were given the name *bertsolariak*. They believe that the devil could not learn this language and quit in frustration after seven years. People are mostly Roman Catholic living in a region that covers parts of France and Spain. They are very independent people and have not been a unified community for centuries. They have managed to maintain autonomy even under foreign rule. Basques were fishermen, farmers, and shepherds or skilled mariners. They were a part of the crew for Columbus and Magellan. Many have moved into industrial jobs while about 20% work at baserria, farms in small villages.

BRETONS:
These Celtic people migrated from the British Islands during 3rd and 4th centuries AD to Brittany, a maritime province on a peninsula in the English Channel. The French authorities limited their autonomy in the 16th century and isolated them from France for more than two centuries. They are progressive farmers, fisherman, and raise livestock in small villages, *treviou* or large settlements called *plous*. The industries of agriculture machinery and food processing offer employment to the Bretons not engaged in farming. The Breton language is derived from the Celtic mixed with Welsh and Cornish. Bretons are Roman Catholics. They honor hundreds of area saints and go on pilgrimage to nine cathedrals. Their religious festivals are called *pardons*.

CATALANS:
There are about ten million Catalans in Catalonia who have retained their identity. *Catalan* is a Romance language that was suppressed under the dictatorial rule of Francisco Franco but

since 1979 has regained the cultural pride. Catalans are Roman Catholic. They honor saints like St. George (Sant Jordi) giving roses and books to loved ones. Ritual papier-mache figures, some 15 feet tall, are used in processions to honor patron saints. The Sardana dance reflects good sense and self-realization.

DUTCH:
People of German, Frisian, and Frankish tribes settled in the Netherlands, meaning 'lowlands' during the pre-Roman era known collectively as Dutch. Much of the lands are reclaimed from the former North Sea inlet, now called IJsselmeer. Although the Dutch are known for growing tulips, only 4% are engaged in farming. Industries like food-processing, petrochemical, and electronics provide work for many people. The Dutch are proud of their well maintained homes and gardens. People differentiate according to their religious affiliation. About 35% are Catholics, 25% Protestants, a majority belongs to the Dutch Reformed Church, and all these religious groups have their own social networks and institutions. This is called *verzuiling* more pronounced in the rural communities where the clergy have greater influence. The peaceful interaction between various groups among 16 million people in Netherlands is based in mutual respect. The Dutch language is Germanic and related to English. The Netherlands became the hub of commerce and trade in the 17th century and is seen in the paitings of renowned artists like Rembrandt, Vermeer, and Frans Hals.

FRISIANS:
Friesland, part of Netherlands is below the sea level including barrier islands in the North Sea. Frisians have to constantly maintain dikes to avoid flooding. They inhabited the area around 400 BCE. Charlemagne established a code of *buorreplicht* , neighbor's duty to help a neighbor in crisis, in 801 CE. Most people are Calvinists, Christianized by the Franks, Frisians during 17th and 18th centuries turned to Reformed sects. Pre-Christian beliefs are called *byleauwe* carrying the stories of *white ladies* that come out at night kidnapping people. Frisians are a farming nation engaged in agriculture and dairying. They

breed cows for milk production. Their dwellings have three
adjoining sections, Living area, barn, and dairy area to handle
milk and its processing.

SOUTHERN EUROPE

ALBANIANS:
Albanian ancestors once controlled the Balkans and parts of
Greece during the 13th century BCE. The Ottoman Empire ruled
from the 14th to the 19th century. The Turks were defeated by the
Russians in the 19th century and the country splintered
becoming part of other nations. Before the communist regime
there were 70% Muslims indicating the influence of the
Ottoman Empire, 20% Eastern Orthodox and 10% Catholic.
Under communist rule, Albania was an Atheist state. Since their
independence in 1990 Christianity has become the main religion.
Muslim Albanians were persecuted in Kosovo. Albanians are
very formal and courteous and polite people with elaborate
greetings involving hand-kissing.

CRETANS:
The Cretans are the descendants of the Minoans representing
the first ancient civilization in Europe that developed on Crete
in 2000 BCE and disappeared by 1450 BCE. They were
dominated by the Greeks, Romans and the Byzantines. In 1669
they were conquered by the Ottoman Empire. They are mainly
Greek Orthodox identified as the Mountains Cretans or the
Plains Cretans engaged in herding and agriculture. They are
weary of the effect of the evil eye and strongly believe in revenge
for transgressions. Their language reflects the influence of past
rulers producing a variation in the Greek language. Women
grieving over the deceased by wailing in verses called the
practice of *keen.*

SICILIANS:
The Sicels, like the Cretans were also dominated by the Greeks,
Romans, Carthaginians, Byzantine Greeks, North African
Muslims, French and the Spanish. The Sicilian language has an
influence of Arabic with Latin. Sicilians are Roman Catholics

devoted to the Virgin Mary and Saint Joseph. They honor their patron saint in each town and observe an annual feast day. Mafia is called *Cosa Nostra* in Sicily meaning our thing. They observe a strict code of silence. Their conviction is difficult.

CENTRAL EUROPE

BOSNIANS:
During the 7th century CE the area now called Bosnia was inhabited by Slavic peoples. Many converted to Islam under the Ottoman rule from 1328 to 1878 so that they could own land, become merchants, and have occupations not allowed to the Christians. Muslims follow the Sunni traditions in Bosnia, in observing a fast during the month of Ramadan culminating in a three day feast called *Bajram* also known as Id al-Fitr. In Bosnia, 44% are Muslims, Serbs make up 31% as Eastern Orthodox, and Croats are Roman Catholic about 17% of the population. Ladies do not wear chadors or burqas in Bosnia. After the reign of President Josip Bronz Tito, Yugoslavia broke up in 1991 into violence and hatred towards Muslims. Ethnic cleansing by the Serbs caused rapes and murders to drive out Muslims during the war in 1992. It left Bosnia in ruins and with high unemployment. The Dayton Peace Accords in 1995 and the help of United Nations and NATO forces brought stability to Bosnia.

CROATS:
Croatia flourished as a state from the 9th century to the early 12th century. The area was invaded by Hungary, Austria, Italy, France and Turkey. During the 19th century Croats managed to stay independent but reluctantly joined the Slavs after WWI when Yugoslavia was created. The communes made under Marshall Tito's rule indicate a socialistic pattern. The majority of the Croatians are Roman Catholics and 11% are Eastern Orthodox. Christmas Eve is *Badnjak* celebrated with lightings.

CZECHS:
The culture of the Czechs reveals Celtic, Germanic, and mainly Slavic influences. Czechs adopted Christianity in the 9th century.

The Bohemian kingdom ushered in the expansion in the cultural and political spheres until the Austrian House of Habsburg took over the kingdom in 1526 CE and ruled until the end of WWI. After the Nazis, the communists controlled Yugoslavia. The Velvet Revolution under Vaclav Havel brought democracy and independence in 1993. Since then Czechs have made marked advances as a market economy. Prague exhibits cultural and political integrity. There are 60% Roman Catholics and 20% Evangelical Lutherans. The traditions show respect for the aged, love for music, food, and embroidered costumes. Czechs and Slovaks mutually understand each other's language but the former are more urbanized.

HUNGARIANS:
The Magyars are the only ethnic group in Hungary that speak *Magyar* language. They were ten tribes identified by the Turks as *on ogur* giving the name Magyars, now 15 million. They came originally from the forests between the Volga River and the Ural Mountains, settling in the Carpathian basin in the 9th century CE. They changed from paganism to Christianity under King Stephen I in 1000 CE. About 62% of the population is Roman Catholic and 25% Protestant. Hungary was dominated by the Turks who forced conversions to Islam, joint monarchy with Austria, the communists until 1989 when the republic was established. Despite a move to the urban areas, farming and industry employ the Magyars. About 75% of women are part of the work force. They have a high divorce rate, and the suicide rate is the highest in the world. 'Hand kissing' tradition is being replaced by verbal greeting I kiss it by saying *Csokolom*.

SERBS:
They moved from the Carpathian Mountains and inhabited the Balkan Peninsula in the 6th century CE. They created a kingdom by 1300 CE. The Turks conquered the area and ruled it for the next four centuries. Serbs pushed the Turks to give them autonomy by the early 19th century. Serbs joined the south Slavs to create their kingdom, and Yugoslavia was formed, but it came under communism until Josip Bronz Tito broke the alliance with the Soviets. He established his own concept of communism

offering more authority to the workers that brought prosperity to people. After the death of President Tito in 1980, ethnic cleansing campaign killed and displaced thousands of Albanian Muslims until the Serbian leader Slobodan Milosevic was taken out with the intervention of UN and NATO which stopped the conflict. It is a male dominated culture, focused on farming and industry. Women are starting to work in jobs held by men. Serbs belong to the Serbian Orthodox Church. Extended family, and *vamilija*, that carries male ancestry in lineage, and the tradition of epic poetry are important to the Serb culture.

SLOVAKS:
They inhabited the area around Danube River in the 5th century. They were under hegemony of the Moravians and then were invaded by Hungarians from 907 CE to WWI. Slovaks were forced to join the Czechs and a new country Czechoslovakia was created. Czechs dissidents elected playwright and activist Vaclav Havel in the Velvet Revolution and toppled the communist regime. Both the Slovaks and the Czechs later became separate independent entities. Slovaks are 60% Roman Catholics, 6% Lutherans, and supported Jews who were targeted during the Holocaust. The Slovaks are mainly engaged in farming and industry. They enjoy music and dancing. Men socialize with men at the bars, and women socialize at home.

SLOVENES:
The Slovene speaking people have inhabited the northwestern hilly area of former Yugoslavia for 1300 years. Under the Frankish rule they were forcibly converted to Christianity during the 8th and 9th centuries. They endured the domination of Germans, Austrians and Hungarians until WWI until Yugoslavia emerged. About half the population lives in urban areas working in industry, forestry and tourism. The hilly terrain is not suitable for agriculture on a large scale. Seventy percent people are Roman Catholic and 5% are Serbian Orthodox or Protestants. Slovenes celebrate Christian and pre-Christian traditions during *pust* the pre-lent Carnival season. With westernized culture, they enjoy a higher standard of living.

369

SORBS: (Wends):

The Sorbs are a small Slavic nation,'Sorbska' living in eastern Saxony and in the region east of Brandenburg in Germany with no contemporary relation to Balcanic Serbs. Sorbs are the descendants of the Western Slavs who controlled north-eastern Germany during 6th to 10th centuries. Sorbs are Lutherans since the Reformation. Their ceremonies include decorated Easter eggs, sing hymns in a procession around the planted fields, and wear national costumes at weddings and funerals. Choral music is important to the Sorbs. White clothes are worn at funeral. Unmarried girls traditionally assemble in groups of twelve and practice 'Spinning Evening' which passes on their culture, folklore and music to the next generation. *Waterman* is a mythical figure which can appear as human, animal, or as fish. Folk tales include ghosts, witches and magical serpents.

EASTERN EUROPE

JEWS:

The Ashkenazic and Sephardic Jews share the Talmud but both traditions differ in language and culture. (See Judaism, p. 120)

ROMA:

They are known as the Gypsy. They came from northwestern India and speak the Romany language. They are nomadic people organized in clans specializing in different trades under a chief. They are talented musicians and dancers and travel in motor homes. They observe Marime code, the code of ritual purity, which has its origins in India. Their spread into Europe is believed to be due to recruitment in 11th century to drive out the Islamic invaders and settle in the Byzantine Empire and Europe. They marry within their clans and exist as marginalized society, always moving from one place to the next. Their numbers are increasing as they marry at an early age. They have joined faiths and traditions of different lands, yet adding their own. There are 8 to 12 million Roma in the world.

RUSSIANS:

Russians developed from the Slavic tribes settled around the Black Sea in the 1st millennium. Vikings established the Kievan Rus by the 9th century. Russians converted to Eastern Orthodox Christianity under the Byzantine Empire in 988 CE. Peter the Great (1672-1725) modernized the culture expanding Russia. Catherine the Great likewise extended the borders adding groups from Finland, Turkey, Siberia and the Baltics, all regarded as Russians. During the 10th century the written Russian language was developed by the Monks Cyril and Methodius by borrowing from Latin, Greek and Hebrew alphabets. Russians are creative people and enjoy music and decorative arts. Their epic songs date back a thousand years called 'byliny', observe liturgical year, and life-cycle rituals.

UKRAINIANS:

Slavic tribes had settled around Kiev as Ruthens controlling the state of Kievan Rus from 9th century till the 13th century. Ukraine became a socialist state under the Soviet rule after WWI. It got independence in 1991. Ukraine was called breadbasket of Europe. The Chernobyl nuclear accident of 1986 polluted the farmlands with radioactivity and could no longer be cultivated. Eastern Orthodox Christianity became the state religion of Kievan Rus in 988 A.D. The decorations on the Easter eggs, *pysanky* is a tradition that comes from pre-Christian times. Easter is the biggest celebration even more elaborate than Christmas. Their greetings are spirited, with tripple kisses, hugs and firm handshakes. They enjoy dancing and singing.

ASIAN CULTURES

Asia is the largest continent with more ethnic diversity than any other continent. China with the highest population is followed closely by India in population density. Apart from hundreds of languages, the migrations and cultural assimilations have created a vast range of customs that were influenced by invasions, religious conversions, assimmilation with indigenous cultures and some preserving the ancient traditions.

ARMENIANS:
There are 3.5 million people of Armenian heritage. The Turks displaced Armenians in 1915 from eastern Antolia and 600,000 people lost their lives. They had adopted Christianity in the 4th century. The Armenian Apostolic Church is independent from but in harmony with the Roman Catholic and the Orthodox Churches. Armenia is an independent nation since 1991.

AZERIS of Azerbaijan:
These people have been Zoroasterians since the 7th century and were followers of the prophet Zoroaster of Iran. They are ethnically and linguistically Turkish. The Zoroastrians believe in a conflict between Good and Evil. At one time they were all over Azerbaijan. The Soviets helped to raise the literacy rate to 95%. Under Glasnost, they became independent in 1991.

BALUCHIS:
The people of the Baluchistan Province are called Baluchis. Five million people have spread to areas of Pakistan, Iran, and Afghanistan. They are of the Middle Eastern descent with a nomadic heritage from the Caspian Sea. A holy Muslim, Sufi mystic or a *pir* is the head of the tribe. They venture long distances for labor into adjoining areas. They tell stories and sing songs of heroism and pride. The Burushos were integrated into Pakistan in 1974. They follow the sect of the Agha Khan and are governed by the descendants of the same family and have no mosques or imams.

KAZAKS of Kazakistan:
Their ethnic background is Turko-mongol and they speak
Turkish. Their country was used by the Russians for nuclear
tests and they out number the local population. Kazaks are an
independent people with a population of 7 million.

PASHTUN (PATHANS) of Afghanistan):
The Afghan people are a tribal nation with 60 tribes speaking 45
languages. About 10 million people live in Pakistan and 8 million
are in Afghanistan. This nation was founded by Ahmed Shah
Durrani in the early 16th century. Pashtuns are proud people
with honor and are known for their hospitality. Their country
was invaded by Persians, Turks, Moghuls, British, and Russians.
It came under the control of fundamentalist regime of the
Taliban and Al Queda set up their training camps for terrorism
until their overthrow and expulsion by the allied forces. In 2006
Afghanistan became a sovereign nation.

TURKS:
The Turks are nomadic herders and regarded themselves as
superior to farmers. They follow the Sunni sect of Islam and
their lineage runs as patriarchal descent. Turks are fine rug
weavers. Their patterns are indicative of their tribe with the
distinctive geometric designs in bright colors. Turks live in
Afghanistan, Iran, Syria and Iraq.

UZBEKS of Uzbekistan):
The country is named after the mongol chief Oz Beg. Islam was
introduced by the Arabs in the 7th century. Genghis Khan's
armed men settled in Uzbekistan and married local women.
Timur, the Turkish conqueror invaded the country in 1380 and
brought learned people to enrich the area. Uzbeks reclaimed
their country by 1501. Russians occupation ended with their
independence in 1991. Uzbeks became successful merchants
being on the commercial route of the silk road where countries
like Russia, China, India and Afghanistan traded goods 2000
years ago.

EAST ASIA

KOREANS:
Sixty eight million people live on the Korean Peninsula. North Korea has half the population of South Korea. Their development was influenced by Chinese culture in the arts and language using Chinese characters up to the 16th century. After that they created *hangul as* their own script. Koreans have one of the world's highest literacy rates. The indigenous faith called *Ch'ondogyo* assimilated teachings and rituals of Confucianism, Daoism, Buddhism, Shamanism, and Catholicism. Now, the traditions of Confucianism and Buddhism also have assimilated Christianity. The Unification Church of Sun Myung Moon has created a sect with millions of followers.

MONGOLS:
Their famous conqueror Genghis Khan raised an army by unifying the clans. With the force of excellent horsemen he was able to conquer large part of Eurasia. They lived in harsh climate and used the circular tents called 'gers' wrapped with felt and canvass. Animals provided most of their diet, shelter, and clothing. Mongols had a close association with Tibet. The title of Dalai Lama was bestowed on the Tibetan leader by a Mongol chieftain. Thousands of monks were killed in 1924 when Mongolia became a communist ally of Russia. Tibetan Buddhism and Shamanism has influenced Mongol culture.

TIBETANS:
The Sherpas of Tibet who assisted Sir Edmund Hillary in the quest for Mount Everest have drawn attention to Tibet. The Tibetans have carried the Buddhist influence into Bhutan, Nepal, northern India, and many Chinese provinces. People of Bhutan are called Drukpas and those of Ladakh named as Ladakhis living in the higher reaches of Himalayas. Buddhism entered Tibet from China. Later the Buddhist missionaries from India joined. Thousands of monasteries sprang up as every family was obligated to have one son to be a monk. The Gelukpa sect has carried the theocratic seat as Dalai Lama since the 17th century. Tibet was independent from 1912 to 1950 when China

occupied Tibet. The Dalai Lama was forced to leave Tibet with his 80,000 followers after the Chinese destroyed many of the monasteries. The Dalai Lama has been in exile at Dharamsala in India since then.

SOUTHEAST ASIA

BALINESE of Bali:
The Balinese believe in spirits and honor gods for self sufficiency in life on the volcanic island of Bali. Indian merchants and traders brought Hinduism to the island during the 7th and 8th centuries. The Balinese resisted conversion to Islam. The main volcano is called *Gunung Agung* and looms large in Balinese culture and its mythology. There is a dramatic rendition of two mythological creatures: *Barong* represents goodness and dancing for joy, the other is *Rangda* representing evil, the witch, queen of death who tries to interrupt celebrations. Ultimately the goodness of Barong triumphs. The play also enacts the epic story of god Rama and struggle with evil Ravan who kidnapped Sita, Rama's wife. The foreign influence with increased tourism has not affected the belief system of the 3 million inhabitants so far.

JAVANESE of Java:
A hundred million people occupy Java island which is smaller in area than Florida. Successful rice cultivation has sustained the inhabitants for 4,500 years. Traders and invaders brought Islam, Buddhism, Hinduism, and Christianity. Hindus built temples between 750 and 900 CE with the Borobudur being the most highly intricate and magnificient of all. Islam in Java did not convert the masses but got blended into the existent Hindu-Buddhist traditions. The Javanese believe in ghosts, spirits, and magic. The mythological stories are shown with puppets. The Javanese are known for Batik printing with religious and artistic motifs on silk or cotton, popular in the fashion industry throughout the world. Printing process involves a wax and dye technique. The Dayak of Borneo survived with little interaction with neighboring clans.The transmigration program under the Indonesian government relocated people from eastern Java into

Borneo. Dayaks attacked the relocated people killing hundreds. The migrants fled and became refugees.

KHMER of Cambodia:
Buddhism and Hinduism together have shaped the people of Cambodia. They have lived along the Mekong River and around the Toule Sap Lake. The Angkor Wat Temple, built between the 9th and 13th centuries, represents Khmer culture's greatest accomplishment. The re-enactment of the celestial nymphs is performed by the temple dancers. The Khmer Rouge revolution between 1975 and 1979 took the lives of 1.5 million people decimating Khmer culture with forced labor, disease, famine, and death. The survivors have preserved the arts and cultural traditions.

MINANGKABAU of Sumatra:
Sumatra is the sixth longest island in the world inhabited by 5 million Muslims. It is a matrilineal society where the titles to property, family name and inheritance passes on to the daughters. Mother's house is the long house where the daughters bring in their husband to live, thus adding to the length of the house with each daughter's marriage. The Bride's family proposes, and a husband leaves his home to go to bride's home to live with her mother. The water buffalo is sacred, its long horns adorn the house.

THAIS:
The people of Thailand are descendants of the Chinese from Yunnan Province. They follow Theravada Buddhism and speak the *Tai* language. Thais spread out to Laos, Myanmar (Burma) and Vietnam. The early Thais settled along the Chao Phraya River by 1238 CE under the Sukhothai Kingdom after the dominance of the Khmer. Lunar calendar is still followed by some Thais. They honor the goddess of rivers *Mae Kongkha*.

NAGAS of Nagaland:
This land covers the area between Myanmar and Brahmaputra River Valley where Nagas occupy villages on hilly bluffs. They speak a Tibeto-buman language. Women always enjoyed high

status and took part in tribal matters of importance. Head hunting was practiced by men with the belief that the head of the warrior enemy brings positive energy to the village. Surrounding areas have Hindu population. Missionaries have converted Nagas to Christianity.

The Harappa culture flourished in the Indus valley and along the five rivers named by the Muslim invaders as Punjab in Northern India. There were many seats of learning in India namely, Varanasi, Ujjain, Prayag, Nalanda, Kanchipuram among others, and the Hindu culture had a rich history of sculpture, architecture, arts, poetry and music. Chandragupta Maurya initiated the records for births and deaths 3500 years ago for all areas. The invasions and plundering of treasures and destruction of monuments by the Muslim raiders diminished the records of India's past. Still the Puranas, Ramayan and Mahabharata are the epic literary treasures of ancient India. The wisdom of the sages is still permeating the west in the form of yoga, massage, meditation and prayer as a part of alternative medical treatment.

OCEANIA TRIBES

French explorer Jules-Sebastien-Cesar Dumont D'Urville (1790-1842) devided tribes in the Pacific in three regions.
   Melanasia: North and east of Australia
   Polynesia: Central Pacific
   Micronesia: East of Philippines in North Pacific

MELANESIA: North and east of Australia

CHIMBU :
In Papua New Guinea, the Chimbu inhabited the Chimbu River valley with highest population in the eastern highlands. The European explorers the Lutherans and Catholics converted the Chimbu to Christianity around 1933 CE. Sweet potatoes were introduced 300 years ago which helped in domesticating large herds of pigs. Along with feathers and shells, pigs were exchanged in the native ceremonies. Men exercise their authority through bravery, strength, and positive social influence. There is no chief or religious head in Chimbu tribe.

ENGA:
The people of Enga tribe occupy the western highlands. They engaged in wars with other groups but after losing a quarter of male population in fights, they adopted exchange of pigs and shells and abandeoned warfare. Women and men are kept segregated. The belief that women's fluids contaminate men instilled fear them. The leadership depends on the ability to manage wealth and the skills of oratory. Ceremonies are called *tee* where pigs and shells are exchanged.

MARIND-ANIM:
This tribe was head hunters. They had practice of assigning a father figure from another tribe called *binahor* who inseminated the boy for male growth, life, and maturity. The belief required the semen of all males of the clan to conceive so woman had sex with all of the males regularly. This caused infection of the genital tract and caused sterility. The low birth rate led to capturing boys during the head hunting raids. The Dutch

stopped that practice and the tribe adopted Christianity.

POLYNESIA – Tribes of the Central Pacific.

HAWAIIANS:
The natives are called Kanaka Maoli who made canoes that took them to the most secluded island groups. They traveled from the Marquesas Islands 1700 years ago. With good farming practices they supported 300,000 natives. The Hawaiian chiefs, men or women, are called *ali'i* and were regarded as descendants from the gods. Kamehameha I became War god by 1810. After his death in 1819, his widow took his place. Protestant missions and commercial entrepreneurs assumed power and deposed the Queen Liliuokalani in 1893. United States annexed Hawaii as the territory in 1898 and became the 50th state in 1959. Hawaiian sea farers built a canoe, *Hokule'a*, in 1976 and navigated it from Caroline Islands by using stars, wind and waves to reach Tahiti as a show of their ethnic pride.

MAORI:
According to the legend, a Maori ancestor set out from Hawaiki Island to hunt a big octopus 1200 years ago. He killed octopus and settled in New Zealand. It was the longest voyage in Polynesia. The social unit, *iwi*, is based on ancestry of men and women. The Maori believed in supernatural beings and chiefs got their power from these deities. An abundance of whales and seals brought Europeans to New Zealand. The Protestant missionaries arrived in 1814. About half million native Maoris make up 10 to 15 percent of the population. It became the territory of England in 1840.

SAMOANS:
The ancestors of the Samoans came to Polynesia 3000 years ago and currently have the largest population of Polynesians. In the *matai* system, the ability and birth determine the title of chief (Ali'i) and orators (tulafale). Half of the natives belong to Congregational Church, 25 percent are Catholics, and others are Methodists, Mormons and of other affiliations.

TAHITIANS:

The early seafaring ancestors came from southeast Asia, crossing Tonga and Samoa to arrive in the Society Islands. The class hierarchy had nobles, commoners, and servants. The nobles claimed to be the descendants of the gods. They converted to Christianity when the Europeans came to the islands. Tahiti became a French Protectorate in 1842 as Overseas Territory of French Polynesia.

TONGANS:

The first sea farers came 3000 years ago and now nearly 100,000 Tongans live on the islands, 70 percent occupying Tongatapu. This tribe was never a territory of any foreign power. The Wesleyan Protestant Mission was started in 1826. The Catholic Missionaries also arrived. Both supported their candidate to be the head of the Tongns. The Protestant candidate won and was established as King George Tupou I according to the British monarchy under the guidance of the Methodist advisors creating the constitution in 1875. Progressive Tongans have moved to New Zealand, USA, and other areas.

The Spanish and the Portuguese started the slave trade around 1750 AD from the West coast of Africa bringing 4 to 5 million Africans to work as farm hands on sugar plantations and mines in Brazil and in the gold and silver mines of Peru. Some of these slaves were captured from Mozambique and Madagascar. Four to 5 million Africans were brought into the Caribbean to work on British plantations. The Indian slaves were also being sold for the plantations. Half a million were shipped into the Southeastern United States and an additional 200,000 were transported to the Mid-West. Nearly 1/3rd of all the slaves were in United States by the middle of 19th century. Spanish South America also brought half a million African slaves for gold and silver mining in Mexico and Peru. They were called *maroons*. However the climate, disease, harsh working conditions and brutal treatment of owners wiped out large numbers. Some who survived were able to preserve their culture and values.

AFRICAN TRIBES

Africa is a continent of great ecological diversity supported by deserts, mountains, valleys and rain forests. Early humans roamed, hunted and flourished as clans and tribes. They developed customs, rituals and traditions. The social and political framework evolved under the guidance and influence of spiritual and political leaders. The Zulu tribe of South Africa created a powerful kingdom. In Western Africa the Asante and Yoruba maintained large states. Tutsi, Buganda and Bunyoro controlled big territories in the East. Some of the relatively smaller states were ruled by the Shona and Tswana tribes of southern Africa. The San of the Kalahari Desert, Mbuti and Efe Pygmies of central Africa are hunter-gatherer tribes without any political organization. The Nuer of Sudan have no leadership hierarchy. The colonial rule in the last three centuries changed the political landscape until the countries got their independence. However, religion always played a major role in all the tribes with unique traditions and rituals involved in their celebrations passed down to the next generation (Peoples of the World, NG, p. 198-242).African tribes have suffered through the indigenous practice of clitoridectomy on women to vaccination for Human Papilloma Virus (HPV) promises to reduce chances of cervical cancer. Education is gradually making people more health conscious. The East African tribes include Amhara, Falasha (Beta Israel), Kikuyu, Masai, Somali and Swahili.

AMHARA
Amhara are an ethnic majority speaking the Amhari language. Ethiopia was the only African nation of 12 million people that escaped European domination during the 20th century. Ethiopeans speak the Amharic language which is closely related to Hebrew. They follow Coptic Christianity under the Ethiopean Orthodox Church established under Greek and Coptic influence in the past. This continued even after the Arab conquest in 7th century CE. Menelik II assumed power as Emperor of Ethiopia in 1889 ruling an area that almost matches the boundaries of the country at this time. The Amharic are the dominant elite with military power which is opposed by the Oromo people who are

subordinate to Amhara.

FALASHA
Falasha are African Jews of Ethiopia belonging to the tribe of Beta Israel, in *Ge'ez* language it means 'gone into exile'. These people practiced Judaism for 2500 years but are now a small population living only in the capital Addis Ababa. The majority of Beta Israel were air lifted to Israel in "Operation Moses" in the 1980s. This tribe was not aware of the white Jews. They did not have access to the Talmud, the Jewish scriptures and were isolated from the other Jews. They carried on the oral interpretations of the Torah. These people could not have crossed at the biblical parting of the Red Sea as they arrived late when waters had already returned. They moved south into Ethiopia. They were a powerful force in the 13th century with a large population until they were conquered by the Solomonic Dynasty of Ethiopia in 1400 CE. By 1700 CE their lands were seized after their defeat. The Falasha observe all the Jewish festivals and Sabbaths. Legata Sanbat, the seventh Sabbath is celebrated with prayers, sanctification service to absolve sins by Kohanim, the community priest and festivities.

KIKUYU
The Kikuyu tribe inhabited Kenya since 1200 CE Jomo Kenyatta, a Kikuyu, became the first President of the Republic of Kenya after Kenya's independence from colonial rule in 1963 after nearly 30 years of struggle and the Mau Mau rebellion. It sent 15,000 Africans to detention camps. The Kikuyu honor a supreme deity named *Ngai*. People feel his presence when they see clouds on Mount Kenya. The founder of the tribe was Gikuyu. They follow groupings of nine, based on the legend of nine daughters of Gikuyu whose families played a dominant role in the tribe. Kikuyu still work on farms and tea plantations although many moved to urban areas. Number 10 is a taboo, so it is counted as 9+1. The kikuyu language, banned during colonial era is now taught in schools including Swahili and English.

MASAI

This culture observes age-set kinship system. The men are categorized as circumcised, uncircumcised, and elders. Women fall in two categories, circumcised and uncircumcised. A bride is secluded after circumcision during the celebration of this sacred event. The elder men enjoy power and prestige. They decide and supervise the rituals and ceremonies to initiate age-sets and recognize the change of status among category sets in the tribe and marriage. Each set belongs to the same generation. Masai rely only on cattle and do not practice farming. Their settlements have cattle enclosures and mud houses. This nomadic tribe keeps moving to grasslands to feed their cattle. Cattle provide milk, blood and meat for rituals and ceremonies. Masai are tall and dark and wear jewelry. Men carry spears as a symbol of manhood. The *eunoto* ritual signifies the status of true adulthood.

SOMALI

These people mainly live in southeast Ethiopia, Djibouti and northeastern Kenya with a population of 200,000. They have inhabited that area for 3000 years. Some Somali clans are genealogically linked to the Sharifs, the Prophet Mohammad's family. Islam was adopted by the Somali tribe in 1400s. The area has seen an encroachment, by Islamic fundamentalism, into the traditional sphere of Sufi mystical orders. Somali clans established loose territorial herding boundaries but are a nomadic tribe where males herd camels and women take care of cows, goats and sheep. The British, Italians and French had territories in Somaliland. Britain and Italy together established Somali Democratic Republic in 1960. In 1977 the French territory became Djibouti after gaining independence.

SWAHILI

Swahili are a coastal tribe, descendants of Arab and Persian traders who married East Africans. This community flourished as brokers between East Africa, Europe, the Middle East and Asia as well as towards central Africa. Their Islamic religion has influenced their language , art and literature. Due to their vast range of business engagements on the entire East coast of Africa they are wealthy and live in well built dwellings with carved doors, symbolic of affluence. They are Muslims with great ethnic diversity. They are active in social and political process for the improvement of their communities. They believe in attractive physical appearance that, according to their belief, symbolizes inner purity. Men have Koranic verses in their amulets. Women have hair styled, wear jewelry and use cosmetics to look pretty.

INTERVIEW WITH RELIGIOUS LEADERS
Virginie Luc, (In God's Name, 2008)
Selected Comments
(courtesy National Geographic Society)

JUDAISM. Rabbi Yona Metzer, Ashkenazi Chief Rabbi of
 Israel.
He has promoted the idea of a Religious United Nations to
represent the religions of the world in a diplomatic way (153).
He who commits suicide loses his place in the next world
according to our religion (197).

CHRISTIANITY.

 CATHOLIC CHURCH. Pope Benedict XVI, Head of the
  Roman Catholic Church.
In every human heart, despite all the problems that exist, is a
thirst for God (5). Starting from this point we must find the way
to meet each other in the family, among generations, and then
among cultures and people as well. We must find a way to
reconciliation and peaceful existence in this world...We will not
find these ways leading to the future if we do not receive light
from above (231)

 CHURCH OF ENGLAND. Dr. Rowan Williams,
  Archbishop of Canterbury and Head.
I am aware of God, everytime I am aware of my own breathing,
my own heartbeat...to draw in your breath is to draw in the
spirit. To let out your breath is to echo God's outpouring and
creation (69).

In response to a question in reference to 9/11: Well, where was
God? Well, God is also in those who are digging out the bodies.
And those who are putting themselves at the service of others.
God is there. That is still true (183).
...We fail to see how very fast our civilization can unravel, both
in terms of environmental disaster and in terms of economic and

military disaster... Wake up. Wake up to how very quickly this could disappear (228).

BAPTIST. Dr. Frank Page, President of the Southern
            Baptist Convention.
There is a common link in all religions. That common link is humanity's desire to touch the divine, to understand that there is a Supreme Creator or designer or architect of the world, of our physical environment, of our society,..One must seek daily a closeness with God (161).

LUTHERAN. Bishop Mark S. Hanson, Presiding Bishop of
            the Evangelical Lutheran Church in America and
            President of the Lutheran World Federation.
I know God most fully in Jesus.

ORTHODOX. Alexi II, Patriarch of Moscow and all Russia.
Last year (2007) in Moscow, we conducted an International Summit of religious activists...Everyone stood as one in condemnation of terrorist acts... Everybody advocated preservation of the moral and spiritual value that religion proclaims (163).

ISLAM.

SHI'ITE. Grand Ayatollah Mohammed Hussein Fadallah,
            Beirut, Lebanon.
Life is a reflection of the energy of our existence. ...Man can, through his intellect, create a new intellectual life, and
through his heart, create a spiritual life, and
through his movement create new and innovative life.
I see God in all the manifestations in the universe (138).

All religions are the same. All religions worship one God.
We believe in Torah, the Bible, and the Koran. They are all books revealed by God (162).

SUNNI. Imam Muhammad Sayyad Tantawi, Grand
            Sheikh of Al-Azhar University, Cairo, Egypt and

Grand Imam of the Al-Azhar Mosque.
Belief means embracing a sound faith represented in worshipping God faithfully and sincerely and believing in the messengers of God, His books, and His angels. Fortunate are those who toil for this world as if they would live for ever, and for the hereafter as if they would die tomorrow (191).
...the best jihad any human can perform in the service of his religion, his country, his homeland, and his family is to spread peace and safety among people (216).

HINDUISM. Amma, Sri Mata Amritanandamayi Devi, Spiritual leader, India, the hugging saint.
When I hold someone, it allows him to experience true unconditional love. What everyone desires is love. For that there is no caste or East or West, no female or male....Love is the same everywhere. I am always in communion with God (41).

BUDDHISM. Tenzin Gyatso, The 14th Dalai Lama, Dharamsala, India.
Whoever I meet, I tell him we are the same, the same. Tibetan people are very practical in doing this job. Then again, they say that through their inner being they have faith in me and consider me holy...It is troublesome if I think I am smart and higher (73).
It is very important to stay peaceful, happy, and conscious...We have a physical body, we need external material development. But we have a mind, and this mind has different emotions...we have to inculcate joy and happiness for ourselves (107).

SIKHISM. Singh Sahib Giani Joginder Singh Vedanti, Jathedar Akal Takht, Supreme Sikh authority, Amritsar, India.
Only the eyes of wisdom and awareness can see the beauty of God. He is Waheguru. He is the ultimate Supreme Guru (48).

Singh Sahib Yogi Bhajan, founder of 3HO (Healthy, Happy, Holy) Foundation, Santa Fe, NM in USA.
(Keeping Up Connections, Ist Quarter, 1990).
Society often segments itself into factions, when one group or ideology proclaims its superiority over another. To live and let

387

live is the experience of mediation. All wars eventually lead to the negotiating table. Don't hate, communicate.

...But one thing which I have learned, and I am telling you, Guru as my guarantee: there is nothing good in living except those personal hours of meditation. Keeping Up Connections, 1st Quarter, 1990.

VIEWS ABOUT SPIRIT OF GUIDANCE
(Interviews by Dveirin and Borysenko 2007)

JUDAISM:

Rabbi Rami admits, he experiences spirit of guidance but feels it is hard to describe it. The contentment and wisdom that emerges from one's true nature can be expressed through music, art, and poetry. He offers what he calls "roadside assistance for spiritual journey". He taught at Middler Tennessee State University.

Rabbi Zalman Schachter-Shalomi believes that guidance is the "intuitive knowing". IN-tuition happens within. He holds ancient lineage and works towards alignment to modernity.

Rabbi Tirzah Firestone of Nevei Kodesh in Colorado believes it to be an encounter with G-d who creates spirituality.

CHRISTIANITY:

Sister Rose Mary Dougherty is a Catholic and a sensei (Zen teacher). The inner direction, the Holy Spirit, we need to listen within and perceive guidance like the Jewish sages.

Father Thomas Keating, a Catholic priest started the Centering Prayer movement. He lives at Benedict's Monastery in Colorado. The guidance comes from listening, reflective mind, surrender, and acceptance of God's will.

Dr. Borysenko, a Harvard trained psychologist experienced visions of divine light, lucid dreams, and manifestation of psychic abilities. When she felt the floating in lucid dream, ego kicked in which block dynamics of that moment. She calls it magnetic deviance which blocks the true nature, the guiding spirit.

ISLAM:

Sheikh Kabir Helminsky is a Sufi of Mevlevi order to which poet–saint Maulana Jalal-ud-ar-Rumi belonged. He is a founder of Threshold Society which promotes experiences of the divine, unity, love, and truth. Divine offers us the understanding.

Hamis Ali, a Ph.D student at Berkeley in 1960 was guided by the Spirit and embarked on the spiritual journey. He teaches the Diamond Approach to Realization through *Ridhwan*, Arabic for manifestation of contentment in the complete human being. The truth of the moment leads you to consciousness and spirituality.

Taj Inayat, a Sufi, was a spiritual companion of the late Pir Vilayat. She described Creation as an exhaltation of a sigh of compassion. God is love, lover, and beloved. Our realization of Universe comes from love.

HINDUISM:

Swami Adiswarananda of the Rama Krishna Vivekananda Center in New York city explained that spiritual path involves an element of divine intervention which leads to awakening, opening doors to the Great Adventure, towards glimpses of truth and his grace.

BUDDHISM:

Ajahn Sona is a Thervadan monk at the Birken Forest Monastery in British Columbia, Canada. He believes that spiritual journey requires to be more conscious, awakened, and compassionate. The soul friend (*Kalyana Mitta*), the beautiful one who loves you, helps to become mindful and serene, vital to attain guidance which comes from wisdom by asking the questions: Does an action involve greed or not, ill will or not, confusion or clarity. This determines if actions are based on ego or wisdom.

Dr. Edward Bastian studied Buddhism and Western Philosophy. He is president of Spiritual Paths Institute. He said that we have the seed of Buddha nature within us. But like acorn in its shell, the obstruction has to be removed for it to sprout and grow. We have to create the condition for the realization and enlightenment. We could all become Moses or Jesus, or Muhammad or Solomon. That is the goal.

SHAMAN:

Cecilia Montero is a psychotherapist, trained as Andean Shaman, and a spiritual guide. Her training involved silence to comprehend the knowledge of sound. According to Inca tradition, *Sami* are waves of Intelligent Creative Force that generates infinite pure life energy which connects to spiritual guidance. It is available to everyone and can be felt in body and mind with meditation. Lower force is based on disharmony and desire.

JOURNEY THROUGH INCARNATIONS:

Dr. Linda Backman was a practicing psychologist for 30 years. She is trained in hypnotherapy, life between lives, spiritual regression therapy, and past-life-regression therapy. From her experience with 600 clients, she explains that we can understand,where we have been and where we are going next. The incarnations are opportunities to seel spiritual guidance.

QUAKERS:

Deanne Butterfield believes when there are five of us together, the presence of spirit is amplified and that is why group worship is preferred rather than individual meditation. The group together feels clarity and authentic spiritual guidance. There are three major groups in Quakers:

> Conservative: have ministers
> Middle Group: like Protestants, have ministers
> Unprogrammed: They have meetings, no ministers

Deanne belongs to Boulder Friends Meeting.

ORIGINS OF
WORLD RELIGIONS

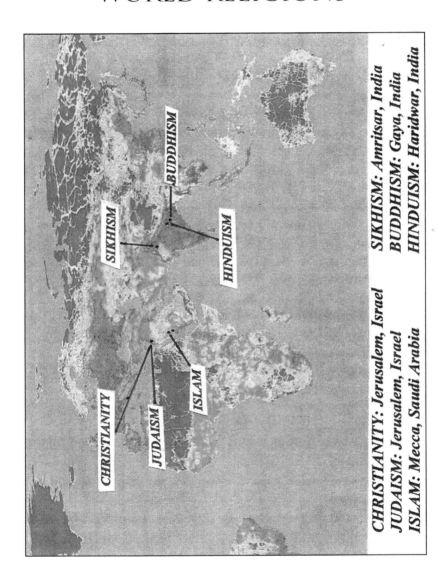

CHRISTIANITY: Jerusalem, Israel
JUDAISM: Jerusalem, Israel
ISLAM: Mecca, Saudi Arabia
SIKHISM: Amritsar, India
BUDDHISM: Gaya, India
HINDUISM: Haridwar, India

Bibliography

Ahmed, Akbar. *Frankness, Sadness and Hope*: Journey into Islam. New York, NY: Brookings Institution Press, 2007.

Albright, Madeleine. *The Mighty & The Almighty*. New York: Harper Collins, 2006.

Armstrong, Karen. *Biography of The Bible*. NPR November 12, 2007.

Baigent, Michael. *The Jesus Papers*. New York, NY: Harper Collins, 2006.

Bhaumik, Mani. *Code Name God*. New York, NY: Crossroad, 2005.

Blackmore, Susan. *Conversations on Consciousness*. New York, NY:Oxford University Press, 2006.

Borysenko, Joan, and Dveirin Gordon. *Your Soul's Compass*. Carlsbad, CA. Hay House, 2005.

Braden, Gregg. *The God Code*. Carlsbad, CA: Hay House, 2004.

Brockman, John, ed. *Intelligent Thought: Science vs. The Design Movement*. New York, NY: Vintage Books, 2006.

Brookhiser, Richard. *Inventing America*. Time: May 7, 2007.

Cannon, Dolores. *Conversations with Nostradamus* . Vol. 1. Huntsville, AR: Zork Mountain Publishers, 1996.

Chahal, Devinder Singh. *Nanakian Philosophy*: Basics for Humanity. Laval, Quebec, Canada : Institute for Understanding Sikhism, 2008.

Chopra, Deepak. *Ageless Body, Timeless Mind*. New York, NY: Harmony Books, 1993.

_____. *How to Know God*. New York, NY: Harmony Books, 2000.

_____. *Life After Death*: The Burden of Proof. New York, NY: Harmony Books, 2006.

_____. *Power, Freedom and Grace*: Living from the Source of Happiness. San Rafael, CA: Amber-Allen, 2006.

Christian, David. *Big History: The Big Bang, Life on Earth, and The Rise of Humanity* (San Diego State University), The Teaching Company Course # 8050, 2008.

Copeleston, Frederick. *Religion & The One*: Philosophies East And West. London: Continuum, 2002.

Dalai Lama, The. *The Universe in a Single Atom*. New York, NY: Morgan Road, Random House, 2005.

Devorkan, David & Robert W. Smith. *HUBBLE –Imaging Space And Time*. Washington, DC: Smithsonian National Air and Space Museum and National Geographic, 2009.

Domhoff, G. William. *The Scientific Study of Dreams*. American Psychological Association, Washington, D.C., 2003.

Dyer, Wayne W. *Wisdom of the Ages*. New York, NY: Harper Collins, 2002.

Eckel, Malcolm D. *Buddhism*. (Boston University). Chantilly, VA: The Teaching Company Course #6105, 2003.

Edgar, Walter. *South Carolina : A History*. Columbia, SC: University of South Carolina Press, 1998.

Esposito, John L. *Islam* . (Georgetown University). Chantilly, VA: The Teaching Company, Course #6102, 2003.

Fakhry, Majid. *A History of Islamic Philosophy* . 3rd ed: Columbia University Press, 2004.

Fisher, Howard & Igor Smirnov. *Molecular Resonance Effect Tecnology: The Dynamic Effects on HumanPhysiology*. Toronto, Ontario: Brittania Printers, 2008.

Friedman, Richard E. *How to Read Bible*. Book review: Biblical Archaeological Review, Jan-Feb, 2008.

Gafni, Isaiah M. *Judaism* . (Hebrew University of Jerusalem). Chantilly, VA: The Teaching Company, Course #6103, 2003.

Gilbert, Mark. *The Evolution of Consciousness* : Spiral Dynamics. Science of Mind, April 2008.

Gingerich, Owen. *God's Universe*. Cambridge: Harvard University Press, 2006.

Goenka, S. N. *Meditation Now: Inner Peace through Inner Wisdom*. Seattle, WA: Pariyatti Publishing, 2003.

Grewal, V. S. *Concepts of Heaven and Hell in World Religions* . Institute for Understanding Sikhism: the Research Journal, Vol. 8, 2006.

Grim, Patrick. *Philosophy of Mind: Brains, Consciousness and Thinking Machines*. (State University of New York at Stony Brook). Chantilly, VA: The Teaching Company, Course # 4278, 2008.

Hancock, Graham. *Finger-prints of the Gods.* New York, NY: Random House, 1995.

Harrell, Keith. *Attitude is Everything.* New York, NY: Harper Collins, 2003.

Harrington, Anne. *The Cure Within: A History of Mind-Body Medicine.* New York, NY: Norton, 2008.

Hieronimus, J. Zohara Meyerhoff. *Kabbalistic Teachings of the Female Prophets : The Seven Holy Women of Ancient Israel.* Rochester, VT:Inner Traditions, 2008.

Holland, Glenn S. *Religion in the Ancient Mediterranean World.* (Allegheny College). Chantilly, VA: The Teaching Company, Course #6340, 2005.

Issacson, Walter. *Einstein & Faith.* Time: April 16, 2007, 44-48.

Johnson, Timothy L. *Christianity.* (Emory University). Chantilly, VA: The Teaching Company, Course #5101, 2003.

Karsh, Efraim. *Islamic Imperialism*: A History. New Haven, CT: Yale University Press, 2006. 9-23.

Kostyal, K. M., ed. *Peoples of the World.* New York, NY: National Geographic Society, Washington, DC, 2001.

Kant, Immanuel. *The One Possible Basis for a Demonstration of The Existence of God.* Lincoln, NE: University of Nebraska Press, 1994.

Klein, Richard G. With Edgar Blake. *The Dawn of Human Culture.* New York, NY: John Wiley & Sons, 2002.

Kraemer, R. S. *Women's Religions in the Greco-Roman World.* New York, NY: Oxford University Press, 2004.

Kyokai, Bukkyo Dendo. *The Teaching of Buddha.*Tokyo: Kosaido Printing Company, 1966.

Lemesurier, Peter. *Nostradamus.* New York, NY: John Hunt, 2003.

Lewis, Bernard. ed. *Islam*: From Prophet Mohammad to the Capture of Constantinople. Oxford University Press, Vol. 1, 1974.

Linden, David J. *The Accidental Mind*: How Brain Evolution has Given us Love, Memory, Dreams, and God. Cambridge, MA: Harvard University Press (Belknap), 2007.

Lipton, Bruce. *Biology of Belief:* unleashing the power of consciousness, matter, & miracles. Santa Rosa, CA: Elite Books, 2008.

Luc, Virginie. Interviews. *In God's Name.* Washington, DC:
    National Geographic Books, 2008.

Mann, Charles C. *1491: New Revelations of the Americas
    Before Columbus.* New York, NY: Vintage Books, 2005.

McNamara, Jo Ann Kay. *Sisters in Arms : Catholic Nuns
    through Two Millennia.* Cambridge: Harvard University
    Press, 1996.

McWhorter, John. *The Story of Human Language.* (Manhattan
    Institute). Chantilly, VA: The Teaching Company,
    Course #1600, 2004.

Miller, Stephen M. *Who's Who and Where's Where in the Bible.*
    Uhrichsville, OH: Barbour Publishing, 2004.

Morris, Jeremy and Nicholas Sagovsky. eds. *The Unity We Have
    and The Unity We Seek*: Ecumenical Prospects for the
    Third Millenium. New York, NY: T & T Clark LTD,
    2003.

Muesse, Mark W. *Hinduism* (Rhodes College). Chantilly, VA:
    The Teaching Company Course # 6104, 2003.

_____. *Religions of the Axial Age.* (Rhodes College). Chantilly,
    VA: The Teaching Company Course, # 6312, 2007.

Murray, Charles. *Human Accomplishments:* Pursuit of
    Excellence in Arts and Sciences 800 BC to 1950. New
    York, NY: Harper Collins, 2004.

Nicholi, Jr, Armand M. *The Question of God : Lewis and
    Sigmund Freud Debate: God, Love, Sex, and the
    Meaning of Life.* New York, NY: The Free Press, 2002.

Ong, Yi-Ping. (Notes) *Tao Te Ching*: Lao Tzu. Barnes & Noble
    Classics, New York, NY: 2005.

Pagels, Elaine and Karen L. King. *Reading Judas*: The Gospel of
    Judas And the Shaping of Christianity. New York, NY:
    Viking, Penguin Group, 2007.

Parnia, Sam. *What Happens When We Die: A Ground breaking
    Study-The Nature of Life and Death.* Carlsbad, CA:
    Hay House, 2006.

Pearl, Eric. *The Reconnection: Heal Others, Heal Yourself.*
    New York. NY: Hay House, 2007.

Pinker, Steven. *The Mystery of Consciousness.* Time: Jan 29,
    2007.

Principe, Lawrence M. *Science and Religion.* (John Hopkins University). Chantilly, VA: The Teaching Company Course #4691, 2006.

Rampa, Lobsang. *Doctor from Lhasa.* Corgi Publishing, 1959.

_____. The Third Eye. Corgi Publishing, 1966.

Ratzinger, Joseph. Pope Benedict XVI. *Jesus of Nazareth.* New York, NY: Double Day, Random House, 2006.

Sachs, Oliver. *Musicophilia: Tales of Music and the Brain.* New York, NY: Knopf, 2007.

Shillinmgton, V. George. *Reading of Sacred Text.* New York, NY: The Continuum Publishing, 2002

Singh, I. J. *The World According to Sikhi*: Toronto, Canada: The Centennial Foundation, 2006.

Singh, Kirpal. *Naam Or Word.* 6th ed. Delhi, India: Ruhani Satsang, 1999.

Soggin, , J. Alberto. *Israel in the Biblical Period.* New York, NY: T & T Clark, 2001

Sorabji, Richard. *Self: Ancient and Modern Insights about Individuality, Life, and Death.* Chicago, IL: University of Chicago Press, 2006.

Spalding, Baird T. *Life and Teaching of the Masters of the East.* Camarillo, CA: De Vross & Company, Vol. 1, 1927; Vol. 3, 1935; Vol. 6, 1996.

Spillar, Jan. *Astrology of the Soul.* New York, NY: Bantam, Random House. 1997.

Stade, George. ed. *Tao Te Ching*: Lao Tzu. New York, NY: Barnes & Nobles Classics, 2005.

Tolle, Eckhart. *The Power of Now.* Vancouver, BC, Canada: Namaste Publishing, and New World Library, 2004.

_____. *A New Earth: Awakening to your Life's Purpose.* New York, NY: Plume, Penguin Group, 2006.

Warren, Rick. *The Purpose Driven Life: What on Earth Am I Here For?* Grand Rapids, MI: Zondervan, 2002.

Waters, Owen. *The Shift: The Revolution in Human Consciousness.* Delaware, USA: Infinite Being Publishing, 2006.

Weil, Simone. *Gravity and Grace.* New York, NY: Routledge Classics, 2002. (First English edition, 1952)

Yogananda, Paramahansa. *Autobiography of a Yogi.* Delhi, India: Jaico Publishing House, 1946.

PERIODICALS

National Geographic. America, Found & Lost. (Jamestown 1606):
May, 2007, 32-41.
_____. Building a Tree of Life (LUCA, NSF >Super Tree=):
      June, 2007, 82-86.
_____. The Maya Glory and Ruin: August, 2007, 68-97.
Time.   Mother Teresa: Her Agony: September 3, 2007, 36-43.
_____. Failing Our Geniuses: August 27, 2007, 41-46.
_____. Einstein & Faith: April 16, 2007.

DOCUMENTARIES A & E Television Networks

The Unexplained: Prophets & Doom, 1997.
The Kings: From Babylon to Baghdad, 2004.
Decoding the Past: The Other Nostradamus, 2005.
Prophecies of Israel: 2005.
Decoding the Past: Mayan Doomsday Prophecy, 2006.
Digging the Truth: New Maya Revelations, 2007.
EGYPT: Engineering An Empire, (H), 2006.
Conversations with God, 2008
History of Sex: Ancient Civilizations. Vol. 1, 1999.
_____: The Eastern World. Vol. 2, 1999.
_____: The Middle Ages. Vol. 3, 1999.
_____: From Don Juan to Queen Victoria. Vol. 4, 1999.

GLOSSARY

JUDAISM

Adam	Hebrew for human, man
Adonai	name of God used during prayer
aggadah	Stories, sermons in Aramaic, semitic language of Babylonian and Palestine Talmud
aqedah	God's command to Abraham to sacrifice son Isaac
ark	holy Chest for Torah, for aron hakodesh
Av	day to mourn destruction of temple
BAR	Biblical Archaeology Review
bar mitzvah	a boy at 13 years of age follows commandments
bat mitzvah	a girl at 12 years of age follows commandments
brit	the Covenant between God and Jewish people
cantor	reciter, singer of liturgical material in Synagogue
Eloh	Elohim, name of God in Aramaic language
emuna	means faith in Hebrew
etrog	a citron, carried in procession during Sukkot
gilgul	Jewish doctrine of re-incarnation
gematria	interpretation of each word , its numerical value
Gentile	non-Jewish people
hagada (h)	liturgical manual used in Seder, Jewish Passover
halaka	Jewish law, custom, practice
goy	Gentiles, non-Jews
Hanukkah	miraculous oil that burned for eight days, festival Commemorates temple
Hashem	the word for God, Orthodox Jews do not say God
Hebrew	name given to people of Israel
kippah	head covering
kohen	cohen, priest
kosher	proper, ritually correct dietary practice
lulab	palm branch used in Sukkot celebration
matzah	unleavened bread (non yeast) used at Passover
masora	books with notes on the sides (small masora), top/bottom (large masora)

menorah	candelabrum
Mezuzah	a parchment scroll with Torah verses in a container, attached on the right door post
midrash	sermon
miqvah	Jewish communal bath (like baptism) by immersion in water
shalom	hello, goodbye
shofar	blowing the horn, commemorates sacrifice
Siddur	prayer book used in Jewish liturgy
Sukkot	commemoration of Exodus, harvest
Talmud	Oral Torah, TaNaK, Jewish Bible
YHWH	sacred name of God revealed to Moses
Zionism	political movement to create a Jewish state.
Zohar	text of the Kabbalah

Source: Http://www.religionfacts.com/judaism/glossary.htm#a

CHRISTIANITY

absolution	forgiveness of sin granted by a priest
A. D.	anno domini, year of the Lord
anabaptists	view that baptism is adequate only for adults who profess faith
Anglicans	Reformation under Henry the 8th in Church of England (Episcopal in USA
agnostic	not knowing (Greek)
allegory	symbolic interpretation of scriptures
altar	raised platform to administe the Eucharist,
Apostle Creed	Christian Creed prior to 'Nicene Creed'
asceticism	rigorous bodily and spiritual discipline to enhance spiritual experiences
assumption	Taking up of a human to heaven , Virgin Mary
atheism	belief that there is no God, no deity
baptism	rite of ritual immersion in water for initiation
BCE	before the common era, a neutral term for BC,
Bible	biblos' (Greek) meaning "Book"
bishop	head of diocese in Roman Catholic and and Eastern Orthodox Church
Canon	the books of the Bible
Cardinal	official appointed by Pope in Roman Catholic Church, a position next to the Pope
catechism	oral instruction in doctrine before baptism
clergy	ordained men permitted to perform pastoral duties
confession	to admit privately ones sin and guilt before God in presence of a priest
consecrate	to bless formally in classical sacraments
crucifixion	crucifix, cross represents death of Jesus.
deity	dues means God in Latin
deify	to make someone or something God-like
denomination	subdivision within religion
duality	polarities e.g. God vs. Satan, good vs. evil,
ecclesiastical	governance and activities in church

ecumenism	to promote Christian initiates worldwide,
episcopal	to signify that responsibility falls on bishop, not general membership
Eschatology	study of ultimate destiny or purpose of mankind, how end will happen
eucharist	sacrament of receiving bread and wine
evangelical	preaches repentance, authority of the Bible
excommunication:	exclusion from church membership
Gentile	non-Christian people
Gospel	the message and writings about Jesus
grace	divine assistance on spiritual path
Holy Spirit	Holy Ghost, presence of God in Church
hellenism	civilization in ancient world (333-63 BCE)
icon	painted religious image
Inquisition	Roman Catholic court for investigating heresy
Jesuits	Roman Catholic order called Society of Jesus (
lent	period of 40 days between Ash Wednesday and Easter
monastery	isolated institution for disciplined quest of monks and nuns
pagan	an irreligious person
penance	rite of repentance and confession to a priest for sins, forgiveness
penitent	prolonged period of seeking forgiveness through prescribed acts
presbyter	lder person in church
purgatory	intermediate state after death to repent for sins for going to heaven
Puritan	movement in 17th century (purifying church)
Yom Kippur	practice of fasting

Source: http://ccat.sas.upenn.edu/~rs002/glossary.html

401

ISLAM

adhan	call from the mosque for prayers
akhlaq	Arabic term for practice of virtue, morality
Allah	God, in Aramaic language
al-akhirah	After-life
Allah u-Akbar	Allah is the Greatest
Al-fatiha(h)	initial sura of Qur'an which serves as prayer
Assalamu Alaikum	Greeting: Peace be with you
	Response: Wa Alaikum Aslam
ayatollah	title in Iranian Shi'ites for honored leader
Bakr	father of Muhammad, the first Caliph,
baraka(h)	spiritual power in holy persons
basmala (Bismila)	Arabic noun, constitutes the first verse of
	every sura (chapter) In the name of God,
	the Merciful, the Compassionate
batin	esoteric internal message of Qu'an by Imam
caliph	Islamic leader , title, in service to God, title
din	religion
dozakh	hell
du'a	sincere prayer to God
fatwa	statement issued by an Islamic authority
faqir	mendicant with spirituality and poverty
fiqh	interpretation of religious law
fitnah	persecution
Gabriel	angel, who revealed Qur'an to Muhammad
hajj	pilgrimage to Mecca, id al-adha
hijra	emigration of Muhammad from Mecca to
	Medina in 622 CE
id al-fitr	Feast: breaking fast during Ramadan
ijtihad	effort of Muslim jurist to reach independent
	religious/legal decision
imam	leader in Shi'ite Islam, religious /political
iman	faith, religious virtue in Koran
islah	reform
Islamic Calendar	Lunar, 354 days a year,100 solar=103 lunar
Jahunnum	hell

jihad	struggle in the work of God, holy war when armed force is employed
jizya	tax levied by Islamic rulers to non-Muslims
kalam	speech in Arabic, Islamic principles
khutba	kalam (Sermon)
Masih	Arabic for Messiah - Isa al-Masih (Jesus)
Masjid	mosque, minarets identify historic sites
mufti	Muslim legal scholar who can deliver 'fatwa'
nabi	Prophet, the holy man
ninbar	the raised pulpit in a mosque
qadi	Islamic religious judge
Qur'an	Islamic scriptures revealed to Muhammad
Rabb	God, Allah
Ramadan	month of fasting, 9th month
sabr	patience
salat	Islamic prayer
salih	righteous, living in the will of God
shukr	gratitude, thankfulness
siddiq	truthful, for Abu Bakr, first Caliph of Islam
Subhan-Allah	glorious is Allah
tawassul	religious practice seeking closeness to Allah
tawbah	repentance for a transgression
tawhid	doctrine of Oneness with God
ummah	country, nation
wali	religious man, friend of God
zahir	external impression about Koran
zakat	Arabic for purification
zulm	cruelty, oppression, exploitation

Source: http://ccat.sas.upenn.edu/~rs.002/glossary.html
          http://en.wikipedia.org

HINDUISM

absolute	supreme consciousness, Ultimate Reality
ahamkar	egoism, independent individuality
anand	blissful feeling
asana	posture during meditation or yoga
atma	the energy force of a person, the divine self
avatar	human endowed with divine power by God
Ayurveda	knowledge of natural medicine for total wellness of body and mind
Bhagavad Gita Arjuna	Holy Scripture, Krishna's teachings to
Bhagavan	God, the Supreme Force
bhakti	devotion to God, to seek God realization
chitta	mind, with the power of discernment
consciousness	awareness of the divine
darshan	to see, to meet, spiritual discernment
deva	manifestation of God in a male human form
devi	manifestation of God in a female human form
dharma	religion, righteousness in thought and action
diksha	transfer of guru's spiritual power to disciple
guna	positive qualities of a person or entity
guru	Human spiritual guide
Ishwara	God, the Supreme Force
japa	recitation of God's Name
Jnana	awareness of God's truth
jyotish	knowledge of a person's past, current, and future events through Astrology
kalpa	expression of time
karma	actions, cause and effect during life cycles
kriya	beneficial actions for body, mind, and soul
kundalini	latent potential to awaken body, mind, and it for full awareness
mahasamadhi	deep meditation beyond bodily awareness
mantra	specific verses, create predictable outcomes
maya	illusion of the physical world that clouds the reality, consciousness of God, truth
meditation	contemplation on God's Name

moksha	salvation, liberation of the soul
Om	Aum, sound principle which created nature
prakriti	force that drives the life force in nature
prana	breath, supports life by regulating body
Pranayama	breathing techniques to energize body
reincarnation	the cycle of birth, death, and rebirth
sadhana	practice, dedication with full mind
samadhi	meditation for stillness of mind, in prayer
samsara	forces of shifting perceptions that influence stability of mind
shakti	power, the cosmic strength that supports life
siddhi	manifestation of the desired actions with acquired spiritual power
tapasaya	meditation, disciplined long term dedication
transcendental	God realization, awareness of the supreme
yoga	practice or exercise to harmonize body/mind
Yuga	epochs of time according to the Vedas

Source: selected from glossary in *The Eternal Way*
(with permission from Roy Eugene Davis, CSA).

BUDDHISM

acariya	religious teacher
anicca	impermanance
bodhi	awakened
brahmavihara	nature of Brahma, divine state of mind
Buddha	Awakened One
chakra	energy centers of human body
chitta	mind and consciousness
dana	practice of giving, a selfless act
dhamma	enlightenment of mind
dharma	refers to the teachings of Buddha
dhyana	absorbed state of mind, meditation
dukkha	suffering
karma	intentionalaction, refers to cause and effect
karuna	compassion
Lama	embodiment of Buddha=s teachings
mahayana	doctrine of emptiness
metta	loving kindness
mudita	taking sympathetic joy in happiness of others
nirvana	freedom from attachments
prajna	consciousness, perception of reality
samsara	journey of the soul through birth/death cycle
sangha	community of Buddhists
samadhi	deep state of meditation, mastery of mind
sankharas	mental reaction
trikaya	three bodies of Buddha (dharma, samboga, nirvana)
Tripitaka	Pali Canon, three baskets (Sanskrit)
upekkha	beyond feelings of outcome, success or failure
vipassana	observing the truth breathing. Art of living
Wu Wei	Taoist concept, action without attachment
yogachara	process of knowing
zagen	meditation in Zen Buddhism

Source: http://buddhism.about.com/od/buddhismglossary/.htm

SIKHISM

AGGS	Aad Guru Granth Sahib, Sikh Scriptures
aad	the beginning
akath	what cannot be described, God
atma	individual soul
akal	eternal
Akal Purakh	God, beyond time and space
ardas	prayer
ateet	unattached
Baisakhi	Identity of devotees as Sikh, established in 1699, celebrated at harvest time.
bakhshish	Divine grace
bole So nihaal, Sat Siri Akal (congregational chant)	Eternal God is True, and exhalting
bandagi	meditation
bharosa	faith, confidence
chanan	illumination, brightness (enlightenment)
chit	mind, thought
darshan	to see, the sight
dharm (religion)	code of principles to be adhered to by a Sikh
dukh	pain, hardship
daya	compassion, mercy, forgiveness
Ek Oankaar	One God, Creator
gurdwara	Sikh temple
gurmukh	who observes Guru's presence every moment
Guru	spiritual guide, godhead
hankaar	ego, false pride
hukamnama	opening verses in Holy Book, daily guidance
kaam	lust, sexual desire
krodh	anger
Kaur	surname for Sikh women, means princess
kudrat	nature
langar	free meals in community kitchen, open to all
lobh	greed
mun	mind
munmukh	who gives in to his or her mind's desires
moh	attachment, love

namaskar	devotional act of submission (bowing head with folded hands)
nimarata	humility
Param Atma	God
Parkash	daily services of opening Holy Book (AGGS)
pachhtawa	repentance
unt	end, doomsday
Punjabi	language of the Sikhs in Punjab state, India
sadhu	saint, who has renounced worldly possessions
sangat	congregation in Gurdwara
Sat Nam	God's Word is Truth
sewa	selfless community service
Shabd	Word, Guru's verses in Sikh Scriptures
SGPC	Sikh Religious Committee, governs historic Sikh shrines.
Sikh	seeker of God, devotee of Sikh faith
Singh	surname of Sikh men, signifies integrity
sukh	pleasure, peace of mind, enjoyment
sukhasan	services of closing Holy Book in the evening
wadyai	praise
Waheguru	wonderous praise for the bounteous God

Source: http://.Gurbanifm.com/index_ishmeet_Singh.

ABOUT THE AUTHOR

At age 3 Ajit walked into the Prayer Room to offer prayer imitating his parents. Growing up, he felt the urgency to read the scriptures. He received the 'word' at the age of 13 from a sage who was the disciple of his grandfather.

He earned his Ph.D from the University of British Columbia, Canada. Professor Ajit Randhawa retired as chairman of Science Division at a South Carolina college after teaching in USA for 29 years, having been recognized with the South Carolina "Governor's Distinguished Professor" award.

His head bows to all faiths which are imbued with spirituality and believes that everyone has an inner voice, the divine awareness, only if one is attuned to it. "Evolution of Faith and Religion – An Exploration" is an avenue to reach the global youth. Young minds, in their purity and innocence offer us hope that they will respect humanity in all its diversity and faiths to experience the innate spark that transcends cultures, politics, and all sectarian divisions and prejudices in the world. Randhawa enjoys inter-faith forums, journals, and spiritual books on the divine link between the world's religions.